50 Jahre Moderne Farbfotografie

50 Years Modern Color Photography

1936 - 1986

photokina

»photokina«
Weltmesse des Bildes, Köln 1986
Bilderschauen
3.-9. September 1986

50 Jahre
Moderne Farbfotografie 1936-1986

Ausstellung

Konzept und Design:
Manfred Heiting, DGPh., Frankfurt

Koordination:
Claudia Leiendecker, Köln

Assistenz:
Ans Otsen, Amsterdam

AV-Präsentation:
Jan van der Horn, Amsterdam

Aufbau:
Brune & Königs, Bergisch-Gladbach

Lichtinstallation:
Elektro Kiesling GmbH., Köln

Satz:
Van Soest Amsterdam

Schrift:
Perpetua normal und kursiv

Katalog

Herausgeber:
Messe- und Ausstellungs-Ges.m.b.H., Köln

Konzept, Design und Redaktion:
Manfred Heiting, DGPh., Frankfurt

Koordination:
Zdena Schmied, Frankfurt
Julia Diebold, Köln

Biografien:
Martina Mettner, DGPh., GDL, Frankfurt

Übersetzungen:
Addison, Randell & Partners, London
Martina Mettner, Frankfurt
Maureen Shepstone, Amsterdam

Layout:
Ger Hudepol, Purmerend

Satz und Druck:
Van Soest Amsterdam

Papier:
Seiten 1-304, 150 g silk-maschinengestrichen Offset
Seiten 305-364, 80 g holzfrei Offset, grau

Schrift:
Perpetua normal, halbfett und kursiv

Lithographie:
Laudert & Co., Vreden

Buchbinderische Verarbeitung:
Stokkink's Boekbinderij bv, Amsterdam

Vertrieb:
Van Soest Amsterdam

Gedruckt in den Niederlanden, Juli 1986.
ISBN 3-9800730-2-5

»photokina«
World's Fair of Imaging Systems, Cologne 1986
Exhibition of Photographs
September 3-9, 1986

50 Years
Modern Color Photography 1936-1986

Exhibition

Concept and Design:
Manfred Heiting, DGPh., Frankfurt

Coordination:
Claudia Leiendecker, Cologne

Exhibition Assistance:
Ans Otsen, Amsterdam

AV-Presentation:
Jan van der Horn, Amsterdam

Construction:
Brune & Königs, Bergisch-Gladbach

Lighting Installation:
Elektro Kiesling GmbH., Cologne

Typesetting:
Van Soest Amsterdam

Typeface:
Perpetua medium and italic

Catalogue

Publisher:
Messe- und Ausstellungs-Ges.m.b.H., Cologne

Concept, Design and Editor:
Manfred Heiting, DGPh., Frankfurt

Coordination:
Zdena Schmied, Frankfurt
Julia Diebold, Cologne

Biographies:
Martina Mettner, DGPh., GDL, Frankfurt

Translations:
Addison, Randell & Partners, London
Martina Mettner, Frankfurt
Maureen Shepstone, Amsterdam

Layout:
Ger Hudepol, Purmerend

Printing and Typesetting:
Van Soest Amsterdam

Paper:
Pages 1-304, 150 grams silk machine-coated offset
Pages 305-364, 80 grams woodfree offset, grey

Typeface:
Perpetua medium, bold and italic

Lithography:
Laudert & Co., Vreden

Binding:
Stokkink's Boekbinderij bv, Amsterdam

Distribution:
Van Soest Amsterdam

Printed in The Netherlands, July 1986.
ISBN 3-9800730-2-5

VORWORT
FOREWORD

Durch den Besuch der Ausstellungen *Farbe im Photo* 1981 in der Kölner Kunsthalle und *Color as Form* 1982 im *International Museum of Photography* im *George Eastman House* in Rochester, wurde ich, neben meiner Begegnung mit der experimentellen Farbfotografie – als Kurator der *International Polaroid Collection* von 1968-1982 – mit der starken Aussagekraft der Farbe als Stilelement auf sehr einprägsame Weise konfrontiert und als Sammler von überwiegend Schwarzweiß Fotografien nachhaltig beeinflußt.

In den nachfolgenden Jahren hatte ich die Gelegenheit mein Wissen über die *neue* Farbfotografie in Amerika und hier speziell durch die Publikationen von Sally Eauclaire – erschienen bei Abbeville Press, New York – zu vertiefen und aufgrund meines wachsenden Interesses an der Farbfotografie bei dem weiteren Aufbau meiner Sammlung die selbstgesteckten Grenzen maßgeblich zu ändern. Ich bin heute davon überzeugt, daß zeitgenössische Fotografie ohne das Stillelement Farbe nur bedingt den Zeitgeist vermittelt und eine moderne Fotosammlung die Farbfotografie nicht mehr ausschließen kann.

Als mir im Juli 1985 der Geschäftsführer der KölnMesse, Hans Wilke, und der Vorsitzende des *photokina* Messeausschußes, Hans Joachim Ernst, die Konzeption und Ausführung der 1986er Bilderschauen mit dem Thema *50 Jahre moderne Farbfotografie 1936-1986* übertrugen, war mir aufgrund der Vorkenntnisse der besondere Stellenwert aber auch die Komplexität dieser Ausstellung bewußt und für das mir entgegengebrachte Vertrauen möchte ich mich recht herzlich bedanken. Das Fortbestehen der Bilderschauen als fester Bestandteil der *photokina* ist nicht zuletzt das Resultat ihres kontinuierlichen Einsatzes, den ich hiermit besonders würdigen möchte.

Bei einer solchen umfangreichen und historisch wichtigen Ausstellung ist es notwendig, dem Besucher alle Facetten der Farbfotografie im Verlauf dieses Zeitraums zu verdeutlichen. Es ist mir sehr daran gelegen, festzuhalten, daß diese Ausstellung keine chronologische Übersicht der verschiedenen Gegenstandsbereiche der Fotografie ist, sondern vielmehr ein Spiegelbild fotografischen Schaffens in dem jeweiligen Jahrzehnt.

Mit den Einführungen in die einzelnen Dekaden sowie bei der Auswahl der Bilder habe ich versucht den besonderen Aspekt des jeweiligen Jahrzehnts – sei es auf Grund technologischer Innovationen, sozio-ökonomischer Entwicklungen oder kreativer Interpretationen – hervorzuheben. Dadurch soll dem Betrachter die Möglichkeit gegeben werden die einzelnen Jahrzehnte mit einander zu vergleichen und ihm gleichzeitig eine historische Entwicklung der Farbfotografie aus sowohl technischer als auch künstlerischer Sicht zu verdeutlichen.

Die Einführungen wurden entsprechend der Bedeutung der jeweiligen Dekade gewichtet. Die Zeit von 1936-1946 ist natürlich durch den Aspekt der Erfindungen stark geprägt, die beinahe gleichzeitig in zwei verschieden Ländern – Deutschland und den USA – gemacht wurden. Dem zufolge haben Gert Koshofer, Publizist und Sekretär der *Deutsche Gesellschaft für Photographie,* Köln und Horst W. Staubach, Fachjournalist aus Stuttgart den Themenbereich sehr ausführlich gestaltet. Diana Edkins Richardson, verantwortlich für das *Condé Nast Archiv* in New York ist vor allem dem Einfluß der Farbe in der Modefotografie der Pionierzeit 1946-1956 gerecht geworden.

The exhibitions *Farbe im Photo,* 1981 at the Cologne Kunsthalle and *Color as Form,* 1982 at the International Museum of Photography at the George Eastman House in Rochester have been an eye opener to me. As curator of the *International Polaroid Collection* from 1968-1982, I had witnessed the development of color in the field of instant photography for many years but these two exhibitions have enhanced my understanding of color photography in general.

During the following years I was able to further increase my knowledge of the *new* color photography in the United States, especially through the books written by Sally Eauclaire and published by Abbeville Press, New York. Thus my growing appreciation for color photography has substantially changed the guidelines for my own collection and I'm convinced today that contemporary photography *is* color photography. Furthermore: a contemporary collection of photographs has to include color photographs.

When in July of 1985 Hans Wilke, Executive Director of the Cologne Fair, and Hans Joachim Ernst, Chairman of the *photokina* Committee, asked me to conceptionalize and execute the 1986 Exhibition *50 Years of Modern Color Photography 1936-1986,* I realized the importance and the complexity of this project and I would like to thank both of them for their faith in me. The future existence of the *photokina* Picture Exhibition as part of the *World's Fair of Imaging Systems* is due to their continuous efforts and appropriate credit should be given to both of them.

A historically important exhibition such as this one makes it necessary to present to the public all aspects of color photography and its development during these 50 years. Therefore the concept of the exhibition was to show the influence of the time, as well as the impact of the technological achievement of that time, on the creative work of that period in order to make a comparison between the five decades, and to demonstrate the evolution of color photography.

With the introductions to the various decades, as well as in the selection of the photographs, I have attempted to emphasize the outstanding attributes of the individual periods – whether based on the grounds of technological innovations, social-economical developments or creative interpretations.

Each introduction is in line with the importance of the specific decade, i.e. the period from 1936-1946 obviously highlights indepth the inventions which took place almost simultaneously in two parts of the world – Germany and the USA. For this reason both Gert Koshofer, science-writer and Secretary General of the *Deutsche Gesellschaft für Photographie,* Cologne and Horst W. Staubach, a respected journalist in the field of photography from Stuttgart, have covered this period extensively.

Diana Edkins Richardson, responsible for the *Condé Nast Archive* in New York, gives full justice to the influence of color in fashion photography in the pioneering times of 1946-1956.

The use of color photography in the advertising world and subsequently the field of reportage and documentary photography, were the outstanding attributes of the years 1956-1966 and 1966-1976. The growing effects of television and the Consumer Society also had a strong impact on color photography during that period.

Das Vordringen der Farbfotografie in die Werbung und dann in die Reportage sind deutliche Merkmale der Jahre 1956-1966 und 1966-1976. Unsere Entwicklung zur Konsumgesellschaft sowie der Einfluß des Fernsehens auf unser tägliches Leben, haben die Farbfotografie in diesen Jahren stark beeinflußt. Die Einführungen von Freddy Langer, freier Journalist aus Frankfurt und Lorenzo Merlo, langjähriger Direktor der *Canon Galerie* in Amsterdam werden diesem Aspekt voll gerecht.

Der besondere Ideenreichtum der zeitgenössischen Fotografie, das explosive Vordringen sämtlicher Stilelemente in die Farbfotografie, sowie die gegenseitige Befruchtung sämtlicher Medien, Kunstrichtungen und Kulturen haben die Zeit 1976-1986 geprägt. Diese Tatsache wird auch in der Zukunft ein maßgeblicher Faktor bei der Entwicklung der Farbfotografie bleiben.

Das besondere Gewicht der zeitgenössischen Farbfotografie in dieser Ausstellung – mit über 300 Fotografien der umfangreichste Teil – wurde durch zwei versierte Kenner der Materie akzentuiert: Sally Eauclaire, Direktor des *Museum of Contemporary Photography, Columbia College* in Chicago und Professor Klaus Honnef vom *Rheinisches Landesmuseum* in Bonn. Mit diesen beiden Essays sollte der starke Einfluß der künstlerischen Fotografie in viele Anwendungsbereiche der Kommunikation der letzten zehn Jahre entsprechend kunsthistorisch untermauert werden.

Entwicklungen und Produkte die die Farbfotografie bzw. das Farbbild maßgeblich beeinflußt haben sind in einer detailierten Chronik (Seiten 357-363) zusammengefaßt worden.

Die Einführungen in die verschiedenen Dekaden sowie die ausführliche Chronik geben dem Besucher der Ausstellung und Leser des Kataloges den notwendigen theoretischen Rahmen zu den 50 Jahren Farbfotografie. Für den sachkundigen Rat und die geleistete Arbeit möchte ich mich bei allen Verfassern bedanken.

Nur mit tatkräftiger Unterstützung vieler Freunde der Fotografie und Experten der Fotografie war es möglich, die über 550 Bilder auszusuchen bzw. zu bestimmen und die entsprechenden Vorlagen und Originale zusammenzutragen.

Da die Ausstellung nicht nur Bilder aus 5 Jahrzehnten sondern außerdem aus 5 Kontinenten (22 Ländern) umfaßt, war der Weg nicht nur 'tief' sondern auch 'weit'.

Die Fotografen sowie die entscheidenden Bilder der ersten 20 Jahre waren besonders schwierig zu ermitteln, da das entsprechende, drucktechnisch adäquate Material nur mit Hilfe gedruckter Vorlagen aus der Zeit zu beschaffen war. An dieser Stelle möchte ich Dr. Karl Steinorth, Kodak AG, Stuttgart; Tenneson Schad, Light Gallery, New York und Harry Lunn, New York, sowie Robert J. Lehmann und Diana Edkins Richardson, Condé Nast, New York, für die Bereitstellung ihrer Resourcen ganz besonders danken.

Die zeitgenössische Fotografie bildet wie bereits angedeutet den umfangreichsten Teil der Ausstellung, und es ist gerade für diese Periode sehr viel Material gesichtet worden. Bei der Vorbereitung und Auswahl haben mir besonders Goro Kuramochi, Goro International Press, Tokyo; Ans Otsen, Amsterdam; Giuliana Scimé, Mailand; Joan Fontcuberta, Barcelona; Daniela Mrazková, Prag; Laurence

The introductions by Freddy Langer, a freelance journalist from Frankfurt, and Lorenzo Merlo, who for many years has been the director of the *Canon Gallery* in Amsterdam, thoroughly cover these aspects.

The tremendous wealth of ideas which have stimulated contemporary photography, the explosion of its multi-style facets, as well as the cross-fertilization between the mass media, and new directions in art and cultures – have marked the period 1976-1986. Indeed, also in the future, this will continue to influence the development of color photography.

The particular weight which the present decade (represented by 300 images) carries in this exhibition is accentuated by two renown experts of contemporary photography: Sally Eauclaire, Director of the *Museum of Contemporary Photography, Columbia College* in Chicago and Professor Klaus Honnef of the *Rheinisches Landesmuseum* in Bonn. Their two essays underline the contribution of artistic photography in many fields of communication during the past 10 years.

Developments and products which have been fundamental to color photography, are summarized in a compact chronology on page 357-363.

The introduction to the various decades, together with the chronology, provide the visitor to this exhibition and the reader of this catalogue with the vital theoretical framework of 50 years of color photography. I wish to thank all contributors for their expertise and effort they have invested in this project.

Only with the active support of many friends and professionals in the field of photography it was possible to choose and/or define the more than 550 images and to compile the necessary material and originals. As the exhibition not only includes images from 5 decades but also from 5 continents (22 countries), the project was not only 'profound' but also 'distant'.

The photographers and the images representing the first 20 years were extremely difficult to trace, and the adequate reproduction material could only be organized with the help of printed material like books and magazines from that period. I would like to express my sincere thanks to Dr. Karl Steinorth of Kodak AG, Stuttgart; Tenneson Schad of Light Gallery, New York and Harry Lunn, New York, as well as Robert J. Lehman and Diana Edkins Richardson of Condé Nast, New York, for lending their knowledge and resources to this exhibition.

Because of its importance and scope, contemporary photography represents the largest part of the exhibition and a vast number of images have been reviewed from this period. To help organize the material, valuable support was given by Goro Kuramochi of Goro International Press, Tokyo; Ans Otsen, Amsterdam, Giuliana Scimé, Milan; Joan Fontcuberta, Barcelona; Daniela Mrzazková, Prague; Laurence LeGuay and James A. Coleman of Photo Publishing Company, Sydney and Arthur Goldsmith, New York. Without their most appreciated help, I would have not been able to finish the project within the available time.

I also would like to express special thanks to the many galleries and photo-agencies who supported the exhibition with information

LeGuay und James A. Coleman, Photo Publishing Company, Sydney sowie Arthur Goldsmith, New York, sehr viel Unterstützung gegeben und es wäre mir ohne deren Hilfe schwergefallen, in dem zur Verfügung stehenden Zeitraum das Gesamtprojekt zu realisieren.

Ein spezieller Dank gilt ebenfalls den vielen Galeristen und Agenturen, die mit viel Verständnis und professionellem Wissen nicht nur ihre Mitarbeit an der Ausstellung tatkräftig bewiesen haben, sondern ebenfalls sehr viel Umsicht und Einsatz für die von ihnen vertretenen Fotografen zeigten.

Eine vollständige Liste sämtlicher Leihgeber und an der Ausstellung beteiligter Galeristen, Agenturen, Archive und Museen ist auf den Seiten 305 bis 306 aufgeführt. Allerdings möchte ich an dieser Stelle die sehr engagierte Mitarbeit von Elizabeth Gallen, Magnum, New York; Christian Caujolle, VU Agence de Photographes, Paris; Sue Davis, Photographers' Gallery, London; Joachim Soyka, The Image Bank, München; Peter McGill, Pace/McGill, New York; Daniel Wolf, New York; Russ Anderson und Maggie Weston, Weston Gallery, Carmel; G. Ray Hawkins, Los Angeles und Barbara Hitchcock, Polaroid Collection, Cambridge, besonders hervorheben.

Ich hatte das Privileg, viele der noch lebenden Fotografen persönlich zu besuchen bzw. mit ihnen zu korrespondieren. Für die mir zur Verfügung gestellte Zeit sowie die erhaltenen Informationen und Originale bin ich allen Fotografen sehr dankbar.

Die endgültige Auswahl der ausgestellten Bilder ist sicher subjektiv und ich bitte alle jene Fotografen um Nachsicht und Verständnis, bei denen meine Wahl nicht die vollste Zustimmung erhalten hat. Es ist sicher garnicht möglich, bei einer Schaffensperiode von manchmal 30 oder selbst 40 Jahren die Arbeit des Fotografen mit ein oder zwei Bildern überzeugend darzustellen. Die Ausstellung kann deshalb nur etwas über die Fotografie und nur bedingt etwas über den Fotografen aussagen.

Auch hinsichtlich der Kurzbiographien bitte ich zu bedenken, das diese nur das wiedergeben können, was von den betreffenden Fotografen an Informationen zur Verfügung gestellt wurde. Leider waren diese oftmals von unterschiedlicher Qualität. Die Biographien erstellte Martina Mettner, Frankfurt und ihre Geduld, Sorgfalt und detailliertes Fachwissen waren bei der Zusammenstellung und Übersetzung eine unabdingbare Notwendigkeit. Ihre Einsatzbereitschaft verdient besondere Anerkennung.

Es war mir nicht möglich, die Arbeiten von allen wichtigen Fotografen oder ganz bestimmte Arbeiten für die Ausstellung zu bekommen. Ich möchte allerdings nicht versäumen, dem Kenner der Farbfotografie die Namen einiger Fotografen die in einer derartigen Ausstellung ihren verdienten Platz haben sollten, jedoch fehlen, zu nennen. Trotz intensivster Versuche waren Richard Avedon bzw. seine Mitarbeiter nicht zu einer Teilnahme zu bewegen. Auftragsfotografien – so die Mitteilung – ständen für Ausstellungen grundsätzlich nicht zur Verfügung... – sicher auch für die Auftraggeber eine enttäuschende Begründung. Bruce Davidson wollte nur nach Überweisung eines vierstelligen Dollarbetrages ein Bild aus einer Reportage ausleihen, was im gegebenen finanziellen Rahmen der Ausstellung nicht möglich war.

and professional advice and who also have shown prudence and engagement regarding the correct presentation of their photographers and artists. A complete list of all participating galleries, photo-agencies, archives and museums who gave most of the originals on loan for the exhibition, can be found on page 305 to 306. I specifically would like to mention the considerable cooperation of Elizabeth Gallen of Magnum, New York; Christian Caujolle of VU, Agence de Photographes, Paris; Sue Davis of The Photographers' Gallery, London; Joachim Soyka of The Image Bank, Munich; Peter McGill of Pace/Mcgill, New York; Daniel Wolf, New York; Russ Anderson and Maggie Weston of Weston Gallery, Carmel; G. Ray Hawkins, Los Angeles and Barbara Hitchcock of The Polaroid Collection, Cambridge.

I had the privilege to meet or correspond with many of the living photographers and I am most grateful to them for the time, the information and the original material they were prepared to give me. The final selection of the images of course is subjective and I would like to ask them for their understanding and tolerance in cases where my choice is not in accordance with their own idea on this matter or if their images were not included in the final selection.

It is also impossible to present a photographer's work of some 30 to 40 years with only one or two images. The exhibition can therefore merely be an impression about photography but not about the photographer. Concerning the short biographies, I would like to remind the reader that we could only use the information which was supplied by the photographers or was available to us from some other sources. The quality of this information varied. The biographies were compiled by the photo-critic Martina Mettner, Frankfurt and her patience, accuracy and extensive knowledge were indispensible ingredients for the completion and translation. Her engagement in this project deserves special recognition.

Unfortunately it was not possible for me to obtain images from all important photographers, or all the specific images vital for the exhibition. However, I am obliged to stress the significance of some of the missing photographers in the field of color photography: Richard Avedon and his team could not be convinced – in spite of many attempts – to participate. Commercial photography – according to their final reply – whether for advertising or for fashion magazines, e.g. Vogue, was not available for exhibitions... A disappointing reason, indeed. Bruce Davidson agreed to lend one image of one of his documentary series, upon payment of a four-digit dollar amount, which was not possible because of budget limitations. The *Time-Life Archives* 'protect' Alfred Eisenstaedts images by means of quite complicated procedures and high costs which likewise exceeded the scope of this exhibition. Because of the very time consuming correspondence and lack of response – maybe due to the limited knowledge about the *photokina* Exhibition – certain photographers or selected images could not be included. In some instances there was no response to the invitation to participate, or contact could not be made at all. Eve Arnold, Bert Stern, Claus Wickrath, Stefan de Jaeger, James Nachtway, David Bailey, Timm Rautert, Stefan Moses, Robert Doisneau for example, should have been represented in this exhibition.

Auch das *Time-Life Archiv* in New York 'schützt' die Bilder von Alfred Eisenstaedt durch eine Mauer von kostenschweren Formular-Prozeduren, die leider nicht befolgt werden konnten.

Durch schleppende Korrespondenz – vielleicht auch aufgrund mangelnder Informationen über die *photokina* Bilderschauen – konnten einige Fotografen bzw. die entsprechenden Bilder aus Zeitgründen nicht mehr aufgenommen werden. Eve Arnold, Bert Stern, Claus Wickrath, Stefan de Jaeger, James Nachtway, David Bailey, Timm Rautert, Stefan Moses und Robert Doisneau z.B., hätten mit ihren Arbeiten sicher die Ausstellung bereichert.

An dieser Stelle möchte ich anmerken, daß der Erfolg der Fotografie und somit auch der Erfolg des Fotografen vom Bekanntheitsgrad durch z.B. Ausstellungen ab hängt und gerade bei steigendem historischen Interesse und sozialem Engagement breiter Schichten unserer Gesellschaft nicht künstlich begrenzt werden sollte.

Die Museen und Privatsammler haben bei der Beschaffung von Exponaten wertvolle Hilfe geleistet. Mein Dank geht besonders an Michael Bischof, Zürich; Marnie Sandweiss, Amon Carter Museum, Fort Worth; Charles E. Fraser, London; Renate und L. Fritz Gruber, Köln; Max Scheeler, Hamburg; Eelco Wolf, Hingham; Michael E. Hoffman, Aperture, New York; und Teresa Rowat, Public Archives of Canada, Ottawa.

Die Ausstellung ist mit ca. 550 Fotografien sicher eine umfangreiche Dokumentation und der vorliegende Katalog war mit einer Gesamtproduktionszeit von nur drei Monaten – vom ersten Gespräch bis zur Auslieferung – ein sehr arbeitsintensives und komplexes Projekt. Die drucktechnische Qualität kann sicher als hervorragend eingestuft werden. Diese Meisterleistung, trotz sehr unterschiedlicher Qualität der Druckvorlagen – vom gedruckten Foto aus den 30er Jahren über das Dup einer Kopie bis zur Vergrößerung – war nur durch das hohe persönliche Engagement sämtlicher am Projekt beteiligten Mitarbeiter der Druckerei *Van Soest Amsterdam,* möglich. Ich hoffe sehr, daß viele Fotografen mit dieser Beurteilung einverstanden sind, und ich möchte mich im Namen aller für die besondere professionelle Leistung bedanken.

Sicher ist selten eine Publikation ganz ohne Fehler hergestellt worden, und auch der vorliegende Katalog wird keine Ausnahme sein. Für die entstandenen Fehler, besonders bei Namen und Daten, sowie seitenverkehrter Druck von Fotografien, die bei der Fülle der Informationen sicher nicht ausbleiben, möchte ich mich entschuldigen und um Ihre Nachsicht bitten.

Es sollte dem Besucher der Ausstellung bekannt sein, daß etwa die Hälfte der gezeigten Bilder nicht vom Fotografen selbst bzw. nicht unter seiner Anleitung hergestellt worden sind. Bei Bildern, die vor 30 oder mehr Jahren entstanden oder zeitgenössischen Arbeiten, die ausschließlich für die Reproduktion hergestellt wurden, ist der für den Kunstbereich zutreffende Begriff des 'Originals' nicht relevant. Damit dem Besucher alle Aspekte des modernen Farbbildes vermittelt werden, sind alle „Abzugstechnologien" – Dye-Transfer, Fresson, Cibachrome; Farbmaterialien der Firmen Agfa, Kodak, Ilford, Polaroid und Fuji; in Aufsichts- und Durchsichtsvorlagen – in verschiedenen Formaten, eingesetzt worden.

The success of photography, with its inherent unlimited reproduction capability – as well as the success of the photographer – depends on communication. In view of the growing interest in history and social engagement of a large section of our society, public showing of photographs should not be artificially limited!

Museums and private collectors have been a valuable help in compiling the exhibits. My sincere thanks goes to: Michael Bischof, Zürich; Marnie Sandweiss, Amon Carter Museum, Fort Worth, Charles E. Fraser, London; Renate and L. Fritz Gruber, Cologne; Max Scheeler, Hamburg; Eelco Wolf, Hingham; Michael E. Hoffman, Aperture, New York; and Teresa Rowat, Public Archives of Canada, Ottawa.

With approximately 550 images, the exhibition and catalogue is a comprehensive documentation of color photography, and with a production time of only three months – from its first inception to final delivery – a very complex and work intensive assignment. I'm sure you will find the printing quality outstanding. This remarkable achievement – especially as the quality of the reproduction material was not always up to standard and varied in quality and type (e.g. printed materials from the 30's to second copies and faded enlargements) – could only be achieved with superior technical skills and the great personal involvement of all members of the project team at the printer, *Van Soest Amsterdam.* I believe that every photographer will agree to a job well done and will join me in thanking all of them for their outstanding and most appreciated performance.

Almost no publication has been produced without any mistakes and this one is no exception. I therefore would like to apologize in advance for any errors which may occur; most of all I regret the possible incorrect spelling of names or mistakes with dates, which might have arisen due to the mass of information and changes involved.

The visitor of the exhibition should be aware of the fact that approx. half of the enlargements in the exhibition have not been made by the photographer himself or to his specifications. Images reproduced from 30 or 40 years old material or enlargements from contemporary work, which were made for magazine or advertising, cannot be called 'originals' as is in the field of art photography.

In order to make visible to the visitor the complete spectrum of modern color photography, all forms of photographic printing techniques, in different forms and sizes, have been included in the exhibition: Dye-Transfer, Fresson, Cibachrome; Color material from Agfa, Kodak, Ilford, Polaroid and Fuji; large and ultra-large formats; reflected and transparent prints, etc.

I would like to extend my special thanks to the specialists of *Fach-Fotozentrum Brieke* in Frankfurt, who had to follow many instructions, and very often had to mediate between the condition of the reproduction material and the available technology. They contributed with unusual personal engagement to the technical quality of the exhibition and without their support, this part of the project would not have been feasible within the given budget.
Fachlabor Helmut Schnepf, Stuttgart and *CCD, Creative Color Dusseldorf,* have supported the exhibition with their assistance.

Mein Dank gilt besonders den Mitarbeitern des *Fach-Fotozentrum Brieke,* Frankfurt, die nicht nur mit sehr viel Können und persönlichem Einsatz den bekannten und sehr oft auch unbekannten Vorgaben und Wünschen der Fotografen Rechnung trugen, sondern es auch ermöglichten, dieses Projekt kostenbewußt zu realisieren. Das Fachlabor Helmut Schnepf, Stuttgart sowie CCD, Creative Color, Düsseldorf haben die Ausstellung ebenfalls durch ihren Einsatz gefördert.

Bedanken möchte ich mich ebenfalls bei den Firmen Kodak, Stuttgart; Ilford, Neu-Isenburg; Canon, Amsterdam; Nikon, Düsseldorf; Agfa, Leverkusen; Leitz, Wetzlar und Polaroid, Cambridge sowie Sony, Köln, für die Bereitstellung von Materialien für die Austellung oder Unterstützung beim Verkauf des Kataloges.

Ein besonderer Dank gilt der Image Bank, München, die für den 'Image Torbogen' mit über 40.000 Kleinbilddias – als Teil der Ausstellungsgestaltung – die nötigen Duplikate zur Verfügung stellte.

Zum Schluß möchte ich mich ganz besonders und mit größter Anerkennung und Respekt für die geleistete Arbeit, bei meinen beiden Mitarbeiterinnen Claudia Leiendecker und Zdena Schmied vom *Fotografie Forum Frankfurt* bedanken. Während der letzten sechs Monate lag die gesamte Tagesarbeit in ihren Händen. Ohne ihren Einsatz, Einsicht, Geduld und Ausdauer wäre es für mich nicht möglich gewesen, dieses Projekt neben meiner eigentlichen Tätigkeit im Medienbereich durchzuführen.

50 Jahre sind sicher ein Grund zum Feiern für alle, die zum Erfolg der modernen Farbfotografie beigetragen haben. Für die Wissenschaftler, Ingenieure und Manager der Fotoindustrie, deren Weitblick, Technologien und unternehmerische Risikobereitschaft diese Entwicklung ermöglicht haben. Für erstaunlich kreative und aufnahmebereite Fotografen – Profis und Amateure – und nicht zuletzt für Sie – den Besucher der *photokina* 1986.

I would additionally like to thank Kodak, Stuttgart; Ilford, Neu-Isenburg; Canon, Amsterdam; Nikon, Düsseldorf; Agfa, Leverkusen; Leitz, Wetzlar; Polaroid, Cambridge and Sony, Cologne for the generous supply of material or support with the distribution of the catalogue.
Special thanks also to The Image Bank, in Munich. They supplied 40.000 duplicates from 35 mm transparencies for the 'Image Arch', which is part of the exhibition design.

Finally, I am very much indebted to Claudia Leiendecker and Zdena Schmied of *Fotografie Forum Frankfurt* and I would like to express my sincere gratitude for all the work they have done. Over the last six months the day to day business was handled completely by them and without their diligence, foresight, patience and endurance, it would not have been possible for me to realize this project in addition to my regular work.

50 years of modern color photography is a good reason to celebrate with all of those who have contributed to its success, with the scientists, engineers and managers of the photographic industry, whose vision, technology and the will to take risks, has made this development possible; with the creative and receptive photographers, professionals and amateurs, who have changed the way we look at life – and last but not least – with you, the visitor to *photokina* 1986.

Manfred Heiting DGPh.,
Frankfurt, 1. September 1986

1936-1946

Gert Koshofer & Horst W. Staubach

Die fotografische Szene des Jahres 1936 war in keinerlei Hinsicht sonderlich bemerkenswert. Fotografie war nach wie vor gleichbedeutend mit Schwarzweiß-Fotografie. Und Farbfotografie war zwar nicht gerade ein Fremdwort, aber sie war eine damals nur von einer verschwindenden Minderheit praktizierte Kunst. Was nicht verwunderlich ist, waren doch die Verfahren jener Zeit entweder recht unzulänglich oder in der Verarbeitung schwerfällig, sehr kompliziert und kostspielig.

Noch war die Farbfotografie recht unzulänglich

Genau genommen war die Farbfotografie 1936 schon 75 Jahre alt: Im Mai 1861 hatte nämlich der schottische Gelehrte James Clerk Maxwell vor den Mitgliedern der Royal Institution of Great Britain erstmals eine Diaprojektion in Farbe demonstriert. Mit den in den dreißiger Jahren erhältlichen Korn-, Linsen- und Linienrasterfilmen deutscher, französischer und englischer Hersteller konnten zwar farbige Diapositive oder Schmalfilme aufgenommen werden, jedoch nur mit Hilfe von Aufnahmefiltern oder optischen Vorsätzen; ihre Lichtempfindlichkeit war niedrig und die Dias wirkten in der Projektion recht dunkel.

Farbige Aufsichtsbilder konnten nur nach äußerst umständlichen und zeitraubenden Verfahren von wenigen Könnern und von Fachlabors hergestellt werden: Ausgehend von drei, meist mit einer sogenannten Strahlenteilerkamera fotografierten Schwarzweißaufnahmen, die jeweils den roten, grünen und blauen Farbanteil eines Motivs enthielten, wurden Farbpapierbilder nach Methoden, die dem Farbdruck ähnelten und viel handwerkliches Geschick erforderten, angefertigt. Alles in allem waren die farbfotografischen Verfahren jener Zeit aber nicht dazu angetan, in weiten Kreisen ein nachhaltiges Interesse zu wecken.

Dr. Rudolf Fischer wies den richtigen Weg

Die vor 50 Jahren von Kodak und von Agfa eingeführten neuen Farbfilme gingen auf Entdeckungen und Vorschläge zurück, die der deutsche Chemiker Dr. Rudolf Fischer zusammen mit seinem Schweizer Kollegen Dr. Hans Siegrist schon 1909-1912 bei der damaligen Firma Neue Photographische Gesellschaft in Berlin-Steglitz gemacht hatte. Als junger Betriebsleiter dieses seinerzeit mit verschiedenen farbfotografischen Verfahren beschäftigten Unternehmens verfolgte Fischer mit seinen Experimenten im Versuchslabor der Firma vor allem das Ziel, dem damaligen Geschmack entsprechende farbig „getönte" Bilder schon in der Entwicklung zu erhalten. Dabei stellte er fest, daß bei der Behandlung eines Schwarzweißbildes mit einer bestimmten Gruppe von Entwicklern sich unter Zusatz von an sich farblosen, aus der Chemie der organischen Farbstoffe her bekannten Substanzen neben dem metallischen Silber zugleich Farbstoffe bilden. Bleicht man das Silber heraus, verbleibt reiner Farbstoff.
In seinem Patent vom 7. Februar 1912 (DRP 253.335)

Dr. Rudolf Fischer

There was nothing at all remarkable about the photographic scene in 1936. Photography still meant black-and-white photography. Color photography was not exactly unheard-of, but it was an art which at that time was practised by a dwindling minority. Hardly surprising, since the processes used in those days were either quite insufficient or clumsy, highly complicated and expensive as regards to processing.

Color photography was still quite inadequate.

To be exact, color photography was already 75 years old by 1936. It was in May 1861 that the Scottish academic, James Clerk Maxwell first demonstrated the projection of color slides to the members of the Royal Institution of Great Britain. The grain, lenticular and line-screen films available from german, french and english manufacturers in the 1930's enabled color slides or narrow-gauge color films to be taken, though this was only possible with the aid of filters or optical attachments; their sensitivity to light was poor, and the slides appeared very dark when projected.

Color positives could only be produced by a few experts and specialist laboratories, using extemely laborious and time-consuming processes. Color prints were prepared from the black-and-white photographs, usually taken with what was known as a one-shot camera, the three photographs showing respectively the red, green and blue color elements of an image, a technique resembling that used for color printing and calling for a great deal of skilled labour. By and large, color photographic processes at that time were not calculated to arouse widespread or lasting interest.

Dr. Rudolf Fischer shows the way

The new color films introduced 50 years ago – in 1936 – by Kodak and Agfa had their origins in discoveries and suggestions made by the German chemist, Dr. Rudolf Fischer and his Swiss colleague, Dr. Hans Siegrist at what was then the Neue Photographische Gesellschaft in Berlin-Steglitz as far back as 1909-1912. As a young man, Fischer had been factory manager at this company, which at the time had been concerned with a variety of color photography processes. His principal aim in his experiments in the company's laboratory was to obtain 'tinted' color photographs to suit contemporary taste, and to do so at the development stage. He found that when a black-and-white image was treated with a certain group of developers, and colorless substances known from the chemistry of organic dyestuffs were added in addition to metallic silver, dyes immediately formed. When the silver is bleached out, pure dye remains.

In his patent of 7th February 1912 (German Patent 253.335) Fischer described how various substances 'couple' with the oxidation product of the developer to form dyes, thus introducing the idea of the 'color coupler'. Fischer and Siegrist had thus laid the foundation stone for modern color photography – although years were to pass before

beschrieb Fischer, wie verschiedene Substanzen mit dem Oxidationsprodukt des Entwicklers zu Farbstoffen „kuppeln" und prägte damit den Begriff des „Farbkupplers".

Fischer und Siegrist hatten damit den Grundstein zur modernen Farbfotografie gelegt – nur war eine Lösung des Problems der Diffusionsechtheit, das heißt der Verhinderung eines Abwanderns der Farbkuppler und Entwickleroxidationsprodukte in andere Schichten noch lange nicht in Sicht. Es konnte erst in den dreißiger Jahren – unabhängig voneinander – von Kodak in den USA und von Agfa in Deutschland bewältigt werden.

the solution was found to the problem of diffusion resistance, in other words preventing the migration of the colour couplers and developer oxidation products into other layers – something which was not achieved until the 1930's, when Kodak in the USA and Agfa in Germany solved the problem independently of one another.

Erste Anzeige für Agfacolor-Neu/*First Advertisement for Agfacolor-New*

Agfacolor-Neu

Für die Aufnahme kann **jede Kleinbild-Camera** verwendet werden.
Es ist **kein Filter** und **keine besondere Optik** notwendig.
Für die Wiedergabe genügt **jeder normale Kleinbild-Projektor.**

Agfacolor-Neu ist **vollkommen kornlos,** der Vergrößerung bei der Projektion sind also keine Grenzen gesetzt. Die Bilder zeichnen sich durch außerordentliche Reinheit und Leuchtkraft der Farben aus.

Agfacolor-Neu wird geliefert in Form von Patronen zu 36 Aufnahmen und ist für alle bekannten Kleinbildapparate, die mit Patronen beschickt werden können, verwendbar • Die Entwicklung ist im Kaufpreis enthalten und wird von der Agfa besorgt • Das Photographieren mit Agfacolor-Neu ist außerordentlich billig, denn

jedes fertige Farbenbild kostet nur 10 Pfg.

Erste Anzeige für Kodachrome/*First advertisement for Kodachrome*

NEW

GORGEOUS, FULL-COLOR, "STILL" PICTURES IN

KODACHROME

for miniature cameras

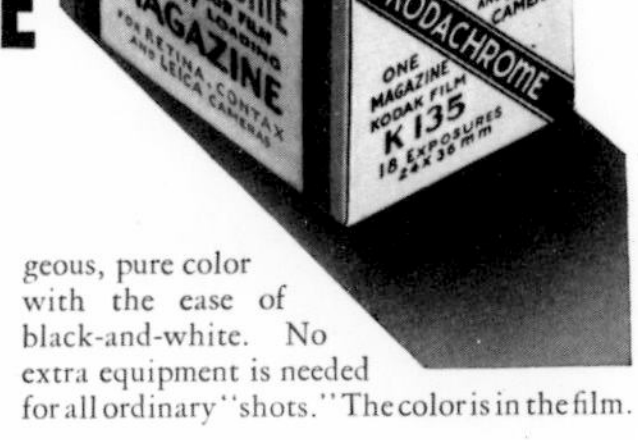

KODACHROME, the unique color film that has created such a sensation among home-movie fans, is now available for the new Kodak Bantam Special; Kodak Retina and similar miniature still cameras. All the lovely hues of nature . . . all the charm of colorful indoor settings . . . can now be yours in "stills."

Kodachrome transparencies may be viewed as they are, or mounted in slides for large-size projection on the home screen. Either way they spell a fascinating new phase of picture making.

Don't miss making Kodachrome "stills" these fine fall days. There has never been a color film like Kodachrome. It gives you gorgeous, pure color with the ease of black-and-white. No extra equipment is needed for all ordinary "shots." The color is in the film.

8-exposure Kodachrome Film No. K828, for Kodak Bantam Special, $1.75. No. K135, for Kodak Retina and similar miniature cameras, 18 exposures, $3.50 . . . at your dealer's. And the price includes processing in the Kodak laboratories at Rochester, N. Y. New Eastman "still" projection accessories to be announced later.

KODAK BANTAM SPECIAL

A brilliant, distinctive miniature camera for black-and-white and Kodachrome pictures

AN entirely new conception in miniature-camera design, with the looks, "feel," and balance of a choice, exquisitely made instrument.

FEATURES . . . Eastman's new super lens—Kodak Anastigmat EKTAR *f*.2. 1/500 Compur-Rapid shutter. Military-type, split-field range finder, coupled with focusing mount. Stainless steel fittings. Brilliant die-cast, machined aluminum body, offering complete protection to operating parts when closed. Makes needle-sharp negatives on Kodak Panatomic or Kodak Super X Film that yield excellent enlargements in black-and-white, the standard, low-cost size being 2¼x4 in. Also makes full-color transparencies on new Kodachrome Film. A remarkable camera, from every viewpoint. Price $110. At your dealer's . . Eastman Kodak Co., Rochester, N.Y.

AGFACOLOR

Gert Koshofer

„Erfindungen lassen sich ebensowenig erzwingen als befehlen. Erfindungen haben ihre eigenen Gesetzmäßigkeiten und entstehen meist aus merkwürdigen Anlässen. Erfinder sind oft Außenseiter, und auch dies ist verständlich, weil sie unbelastet und unvoreingenommen sind."

Diese Bemerkungen machte Dr. Wilhelm Schneider, als er nach dem Kriege in einem für die amerikanische Besatzungsmacht in Deutschland verfaßten Manuskript auf seine Arbeiten am Agfacolor-Verfahren zurückblickte. Anders als die „Väter" von Kodachrome, Godowsky und Mannes, war Schneider zwar von Beruf Chemiker, doch in bezug auf die Farbfotografie war auch er zunächst ein Außenseiter gewesen. 1929 in die Agfa-Filmfabrik in Wolfen eingetreten, befaßte er sich dort zunächst nur mit Feinkorn-Entwicklersubstanzen, Filterfarbstoffen und Sensibilisatoren, also lichtempfindlich machenden Zusätzen, für die Schwarzweißfotografie – für Farbfilme war seine Abteilung, das Organisch-Chemische Technikum innerhalb der von Dr. Gustav Wilmanns geleiteten Technisch-Wissenschaftlichen Abteilung der Agfa, überhaupt nicht zuständig.

Die Aufgabe, farbfotografische Verfahren zu entwickeln, stand vielmehr dem Wissenschaftlichen Zentrallaboratorium zu, und dort befaßte man sich hauptsächlich mit dem sicherlich besonders wichtigen Gebiet des farbigen Kinofilms. Dabei galt es, nach eleganteren neuen Aufnahme- und Kopierverfahren zu suchen, lieferte die Agfa doch für die Farbfotografie schon seit 1916 ihre Farbrasterplatten und später auch -filme. Damit ließen sich immerhin recht leidliche Farbdias – seit 1933 sogar im Kleinbildformat – aufnehmen.

Dr. Wilmanns und Dr. Schneider „erfinden" Agfacolor

1934 aber hatte die IG Farbenindustrie, zu der die Agfa damals gehörte, ihrem Fotobereich den Auftrag erteilt, beschleunigt bessere Farbfotoverfahren zu entwickeln. Das Wissenschaftliche Zentrallaboratorium der Agfa suchte nun nach neuen Wegen, ohne jedoch den von Dr. Rudolf Fischer aufgezeigten und bei Kodak bereits in Angriff genommenen zu verfolgen. Dr. Wilhelm Schneider war noch damit beschäftigt, die Feinkörnigkeit von Schwarzweißfotos zu verbessern; aus diesen Arbeiten entstand der heute noch hergestellte Atomal-Entwickler. In seiner Abteilung glaubte man, die Feinkörnigheit weiter steigern zu können, indem statt Bilder aus Silber solche aus Farbstoff erzeugt würden. Dazu griff Schneider auf die Arbeiten von Fischer zurück – und entwickelte Filmstreifen in einzelnen Farben. Sie waren allerdings grobkörniger als zuvor bei herkömmlicher Entwicklung.

Als sein Chef Dr. Wilmanns die Filmstreifen auf dem Leuchttisch liegen sah, fragte er Schneider: „Können wir damit nicht Farbfotografie machen?" Daran hatte Schneider tatsächlich gedacht. Und so sprach Wilmanns nun bei seinem Vorgesetzten Dr. Alfred Miller vor, der nach der Devise „Der Erfolg entscheidet" der eigentlich unzuständigen Abteilung grünes Licht gab.

Das war im Herbst 1934 gewesen, und schon am 10.4. 1935 wurde das erste Agfa-Patent zu diffusionsfesten, also fest in dem Filmschichten verankerten Farbkupplern angemeldet. Es beschrieb

"Inventions cannot be forced, any more than they can be made to order. Inventions have their own laws, and in most cases spring from significant causes. Inventors are frequently outsiders, and this is also understandable, because they are free from encumbrances and prejudice."

These remarks were made by Dr. Wilhelm Schneider, when, after the war, in a manuscript drafted for the American occupying power in Germany, he looked back on his work on the Agfacolor process. In contrast to the 'fathers' of Kodachrome: Godowsky and Mannes, Schneider was by profession a chemist, but as far as color photography was concerned he too had in the first instance been an outsider. Having joined the Agfa film factory in Wolfen in 1929, he was initially involved only with fine-grain developer compositions, filter dyes and sensitizers, i.e. additives creating sensitivity to light, for black-and-white photography. His department, the Organic Chemistry Laboratory within the Technical and Scientific Division of Agfa, which was managed by Dr. Gustav Wilmanns, had no responsibility whatsoever for color films.

The task of developing processes for color photography was actually the responsibility of the Central Scientific Laboratory, and the staff there were principally concerned with the area – which was certainly of particular importance – of color cine film. In this connection, the important function was to look for more elegant new exposure and printing processes, although Agfa has been supplying its grain screen color plates for color photography ever since 1916, and lenticulated films were added later. With these materials, it was indeed possible to take quite reasonable color slides – from 1933, even in 35 mm format.

Dr. Wilmanns and Dr. Schneider 'invent' Agfacolor

In 1934, however, IG Farbenindustrie, to which Agfa belonged at that time, had instructed its photographic division to accelerate the operation of developing improved processes for color photography. The Central Scientific Laboratory of Agfa now looked for new ways, without however pursuing those indicated by Dr. Rudolf Fischer and already taken up at Kodak. Dr. Wilhelm Schneider was still involved in improving the fine-grain properties of black-and-white photographs; this work led to the formulation of the Atomal developer, which is still manufactured today. The prevailing view in his department was that it was possible to achieve a further increase in the fineness of the grain by producing images from dye, rather than from silver. In this connection, Schneider had recourse to the work of Fischer and developed film strips in individual colors. They were, however, of coarser grain than previously obtained with conventional development.

When his principal Dr. Wilmanns saw the film strips lying on the viewing desk, he asked Schneider: "Can't we use these to make color photographs?" Schneider had in fact thought of this. It thus came about that Wilmanns discussed the matter with his superior, Dr. Alfred Miller, who, adopting the maxim "Success shall decide", gave the green light to the department which in fact was not actually responsible. That was in autumn 1934, and by as early as April 10, 1935

zwar die richtige Grundlage, die darin als Beispiele genannten Farbkuppler erwiesen sich aber als kaum tauglich – ein Zeichen dafür, mit welcher großen Eile die Arbeiten am dem neuen Verfahren vorangetrieben wurden. Die Zahl der Mitarbeiter Schneiders war stark erhöht worden, Tausende von Farbstoffen der kompliziertesten Zusammensetzung wurden hergestellt, Zehntausende von Filmemulsionen wurden gegossen.

Bei der Lösung der schwierigen Aufgabe, Substanzen zu finden, die farbige Bilder ergeben, die nicht verschwommen ober verwaschen sind, waren Schneider seine bereits 1932 angestellten Versuche mit Farbstoffen, die die Bildschärfe in Schwarzweißfilmen verbessern sollten, behilflich. Der Trick, die Farbkuppler am Abwandern aus den Filmschichten zu hindern, bestand schließlich darin, ihnen eine sperrige Kohlenwasserstoff-Kette anzuhängen, den sogenannten Fettschwanz, der sie als „Anker" in der Gelatine festhielt. Damit war es der Agfa möglich, die Farbkuppler gleich bei der Fabrikation und nicht erst – wie bei Kodachrome – während der Entwicklung den Filmschichten beizufügen. Das vereinfachte nicht nur die Verarbeitung, sondern machte das Agfacolor-Verfahren universell: Neben Umkehrfilmen für Dias und Schmalfilme konnten bald auch Aufnahme- und Kopiermaterialien für den farbigen Kinofilm und Bilder auf Colorpapier hergestellt werden.

„Natürlich waren unsere ersten Bilder alles andere als schön, und wenn man sie sich heute ansieht, wundert man sich, daß die ersten Resultate uns nicht entmutigten, zumal nun unentwegt die weisen Theoretiker kamen und uns in höflicher Form ihre wohlbegründeten Zweifel bewegt vorstellten", sagte Wilmanns 1941 zurückblickend in einem Buchbeitrag. Er spielte damit auch auf interne Meinungsverschiedenheiten in der Filmfabrik an. Einflußreiche Kollegen glaubten nämlich, die Vorschläge Fischers ließen sich nicht verwirklichen.

Vorsichtshalber trat die Agfa daher – wie auch Kodak – mit der englischen Firma Dufay-Chromex in Lizenzgespräche, um gegebenenfalls den Dufaycolor Linienrasterfilm zu übernehmen. Doch beteiligten sich seit Ende 1935, nachdem die Konzernleitung beschlossen hatte, das neue Verfahren zunächst in Form des damals recht populären Umkehrfilms für Dias und Schmalfilme zu entwickeln, alle Abteilungen der Filmfabrik an den Arbeiten.

Zur Herstellung des Mehrschichtenfilms mußten erst neue Gießmaschinen und -verfahren entwickelt werden. Immerhin mußten drei jeweils 5/1000 Milimeter dünne Filmschichten übereinandergegossen werden, zwischen denen noch 2/1000 mm starke Trennschichten lagen; die drei Farbschichten zusammen erreichten nur etwa die halbe Dicke eines Frauenhaares! Aus einer Vielzahl von Möglichtkeiten mußten die am besten geeigneten Farbkuppler herausgesucht werden; sie wurden von den Farbwerken Hoechst geliefert, die auch zum IG-Farben-Konzern gehörten.

Dr. Gustav Wilmanns

the first Agfa patent application had been filed concerning color couplers which were resistant to diffusion, i.e. firmly bound in the film coatings. It did actually describe the correct principle, but the color couplers mentioned in the application as examples proved very unsuitable; this was an indication of the great haste with which the work on the new process was carried out. The size of Schneider's team had been greatly increased, thousands of dyes of the most complicated composition were produced, and tens of thousands of film emulsions were coated.

The achievement of the difficult objective of finding substances that produce color pictures which are not blurred or washed out was assisted, as far as Schneider was concerned, by his experiments, commenced as early as 1932, with dyes intended to improve the image sharpness in black-and-white films. The trick of preventing the color couplers from migrating out of the film coatings finally consisted of attaching them to a long chained hydrocarbon residue, the so-called fatty tail, which 'anchored' them in the gelatine. In this manner, it was possible for Agfa to add the color couplers to the film coatings at the production stage and not – as in the case of Kodachrome – during subsequent development. This not only simplified processing, but made the Agfacolor process universal: in addition to reversal films for slides and narrow-gauge films, it was soon also possible to produce recording and printing materials for color cine film and pictures on color paper.

"Naturally, our first pictures were anything but beautiful quality, and, so examining them today, it is surprising that the first results did not discourage us, particularly since the wise theoreticians were constantly coming and expressing to us in a polite manner their well founded doubts," said Wilmanns in 1941, while reminiscing in a contribution to a book. He referred to internal differences of opinion in the film factory. Influential colleagues did indeed believe that Fischer's proposals could not be implemented.

By way of a precaution, Agfa accordingly – just like Kodak – entered into licensing negotiations with the english company Dufay-Chromex, in order possibly to take over the Dufaycolor line screen film. However, all departments of the film factory participated in the work from the end of 1935, after group management had decided to develop the new process in the first instance in the form of the reversal film for slides and narrow-gauge films which was then very popular.

In order to produce multi-coated film it was first of all necessary to develop new coating machines and processes. Indeed, it was necessary to apply three film coatings, each only 5/1000 mm thick, one on top of the other. Between these coatings, there were separating layers only 2/1000 mm thick; the three color coatings together reached a thickness of only about half that of a woman's thread of hair! The most suitable color couplers had to be selected from a

Premiere am 17. Oktober 1936

Im Frühjahr 1936 sahen Pressevertreter erste Proben des neuen Agfacolor-Verfahrens, und die Sommerolympiade im Juli in Berlin diente schon als ideales Experimentierfeld für die Versuchsproduktion – zu den Testfotografen gehörte auch Dr. Wilhelm Schneider selbst. So standen dann viele Dias und 16mm Filme zur Verfügung, als am Samstag, dem 17. Oktober 1936, die ins *Haus der Deutschen Presse* in der Berliner Tiergartenstraße, also im alten Diplomatenviertel, eingeladene Tages- und Fachpresse die offizielle Premiere erlebte: „Ein Film von den olympischen Schwimmwettbewerben und andere von der Ostsee führen eine schimmernde Klarheit des Wassers vor, wie man sie mit künstlichen Mitteln nicht für erreichbar halten sollte. Eine Nachtaufnahme des farbig leuchtenden Berlin führte zu einem spontanen Beifallsausbruch der Zuschauer" beschrieb das *Berliner Tageblatt* die Vorführung, und eine andere Zeitung ergänzte unter der Schlagzeile „Proben, die Appetit machen": „...blaugrün das Meer, bunt die verschiedenen Strandanzüge, ja selbst die braungebrannten Menschen waren von den frisch angekommenen genau zu unterscheiden. Man möchte es als ein Wunder bezeichnen, wenn man es nicht selbst alles erlebt hätte."

Ja, die Presse feierte – ganz im Stil jener Zeit – den „neuen Triumph der deutschen Chemie", ein Verfahren, dem man „drei große Vorzüge nachrühmte: einfach, billig und rein deutsch zu sein" *Kölnische Volkszeitung.* Das Blatt *Der deutsche Kaufmann* stellte fest: „Es wird bunt in der Lichtbildnerei", und der *Berliner Lokal-Anzeiger* meinte sogar: „Jeder soll farbig knipsen können".
Ein anderes Blatt forderte gleich auf: „Künftig knipst du bunt"! Und selbst ein kritischer Beobachter wie der Redakteur der Fachzeitschrift *Kleinfilm-Foto,* Curt Emmerman, mußte zugeben: „Mit diesem Verfahren scheint ein markanter Wendepunkt der Farbenphotographie erreicht zu sein. Das wagen wir zu erklären, obwohl wir im Laufe der Jahre immer wieder erlebt haben, daß die Farbenphotographie 'endgültig und unwiderruflich zum letzten Mal' erfunden wurde..."

Dr. Wilhelm Schneider

Anfangserfolge und -probleme

Schon kurz nach seiner offiziellen Vorstellung kam der Agfacolor Kleinbildfilm im November 1936 auf den deutschen Markt. Sein Kaufpreis – nur 3,60 Reichsmark einschließlich Entwicklung für die Patrone mit 36 Aufnahmen – hielt ein bei seiner Ankündigung gegebenes Versprechen, so „volkstümlich" zu sein, „daß keine Luxuspreise den großen Gewinn der Farbe für den Amateur wieder herabsetzen wird", wie die Zeitschrift *Licht-Bild-Bühne* am 19.10.1936 geschrieben hatte. Das einzelne Farbdia kostete also nur 10 Pfennige. Hinzukamen bei Agfacolor-Neu, wie der Film zur Unterscheidung von den noch auf dem Markt befindlichen gleichnamigen Korn- und Linsenrasterfilmen der Agfa zunächst hieß, noch weitere Vorzüge

multiplicity of possibilities; they were supplied by Farbwerke Hoechst, which also belonged to the IG Farben Group.

First showing on October 17, 1936

In spring of 1936, representatives of the press saw some initial samples of the new Agfacolor process, and the Summer Olympics in July in Berlin served as an ideal experimental opportunity for the test production – the test photographers included Dr. Wilhelm Schneider himself. On this occasion, many slides and 16 mm films were thus available, when, on Saturday October 17, 1936, the daily and trade press which had been invited to the *Haus der Deutschen Presse* in Tiergartenstrasse, Berlin (the old diplomatic quarter), experienced the official first showing: "A film of the Olympic swimming events and others of the Baltic Sea show water with shimmering clarity, such as was considered impossible with artificial means. A night-time exposure of Berlin, with its colored lights, caused a spontaneous outbreak of applause on the part of the spectators." This was how the *Berliner Tageblatt* described the demonstration, and another newspaper added, under the headline "samples which really whet your appetite:"... the sea blue-green, the various bathing costumes in many colors, even the sun-tanned people could easily be distinguished from those who had just arrived. You would call it a miracle, if you hadn't experienced it all for yourself."

Yes, the press extolled - in the particular style of that time - the "new triumph of German chemistry", a process which was praised for its "three great advantages: it is simple, cheap and entirely German" *Kölnische Volkszeitung.* The publication *Der deutsche Kaufmann* stated: "Lots of color has come into photography", and the *Berliner Lokal-Anzeiger* printed the following: "Everyone should be able to take color snaps." Another newspaper issued the same invitation: "In future, you'll be snapping in color"! Indeed, even a critical observer such as the editor of the trade magazine *Kleinfilm-Foto,* Curt Emmermann, had to admit: "It seems that this process represents a significant turning point in color photography. We dare say so, although over the years we have repeatedly seen color photography invented 'finally and irrevocably for the last time'..."

Initial successes and problems

A short time after its official presentation, the Agfacolor 35 mm film came onto the German market in November 1936. Its purchase price - only 3.60 Reichsmark including processing for the cartridge of 36 exposures - kept a promise, made at the time when the film was announced, that it would be so "popular... that no luxury prices would reduce the great benefit of the film to the amateur", as the magazine *Licht-Bild-Bühne* had stated on October 19, 1936. Each individual color slide thus cost only 10 Pfennig. In the case of Agfacolor-Neu, as the film was initially known in order to distinguish it from the similarly

gegenüber den alten Farbfilmen. Sie wurden in der ersten Anzeige (Abb. Seite 8) herausgestellt:
„Für die Aufnahme kann jede Kleinbild-Camera verwendet werden. Es ist kein Filter und keine besondere Optik notwendig. Für die Wiedergabe genügt jeder normale Kleinbild-Projektor..."

Und in einem Prospekt teilte die Agfa mit: „Alles ist genauso leicht wie in der Schwarzweißphotographie, ja noch leichter, denn... auch die Fertigstellung der Aufnahmen besorgt die Agfa." Dazu führte die Tageszeitung *B.Z. am Mittag* am 19.10.1936 aus: „Durch Zusammenführen der im ganzen Reich anfallenden Aufnahmen an die Zentralstelle der Agfa wird man wirtschaftlicher arbeiten können. Wenn sich der neue Film erst gut eingeführt hat, können selbstverständlich auch die Fotohändler und Amateure für das Entwicklungsverfahren angelernt werden." Damit bezog sie sich auf die Einfachheit des Agfacolor-Verfahrens in seiner Verarbeitung. Wenn diese aber zunächst ausschließlich durch die Filmherstellerin selbst erfolgen sollte, so ging die Agfa in erster Linie davon aus, „daß es für den einzelnen in der Anlaufzeit noch nicht immer lohnend genug sein wird, das Spezialentwicklungsbad anzusetzen."
Daher trafen im Agfacolor-Labor in der Lohmühlenstraße in Berlin-Treptow schon 1937 soviele Filme ein, daß es aus Personalmangel und wegen der auf solche Filmmengen nicht eingestellten technischen Einrichtung einige Tage dauerte, bis sie entwickelt waren.
Die Folge waren Waschkörbe voller Reklamationen... Die Begeisterung der Anhänger des neuen Farbfilms wurde aber auch kaum dadurch getrübt, daß, wie die von der Agfa herausgegebenen *Photoblätter* (Heft 5, 1938) selbst einräumten, „die ersten Filme... mitunter eine gewisse Farbstichigkeit – meist etwas nach Blau oder Grün – aufwiesen."

Auch die zunächst noch sehr niedrige Filmempfindlichkeit von nur „7/10 °DIN", was nach der gegenwärtigen Empfindlichkeitsnorm ISO 2,5/5° entsprechen würde (zum Vergleich: Ein heutiger Standard-Diafilm hat ISO 100/21°!), dämpfte nicht die Freude am neuen Aufnahmematerial. Man hatte damals ja auch nur die alten Farbverfahren als Vergleichsmaßstab, und denen gegenüber „ermöglicht die hohe Empfindlichkeit Momentaufnahmen mit billigen Apparaten".
Bei Sommersonne genügte schon ein Objektiv von der Lichtstärke 6.3, um „Momentbilder von 1/25 Sek. zu machen", wie die Agfa in ihrem ersten Prospekt *Die Photographie in natürlichen Farben mit dem neuen Agfacolor-Film* feststellte.

Als im Sommer 1938 die Empfindlichkeit des Agfacolor Diafilms auf „15/10 °DIN" erhöht werden konnte, erschlossen sich der Farbfotografie neue Gebiete. Diese Steigerung um fast das Achtfache ohne Vergröberung der Kornstruktur des Bildes war dem von dem Agfa-Chemiker Dr. Robert Koslowsky entdeckten "Goldeffekt" zu verdanken gewesen. Er hatte den fotografischen Emulsionen Spuren von Gold zugefügt – bis Kriegsende ein sorgsam gehütetes Fabrikationsgeheimnis der Agfa.

named grain screen and lenticulated films from Agfa which were still available on the market, there were also further advantages as compared with the old color films. They were set out in the first advertisement (see page 8): "Any miniature camera can be used to take the picture. No filter and no special lens are required. Any normal miniature projector can project your slides..."

Furthermore, Agfa gave the following information in a brochure: "Everything is just as easy in black-and-white photography, or even easier, because ... Agfa also takes care of the production of the pictures." On this subject, the daily newspapier *B.Z. am Mittag* printed the following on October 19, 1936: "By collecting the pictures taken throughout the Reich at the central offices of Agfa, it will be possible to operate more economically. When the new film has become established, it will of course also be possible to train the photographic dealers and amateurs in the development process." This was a reference to the simplicity of the Agfacolor process as regards the processing of films. Although, however, this was in the first instance to be carried out exclusively by the film manufacturer itself, Agfa was

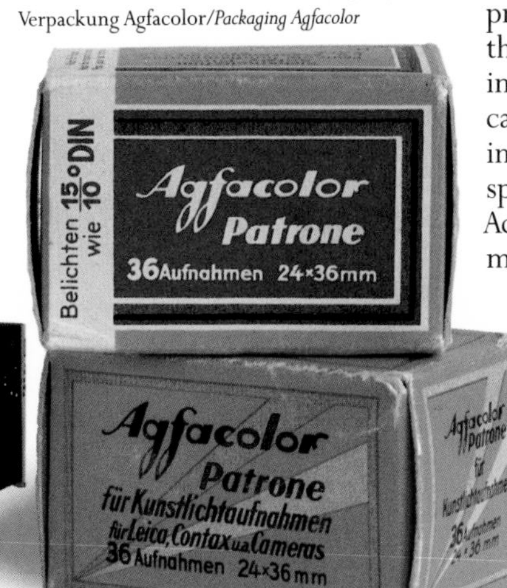

Verpackung Agfacolor/*Packaging Agfacolor*

proceeding fundamentally on the basis "that during the initial period it will not in all cases be worth while for an individual to prepare the special developing bath". Accordingly, already in 1937, so many films were received in the Agfacolor laboratory in Lohmühlenstrasse in Berlin-Treptow that, on account of the lack of staff and by reason of the technical equipment not being designed for such large numbers of films, development required a period of several days. This resulted in baskets full of complaints... However, the enthusiasm of the devotees of the new color was not much dampened even by the fact that, as the *Photoblätter* (No. 5/1938) published by Agfa admitted, "The first films ... exhibited in some cases a certain color cast – mostly showing a tendency towards blue or green." Not even the initially very low film speed of only 7/10° DIN, which would correspond to ISO 2.5/5° according to the present speed standard (for comparison, it should be noted that a present-day standard slide film has a speed of ISO 100/21°!), could spoil the pleasure experienced with the new exposure material. At that time, only the old color processes were available as a scale for comparison, as compared with these, "the high speed permits instantaneous exposures with cheap cameras". Under sunny conditions in summer, a lens of aperture 6.3 was actually adequate "to make instantaneous exposures of 1/25 sec., as was stated by Agfa in its first brochure *Photography in Natural Colors with the new Agfacolor film.*

Im selben Jahr 1938 erschien auch ein Agfacolor Kunstlichtfilm. Ein solches auf die damals üblichen Fotolampen vom Typ Nitraphot-B oder Osram-S abgestimmtes spezielles Filmmaterial erfreute sich mangels Blitzgeräten im heutigen Sinne bei den Fotografen in jenen Jahren für Personenaufnahmen im Heim noch großer Beliebtheit. „Die Farbenwiedergabe ist bei dem neuen Material als gut zu bezeichnen. Auch schwierige Fleischtöne kommen überzeugend heraus" stellte die Zeitschrift *Kleinfilm-Foto* (Heft 5, 1938) fest. Wenn man den ursprünglichen Farbcharakter von Aufnahmen aus den Anfangsjahren der modernen Farbfotografie noch gut erahnen will, dann muß man allerdings auf Abbildungen in Büchern zurückgreifen. Bei vielen Agfacolor-Dias ist nämlich der gelbe Farbstoff mehr oder weniger ausgeblichen, woran häufig auch ungünstige Lagerungsverhältnisse in der Kriegs- und Nachkriegszeit schuld waren. So sind Veröffentlichungen wie das Ende 1938 erschienene „erste und grundlegende Agfacolor-Buch", das von Eduard von Pagenhardt herausgegebene Werk *Agfacolor, das farbige Lichtbild – Grundlagen und Aufnahmetechnik für den Liebhaberphotographen* mit 64 Farbfotos bekannter Fotografen recht interessant. Im selben Jahr brachte ebenfalls der Münchner Verlag Knorr & Hirth ein Buch heraus, das bewies, daß "trotz der offiziellen Warnung der Agfa, den neuen Farbfilm vorerst nicht in tropischen Ländern zu verwenden", in Afrika erfolgreich auf Agfacolor fotografiert worden war: Reisebuch *Zu den Palmen Libyens* von Max Geysenheyner.

Der höherempfindliche Agfacolor Film, vor allem als Kunstlichttyp, kam einer Pionierleistung des bekannten Leica-Fotografen Dr. Paul Wolff zugute, der für das 1940 erschienene Buch *Im Kraftfeld von Rüsselsheim* in den Opel-Werken erstmals farbige Industrieaufnahmen machen konnte. Wolff schilderte dann 1942 in seinem bekanntesten Farbfotobuch *Meine Erfahrungen – farbig.* Zu den bedeutendsten Fotografen, der weiteren vor Kriegsende erschienenen über 20 Bücher und Bildbände mit Agfacolor-Aufnahmen, gehören Kurt Peter Karfeld und Erich Retzlaff. Agfacolor Filme waren bald auch in den Export gegangen. 1940 bestanden bereits Entwicklungsanstalten in Wien, London, Arnhem (Holland), Brüssel, Paris, Mailand, Zürich, Prag, Zagreb, Budapest, Stockholm und in Binghamton, N.Y., USA, wo der Film schon 1938 von der amerikanischen IG-Farben-Tochterfirma Agfa Ansco Corp. unter dem Namen "Ansco Color" eingeführt worden war. Doch mit fortschreitendem Krieg wurde Agfacolor für zivile Fotografen immer rarer: Tausende von Filmen wurden für die Arbeit der Kriegsberichterstatter an den Fronten benötigt. In den PK-Kompanien der deutschen Wehrmacht hielten viele bekannte Fotografen das Kriegsgeschehen in Farbfotos fest, zur Auswertung „nach dem Endsieg"... Einige Bilder wurde auch bereits in der für das Ausland bestimmten, journalistisch gut gemachten Propagandazeitschrift *Signal* abgedruckt, die sich schon früh der Farbfotografie bedient hatte.

Ansco Printon

When, in summer 1938, it became possible to increase the speed of the Agfacolor slide film to 15/10 DIN, new areas were opened up for color photography. This increase by a factor of almost eight without any increase in the coarseness of the grain structure of the image had been due to the 'gold effect' discovered by the Agfa chemist Dr. Robert Koslowsky. He had added traces of gold to the photographic emulsions – until the end of the war, a carefully guarded manufacturing secret at Agfa.

In the same year, 1938, an Agfacolor for artificial light film also appeared. This type of special film material adapted for the photographic lamps of the tungsten type which were customary, still enjoyed great popularity in those years of portraits at home, in the absence of flashguns in the current sense of the term. "With the new material, the color reproduction can be described as good. Even flesh tones which present difficulty are rendered convincingly," said the magazine *Kleinfilm-Foto* (No. 5, 1938). To get any clear idea today of the original nature of the colors of photographs taken during the initial years of modern color photography, one has to turn to book illustrations. In the case of many Agfacolor slides, the yellow dye has to some extent been bleached out, and in many cases this was due to unfavourable storage conditions during the war and in the post-war period. Thus, publications such as the *First and Fundamental Agfacolor Book,* which appeared at the end of 1938, and the work *Agfacolor, das farbige Lichtbild Grundlagen und Aufnahmetechnik für den Liebhaberphotographen* (Agfacolor, the Color Photograph, Principles and Exposure Technique for the Photographic Enthusiast) with 64 color photos of well known photographers are of great interest. In the same year, the Munich publishing house Knorr and Hirth also published a book, which proved that "in spite of the official warning by Agfa not to use the new color film at first in tropical countries", photographs had been successfully taken in Africa with Agfacolor: the travel book *Zu den Palmen Libyens* (Palms of Libya) by Max Geysenheymer.

The higher-speed Agfacolor film, principally in the form of the artificial light type, proved to be very useful for pioneering work undertaken by the well known Leica photographer Dr. Paul Wolff, who was able to take color pictures of industry for the first time in the Opel works for the book *Im Kraftfeld von Rüsselsheim,* which appeard in 1940. Then, in 1942, Wolff's best known book on color photography described *Meine Erfahrungen - farbig* (My Experiences - In Color). The most significant photographers responsible for over 20 further books and picture books containing Agfacolor photographs which were published before the end of the war include the work of Kurt Peter Karfeld and Erich Retzlaff.

Agfacolor films had soon also started to be exported. In 1940, developing laboratories already existed in Vienna, London, Arnhem (Holland), Brussels, Paris, Milan, Zurich, Prague, Zagreb, Budapest, Stockholm and Binghamton N.Y., USA, where the film had been introduced as early as 1938

Die Kriegsberichter gehörten auch zu dem auserwählten Kreis von Fotografen, die bereits eine weitere Farbfilmsorte nutzen konnten, die der Öffentlichkeit noch nicht zur Verfügung stand: den Agfacolor Negativfilm für farbige Papierbilder.

Vom farbigen Kinofilm zu Papierbild

„Das Endziel der Farbenphotographie ist das naturfarbige Papierbild, dessen Herstellung genauso einfach sein muß, wie die Anfertigung einer Schwarzweiß-Kopie oder -Vergrößerung von einem Schwarzweiß-Negativ. Man könnte daran denken, daß ein Papier, welches die gleichen drei Schichten besitzt wie der Agfacolor Film, von dem Farbennegativ auch ein Farbenpositiv ergibt..." schrieben die *Photoblätter* der Agfa im Jahre 1938. Seit der Ankündigung der umfassenden Möglichkeiten des Agfacolor-Verfahrens auf den Pressekonferenzen am 17. Oktober 1936 hatte die Diskussion um das bevorstehende neue Negativ/Positiv-System nämlich in Fachkreisen angehalten. Teils waren die Erwartungen vorsichtig, teils recht hoch.

Immerhin – aber das war öffentlich unbekannt – hatten die ersten praktischen Farbfilmversuche von Schneider und Kollegen schon im Sommer 1935 einem farbigen Negativ gegolten, und war schon 1936/37 die Herstellung von Agfacolor-Papier in der Agfa Photofabrik in Leverkusen gelungen. Für die Negativ/Positiv-Materialien hatte man auf Grund ihrer vom Diafilm abweichenden Voraussetzungen und Eigenschaften andere chemische Bausteine suchen müssen. Vorrang genoß aber ein ehrgeiziges Projekt, das von höchsten deutschen Regierungsstellen gefordert und gefördert wurde: der mit dem amerikanischen Technicolor konkurrenzfähige, aber einfacher zu handhabende farbige Kinofilm. Bis dahin hatte es nämlich nur komplizierte Aufnahme-, Kopier- und Wiedergabe-Verfahren gegeben.
Das blieb im Ausland auch so bis nach Kriegsende, während es in Deutschland schon kurze Zeit nach der Einführung der modernen Farbfotografie gelang, Farbnegativ- und entsprechende -positivfilme für die Kinofilmkopie herzustellen, wie sie heute allgemein üblich sind. So konnten den Filmstudios – allen voran die UFA – bereits ab Sommer 1939 Agfacolor Filme zur Verfügung gestellt werden. Am 31. Oktober 1941 erlebte der erste abendfüllende farbige Spielfilm *Frauen sind doch bessere Diplomaten* seine Uraufführung. Als ein Jahr später der zweite, *Die goldene Stadt,* folgte, konnte auf der Dresdner Fachtagung *Film und Farbe* gleichzeitig mit seiner deutschen Erstaufführung das Agfacolor-Papier der Öffentlichkeit vorgestellt werden.

In einer kleinen Ausstellung waren Agfacolor-Vergrößerungen in den Formaten 24 x 30 und 30 x 40 cm von Kleinbild- und Rollfilm-Aufnahmen zu sehen, die – wie es im Tagungsband hieß – „die dargestellten Gegenstände in vollkommener Farbenrichtigkeit und Farbschönheit bei kräftiger, leuchtender Farbgebung" zeigten. Anders als in den USA hatte man sich in Deutschland nicht mit dem Weg befaßt, zu den Dias ein entsprechendes Kopiermaterial zu schaffen, weil man den Gang über das Negativ/Positiv-Verfahren für einfacher und auch für „unbedenklich der Allgemeinheit zugänglich" hielt. Beim Agfacolor-Verfahren mit den in den Filmschichten eingelagerten

by the American IG Farben subsidiary Agfa Ansco Corp. under the name 'Ansco Color'. However, as the war progressed, Agfacolor became increasingly scarce for civilian photographers: thousands of films were required for the work of the war reporters at the front. In the so called 'propaganda' companies of the German forces, many well known photographers recorded the events of the war in color for evaluation "after the final victory"... Some pictures had also been printed in the propaganda periodical *Signal,* which was intended for foreign countries, and well prepared from the journalistic point of view and had made use of color photography from an early stage. The war reporters also belonged to the select group of photographers who could already use another type of color film which was not yet available to the public: Agfacolor negative film for color prints.

From color cine film to the print

"The ultimate objective of color photography is a print, which is in natural colors and the production of which must be just as simple as the preparation of a black-and-white copy or enlargement from a black-and-white negative. One might think that a paper which has the same three coatings as the Agfacolor film should also produce a color positive from the color negative..." wrote the Agfa *Photo blätter* in 1938. Since the announcement of the extensive possiblities of the Agfacolor process at the press conferences on October 17, 1936, the discussion about the forthcoming new negative/positive system had indeed been pursued in expert circles. In some cases, the expectations were cautious, but in some cases they were very high.

Anyway – but this was not known to the public – the first practical color film tests by Schneider and his colleagues back in the summer of 1935 had been intended for the production of a color negative, and as early as 1936/37 success had been achieved in the production of Agfacolor paper in the Agfa photographic production facility in Leverkusen. Where the negative/positive materials were concerned, their requirements and properties which differed from those of the slide film, had made it necessary to look for different chemical components. However, priority was given to an ambitious project, which was requested and promoted by the highest levels of the German Government: the color cine film which would be able to compete with the american Technicolor but which would have simpler handling properties. Until then, there had really only been complicated exposure, printing and reproduction processes. This continued to be the case in foreign countries until after the end of the war, while in Germany, only a short time after the introduction of modern color photography, success was achieved in producing color negative and corresponding positive films for cine film copies, in the form in which they are generally customary today. Thus, it was possible to provide the film studios – first and foremost, the UFA - with Agfacolor films from summer 1939 onwards. On October 31, 1941, the first full-length color feature film *Frauen sind doch bessere Diplomaten* was given its first showing. "When, one year later, the second film *Die goldene Stadt* followed, the Agfacolor paper could be presented to the public at the Dresden trade congress *Film und Farbe* (Film and Color) at the same time as its first showing in Germany.

Farbkupplern stand ja von vorneherein die Möglichkeit zur Verfügung, den Film zum Negativ zu entwickeln. Doch mußte der Verbraucher leider noch lange darauf warten.

Die in der Wolfener Filmfabrik schon 1939 eingerichtete Fabrikationsanlage für das neue Papier mußte, wie überhaupt ein Großteil der Produktionskapazität „kriegswichtigeren Zwecken" zugeführt werden. Daher konnte die Erfüllung des Wunsches nach farbigen Papierbildern im neuen Verfahren – von Dias waren sie nach umständlichen und kostspieligen Spezialverfahren wie Duxochrom oder Coloprint durchaus schon möglich – von der Agfa schließlich erst für die Zeit nach Kriegsende in Aussicht gestellt werden. Dann aber sollten sowohl Tages- als auch Kunstlichtfilme in allen Formaten sowie das Colorpapier in verschiedenen Gradationen (Kontrasten) und Oberflächen erhältlich sein; auch an eine Freigabe der Verarbeitung für das Heimlabor wurde bereits gedacht.

Aber erst 1949 war es für die deutschen Fotografen soweit, nachdem schon vor 1945 einige wenige Berufsfotografen beim Militär, in der Industrie, in den Filmstudios und nicht zulezt im Auftrage der Agfa selbst Gelegenheit hatten, das Agacolor Negativ/Positiv-Verfahren gut kennenzulernen.

Aber auch die Diafilme wurden weiter verbessert, denn bis 1945 arbeiteten über 50 Chemiker, Physiker und Ingenieure trotz der immer einschneidenderen Kriegseinwirkungen bei der Agfa an der Fortentwicklung der Farbfotografie und konnten bis dahin rund 270 Patente anmelden.

Wie hatte doch Dr. Gustav Wilmanns schon 1941 in seinem Beitrag zum *Farbfoto-Buch vom Film* von Charlott Serda vorausgesagt?: „Als schöpferische Techniker wissen wir, daß nur der Wechsel beständig ist. Daher halten wir es bei allem Stolz auf das, was wir verwirklichen konnten, immerhin für möglich, daß spätere Jahre den von uns eingeschlagenen Weg auch wieder einmal verlassen..."

Doppelporträt Schneider/Wilmanns (Bronze-Ehrentafel der UFA 1942)
Doubleportrait Schneider/Wilmanns (UFA bronce-plaque 1942)

In a small exhibition, Agfacolor enlargements size 24 x 30 and 30 x 40 cm from 35 mm and roll film pictures were on view, and these – as was stated in the conference programme – "showed the portrayed objects in completely accurate colors and with perfection as far as color was concerned, with strong, bright colors". In contrast to the USA, the choice in Germany was not to follow the path of producing a copying material appropriate for slides, because the route via the negative/positive process was considered to be simpler and also"accessible to the public without difficulty". With the Agfacolor process, with the color couplers embedded in the film coatings, it was actually possible from the outset to develop the film into a negative.The public unfortunately had to wait a long time for this.

The production facility for the new paper, set up as early as 1939 in the Wolfen film production plants had to be designated, just like any large proportion of the production capacity, to "purposes which were more important in terms of the war effort". Accordingly, the fulfilment of the desire for color prints in the new process - these could in fact already be made from slides by means of cumbersome and costly special processes such as Duxochrom or Coloprint - could finally be regarded by Agfa as only being a possible prospect for the period after the end of the war. However, both daylight and artificial light films in all formats and color paper in various degrees of contrast and surfaces were to be available; the possibiltiy of releasing the processing for the home darkroom was also already under consideration.

But not until 1949 was this degree of progress made for the benefit of german photographers, bearing in mind that, even before 1945, a few professional photographers in military service, in industry, in the film studios and, not least, acting for Agfa itself, had an opportunity to become well acquainted with the Agfacolor negative/positive process.

However, slide films were also being further improved: until 1945 over 50 chemists, physicists and engineers worked at Agfa on the further development of color photography, in spite of the increasingly drastic effects of the war, and by that time were able to apply for about 270 patents.

What was Dr. Gustav Wilmann's prediction, as long ago as 1941, in his contribution to the *Farbfoto-Buch vom Film* (Color Photography Book from film) by Charlott Serda: "As creative engineers, we know that only change is constant. For all our pride in what we were able to archieve, we still think it possible that later generations may once more turn away from the road on which we set out . . "

Kodachrome

Horst W. Staubach

Für die meisten Menschen war der 15. April 1935 sicherlich ein Tag wie jeder andere. Für die fotografische Welt hingegen war es ein denkwürdiger Tag, wurde doch an diesem 15. April der erste Mehrschichtenfarbfilm der Welt, der Kodachrome, vorgestellt. Ab sofort konnte jedermann mit diesem Film ohne mechanische oder optische Hilfsmittel Schmalfilme in natürlichen Farben drehen (im August 1936 folgte dann der Kodachrome Kleinbildfilm für Stehbildaufnahmen). Die "ungewohnte" Naturtreue der Farbwiedergabe des Films und die Einfachheit, mit der sie erreicht werden konnte – das war für das Publikum das Faszinierende am Kodachrome Film. Bezeichnend für den Eindruck, den ein Vorführfilm bei den Zuschauern hinterließ, ist die Äußerung eines Schmalfilmers: "Es war, als hätte man durch ein Fenster auf das wirkliche Leben geblickt."

Anläßlich der offiziellen Vorstellung des Kodachrome Films in Rochester hielt Dr. Mees, damals Vizepräsident und Chef der Forschungslaboratorien der Eastman Kodak Company, eine Ansprache, in deren Verlauf er eine für die meisten Anwesenden erstaunliche Mitteilung machte. "Der Prozeß", sagte er, "ist die Erfindung von Leopold Mannes und Leo Godowsky jr., beide in der Welt der Musik als Künstler gut bekannt, die vor einigen Jahren als Hobby Forschungsarbeiten auf dem Gebiet der Farbfotografie aufnahmen." Dr. Mees gebrauchte das Wort "Hobby", und in der Tat konnte die Beschäftigung mit der Farbfotografie für die beiden Freunde nur eine Freizeitbeschäftigung sein. Denn ihren Lebensunterhalt mußten sie sich als Musiker, Mannes als Pianist, Godowsky als Violin-Solist, verdienen. So weit so gut. Doch was in aller Welt konnte zwei junge Menschen, beide aus bekannten Musikerfamilien stammend, dazu bewegt haben, sich ausgerechnet mit einem so amusischen Gebiet wie farbfotografischen Forschungsarbeiten zu befassen?

Ein Kinobesuch und seine Folgen

Den Anstoß gab ein Kinobesuch im Jahre 1917 in New York. Man zeigte den Dokumentarfilm "Our Navy", an dem die beiden Freunde in erster Linie die Tatsache interessierte, daß er als Farbfilm angekündigt worden war. Doch ihre hochgespannten Erwartungen wurden bitter enttäuscht: die Bilder auf der Leinwand waren unscharf, die Farben unschön und verwaschen. Noch auf dem Heimweg beschlossen die beiden Freunde, ein besseres Farbverfahren zu entwickeln. Ein kühner, ja geradezu abenteuerlicher Entschluß, denn das Gebiet der Farbfotografie war damals weitestgehend Neuland, war auf der Landkarte der Fotochemie noch ein großer weißer Fleck.

Für ihre ersten Schritte in das Neuland war beiden Freunden unabhängig voneinander die gleiche Idee gekommen. Es war – was sie allerdings erst sehr viel später entdeckten – die gleiche Idee, die reichlich ein halbes Jahrhundert vor ihnen der schottische Gelehrte James Clerk Maxwell den staunenden Mitgliedern der Royal Institution of Great Britain praktisch demonstriert hatte: die additive Farbenfotografie (ein Begriff, den es zu Maxwells Zeit freilich noch nicht gab).

For most people, April 15, 1935 was just a day like any other. But for the photographic world it was a day to remember; the day which saw the launching of Kodachrome, the world's first multi-layer color film. From that moment on, anyone could use this film – with no mechanical or optical aids – to shoot narrow-gauge films in natural colors (the Kodachrome miniature film for still photography came later, in August 1936). What fascinated the general public about Kodachrome film was the (unaccustomed) faithfullness of the natural colors it reproduced, and the simplicity with which this was achieved. One maker of narrow-gauge films said, 'It was as if we had a glimpse of real life through a window,' a comment which typifies the impression which the demonstration film made on those who saw it.

At the official launch of the Kodachrome film in Rochester, Dr. Mees, then Vice-President of the Eastman Kodak Company and head of its research laboratories gave an address which astonished most of those present. 'The process,' he said, 'is the invention of Leopold Mannes and Leo Godowsky Jr., who were musicians well known in the musical world when some years ago they commenced the study of color photography as a hobby.' And in fact the two friends' interest in color photography could have been no more than a hobby, since they both had to earn their living as musicians – Mannes as a pianist, Godowsky as a solo violinist. So far so good. But what on earth could have prompted these two young men – both members of well-known musical families – to have interested themselves in such a conspicuously non-musical field as research into color photography?

A Movie-Film and its Consequences

The impetus came from a visit to a New York cinema in 1917. The film being shown was a documentary, *Our Navy*, and its principal interest for the two friends was the fact that it was advertised as a color film. But their high hopes were bitterly dashed: the images on the screen were blurred, the colors ugly and feeble. Before they had even reached home, the two friends made up their minds to develop a better color process. It was a bold, even adventurous decision, since color photography at the time was very largely unexplored territory, a large empty space on the map of photo-chemistry.

The two friends' first steps on this uncharted shore were guided by an idea which had come to both of them independently. It was – as they themselves only learnt much later – the same idea as that demonstrated by the Scottish academic, James Clerk Maxwell to the astonished members of the Royal Institution of Great Britain a good half-century earlier: additive color photography (though of course the term was unknown in Maxwell's day).

In the Footsteps of Maxwell

Leopold Mannes and Leo Godowsky, 18 and 17 years old respectively, were then pupils at Riverdale County School in New York. Obtaining permission to use the school's physics laboratory, they began their experiments in color photography. Even though the results of their first efforts were no more than a repetition of Maxwell's method, they did achieve one substantial improvement – they had contrived a device which accurately centered and focussed

Auf den Spuren Maxwells

Der 18jährige Leopold Mannes und der 17jährige Leo Godowsky waren damals Schüler der Riverdale Country School in New York. Im Physiklabor der Schule begannen sie mit ihren farbfotografischen Experimenten. Wenn auch das Ergebnis ihrer ersten Versuche nichts anderes war als eine Wiederholung der Maxwellschen Methode, so gelang ihnen doch insofern eine wesentliche Verbesserung, als sie eine Einrichtung zur exakten Zentrierung und Fokussierung der drei Teilbilder ausgeklügelt hatten, die bewirkt, daß die störenden Farbsäume, die sich bei der Übereinanderprojektion gewöhnlich ergeben, nicht mehr auftreten können. Und darauf ließen sie sich ein Patent erteilen. Es war das erste von rund 40 Patenten, die sie im Laufe der folgenden Jahre erworben haben.

Zunächst aber konnten sie keinerlei weiteren Erfolge verzeichnen. Im Gegenteil. Im Jahre 1919 hatten sie einen (ebenfalls auf der additiven Farbmischung fußenden) experimentellen Kinofilm fertiggestellt. Das Ergebnis ihrer Bemühungen war jedoch niederschmetternd: Farben und Schärfe waren um keinen Deut besser als die des Dokumentarfilms, der ihren erfinderischen Ehrgeiz ausgelöst hatte. Und mit diesem Fiasko waren sie an einem Scheideweg angelangt. Sie standen vor der Frage, ob sie weitermachen und ihr Heil in der Verbesserung des von ihnen gewählten Verfahrens suchen sollten. Oder ob es besser sei, das Handtuch zu werfen und ihre junge und bis dahin wenig hoffnungsvolle Erfinderlaufbahn zu beenden. Nun, sie taten weder das eine noch das andere. Vielmehr beschlossen sie, wie Godowsky es später einmal formulierte, "von einem Mehrfachlinsensystem hinüberzuwechseln zu einem Mehrschichtenfilm", mit anderen Worten also von einer optischen zu einer chemischen Lösung des Problems, zum subtraktiven Farbverfahren überzugehen.

Leopold Mannes & Leo Godowsky

Zweischichtenplatten – Sprungbrett zum Dreischichten-Farbfilm

Für den Anfang beschränkten sie sich auf ein Zweischichtenverfahren, "aber nicht deswegen", so Godowsky, "weil wir uns auf zwei Farben beschränken wollten, sondern weil wir erst einmal die Probleme eines Zweifarbenverfahrens beherrschen mußten, bevor wir an einen Dreischichtenfarbfilm denken konnten."

Zunächst arbeiteten sie unter unglaublich primitiven Bedingungen: Badezimmer oder Küchen der elterlichen Wohnungen dienten den beiden Leopolds als behelfsmäßige Dunkelkammern. Die erforderlichen Zweischichtenplatten mußten sie selbst in einer mühseligen Prozedur herstellen: Von handelsüblichen Diaplatten schabten sie vorsichtig die vorher aufgeweichten Emulsionen ab, schmolzen sie ein, sensibilisierten sie für zwei Bereiche des Lichtspektrums – Rotorange und Blaugrün – und gossen sie auf eine Glasplatte. Und zumindest im Prinzip war das Verfahren so vielversprechend, daß Mannes und Godowsky sich bereits im Oktober

the three part-images, with the result that the troublesome chromatic fringes usually encountered with superimposed projection could no longer occur. On this basis, they obtained the grant of a patent, the first of some 40 patents which they were to acquire during the years which followed.

At first, though, they made no further progress. If anything, the reverse was true. In 1919 they had completed an experimental cine-film, again based on the additive color-mixing process, but the result of their efforts was shattering: the colors and sharpness of their film were not one iota better than those of the documentary film which had fired their inventive ambition. This fiasco brought them to a crossroad. Should they carry on and hope to find their salvation by improving the process they had selected? Or would it be better to give up and abandon their new – and not very promising – careers as inventors? In fact, they did neither. Instead, as Godowsky later put it, they decided to 'switch from a multiple-lens system to a multi-layer film', in other words to solve the problem by chemical rather than optical means – the subtractive color process.

Bi-pack Plates – a Springboard to the Tri-pack Color Film

To start with, they confined themselves to a double-coat process, 'but not', said Godowsky, 'because we wanted to confine ourselves to two colors, but because we had to master the problems of the two-color process before we could think in terms of a tri-pack color film.' At first the two Leopolds worked under incredibly primitive conditions, using the bathrooms or kitchens of their parents' homes as makeshift darkrooms. They had to make their own doublecoated plates, a laborious procedure: they obtained ordinary commercial transparency plates, softened the emulsions, scraped them off carefully, melted them down, sensitized them for two parts of the light spectrum – red-orange and blue-green – and then coated them one after another onto a glass plate. The coats had to be dyed after developing, and here they benefitted from their school experience with the metal-salt or mordant toning processes which were known at that time. In principle, at least, the process was so promising that Mannes and Godowsky took out a patent (US Patent 1/538/996) for their double-coat process as early as October 1921. In another patent (US Patent 1/516/824), filed at the end of February 1923, they described for the first time the principle of controlled diffusion, which was later to play a crucial part in the first Kodachrome process. Although the two friends had now recorded their first successes, they didn't earn enough to meet the expenditure for rent and the experimental materials, they needed.

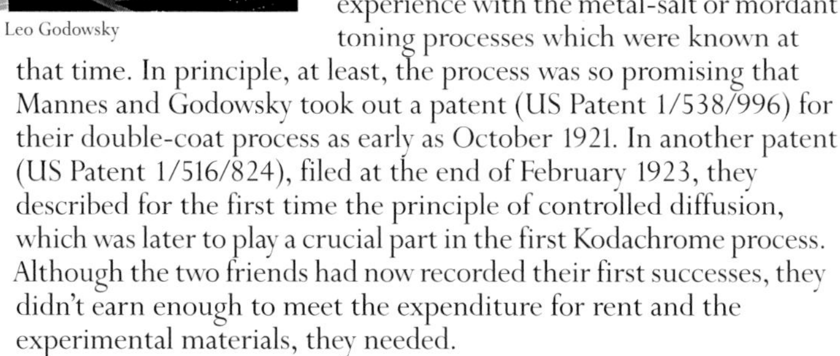

Sponsors and Rescuers from Material Hardships

One day in the late autumn of 1922 a Mr. Lewis L. Strauss,

1921 auf ihr Zweischichtenverfahren ein Patent (USP 1/538/996) erteilen ließen. In einem weiteren Patent (USP 1/516/824), das sie Ende Februar 1923 einreichten, beschrieben sie zum erstenmal das Prinzip der kontrollierten Diffusion, das später beim ersten Kodachrome-Prozeß eine entscheidende Rolle spielen sollte. Die beiden Freunde konnten nun zwar erste Erfolge verzeichnen, aber ihnen fehlten die Mittel, um die Kosten für Miete und die benötigten Versuchsmaterialien bestreiten zu können.

Förderer und Retter aus materiellen Nöten

Da stellte sich an einem Spätherbsttag des Jahres 1922 ein Mr. Lewis L. Strauss, Junior-Partner des New Yorker Bankhauses Kuhn, Loeb & Co., in der Wohnung der Familie Mannes ein. Er hatte von den Farbexperimenten der beiden Freunde gehört und wollte Näheres darüber erfahren. Offensichtlich hatte Strauss einen guten Eindruck gewonnen und die Erfolgschancen der jungen Erfinder günstig beurteilt, denn wenig später wurden Mannes und Godowsky in das Bankhaus gebeten, wo ihnen zu ihrer großen Freude eröffnete wurden, daß man bereit sei, ihnen zur Finanzierung ihrer Forschungsarbeiten ein Darlehen von knapp 20.000 Dollar zur Verfügung zu stellen.

Im gleichen Jahr löste die von einem Bekannten vermittelte Begegnung mit Dr. C.E. Kenneth Mees, dem leitenden Direktor der Kodak Forschungslaboratorien in Rochester, ein weiteres Problem: Mees versprach, den Freunden verschiedene Materialien, vor allem fotografische Platten, die nach ihren Spezifikationen angefertigt würden, zur Verfügung zu stellen. Als Gegenleistung erwartete er, vom Fortgang ihrer Arbeiten auf dem Laufenden gehalten zu werden.

Farbkuppler eröffnen neue Perspektiven

Eines Tages – es war im Jahr 1925 – wurden Mannes und Godowsky auf das Werk *History of Color Photography* von E. J. Wall aufmerksam gemacht, weil der Autor auch das von ihnen entwickelte Verfahren der "kontrollierten Diffusion" beschrieben hatte. Natürlich fühlten sich die jungen Leute geschmeichelt, fasziniert aber waren sie, als sie bei eingehender Lektüre des Bandes auf einen Bericht über die von dem deutschen Wissenschaftler Dr. Rudolf Fischer entdeckten Farbkuppler stießen. Sie erkannten sofort, daß sie Farbkuppler, kombiniert mit ihrem Prinzip der kontrollierten Diffusion ihrem Ziel, dem Dreischichten-Farbfilm einen großen Schritt näherbringen würden. Sie zögerten daher auch nicht lange, die Idee aufzugreifen. Weil sich die von Fischer beschriebenen Farbkuppler als ungeeignet erwiesen, engagierten sie einen jungen Chemiker, dessen einzige Aufgabe es war, für sie neue Farbkuppler zu entdecken. Und sie hatten Glück: Ihr Chemiker wurde bald fündig und bescherte ihnen unter anderem einen sehr guten Gelbkuppler.

Als sie Dr. Mees gelegentlich eines seiner häufigen Besuche in New York ihre jüngsten Ergebnisse vorstellten, war Dr. Mees so beeindruckt, daß er ihnen vorschlug, ihr Projekt als seine Mitarbeiter in den Kodak Forschungslaboratorien fortzusetzen. Die Vertragsbedingungen waren generös, Mannes und Godowsky willigten ein und siedelten im Juli 1931 nach Rochester über. Dr. Mees erläuterte

junior partner in the New York banking house of Kuhn, Loeb & Co., turned up at the Mannes family home. He had heard of the two friends' experiments with color, and wanted to find out more about it. Evidently Strauss formed a favourable impression of the two friends and of their prospects of success. Shortly after this, Mannes and Godowsky were summoned to the bank, and were delighted to learn that it was willing to advance them a loan of almost 20,000 dollars to finance their research.

That same year, an acquaintance arranged for them to meet Dr. C.E. Kenneth Mees, Managing Director of the Kodak Research Laboratories in Rochester, and another problem was solved: Mees promised to supply the friends with various materials, especially photographic plates, which would be made to their specifications. In return, he expected to be kept up-to-date with their progress.

Color Couplers Open up New Perspectives

One day in 1925 the attention of Mannes and Godowsky was called to E. J. Wall's *History of Color Photography,* because the author had also included a description of the process of 'controlled diffusion' which they had developed. The two young men were naturally flattered, but they were fascinated, on closer study of the book, to come across a report referring to the color couplers discovered by the German scientist Dr. Rudolf Fischer. They immediately realised that color couplers, combined with their principle of controlled diffusion, would bring them very much closer to the triple-coated color film. And so they wasted little time in pursuing the idea. Since the color couplers described by Fischer proved unsuitable, they engaged the services of a young chemist whose sole task it was to discover new color couplers for them. And luck was on their side: their chemist soon delivered the goods, presenting them – among others – with a very good yellow coupler.

When they showed Dr. Mees their latest results during one of his frequent visits to New York, he was so impressed that he invited them to work for him, continuing their project at the Kodak Research Laboratories. The terms offered were generous, and Mannes and Godowsky agreed. They moved to Rochester in July 1931. Dr. Mees explained later why the move was necessary: 'As a result of collaboration between them (Mannes and Godowsky) and the Kodak research laboratories in Rochester for a number of years it was evident that the work could be brought to a successful conclusion only by a full utilization of the research and manufacturing facilities available at Kodak Park'. (*Rochester Evening Journal,* 12th April 1935).

Final Spurt in Rochester

The move to Rochester brought profound changes in the lives of the two friends. Previously their time had literally been split between music and research: as orchestral players or soloists they earned the money they needed to live and to continue their experiments in color photography. But in Rochester, for the first time, they were able to devote themselves completely to their research – not just on public holidays and at weekends, but also on quite ordinary working days. They also had a laboratory of their own at their disposal.

die Notwendigkeit dieses Wechsels später so: "Die jahrelange Zusammenarbeit zwischen ihnen (Mannes und Godowsky) und den Kodak Forschungslaboratorien machte deutlich, daß der erfolgreiche Abschluß der Arbeit nur durch die volle Nutzung der Forschungs- und Fertigungskapazität von Kodak möglich war" (*Rochester Evening Journal* vom 12.4.1935).

Endspurt in Rochester

Rochester brachte einen tiefgreifenden Wandel im Leben der beiden Freunde mit sich. Vorher spielte sich ihr Leben buchstäblich zwischen Musik und Forschung ab: als Orchestermitglieder oder Solisten verdienten sie Geld, um leben und ihre farbfotografischen Experimente fortführen zu können. In Rochester aber konnten sie sich zum erstenmal in ihrem Leben uneingeschränkt ihrer Forschungsarbeit widmen, nicht, wie früher, an Feierabenden und Wochenenden, sondern an ganz gewöhnlichen Arbeitstagen, dazu noch in einem eigenem Labor, das ausschließlich ihnen zur Verfügung stand. Sie waren niemandem gegenüber verantwortlich, außer Dr. Mees – und sie konnten sich auf ein großes Team hochspezialisierter Wissenschaftler stützen.

Der Zeitpunkt, zu dem Mannes und Godowsky mit ihrer Arbeit in den Kodak Forschungslaboratorien begannen, konnte kaum günstiger sein. Kodak Wissenschaftler hatten nämlich zu Anfang der 30er Jahre neue Sensibilisatoren entdeckt. Die bis dahin bekannten Verbindungen hatten die unangenehme Eigenschaft, zu diffundieren, d.h. von einer Schicht in der andere zu "wandern", so daß eine exakte spektrale Absorption in der jeweiligen Emulsionsschicht nicht gewährleistet war.

Die neuen Sensibilisatoren hingegen hatten "Stehvermögen", und das heißt, daß sie in den ihnen zugewiesenen Schichten verblieben. Außerdem hatten Kodak Wissenschaftler in dieser Zeit auch neue Farbkuppler gefunden, die während der Entwicklung relativ stabil blieben.

Wenn ihr erklärtes Ziel auch ein Dreischichten-Farbfilm war, so arbeiteten Mannes und Godowsky auch in Rochester zunächst mit experimentellen Materialien, die nur zwei Schichten hatten – eine Vereinfachung, die eine zeitsparende Verkürzung der einzelnen Experimente mit sich brachte. Der Faktor Zeit spielte bei der Durchführung ihrer zahlreichen Versuchsserien auch in anderer Beziehung eine wichtige Rolle: Beim Entwicklungsprozeß, dem ja das Prinzip der kontrollierten Diffusion zugrundelag, kam es entscheidend darauf an, die Einwirkungsdauer des Bleichfixierbades auf die jeweilige Emulsionsschicht exakt festzulegen bzw. einzuhalten. Da sie aber in absoluter Dunkelheit arbeiten mußten, konnten sie die Zeiten nicht mit einer Uhr kontrollieren.
Als Musiker mit einem ausgeprägten Gefühl für den Takt eines ihnen wohlbekannten Musikstücks wußten sie sich aber zu helfen: Sie pfiffen, die Takte zählend, die Melodie des letzten Satzes der Brahms-Sinfonie c-moll so lange, bis sie die erforderliche Zeitdauer erreicht hatten.

They were responsible to no one except Dr. Mees – and they had a large team of highly specialized scientists for their support.

Mannes and Godowsky could hardly have chosen a better time to start their work at the Kodak Research Laboratories: Kodak scientists had discovered new sensitizers early in the 1930's. The compounds known up until that time had the unpleasant property of diffusing, in other words 'migrating' from one coating into the other, so that precise spectral absorption in the particular emulsion layer was not guaranteed.

By contrast, the new sensitizers had 'staying power', meaning that they stayed in the layers to which they were allocated. Not only that, but Kodak scientists had also recently discovered new color couplers which remained relatively stable during developing.

Although their stated aim was to produce a triple-coated color film, Mannes and Godowsky began work at Rochester using experimental materials with only two layers – a simplification which saved time by shortening the individual experiments.

Verpackung Kodachrome/*Packaging Kodachrome*

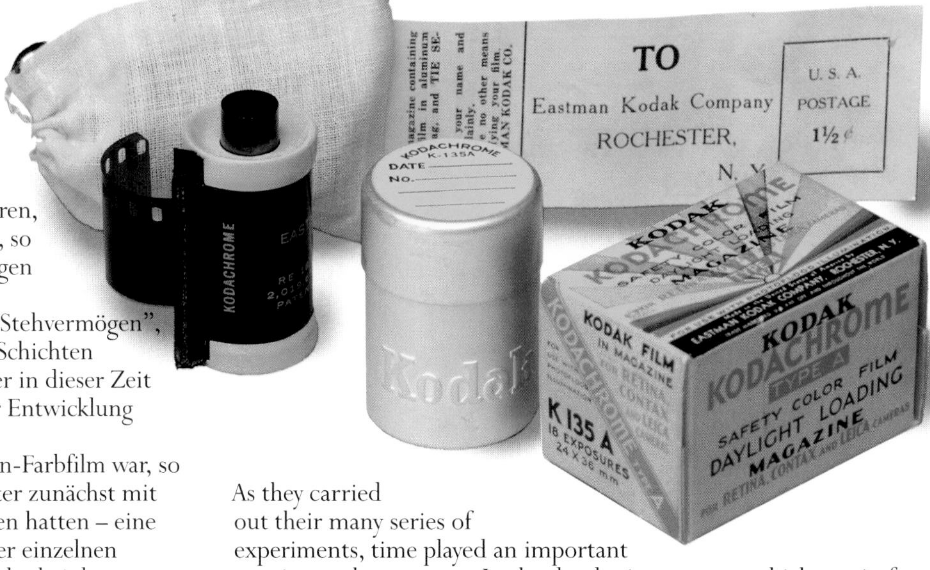

As they carried out their many series of experiments, time played an important part in another way too. In the developing process, which was in fact based on the principle of controlled diffusion, the critical thing was to determine, and comply with, the exact period for which the bleaching-fixing bath should act on each layer of emulsion. Since they had to work in total darkness they could not monitor times with a watch. As musicians, however, they had an unusually keen sense of the rhythm of a familiar piece of music, and this gave the answer: counting the beats, they whistled the melody of the last movement of the Brahms C minor symphony until the necessary time had passed.

It was hardly surprising that word went around the Kodak Research Laboratory that 'those musicians' were always whistling instead of getting on with the job, as some academic colleagues contemptuously put it.

Natürlich sprach es sich in den Kodak Forschungslaboratorium herum, daß "diese Musiker" dauernd pfiffen statt – wie einige akademische Kollegen mißbilligend meinten – ernster Arbeit nachzugehen. In Wirklichkeit aber arbeiteten sie mit Hochdruck, denn schließlich erwartete man von ihnen doch möglichst bald greifbare Resultate, Ergebnisse, die ein verkaufsfähiges Produkt herzustellen erlauben sollten.

Dreischichtenfilm macht das Rennen

Anfang 1933 konnten die beiden Leopolds, wie Dr. Mees seine Schützlinge oft nannte, ihrem Chef einen Zweischichten-Farbprozeß vorstellen, der ihm einen Eindruck davon vermitteln sollte, welche Wirkung ein um das fehlende Gelb angereicherter Dreischichten-Farbfilm haben würde. Was sie Dr. Mees damals demonstrierten, waren Platten, deren zwei Schichten für die Farben Rotorange und Blaugrün sensibilisiert waren. "Die kristallklaren Kupplerfarben", erinnerte sich Godowsky später, "waren allen damals in der Fotografie verwendeten Farben überlegen. Auch waren Schärfe und Auflösungsvermögen der Bilder besser." Dr. Mees war von dem, was er sah, so beeindruckt, daß er bei einem seiner Emulsionäre einen Zweischichtenfilm in Auftrag gab. Der Film wurde geliefert, Mannes und Godowsky machten mit ihm Außenaufnahmen, und als sie Dr. Mees den entwickelten Film vorführten, entschied er: "Diesen Film bringen wir auf den Markt!"

Die beiden Freunde waren konsterniert. Schließlich war das Ziel doch ein Dreischichtenfilm. So war diese Entscheidung von Dr. Mees nur dazu angetan, ihren Ehrgeiz noch mehr anzustacheln. Während die langwierigen Vorproduktionstests für den Zweifarbenfilm in vollem Gange waren, arbeiteten Mannes und Godowsky mit verbissener Energie am Dreischichtenfarbfilm weiter. Für sie stand fest: Der Dreifarbenfilm mußte das Rennen gewinnen. Dabei hatten sie allerdings auch die volle Unterstützung von Dr. Mees, der angeordnet hatte, daß alle Kräfte aus den Bereichen Forschung, Produktion und Entwicklung in den Dienst des Farbfilmprojekts gestellt werden sollten. Es hatte absolute Priorität, und wenn sie es wünschten, standen ihnen sämtliche Spezialisten des Unternehmens mit Rat und gegebenenfalls auch tätiger Unterstützungen zur Seite.
Noch ehe mit der Produktion des Zweischichtenfarbfilms begonnen werden konnte, war ein Dreischichtenmaterial, der Kodachrome Film, produktionsreif geworden. Beinahe hätte es einen Vorläufer mit zwei Farbschichten gegeben, aber schließlich machte der Kodachrome Film mit seinen drei Schichten Anfang 1935 das Rennen.

Beginn einer neuen Ära

Im Prinzip ist der Kodachrome ein Schwarzweißfilm mit drei übereinander gegossenen Schichten, von denen jeweils eine für die Farben Blau, Grün und Rot empfindlich ist. Wie dann die Farben in den Film gelangen, erläuterte Dr. Mees so: "Wie bei einem gewöhnlichten Schwarzweißfilm werden erst einmal die Bilder der drei Schichten entwickelt und dann werden diese Bilder in einer Folge von Behandlungsprozessen zu farbigen Positiven umgewandelt. Schließlich werden alle Silbersalze aus den Schichten entfernt, und

The Tri-pack Film wins the Race

Early in 1933, the two Leopolds – as Dr. Mees often called his protégés – were able to show their boss a double-coat color process intended to give him an idea of what a triple-coat color film would look like when the missing yellow was added. What they actually demonstrated to Dr. Mees were plates whose two coatings were sensitized for red-orange and blue-green. The 'crystal-clear coupler colors,' Godowsky recalled later, 'were superior to any colors used in photography at that time. The sharpness and resolution of the images were better, too.' So impressed was Dr. Mees by what he saw that he commissioned a double-coated film from one of his emulsion makers. The film was delivered, Mannes and Godowsky used it to take some outdoor photographs, and when they showed the developed film to Dr. Mees he simply decided: 'We are going to market this film!'

The two friends were dumbfounded. The ultimate objective, after all, was a triple-coated film. So this decision taken by Dr. Mees was merely calculated to fire their ambition even further. While the laborious pre-production tests on the two-color film were in full swing, Mannes and Godowsky continued their work on the triple-coated color film with even greater determination. They had no doubts: the three-color film had to win. Their efforts were fully supported by Dr. Mees, who had arranged for all the resources of the Research, Production and Development Divisions to be put at the disposal of the color film project. It took absolute priority: Mannes and Godowsky could call on any specialist they liked within the company for advice and, if necessary, practical assistance. Before a start had even been made on production of the double-coated film, a triple-coated material – the Kodachrome film – had reached the production stage. It had only just missed having a predecessor with two coatings, but eventually it was the triple-coated Kodachrome film which crossed the line first, early in 1935, to the great satisfaction of all involved.

The Start of a New Era

In principle Kodachrome is a black-and-white film with three superimposed layers, each of which is sensitive to a different color – blue, green and red respectively. Dr. Mees once explained how the colors get into the film: 'What happens is that the images on the three layers are first developed, as in a standard black-and-white film, and then converted to color positives in a sequence of treatment processes. Finally, all the silver salts are removed from the layers, so that what is left is the composite image built up from the three superimposed colored part-images.'
This is a very over-simplified description of a development process which – at least in the early days – was extremely complex and time-consuming.

In 1935 it took no less than three and half hours, and a grand total of 27 working stages, to obtain a finished, developed film. Over the years, admittedly, the process has been simplified several times, but even today it is still highly complicated with films taking 36 minutes to develop. This, in a manner of speaking, is the tribute

zurück bleibt das aus drei übereinander liegenden farbigen Teilbildern bestehende Gesamtbild." Das ist die stark vereinfachte Darstellung eines Entwicklungsprozesses, der – zumindest in der ersten Zeit – äußerst kompliziert und zeitaufwendig war.

Er dauerte 1935 nicht weniger als dreieinhalb Stunden und erforderte die stattliche Anzahl von 27 Arbeitsgängen, um einen fertig entwickelten Film zu erhalten. Im Laufe der Jahre wurde der Prozeß zwar mehrfach vereinfacht, aber er ist auch heute bei einer Gesamtdauer des Entwicklungsprozesses von 36 Minuten immer noch sehr kompliziert. Das ist gewissermaßen der Tribut, den das chemische Konzept des Kodachrome Films dem Entwicklungsprozeß abverlangen muß. In den drei Schichten des Films sind nämlich keine farbbildenden Komponenten (Farbkuppler) eingelagert. Sie sind vielmehr Bestandteile der Entwicklerlösungen, in denen die farbigen

which the chemical concept of the Kodachrome film has to levy from the development process. The fact is that the film's three layers contain no color-forming components (color couplers). Instead, the couplers are components of the developer solutions in which the colored part-images are gradually built up. Although this is technically a very costly procedure, the disadvantage in terms of process engineering does have one vital virtue: in this form of color development, the exposed silver grains are surrounded by particularly small clouds of dye, ultrafine image elements, which combine to produce a complete color image characterized by exceptionally fine grain, great sharpness and high resolution of detail.
These features, particularly characteristic of the Kodachrome film, have not so far been matched – and certainly not surpassed – by any other Kodak film.

George Sheedy: Erste Farbreportage für den *Sunday-Mirror* aus Anlaß des Zeppelin-Unglücks in Lakehurst; *First color-reportage for the Sunday-Mirror of the "Hindenburg" disaster at Lakehurst,* 1937

Page 4 MAY 23, 1937 SUNDAY MIRROR MAGAZINE SECTION MAY 23, 1937 Page 17

DEATH OF A GIANT: The Exclusive Colorphoto Record of the Destruction of the HINDENBURG

To View These Pictures with Maximum Effectiveness, Look at This Page Together with Page 17.

To View These Pictures with Maximum Effectiveness, Look at This Page Together with Page 4.

DIVING INTO THE FLAMES! A Moment After the Giant Dirigible Struck the Ground in Flames, Members of the Ground Crew—Composed Chiefly of U. S. Navy Men—Rushed to the Wreckage to Drag Out Survivors of the Blast. The Colorphoto Above Was Taken Two Minutes After the One on the Cover.

THE FIRE TRUCK ARRIVES. First Fire Apparatus to Reach the Fiery Carcass of the World's Largest Airship Was This Truck, Stationed at the Lakehurst Naval Air Station.

TOO HOT FOR COMFORT. Only a Small Bit of the Giant Airship's Fabric, Discernible in the Center of This Colorphoto, Remains as the Flames Roar On. The Object in the Foreground Is a Discarded Fire Extinguisher, Useless Against the Blaze.

MULTI-COLORED FLAMES from the Burning Gas, Fuel Oil, Fabric and Other Parts of the Dirigible! Only by Natural-Color Photography Could This Spectacle Be Reproduced.

DENSE CLOUDS OF SMOKE from the Crude Fuel Oil, Used to Run the Hindenburg's Diesel Engines, Mounted Skyward as the Once Mighty Craft Lay Wrecked, a Blazing Skeleton.

A MONSTER'S END. Burned to a Bare Skeleton of Steel Lies Germany's Pride-of-the-Skies, the Largest Airship Ever Built—and the Last, Very Probably, Ever to Be Filled with Hydrogen.

—All Colorphotos Copyright, 1937, by Daily Mirror, Inc. (Sunday Mirror Magazine Section.) Reproduction in Whole or in Part Forbidden.

ALL the world now knows that, on its first voyage to the United States this year, the hydrogen-filled rigid dirigible airship Hindenburg blew up and burned while nearing its mooring mast at Lakehurst, N. J.

On the scene when the disaster occurred was Gerard ("Jerry") Sheedy, staff color-cameraman of the Sunday Mirror Magazine Section. Knocked flat by the force of the explosion, 220-pound Sheedy was forced to run for his life—but not before he had recovered his camera, which the blast had blown from his hands. That camera, a miniature one of a standard "candid" type, was loaded with Kodachrome natural-color film and this fortunate circumstance, combined with his own daring, enabled Sheedy to obtain the colorphotos reproduced in this issue—the only such photos to be taken.

The colorphotos were flown to Rochester, N. Y., for developing and processing at the plant of the Eastman Kodak Company, and flown back to New York. Thomas J. Craig, process manager of that company, pronounced them "the finest colorphotos ever made."

Each of the colorphotos reproduced is an enlargement from an original less than one by one-and-a-half inches, including the colorphoto reproduced on the front and back covers—an enlargement of more than 225 times!

Having pioneered in colorphotography for more than five years, having been first among newspapers to reproduce natural-color photos successfully and first to "cover" spot-news assignments with the color camera, the Sunday Mirror Magazine presents them on these pages and on the front and back covers of this issue—as another of its "firsts."

Because mechanical facilities made it impossible to increase the number of color pages in this issue in the limited time at hand, we are leaving out of this issue—to make room for these colorphotos—two of our regular weekly color features, the natural-color photographic portrait of a Hollywood screen star and the reproductions of famous paintings under the title "The Bible in Classic Art." Both these interrupted series will be resumed in our next issue.

Teilbilder, Schritt für Schritt, hervorgerufen werden. Das ist zwar ein in technischer Hinsicht sehr aufwendiger Vorgang, doch hat dieser prozeßtechnische Nachteil einen entscheidenden Vorteil aufzuweisen: Bei dieser Form der Farbentwicklung bilden sich nämlich um die belichteten Silberkörner herum besonders kleine Farbstoffwölkchen, allerfeinste Bildelemente, die in ihrer Summe ein farbiges Gesamtbild ergeben, das sich durch außerordentlich feines Korn, große Schärfe und hohes Detailauflösungsvermögen auszeichnet. Diese für den Kodachrome Film besonders charakteristischen Merkmalen wurden bisher von keinem anderen Kodak Film erreicht, geschweige denn übertroffen.

Kleinbilddias erobern die Druckmedien

Eine Nachricht, die Millionen erschütterte: Mitte Mai 1937 explodierte das deutsche Luftschiff LZ 129 "Hindenburg" beim Andocken auf der US-Basis Lakehurst in New Jersey. 36 Menschen kamen dabei in den Flammen um. Der Fotoreporter George Sheedy, den die gewaltige Explosion zu Boden geschleudert hatte, kam mit dem Schrecken davon. Seine Kleinbildkamera, die den Sturz unbeschadet überstanden hatte, war mit "Kodachrome natural-color film" geladen, und geistesgegenwärtig begann er sofort, Aufnahmen vom Hergang der Katastrophe zu machen. Sechs seiner Fotos wurden auf einer Doppelseite der Sonntagsausgabe des *New York Daily Mirror* vom 23. Mai 1937 veröffentlicht. Es war die erste aktuelle Farbreportage der Welt (Abb. Seite 22).

Daß ein Fotoreporter eine Kleinbildkamera verwendete, war in jenen Jahren recht ungewöhnlich. Schließlich war damals das Standardformat des Pressefotografen 4x5 ″, und fotografiert wurden auf Schwarzweißmaterial. Aktuelle Farbaufnahmen gab es zu dieser Zeit noch nicht. Zwar hatte man Mitte der 30er Jahre bereits ein gerüttelt Maß an Erfahrung auf dem Gebiet des Farbdrucks nach Aufnahmen mit einer Strahlenteilerkamera, aber das farbige Kleinbilddia war ein absolutes Novum und die Verwendung eines Kodachrome-Dias als Druckvorlage war bislang Neuland. Die Problematik war doppelter Natur: Da war einmal das ungewohnt kleine Bildformat von nur 24 x 36 mm, und zum anderen mußten vom entwickelten Kodachrome-Dia erst nachträglich die für den Druck erforderlichen Farbauszüge hergestellt werden – genug Gründe für viele Drucker, die Verarbeitung von Kleinbilddias rundweg abzulehnen.

Der Amerikaner Ivan Dmitri dürfte der erste gewesen sein, der die Verwendbarkeit des Kodachrome Films als Druckvorlage eingehend testete. Den Anstoß dazu gab ein Auftrag, der ihn im Herbst 1936 nach Südamerika führen sollte. Dabei sollte ihn seine Leica und eine Anzahl der gerade auf den Markt gekommenen Kodachrome Filme begleiten. Doch er wollte die weite Reise nicht antreten, ohne sich davon überzeugt zu haben, daß von Kodachrome Dias auch gute Farbdrucke hergestellt werden können. Daß Dmitri dabei sehr gründlich vorging, geht aus einem Erfahrungsbericht hervor, der in der amerikanischen *Leica Photography* vom Juni 1937 veröffentlicht wurde. Einige Repro-Unternehmen, mit denen er sich in Verbindung gesetzt hatte, waren nicht bereit, einen Versuch zu machen, andere wiederum setzten ihren Ehrgeiz darein, möglichst

Miniature Film Conquers the Printed Media

The news stunned millions: in mid-May 1937 the German Airship LZ 129 *Hindenburg* exploded while docking at the US Lakehurst Base in New Jersey. 36 people died in the flames. Photo reporter George Sheedy, who had been thrown to the ground by the massive explosion, escaped with a severe fright. His camera, which had survived his fall undamaged, was loaded with 'Kodachrome natural-color film', and with great presence of mind he immediately began to photograph the aftermath of the disaster. Six of his pictures appeared as a double-page spread in the Sunday edition of the *New York Daily Mirror* on 23rd May 1937. This was the world's first news photography in color (see pag 22).

The fact that a photo reporter was using a 35 mm camera was highly unusual in those days. Press photographers at that time normally used a 4x5 ″ format and worked in black-and-white. There were no on-the-spot color photographs at that time. True, people in the mid-1930's already had a fair amount of experience in color printing from photographs taken with a one-shot camera, but the 35 mm color slide was a complete novelty, while the use of the Kodachrome slide as an original for printing was unexplored territory. It presented two types of problems: firstly, the picture format was unusually small, a mere 24 x 36 mm; secondly, the color separations necessary for printing could only be produced from the Kodachrome slide after it had been developed – sufficient reasons for many printers to want to have nothing to do with the processing of 35 mm slides.

The American Ivan Dmitri was probably the first to conduct extensive tests into the possibility of printing from the Kodachrome film. What prompted him to do so was a commission he received in the autumn of 1936, which was to send him to South America, where he would be taking with him his Leica and a number of the Kodachrome films which had just appeared on the market. However, he was reluctant to undertake the long journey without first convincing himself that good color printing would be achieved using Kodachrome slides. He went about it very thoroughly, as is clear from a report of his experiences which appeared in the American *Leica Photography* of June 1937. Some of the reprographic companies he approached were not prepared to make the effort. Whereas others regarded it as a challenge to achieve the best possible results. At the end of the day, Dmitri's tests demonstrated that Kodachrome slides reproduce very well in both offset and letterpress printing. Early evidence of this can be found in Dmitri's photograph of a red racing car with its driver, which appeared on the front page of the *Saturday Evening Post* of May 27, 1937. *Leica Photography,* too, published many Kodachrome photographs (including some brought back by Dmitri from South America) to show what good results can be obtained with a 'precision 35 mm camera' like the Leica.

Other pioneers of printing from Kodachrome slides in the early days include the Munich publishing house, Knorr & Hirth, which in 1937 published *Das farbige Leica-Buch* with photographs by Anton F. Baumann. Baumann had first come across the Kodachrome film at a narrow-gauge film showing he attended during a stay in the USA in June 1936. He was about to visit the National Parks of the American

gute Resultate zu erzielen. Unterm Strich ergaben Dmitris Tests, daß sowohl im Offset- als auch im Buchdruckverfahren sehr gute Druckwiedergaben von Kodachrome Dias zu erzielen sind. Ein früher Beweis dafür ist Dmitris Aufnahme eines roten Rennwagens mit Fahrer, die auf der Titelseite der *Saturday Evening Post* vom 27. Mai 1937 veröffentlicht wurde. Auch in der *Leica Photography* wurden 1937 zahlreiche Kodachrome Aufnahmen veröffentlicht (darunter Fotos, die Dmitri aus Südamerika mitgebracht hatte), um zu zeigen, welch gute Ergebnisse sich mit einer "Präzisions-Kleinbildkamera" wie der Leica erzielen lassen.

Zu den Pionieren des frühen Farbdrucks nach Kodachrome-Dias gehört auch der deutsche Verlag Knorr & Hirth in München, der 1937 *Das farbige Leica-Buch* mit Aufnahmen von Anton F. Baumann herausbrachte. Baumann hatte während eines Aufenthalts in den USA im Juni 1936 erstmals Bekanntschaft mit dem Kodachrome Film gelegentlich einer Schmalfilmvorführung gemacht. Im Begriff, die amerikanischen Nationalparks im Westen Amerikas zu besuchen, hörte er, daß der Kodachrome inzwischen auch als Kleinbildfilm zu haben war. Der passionierte Leica-Fotograf "Toni" Baumann griff sofort zu und stellte ein Jahr später seine besten Kodachrome Fotos in dem bereits erwähnten Bildband vor. Im Impressum des Bandes ist folgender stolzer Kommentar des Verlags abgedruckt: "Dieses erste große Werk mit farbigen Momentaufnahmen wurde im Vierfarbendruck hergestellt von der Firma Knorr & Hirth. Die Farbklischees stellte Brend'amour Simhart & Co., München, her. Sämtliche farbigen Aufnahmen sind unmittelbar vom Originalfilm – also vom 24x36 mm Dia – ohne Retusche auf die Druckstöcke übertragen. Die Farben des Original-Kodachrome Dias sind also naturgetreu erhalten."

Farbbilder für Album und Brieftasche

1935 wettete Dr. Mees mit dem damaligen Kodak-Präsidenten Lovejoy, daß der Verkauf von Kodachrome Filmen den von Schwarzweißfilmen innerhalb von fünf Jahren prozentual überflügeln würde. Bereits 1938 kreuzten sich die Umsatzkurven, Dr. Mees hatte seine Wette lange vor der Zeit gewonnen. Doch so erfolgreich der Kodachrome auch war – Dr. Mees war sich schon bald nach seiner Einführung darüber im Klaren, daß sich der "Mann auf der Straße" Papierbilder wünscht.

Bereits 1937 hatte in den Kodak Forschungslaboratorien die Arbeit an einem Farbverfahren begonnen, bei dem – im Gegensatz zu Kodachrome – die Farbkuppler in die Emulsionsschichten eingelagert wurden. Auf diesem Verfahren beruhte unter anderem der am 31. Dezember 1941 angekündigte Kodacolor Film. Der Kodacolor Film war der erste Amateur-Farbnegativfilm der Welt. Im Verein mit einem gleichzeitig auf den Markt gebrachten Farbpapier bot er dem Amateur die Möglichkeit, von seinen Aufnahmen Farbpapierbilder für Album oder Brieftasche anfertigen lassen zu können. Auch für diesen Film galt – zumindest damals und in den ersten Jahren – der alte Kodak-Slogan: "Sie drücken auf den Knopf – den Rest erledigen wir": Kodacolor Filme mußten nämlich zur Entwicklung und Ausarbeitung der Farbbilder nach Rochester eingeschickt werden.

West when he heard that Kodachrome was now also available as a miniature film. 'Toni' Baumann, a fervent Leica enthusiast, immediately took up the challenge; his best Kodachrome photographs appeared a year later, in the illustrated book mentioned above. In the imprint, the publishers observed proudly: 'This first major work containing color photographs has been produced in four-color printing by Knorr & Hirth. The color blocks were made by Brend'amour Simhard & Co. of Munich. All the color photographs have been transferred direct from the original film – 24 x 36 mm slides – to the plates, without retouching, so that the natural colors of the original Kodachrome slides have been faithfully preserved.'

Color Pictures for Albums and Wallets

In 1935 Dr. Mees bet the then President of Kodak, Mr. Lovejoy, that sales of Kodachrome films would outstrip those of black-and-white in percentage terms within five years. In fact the sales curves intersected before the end of 1938, and Dr. Mees had won his bet well ahead of schedule. Yet, successful as Kodachrome was, it had not been on the market long before Dr. Mees clearly perceived that the man on the street wanted color prints.

As far back as 1937, work had begun in the Kodak Research Laboratories on a color process in which – in contrast to the Kodachrome process – the color couplers were put into the emulsion layers. Results obtained with this process included Kodacolor film, were announced on December 31, 1941. Kodacolor film was the world's first color negative film for amateurs. Combined with a color paper which came on the market at the same time, it offered the amateur the chance to have color prints made of his photographs for his album or wallet. This film, too, was covered – at least in the early years – by the old Kodak slogan: 'You press the button – we do the rest.' Kodacolor films did in fact have to be sent to Rochester for processing and printing.

Although Kodacolor film was based on what was then the most up-to-date emulsion technology, it did have certain weaknesses in the early stages: its sensitivity was only 20 ASA (about 14 DIN), the color reproduction left something to be desired, and its grain and sharpness were not good enough for the 35 mm format (still seldom used at the time), so that it was initially produced only in the form of roll film (in more than a dozen of the then current sizes). But it was not long before improvements began to be made to Kodacolor: from 1943 the film was produced with an integrated silver mask, which helped to improve the brilliance of the color. A later achievement, the elimination of the so-called 'secondary absorption', making for a decisive improvement in color reproduction, was brought about by a clever manipulation of emulsion technology: Dr. Hanson – then a senior member of staff at the Kodak Research Laboratories – had the inspiration in 1943 to combine two of the color couplers used in Kodacolor film with azo dyestuffs, which automatically form color masks when the film is developed. Although a patent (US Patent 2/449/966) was applied for as early as 1944, it was not until 1949 that the process was used to produce a greatly improved Kodacolor film.

Der Kodacolor-Film – obwohl nach dem jüngsten Stand der damaligen Emulsionstechnologie gefertigt – hatte anfangs gewisse Schwächen: Seine Empfindlichkeit betrug nur ASA 20 (etwa 14 DIN), die Farbwiedergabe ließ zu wünschen übrig, und weil Korn und Schärfe für das (damals noch wenig gebräuchliche) Kleinbildformat nicht ausreichten, kam er zunächst nur als Rollfilm (in mehr als einem Dutzend der damals gängigen Formate) heraus. Doch die erste Verbesserung des Kodacolor-Films ließ nicht lange auf sich warten: Ab 1943 wurde der Film mit integrierter Silbermaske hergestellt, die zur Erhöhung der Farbbrillanz beitrug. Die Beseitigung der sogenannten Nebenabsorptionen und die dadurch mögliche entscheidende Verbesserung der Farbwiedergabe wurde später durch einen emulsionstechnischen Kunstgriff erreicht: Dr. Hanson – damals in leitender Position in den Kodak Forschungslaboratorien tätig – hatte 1943 den genialen Einfall, zwei der im Kodacolor Film verwendeten Farbkuppler mit Azo-Farbstoffen zu verbinden, die bei der Filmentwicklung automatisch Farbmasken bilden. Das Verfahren wurde zwar schon 1944 zum Patent (USP 2/449/966) angemeldet, aber erst 1949 zur Herstellung eines wesentlich verbesserten Kodacolor-Films ausgenützt.

Farbumkehrfilm für professionelle Zwecke

Hergestellt wurde der Kodak Ektachrome-Film schon lange bevor er frei (an zivile Verbraucher) verkauft wurde. Zunächst hatte sich die U.S. Army eine Option auf diesen Film geben lassen. Was die Militärs 1940 von Kodak haben wollten, war ein spezieller Film für die Luftaufklärung, und und es mußte ein Farbfilm sein, weil er gegenüber Schwarzweißfilm einen höheren Informationsgehalt aufweist. Wichtig war ferner, daß der Film an Ort und Stelle zu einem positiven Durchsichtsbild entwickelt werden kann, so daß er sofort ausgewertet werden konnte. Im Herbst 1941 war es dann so weit: Kodak stellte den Kodacolor Aero Reversal Film vor. Es handelte sich (trotz der Bezeichnung Kodacolor) um einen Farbumkehrfilm mit eingebauten Farbkupplern. Auf Grund seiner steilen Gradation war er für Luftbildaufnahmen besonders geeignet.

Bereits 1938 hatte Kodak einen Kodachrome Professional Film eingeführt, der als Planfilm in Formaten bis 28x35 cm erhältlich war. Bekannte Fotografen wie Cecil Beaton, Horst P. Horst, Victor Keppler, Irving Penn, Edward Steichen, Edward Weston und andere arbeiteten mit ihm. Doch der Kodachrome Film hatte, so gut er sonst auch war, einen für den Profi sehr störenden Nachteil: Jeder belichtete Planfilm mußte nach Rochester zur Entwicklung eingeschickt werden, und ein Fotograf, der seinen Sitz beispielsweise an der Westküste hatte, mußte ungebührlich lange auf die Rückkunft seiner entwickelten Filme warten. Schon aus diesem Grunde ist es verständlich, wie positiv der Ektachrome Film von Profis aufgenommen wurde, den Kodak ab August 1946 in den gängigen Planfilmformaten lieferte.

Color Reversal Film for Professional Use

Kodak Ektachrome film was produced long before it was freely available (to civilian users). In the first instance, the US army had taken out an option on this film. What the military wanted from Kodak in 1940 was a special film for aerial reconnaissance; it had to be a color film, which was capable of supplying more information than black-and-white film. Another important point was that it had to be possible to develop the film on the spot and obtain a positive transparency which could be evaluated immediately. That was the situation in the autumn of 1941, when Kodak introduced the Kodacolor Aero Reversal film. Despite the 'Kodacolor' designation, this was a color reversal film with built-in color couplers. Its steep gradation made it particularly suitable for aerial photography.
Kodak had introduced a Kodachrome Professional Film as early as 1938, which was obtainable as sheet film in sizes up to 28 x 35 cm. It was used by well-known photographers such as Cecil Beaton, Horst P. Horst, Victor Keppler, Irving Penn, Edward Steichen, Edward Weston and others. But, good as it was in other respects, the Kodachrome film did have one very inconvenient drawback for the professional: every exposed sheet of film had to be sent to Rochester for development, and a photographer based, for example, on the West Coast had to wait an unacceptably long time for the return of his developed films. This alone makes it easy to understand the warm welcome given by professionals to the Ektachrome film when Kodak began to supply it in the current sheet-film formats in August 1946.

Alfred Hennig, 1936
Deutschland/*Germany*

Erich Bauer, 1938
Deutschland/*Germany*

Helmut & Erna Blenck, 1939
Deutschland/*Germany*

Paul Outerbridge, 1940
USA

Erich Retzlaff, 1937
Deutschland/*Germany*

Dr. Paul Wolff, 1936
Deutschland/*Germany*

Erich Bauer, 1938

Deutschland/*Germany*

Hanns Hubmann, 1937
Deutschland/*Germany*

Horst P. Horst, 1946
USA

Edward Steichen, 1936
USA

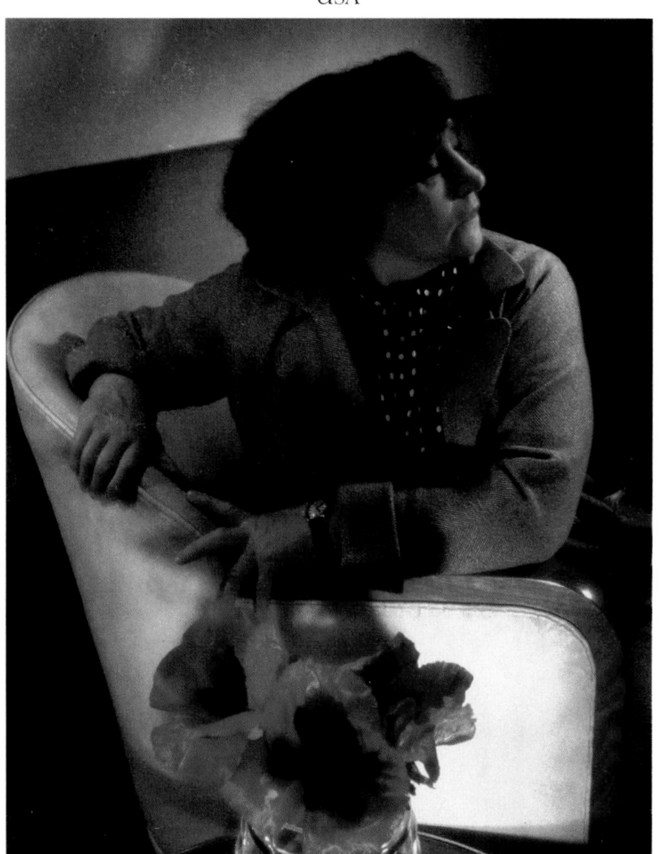

John Rawlings, 1946*
USA

*Erstes Farbfoto per Radiosignale gesendet
First color photograph transmitted by radio

Edward Steichen, 1938
USA

Jack Delano, 1941
USA

Erich Retzlaff, 1938
Deutschland/*Germany*

Manuel Alvarez Bravo, o.D./*n.d.*
Mexiko/*Mexico*

Paul Strand, 1945
USA

Anton F. Baumann, 1937
Deutschland/*Germany*

Jack Delano, 1941
USA

Jack Delano, 1940
USA

Russell Lee, 1940
USA

John Vachon, 1940
USA

Marion Post-Wollcott, 1940
USA

Marion Post-Wollcott, 1940
USA

Keld Helmer Petersen, 1944
Dänemark/*Denmark*

Alfred Tritschler, 1938
Deutschland/*Germany*

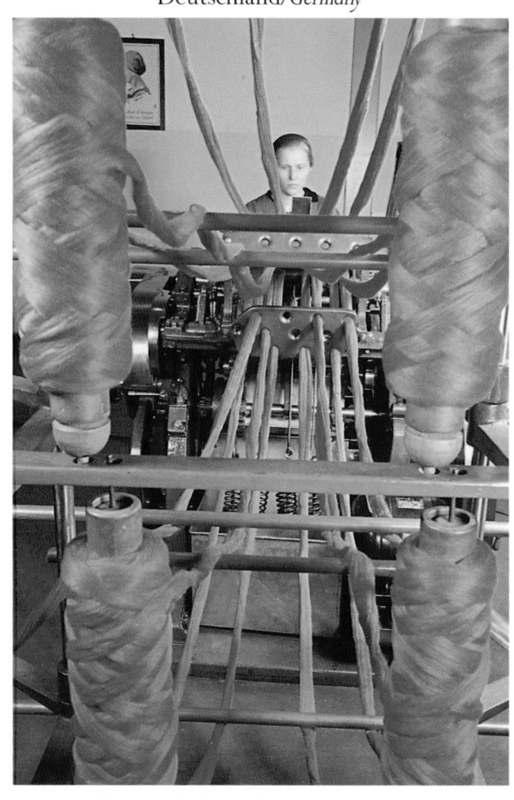

John Vachon, 1940
USA

Marion Post-Wollcott, 1941
USA

Paul Strand, 1945
USA

Dr. Giséle Freund, 1939
Frankreich/*France*

Martin Munkacsi, 1941
USA

Russell Lee, 1940
USA

John Rawlings, 1942
USA

Laura Gilpin, 1941
USA

Drahomir Josef Růžička, 1940
CSSR

Ivan Dmitri, 1937
USA

Anonym/*Anonymous*, 1938
Deutschland/*Germany*

Drahomír Josef Růžička, 1940
CSSR

Toni Frissell, 1937
USA

John Rawlings, 1946
USA

46

Horst P. Horst, 1940
USA

1946-1956

Diana Edkins Richardson

Europas Vorherrschaft als Zentrum der Kunstwelt endete mit dem Zweiten Weltkrieg. Gegen Ende der 40er Jahre hatten sich die sozialen und politischen Verhältnisse in Europa drastisch verändert, während im Amerika der Nachkriegszeit ein ökonomischer und künstlerischer Aufschwung stattfand, der eine Periode intensiver künstlerischer Experimente hervorbrachte. Die Vereinigten Staaten erlebten einen Zustrom von kreativen Kräften, wie z.B. von Alexander Liberman, Horst P. Horst, Erwin Blumenfeld, Ilse Bing, André Kertész u.a. Diese Künstler brachten Ideen mit, die dazu beitrugen, den Aufstieg der amerikanischen Mode-, Werbe- und Kunstfotografie vorzubereiten.

Der Kodachrome-Film kam 1936 auf den Markt. Dies bedeutete einen qualitativen Fortschrift in der Farbwiedergabe und er machte die Farbe in einer praktikablen Form Millionen zugänglich. Die Farbe unterstrich und betonte die Abbildungsfähigkeit der Kamera. Sie begründete eine lebendige und typisch amerikanische Kunstform, deren konsequentes Ergebnis das schnelle Anwachsen der Illustrierten jener Zeit war. Die Hinwendung zur Farbe war unausweichlich, aber die Kosten waren immens und die Wiedergabe problematisch. So war die Farbfotografie aufgrund ihrer Kosten in erster Linie der Werbung und der Welt der Illustrierten vorbehalten.

Liberman nannte die Illustrierten im Vorwort zu seiner wegweisenden Publikation über *die Kunst und Technik der Farbfotografie*, "das Phänomen unserer Zeit. Sie sind der Sammelpunkt aller Talente, sie sind ein neuer Salon, in dem die ganze Welt ausgestellt wird." Durch ihren Erfolg wurden die Illustrierten die Mäzene einer neuen Kunst, und den Fotografen standen die materiellen Möglichkeiten zur Verfügung, etwas Neues zu entwickeln, zu suchen und zu gestalten. Die großen Magazine, wie *Vogue, House & Garden, Glamour, Harper's Bazaar, Life* und später auch *Fortune*, zogen sich Farbfotografen heran und gaben ihnen künstlerische Freiheit.

Die Redaktionsfotografen der Illustrierten setzten in den 40er Jahren meist die Arbeit mit der 8 x 10" Großbildkamera fort, was die Belichtungszeit noch mehr verlängerte, da die Farbfilme noch sehr niedrigempfindlich waren. Jede Packung Planfilm mußte vor dem Gebrauch getestet werden, weil die Emulsionen so unterschiedlich ausfielen. Viele Drucker bestanden darauf, daß die Farb reproduktion vom Kleinbilddia unpraktisch, wenn nicht unmöglich sei. Sie verlangten in der Regel Originale in der Größe der späteren Reproduktion. Entsprechend hatten die in Farbe arbeitenden Fotografen die Tendenz, sich auf statische Motive zu beschränken oder sie benutzten grausam strenges und kompliziert arrangiertes künstliches Licht.

Die Farbe wurde nicht nur begrüßt, sie wurde obligatorisch. Es war neu und aufregend, in Farbe zu arbeiten. Die Farbfotografen vertrauten fest auf eine Welt, reichhaltiger und strahlender als unsere, sie gaben entweder eine überhöhte oder eine stumme Wirklichkeit wieder. Viel der Arbeiten aus den 40er Jahren von Cecil Beaton und anderen wirken heute wie Dekorationsstücke (z.B. Beatons Bild der Irren von Chaillot in allen Regenbogenfarben. Seite 64). Beaton sagte selbst über die Farbe: "Wenn wir nicht nach Realismus streben, können wir das Bild unvoreingenommener betrachten." Dieses Werk wirkt auf uns heute kalt und künstlich.

Europe's reign as the capital of the art world ended with World War II. By the late 1940's social and political conditions in Europe had changed dramatically while post-war America was booming both economically and artistically, producing a formative period of intense, artistic experimentation. New York City became the core of the art, advertising, publishing and fashion worlds. The United States witnessed an influx of creative artists including Alexander Liberman, Horst P. Horst, Erwin Blumenfeld, Ilse Bing, André Kertész and others and with them came ideas that helped set the stage for the rise of American Fashion, commercial and art photography.

Kodachrome was introduced in 1936. It represented a qualitative advance in the state of color reproduction, making color available in a practical form to millions. Color underlined and emphasized the sheer descriptive power of the camera. It pioneered a vital and particularly American art form which logically found its outlet in the fast growing magazines of the time. The move to color was inevitable but cost was high and printing difficult. Color photography was limited primarily to the advertising and editorial magazine worlds due to its expense.

Liberman in his foreword to the landmark publication *The Art and Technique of Color Photography* called the magazine 'the phenomenon of our age. It is the meeting place of all talents, a new salon where the whole world is on exhibition'. Through their success magazines have become the patrons of the new art, and material means have been put at the disposal of the photographers to develop and search and create. The major magazines such as *Vogue, House & Garden, Glamour, Harper's Bazaar, Life* and later *Fortune* all nurtured color photographers and gave them artistic license.

Editorial magazine photographers in the 1940's generally continued working with the large format 8 x 10" cameras, making exposures even longer because color-film emulsions were still very slow. Each batch of film prior to the shoot had to be tested for accuracy as the emulsions were so uneven. Many printers insisted that color reproduction from 35 mm transparencies was impractical if not impossible. They normally required camera originals made to the size of the reproduction. Consequently, photographers using color had a tendency to confine themselves to static subjects or else use ferociously strong artificial and highly orchestrated lights.

Color was welcome if not imperative. It was new and exciting to be working in color. Color photographers relied heavily on a world richer and more lustrous than our own -therefore relaying either to a heightened or a muted reality. Many of the works done in the 1940's by Cecil Beaton and others seem today like set pieces (i.e. Beaton's purple picture of the 'Mad Woman of Chaillot' made with every color under the rainbow on page 64). Beaton in his own words said of color 'if we are not straining after reality we can look at the picture with a less prejudiced eye.' The work looks cold and plastic to us today.

The technical experiments are obvious, stressing the abstract dream worlds, holdouts from the Thirties. Horst says 'you had to be a colorist – the color surrounding the main object should emphasize it. You wanted to make the picture as strong and as simplified as possible.' Like Horst, Louise Dahl-Wolfe, having a flawless instinct

Die technischen Experimente konzentrierten sich ganz offensichtlich auf Abstraktionen und Traumwelten, Überreste der 30er Jahre. Horst sagte, "man mußte ein Kolorist sein – die Umgebungsfarbe sollte die Hauptsache herausstellen. Man wollte das Bild so streng und einfach wie möglich machen". Wie Horst, so hatte auch Louise Dahl-Wolfe einen untrüglichen Sinn für Farbkombinationen. Auch sie folgte dem Diktum, daß ein Bild aus Farbflächen und weniger aus Objekten aufgebaut wird.

Bei der Arbeit für die Illustrierten waren Vitalität, Erfindungsreichtum und Experimentierlust offensichtlich. Ein Handwerker, unermüdlicher Experimentator und Meister in der Dunkelkammermanipulation war Blumenfeld, berühmt für die ungewöhnlich lange Zeit, die er in die Produkton eines, wirklich einmaligen Fotos investierte; für ihn war die Beherrschung der Farbe eine zwingende Notwendigkeit. Das Hauptproblem der Farbfotografen jener Zeit war, die Technik dieses neuen Mediums in den Griff zu bekommen, die Farbe unter Kontrolle zu bringen und sich nicht dem Medium auszuliefern. Marina Schinz sagte über die Fotografen der späten 40er Jahre: "Das Ziel war, ein korrektes Resultat zu erhalten. Man könnte es mit dem Problem der Perspektive in der italienischen Frührenaissance vergleichen – erst nach der Bewältigung der Probleme konnte man an den Unzulänglichkeiten des Materials entlang experimentieren."

Die Illustrierten widmeten, wie die Amateurzeitschriften, immer mehr Seiten der Farbe. Edward Steichen, damals Leiter der Fotoabteilung am Museum of Modern Art, veranstaltete drei große Ausstellungen mit Farbarbeiten. Eine davon war "All Color Photography" von 1950 mit 342 Aufnahmen von 75 Fotografen. *Life* und *Fortune* rückten von ihrem langewährenden Vorurteil gegen Nachrichten- und Dokumentarfotos in Farbe ab und publizierten Arbeiten von Eliot Elisofon und sogar vom Meister schlechthin, von Walker Evans. In Kinofilmen, wie in John Hustons „Moulin Rouge" und in Kinugasas „Gate of Hell" wurde die Farbe zweckent sprechend eingesetzt. Paradoxerweise förderte gerade die Beschränkung des Fernsehens auf Schwarzweiß das Anwachsen der Werbeanzeigen in Farbe.

In den frühen 50er Jahren wurde der Ektachrome eingeführt, ein Film der gleichmäßiger und auch mit kürzeren Belichtungszeiten funktionierte und sofort verarbeitet werden konnte. Eine Anzeigenkampagne von Kodak spielte auf die erreichte Realitätsnähe an mit dem Slogan "Alle Wunder des erwachenden Lebens". Für den Schnappschußfotografen war der Kleinbilddiafilm von großem Reiz. Frances McLaughlin-Gill war eine Pionierin der Kleinbildfotografie in Farbe. Irving Penn, Vogues wichtigster Fotograf zu dieser Zeit, repräsentierte einen Neuanfang. Er wußte intuitiv, wie man außerordentlich Künstliches ganz natürlich aussehen läßt. Mit der sparsamen, vollständig "realistischen" Darstellung seiner Motive, bewies Penn nicht nur Selbstverständlichkeit im Umgang mit diesem trügerischen Medium, sodern auch seine Aussage in dem Buch *The Art and Technique of Color Photography:* "Er (der zeitgenössische Farbfotograf) benutzt den Hypernaturalismus, der seinem Material eigen ist, und macht sich die Neigung der Leute zunutze, alles für die Realität zu halten, was sie auf Fotos sehen. Er wird der Bildner einer bemerkenswerten Welt...", womit er die "bemerkenswerte Welt" vorausahnte.

for color combinations, followed the dictum that a picture be built up of colored planes rather than objects.

It was in editorial work where the vitality, ingenuity and experimentation was evident. As a craftsman, an indefatigable photographic experimenter, a master of darkroom manipulation, Blumenfeld was famous for the extraordinary lengths to which he would go to produce an utterly unique image. He strongly felt the need for controls when working in color. The single outstanding issue of concern for all color photographers at the time was coming to grips with the technicality of this new medium and being able to exercise personal command over the color not to be controlled by the medium. Marina Schinz has said about the photographers of the late Forties 'The main issue was to come up with a correct result. It was similar to early primitive Italian painting, about conquering perspective - only after you did that could you experiment by being guided by the shortcomings of the material.'

Magazines devoted many more editorial pages to color as did amateur camera magazines. Edward Steichen, then director of the photography department at the Museum of Modern Art had three major exhibitions where he included color work. One was in 1950 titled 'All Color Photography' containing 342 photographs by 75 photographers. *Life end Fortune* shifted from their long established bias against news or documentary color photography and published works by Eliot Elisofon and even the master himself, Walker Evans. Movies used color judiciously as in John Houston's 'Moulin Rouge' and Kinugaso's 'Gate of Hell'. Ironically, the black and white limitation of television, in fact, promoted a continued growth of color print advertising.

The early 1950's saw the introduction of Ektachrome, a film which was more stable and where the turn-around time was faster and could be processed immediately. A Kodak advertising campaign played on the idea of an achieved reality with the slogan 'all the wonders of awakening life.' To the snapshooter the 35 mm transparency had great appeal. Frances McLaughling Gill, pioneered the use of color with the smaller camera. Irving Penn, Vogue's principal photographer then, represented a new beginning.
He knew instinctively how to make elaborate artifice seem natural. With his sparse totally 'realistic' rendering of his subject he proved not only his comfort with this illusive medium but also his own quote from *The Art and Technique of Color Photography,* 'He (the contemporary color photographer) can take the hypernaturalism inherent in his materials, and making good use of the inclination people have for believing true anything they see in a photograph; he becomes the imager of a remarkable world...' foreshadowed the 'remarkable world' to come.

Clifford Coffin, 1949
USA

Irving Penn, 1950
USA

Clifford Coffin, 1950
USA

Erwin Blumenfeld, 1949
USA

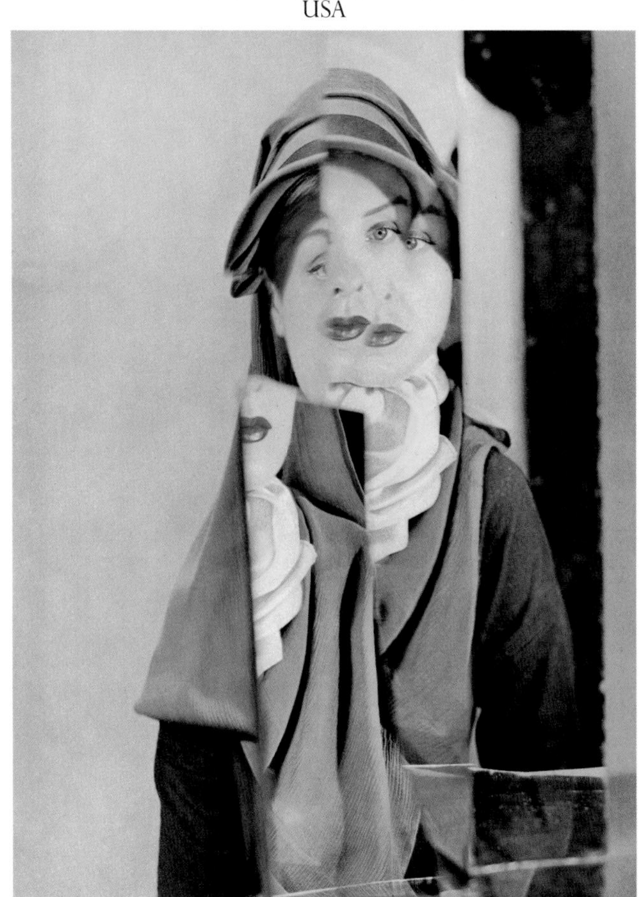

Constantin Joffé, 1950
USA

Cecil Beaton, 1949

Großbrittannien/*Great Britain*

Norman Parkinson, 1949
Großbritannien/*Great Britain*

Serge Balkin, 1950
USA

Frances McLaughlin-Gill, 1949
USA

Gjon Mili, 1950
USA

Dr. Giséle Freund, 1948
Frankreich/*France*

Arthur Siegel, 1949
USA

Walther Benser, 1953
Deutschland/*Germany*

Erwin Fieger, 1955
Deutschland/*Germany*

Anton Bruehl, 1951
USA

Carel Blazer, 1955
Niederlande/*The Netherlands*

Paolo Monti, 1947

Italien/*Italy*

Man Ray, 1950
Frankreich/*France*

Max Yavno, 1955
USA

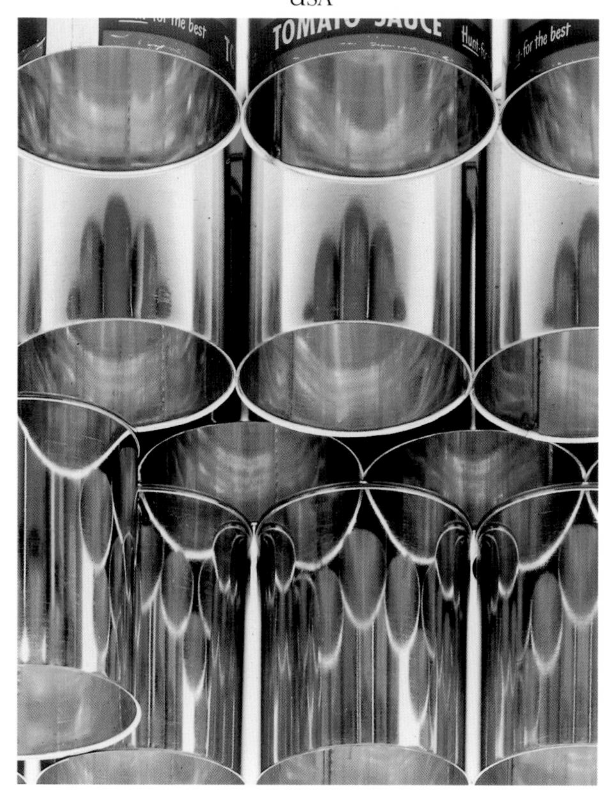

Franco Grignani, 1950
Italien/*Italy*

Irving Penn, 1949
USA

Arthur Siegel, 1946
USA

Hans Hinz, 1951

Schweiz/*Switzerland*

Leslie Gill, 1946
USA

Cecil Beaton, 1950
Großbritannien/*Great Britain*

Josep Renau, 1951
Spanien/*Spain*

Fritz Henle, 1950
Deutschland/*Germany*

Ferenc Berko, 1950
USA

Martin Bruehl, 1946
USA

Erwin Blumenfeld, 1951
USA

Pan Walther, 1947
Deutschland/*Germany*

Richard Rutledge, 1949
USA

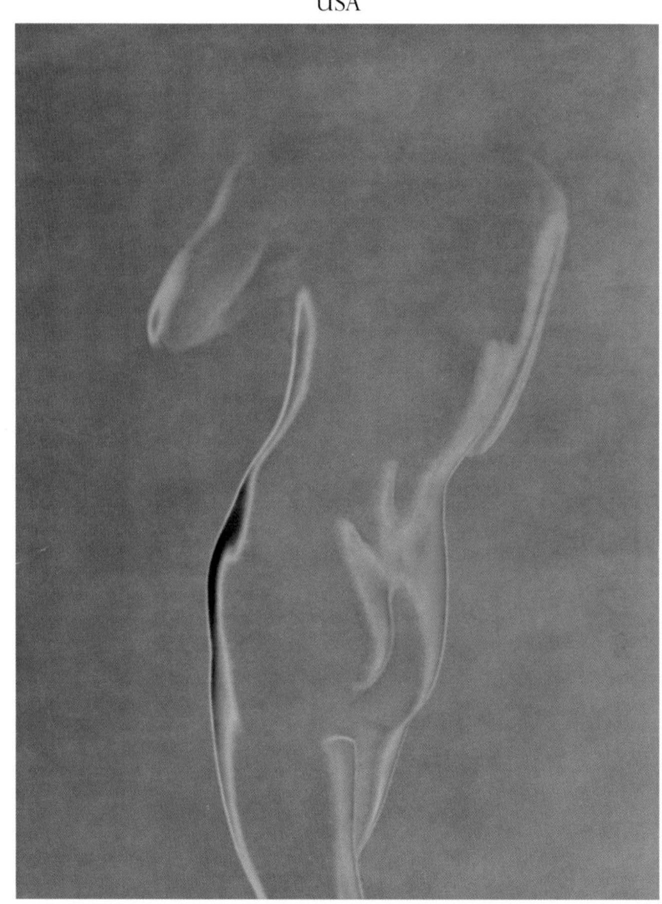

Fritz Henle, 1953
Deutschland/*Germany*

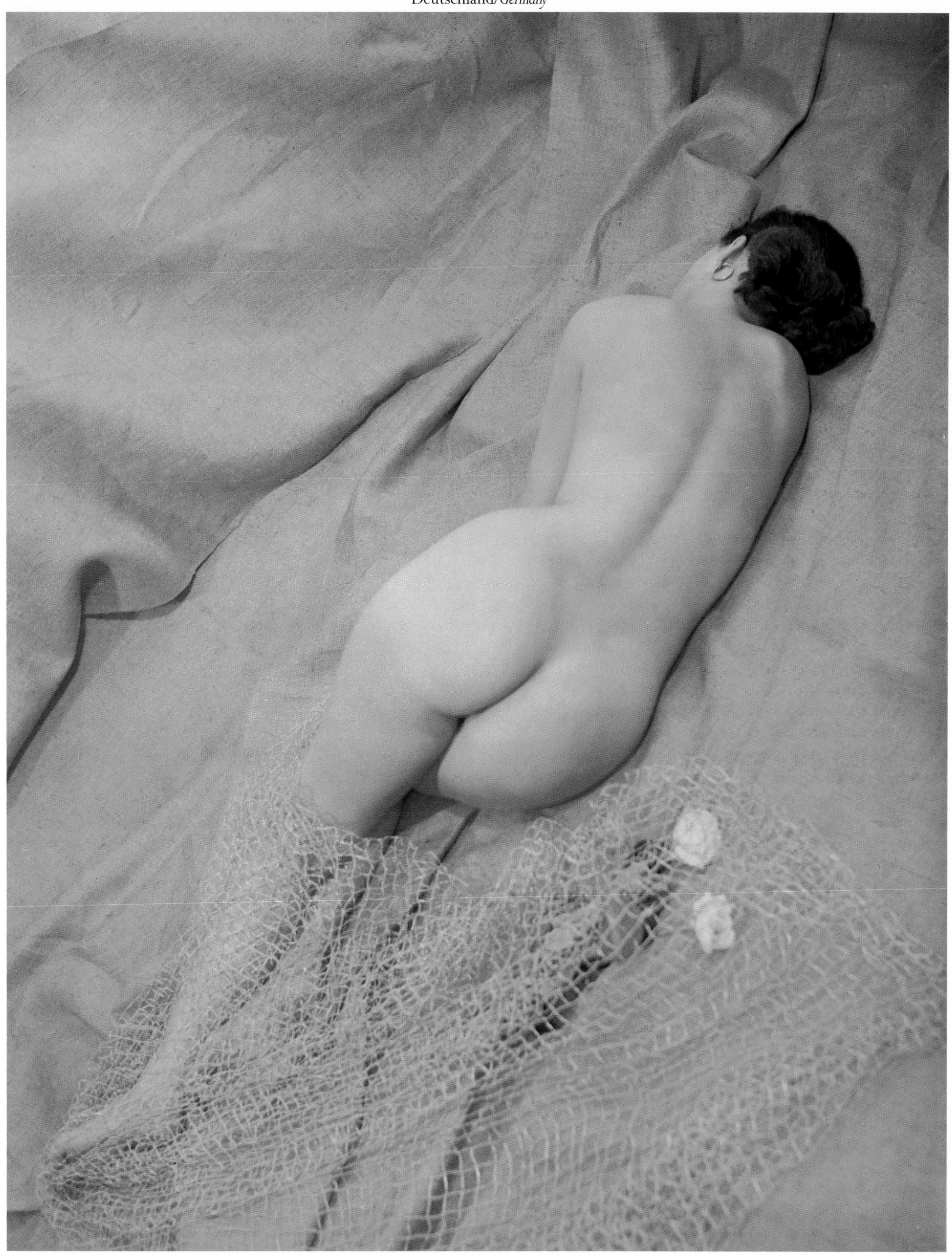

Alexander Liberman, 1949
USA

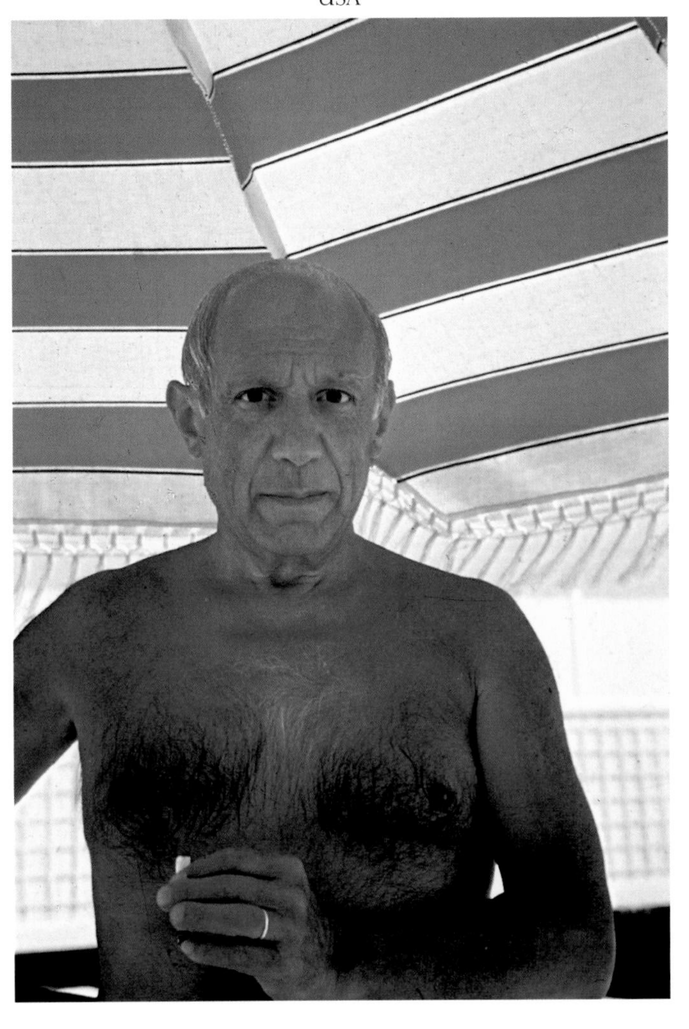

André Kertész, 1948
USA

Victor Keppler, 1954
USA

Leslie Gill, 1948
USA

Edward Weston, 1948
USA

Kryn Taconis, o.D./*n.d.*
Kanada/*Canada*

1956-1966

Freddy Langer

Natürlich hat Raoul Hausmann übertrieben, als er 1956 in der Schweizer Zeitschrift *Camera* konstatierte: "Die Farbfotografie hat nur selten das Stadium der farbigen Postkarte überschritten." Aber der selbstkritische Ton war durchaus charakteristisch für eine Generation, die verstört war durch die Wirren der Kriegs-und Nachkriegszeit und nun Ausschau hielt nach neuen Maßstäben und Wertsystemen – auch in der Ästhetik. Dabei galt es nicht allein, sich von ideologisch befrachteten Werturteilen zu trennen, sondern gleichfalls jenen Konventionen den Rücken zu kehren, die von Amateurzeitschriften noch auf Jahre hinweg als erfolgssichere wie unumstößliche Regeln proklamiert werden sollten: die Notwendigkeit einer authentischen Farbwiedergabe, die Betonung von Komplementärkontrasten und die schon sprichwörtliche Unentbehrlichkeit eines roten Farbtupfers im Bildvordergrund.

Daß die deutschen Farbfotografen mit ihren Arbeiten qualitativ weit hinter denen ihrer amerikanischen Kollegen zurücklagen, mußten sie schon 1952 feststellen, als der Bildband *The Art and Technique of Color Photography* hierzulande in die Buchhandlungen kam.

Aber bereits 1960 konnten auch sie mit respektablen Ergebnissen aufwarten. Unter dem Titel *Magie der Farbe* präsentierte Dr. Walter Boje während der *photokina* zehn deutsche Farbfotografen mit jeweils einem Bild-Essay. Die Themen waren so weit gestreut wie die Darstellungsmittel; sie reichten von Industrieaufnahmen über Balletfotografie bis hin zu Stilleben und wurden interpretiert aus nüchterner Distanz oder mit bewußten Unschärfen, Farbverfremdungen und Verwischungen. Daß dabei an die entgegengesetzten Tendenzen der späten zwanziger Jahre angeknüpft wurde, die *Neue Sachlichkeit* eines Renger-Patzsch einerseits und die Experimentierfreude Moholy-Naggys andererseits, wurde vielen erst in der Retrospektive bewußt.

Der Aufschwung setzte sich auch im folgenden Jahr fort, als wiederum Boje die Bilderschau "Abstraktion und Dokumentation im Farbfoto" zusammenstellte – zum großen Teil mit denselben Autoren. "Fotografie wird heute nicht nur als Abbildungs- und Darstellungsmittel, sondern auch als Ausdrucksmittel anerkannt. Sie ist einer Klaviatur vergleichbar, deren Reichtum an Klangmöglichkeiten man bisher – nur mit einer Hand und in einer Oktave spielend – nicht ausnutzte und erst jetzt zu erproben beginnt", hieß es in dem Begleittext dieser Ausstellung. Nicht mehr allein das Motiv, sondern die Farbe selbst wurde fortan thematisiert. Auch in Deutschland hatte man also erkannt, was Ernst Haas im *Color Annual 1957* so formuliert hatte: "Farbige Fotografien sind die Summe aus schwarzweißen Gegenstand plus Farbe, Farbfotos dagegen eine gleichung, in der das Subjekt Farbe ist."

Nicht minder entscheidend als das Bewußtsein, neue Wege gefunden zu haben, waren für die weitere Entwicklung der Farbfotografie neue und billigere Druckmöglichkeiten. Auch dem Bildband *Magie und Farbenfotografie*, identisch mit der Ausstellung von 1960, kommt somit die Stellung einer Wendemarke zu, hatte es doch vorher kaum ein Forum für Farbfotografie gegeben, das über die Präsentation an Galeriewänden hinausreichte.

Einzig die Werbeseiten wurden in den Zeitschriften der fünfzige Jahre regelmäßig in Farbe gedruckt, denn nur die hohen Budgets der

Naturally Raoul Haussmann was exaggerating when in 1956 he stated in the Swiss magazine, *Camera* that: 'Color photography has seldom surpassed the color postcard stage. 'Nevertheless, this critical attitude was quite characteristic for a generation, confused by the chaos of the war and post-war period and now searching for new standards and new sets of values, also in aesthetics. It was after all not simply a matter of ridding oneself of ideologically dubious values; it actually meant turning one's back on every convention which – yet for years to come – was to be promoted by amateur magazines, as the irrefutable road to success. It involved the need for authentic color reproduction, emphasis on complementary contrasts and the already proverbially indispensible red color splash in the foreground of the picture.

That the work of German photographers was qualitatively behind that of their American colleagues, became evident in 1952 when the photographic album, *The Art and Technique of Color Photography* appeared in German bookstores.

Still, by 1960 they too could show some admirable achievements. During the *photokina* exhibition, Dr. Walter Boje presented ten German color photographers, each with a photo essay. The themes were as diverse as the medium used to portray them; they covered everything from industrial photography to ballet shots and still-lifes, and were either soberly interpreted or deliberately out-of-focus, discolored or smudged. That the two styles of the late Twenties merged into this period – with a Renger-Patzsch *Neue Sachlichkeit* on one hand, and Moholy-Nagy's experimentations on the other – was something that was only discovered much later.

This development escalated in the years to come, when Boje again put together the exhibition, *Abstraction and Documentation in Color Photography*, predominantly with the same photographers. 'Today photography is not just considered a means of copying and interpreting, but also a means of self-expression. It can be compared to a keyboard, which has only been played lightly with one hand, in one octave and its wealth of possiblities therefore still waits to be explored', was part of the introductory text to this exhibition. From that point onwards not only the subject matter but also color became the theme. In Germany too, people had come to realize what Ernst Haas so aptly wrote in the *Color Annual 1957*: 'Coliferous photographs equal the sum total of black and white objects plus color – while in color photographs, the subject is color.'

New and less expensive printing possiblities were as vital to the further development of color photography, as the acknowledgement that new ways of photography had been discovered. The catalogue covering the 1960 exhibition, *Magie der Farbenfotografie* became historical since it presented the first forum for color photography, outside its display in galleries, of course.

Only the advertising pages of the magazines of the Fifties, were regularly printed in color, since apart from the big budgets of larger corporations and the fashion industry, few could afford the exorbitant ten-to-thirty-fold higher printing costs which color photography involved. The criterium that form and tones of products should be accurately reproduced, soon generated a craze for experimentation

Großunternehmen und der Modebranche gestatteten es, die zehn- bis dreißigmal höheren Druckkosten gegenüber einem Schwarzweiß-Klischee zu bezahlen. Der Anspruch, Form und Farbton der Produkte präzis widerzugeben, wich hier schon bald einer Freude am Experiment und einer Neigung zu grellen Übertreibungen. Fern von jeder Exaktheit stellten die Firmen statt ihrer Produkte immer häuftiger Stimmungen vor.

Ihren Höhepunkt fand diese Tendenz während der Beat- und Pop-Ära. Genauigkeit war allenfalls noch in der wissen schaftlichen Fotografie gefragt. Für die Fotoreportagen der Magazine setzte sich Farbe erst in der zweiten Hälfte der sechziger Jahre durch.

and an inclination towards gross exaggeration. Instead of presenting their products, more and more companies ended up presenting a mere conception. This trend reached its peak during the beat and pop era. Accuracy was exclusively expected in scientific photography. For the magazine photo-reporters however, color only fought its way through during the second half of the Sixties.

Walker Evans, 1957
USA

Walker Evans, 1962
USA

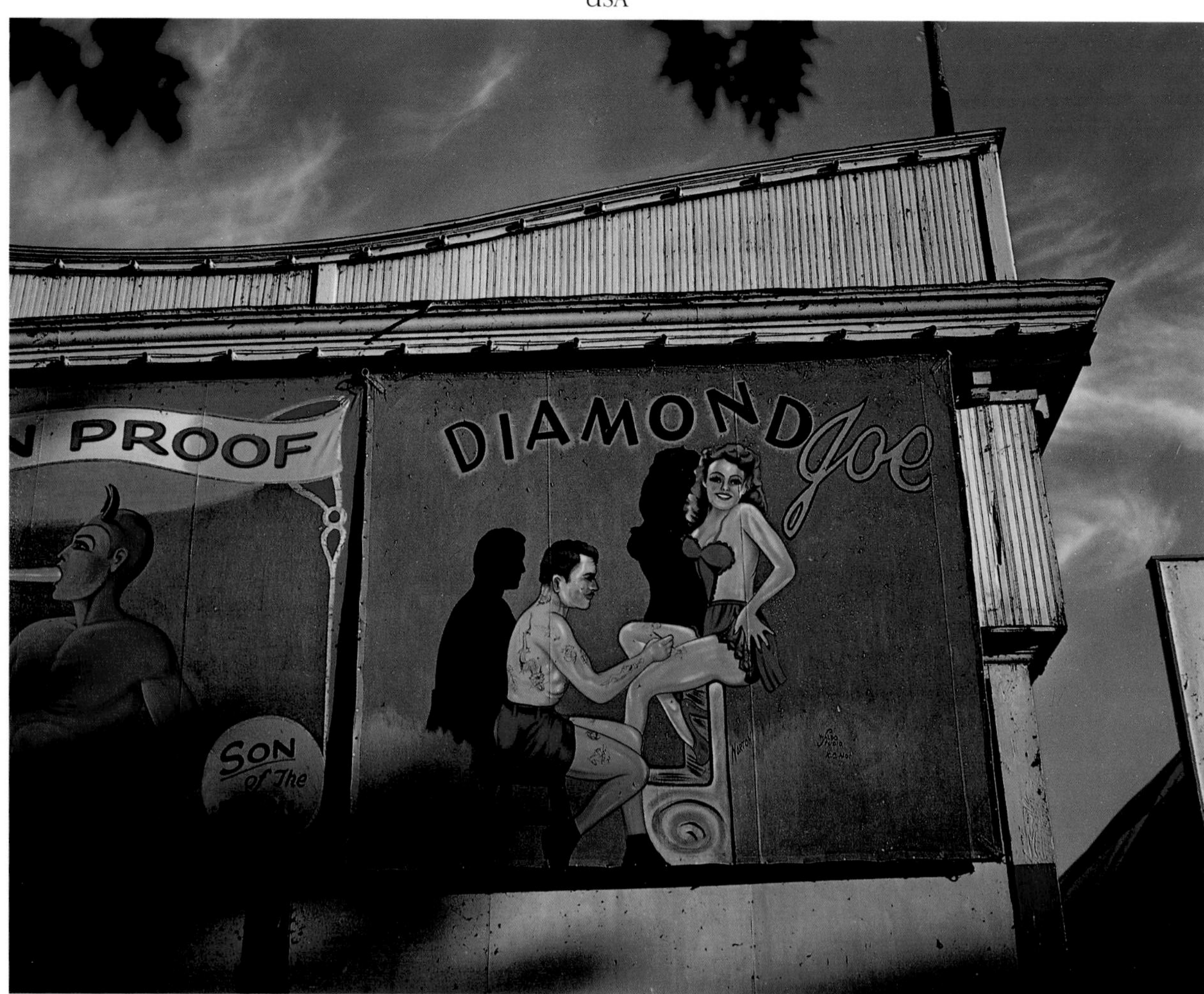

Osamu Hayasaki, 1964
Japan

Will McBride, 1964
Deutschland/*Germany*

Leni Riefenstahl, o.D./*n.d.*
Deutschland/*Germany*

Franz Lazi, 1953

Deutschland/*Germany*

F. C. Gundlach, 1966
Deutschland/*Germany*

Paul Huf, 1954

Niederlande/*The Netherlands*

Yasuhiro Ishimoto, 1965
Japan

Robert Häusser, 1958
Deutschland/*Germany*

Ilse Bing, 1957
USA

Peter Keetman, 1961
Deutschland/*Germany*

Harold E. Edgerton, 1964
USA

Alfredo Libero Ferretti, 1958
Italien/*Italy*

Marta Hoepffner, 1957
Deutschland/*Germany*

Dr. Walter Boje, 1958
Deutschland/*Germany*

Laurence LeGuay, o.D./*n.d.*
Australien/*Australia*

Wynn Bullock, 1962
USA

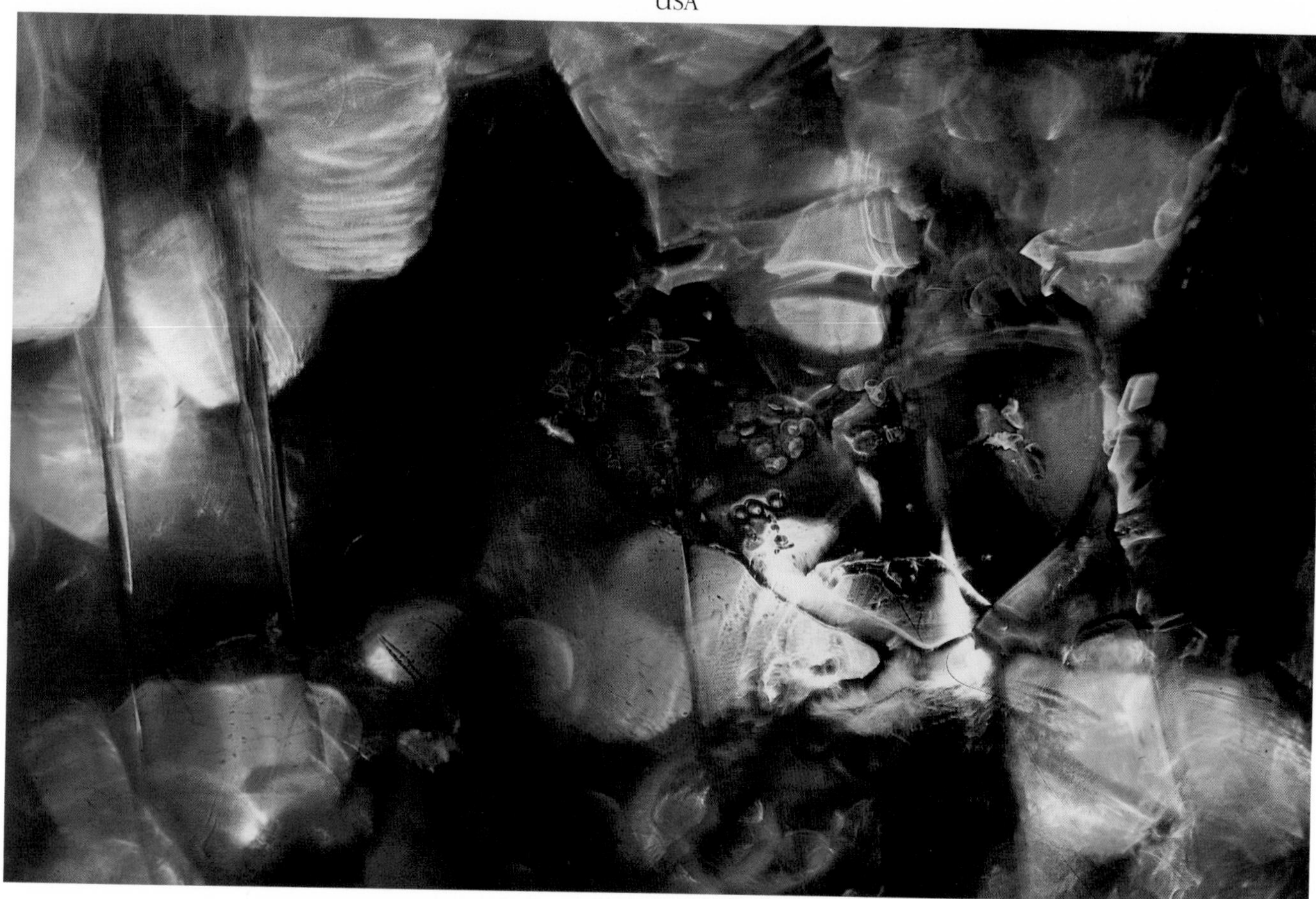

Ernst Haas, o.D./*n.d.*
USA

Ansel Adams, 1964
USA

Cole Weston, 1962
USA

Ansel Adams, 1964

USA

Eliot Porter, 1963

USA

Pete Turner, 1965
USA

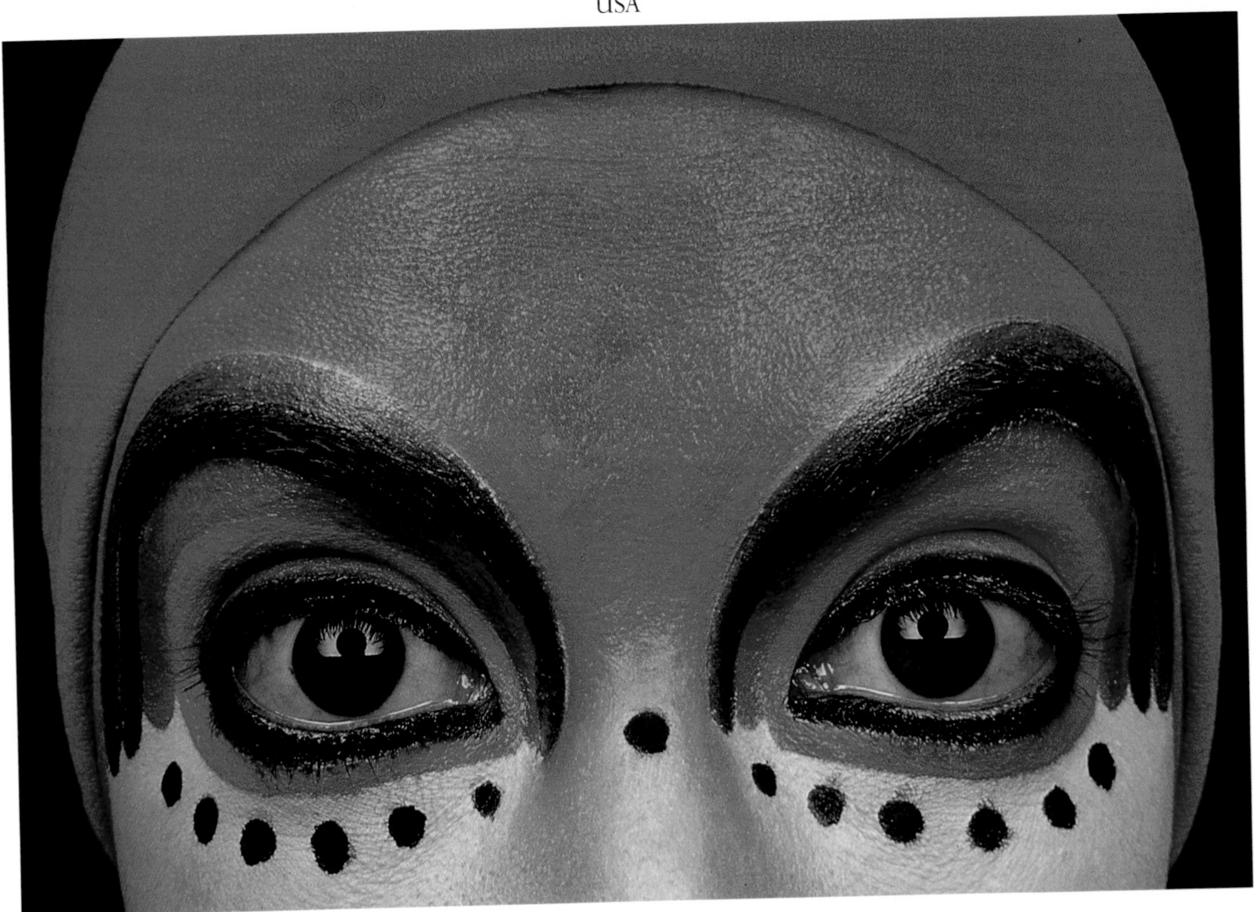

Eliot Elisofon, 1959
USA

Herbert List, 1960
Deutschland/*Germany*

Werner Bischof, 1957
Schweiz/*Switzerland*

Rene Burri, o.D./*n.d.*
Schweiz/*Switzerland*

90

1966-1976

Lorenzo Merlo

Mit dem Tod ihrer großen Meister und der verminderten Arbeitsleistung der verbleibenden Fotografen, geht die Welt der Schwarzweßfotografie langsam unter. Die neunziger Jahre werden dies bestätigen.

Das Jahrzehnt von 1966 bis 1976 stand noch unter dem Einfluß der Pop Ära, dem Siegeszug des Farbfernsehens und dem Verschwinden der Schwarzweißfilme aus den Kinos. Es gab eine florierende Zeitschriftenproduktion mit hohen Auflagen und mehr Anzeigen, alles mit dem Erfolg einer Verbreitung der Farbe. Die bereits etablierten Berufsfotografen wie Arnold Newman, Alfred Eisenstaedt und Philippe Halsman, paßten sich der veränderten Auftragslage an, so daß die junge Generation sie für einen Teil der Farbära halten muß.

Die Freiberufler, jene Fotojournalisten von wohlverdientem Ruhm, gruppiert um Fotoagenturen wie Magnum, Rapho, Sipa und andere, waren vorsichtiger. Sie verbanden – ohne viel darüber nachzudenken – die Farbfotografie mit Postkarten, dem National Geographic, Kalendern, Touristenfotos, Werbe- und Modeaufnahmen. In den Familienfotoalben war die Schwarzweißfotografie von der Farbe langst verdrängt worden, denn für die große Masse der Amateurfotografen bedeutete Farbe schlicht die Abbildung der Welt in ihrer ganzen Schönheit.

Das heißt also, die Absage an die Farbfotogafie kam hauptsächlich von den "Autoren Fotografen", die an die Darstellung der Realität in Schwarzweiß gewohnt waren. Für sie war Farbe eine Übertreibung, Grau aber die Farbe des Taktes, die Sphäre der unverblümten Wahrheit.

Bis in die Mitte der 60er Jahre sah es noch so aus, als würde es nie eine aktuelle Berichterstattung in Farbe geben, da die führenden Zeitungen und Illustrierten mit konservativen Fotografen arbeiteten. David Douglas Duncan brichtete, daß er Kriegsfotos nie in Farbe gemacht habe, weil er der Ansicht sei, dies würde die Grenze des Schicklichen und Erträglichen überschreiten.
Die Überzeugungen der Duncans dieser Welt entsprechen nicht mehr den tatsächlichen Verhältnissen, weil die Farbe inzwischen ein genaues und prägnantes Nachrichtenmedium ist. Die ersten großen Nachrichtenfotos in Farbe entstanden während des Vietnamkrieges. Fotografen wie Ron Haberles oder Larry Burrows markierten den beginn einer neuen Ära in der Reportagefotografie.

Die sensationellen erotischen und aufregenden Modefotos von Guy Bourdin waren der Ausgangspunkt einer aufgeschlossenen Modefotografie in den Illustrierten der frühen 70er Jahre. Da Modefotos gemacht werden, um Interesse am Gegenstand zu wecken, mußten neue Wege in der Gestaltung gefunden werden. Veränderungen in den sozialen Verhältnissen, dem Publikumsgeschmack und in der finanziellen Lage der Modemagazine brachten ein neues Verhältnis zur Modefotografie mit sich.

Bourdins Modefotografien handeln nicht nur von Sexuellem, Mord, Vergewaltigung, Homosexualitat und Transvestiten, sondern repräsentieren auch den Alptraum der Frauen, verlassen zu werden, sind eine romantische Darstellung der in Gedanken versunkenen, einsamen Frau, die sich in einer zur Liebe wie geschaffenen Umgebung befindet.

The generation of black & white photographers is vanishing throughout the world as many of its great masters pass away and the work of those who are left, naturally slows down. The Nineties will surely prove this prediction.

The decade spanning the period 1966-1976 confirmed the influence of the pop art era, the definite acceptance of color television and the fast disappearing of black & white movies. The media was transformed into a flourishing magazine business with bigger circulations and more advertising; all of them aiming to carry color spreads. The old, established professional photographers such as Arnold Newman, Arthur Eisenstaedt, and Philippe Halsman adapted themselves to the change – with the result that the new generation now considers them part of this color era.

The freelance professionals, those photo-journalists of well-deserved fame, grouped together by Magnum, Rapho, Sipa and other agencies, and creating the history of photography, were more cautious. Without much reflection they still associated color photography with postcards, National Geographic, calendars, touristic snapshots, commercial work and fashion. Yet there was no doubt, family albums were already featuring color pictures, replacing the black & white images in this homey contest. The large mass of amateurs simply saw more promise in color as a means of recording the world in all its sensory magnitude.

This goes to say that the refusal to consider color photography was mainly restricted to the world of art photographers, who were used to the black & white rendering of life. To them color was an overstatement. They believed that gray was the color of tact, the realm of blunt truth.

Up until the mid Sixties, it seemed that news photography would never be brought in color since the leading newspapers and magazines were populated by a staff of conservative and concerned photographers. David Douglas Duncan stated that he never took combat pictures in color because to his mind, that would violate to many human decencies and above all, invade the privacy of the battlefield.
The convictions of the Duncans of this world are no longer realistic today because color is a far more explicit and poignant news medium. The first great news photographs in color were made during the Vietnam war. Photographers like Ron Haberles or Larry Burrows were cornerstones of the new era of reportage photography.

In fashion photography Guy Bourdin's sexual, sensational and violent fashion photographs were an important turning point in the early Seventies. Since fashion photography is intended to create interest in its subject, new ways of creating memorable material had to be found. Changes in social conditions, public taste and the economics of fashion-publishing created new attitudes in fashion photography towards sexual expression.

Bourdin's fashion photographs do not only deal with forms of sexual expression, murder, rape, homosexuality and transvestism but also represent woman's living nightmare of 'vulnerability'; an almost romantic visualization of the pensive and abandoned woman, as in a just-terminated lovemaking atmosphere.

Zur selben Zeit begann sich ein anderer großer Modefotograf mit der Farbe zu befassen: Helmut Newton. Seine Modefotos sind die Antithese zu denen von Guy Bourdin. Newtons Fotografien handeln von dem für die 70er Jahre typischen neuen Verhältnis der Frauen zu ihrer eigenen Sexualität.

Andere wichtige Modefotografen kamen in dieser Zeit nach oben: Chris von Wangenheim, Sarah Moon, Oliviero Toscani, Art Kane und Hiro, um nur einige Namen zu nennen, die den Ton in der Modefotografie angaben. Die Modefotografie dieses Jahrzehnts wurde von der Gleichstellung der Farbfotografie stark beeinflußt, weil die großen Modehäuser Aufträge für innovative Werbefotos gaben. Durch die vielen Publikationen in den Fotozeitschriften wurde auch beim Amateur das Verständnis für das Farbbild gefördert.

Natürlich beschränkte sich die Emanzipation der Farbe nicht nur auf den Bereich der Gebrauchsfotografie. Neue technische Errungenschaften und die vielen jungen Künstler, die ausschließlich in Farbe arbeiten, sind ein Indikator dafür, daß eine neue Ära der Fotografie beginnt, zusammen mit der ständigen Weiterentwicklung anderer Medien wie Video, Film, Zeitschriften und vielen anderen. Durch die Fortschritte in der fotografischen Technik wird die Produktion von Farbfotos weiterhin qualitativ verbessert und die Tendenz geht mit der Einführung der SX-70 zum perfekten Sofortbild in Farbe. Mit anderen Worten, dies ist der Beginn der totalen Farb-Ära.

Viele neue Fotografen dieser Zeit sind heute die erwachsenen Benutzer des Farbfilms.

Da ist zuerst Neal Slavin mit seinem anthropologischen Ansatz, die Gesellschaft zu betrachten, die sich zum Kollektiv hin orientiert, und weniger die Individualität des Einzelnen betont. Franco Fontana, der Erneuerer der Landschaftsfotografie; seine Bilder zeigen landschafliche Flächen in grafischer Komposition, deren intensive Farben von dem dunkelblauen Himmel abstechen – mehr wie mit Wasserfarben gemalt, denn fotografiert wirkend.

Stephen Shores Fotos von ländlichen Gebieten und aus den amerikanischen Kleinstädten sind die Fotos eines Reisenden, aber von Touristenfotos weit entfernt.

Die durch das Blitzlicht hervorgerufenen Farbwirkungen sind das Haupthema der Bilder von Joel Meyerowitz. Auf den ersten Blick wirken seine Fotos wie die Zufallstreffer eines Amateurs, aber bei näherer Betrachtung erkennt man ihre aussagestarken Strukturen, und stellt fest, daß die belebten Straßenszenen von unvergleichlicher Poesie sind.

Die erwähnten sind nur einige der wichtigen Fotografen dieser Periode. Es gibt andere wie John Pfahl, Ikko Narahara, Marie Cosindas, Paul Fusco, Burt Glinn, Georges Tourdjman und Ruth Orkin, die der Farbe durch ihre Beiträge in den 70er Jahren zu Ansehen verhalfen, bevor sich die Farbfotografie im folgenden Jahrzehnt zu einer eigenen Kunstform entwickelte.

In that same period, another great fashion photographer got involved with color: Helmut Newton. His fashion work is an antithesis of Guy Bourdin's work. Newton's photographs are essentially concerned with the re-definition of woman's sexual relationships, typical of the Seventies.

Other important fashion photographers have in this period come forward strongly: Chris van Wangenheim, Sarah Moon, Oliviero Toscani, Art Kane, Hideki Fujii, and Hiro are just a few names amongst the leading group which set the direction in fashion photography. Fashion photography in this decade is strongly influenced by the emancipation of color photography because of the new and innovative use of photographs for advertising, commissioned by the most important fashion houses. This allows a better understanding of color images for the large mass of photo-amateurs via the numerous publications appearing in the best photographic magazines.

Of course, the emancipation of color photography did not only evolve in the world of applied photography. New technical improvements and the appearance of many young artists working exclusively in color, were an indication that a new era of photography was dawning, together with the continuous development of other media such as video, films, television, magazines and an ernormous gamma of objects. Also, the technical progress of photographic equipment was, and still is, developing towards a better production of color photographs and – in an incredibly sophisticated way – with the introduction of the SX-70 system towards a perfect instant color image. In other words, this is the start of the 'full color' era.

Many new photographers of this period are today's grown-up users of color film.

Firstly, there is Neal Slavin with his anthropological approach of a giant society oriented towards collective rather than individual identity. Franco Fontana is the innovator of landscape photography; his images are graphical compositions of horizontal layers of land, intensified in their colors against a deep and dark blue sky; more like strokes of watercolor than photographs.

Stephen Shore's rural landscapes and small towns of America are the photographs of a traveler, taken in a spirit far removed from that of a tourist.

The dense color contents of the stobe flash slides are the main ingredient of Joel Meyerowitz's images. On first sight his pictures would seem to be the lucky shots of an amateur but on further study, one has to recognize their vigorous structures and notice how people and street architecture alike are caught in unpredictable lyricism.

The photographers I have mentioned are only some of the important ones of this period. There are others such as John Pfahl, Ikko Narahara, Marie Cosindas, Paul Fusco, Burt Glinn, Georges Tourdjman and Ruth Orkin, who were the people to help put color photography into perspective around the Seventies, introducing a more qualitative visual statement, and one which was to emerge into a distinct art form in the decade to come.

Marie Cosindas, 1966
USA

Arnold Newman, 1974

USA

Arthur D'Arazien, o.D./*n.d.*
USA

J. P. Goell, 1973
USA

Auke Bergsma, 1976
Niederlande/*The Netherlands*

Regina Relang, 1967
Deutschland/*Germany*

Helen Levitt, 1973
USA

Helen Levitt, 1972
USA

Sarah Moon, 1972
Frankreich/*France*

Art Kane, 1972
USA

Hiro, 1971
USA

Pit Ludwig, 1973

Deutschland/*Germany*

Hideki Fujii, 1973
Japan

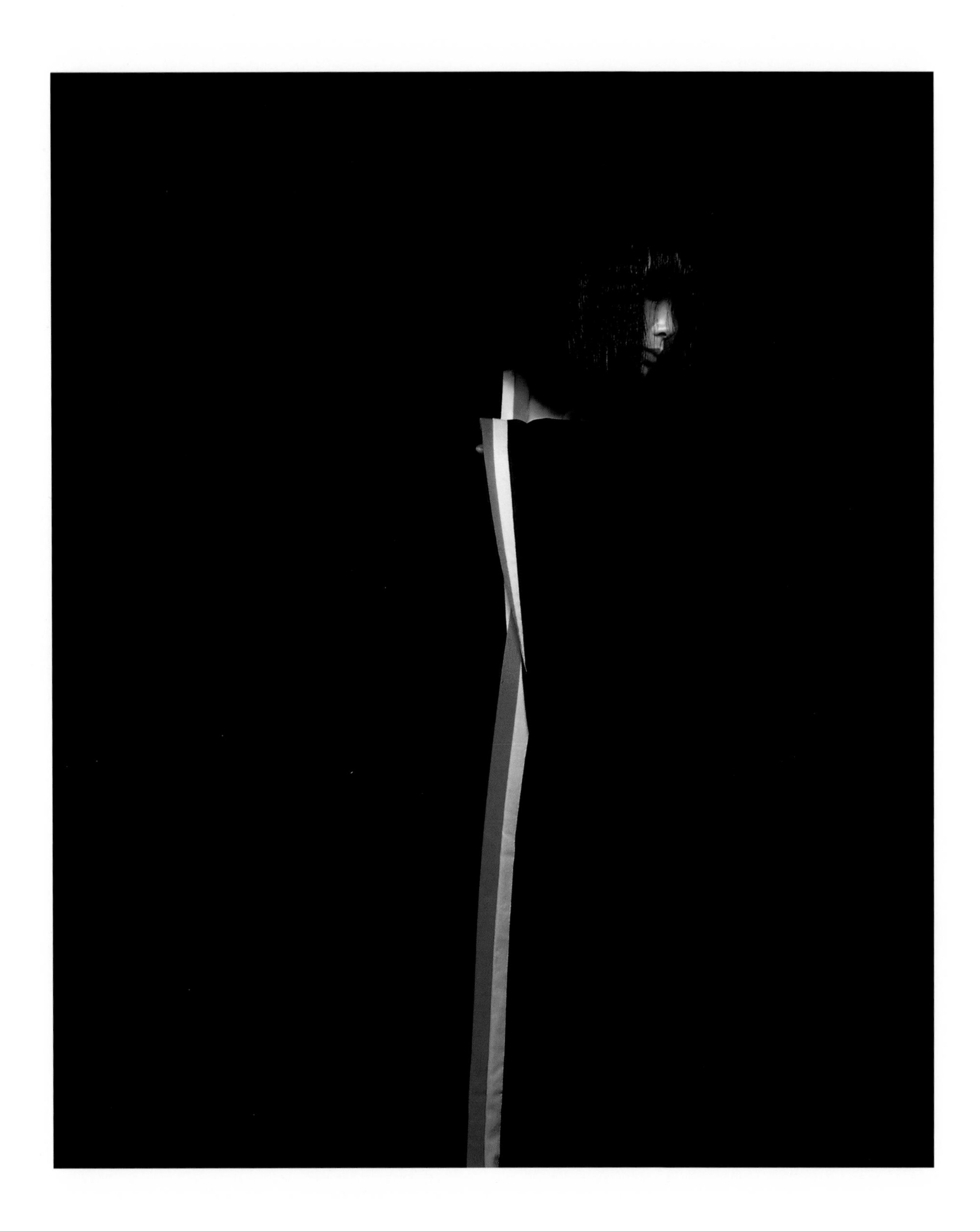

Inge Morath, 1974
USA

Cees van Gelder, 1975
Niederlande/*The Netherlands*

Ikko Narahara, 1968
Japan

Chris von Wangenheim, 1975
USA

Georges Tourdjman, 1970
Frankreich/*France*

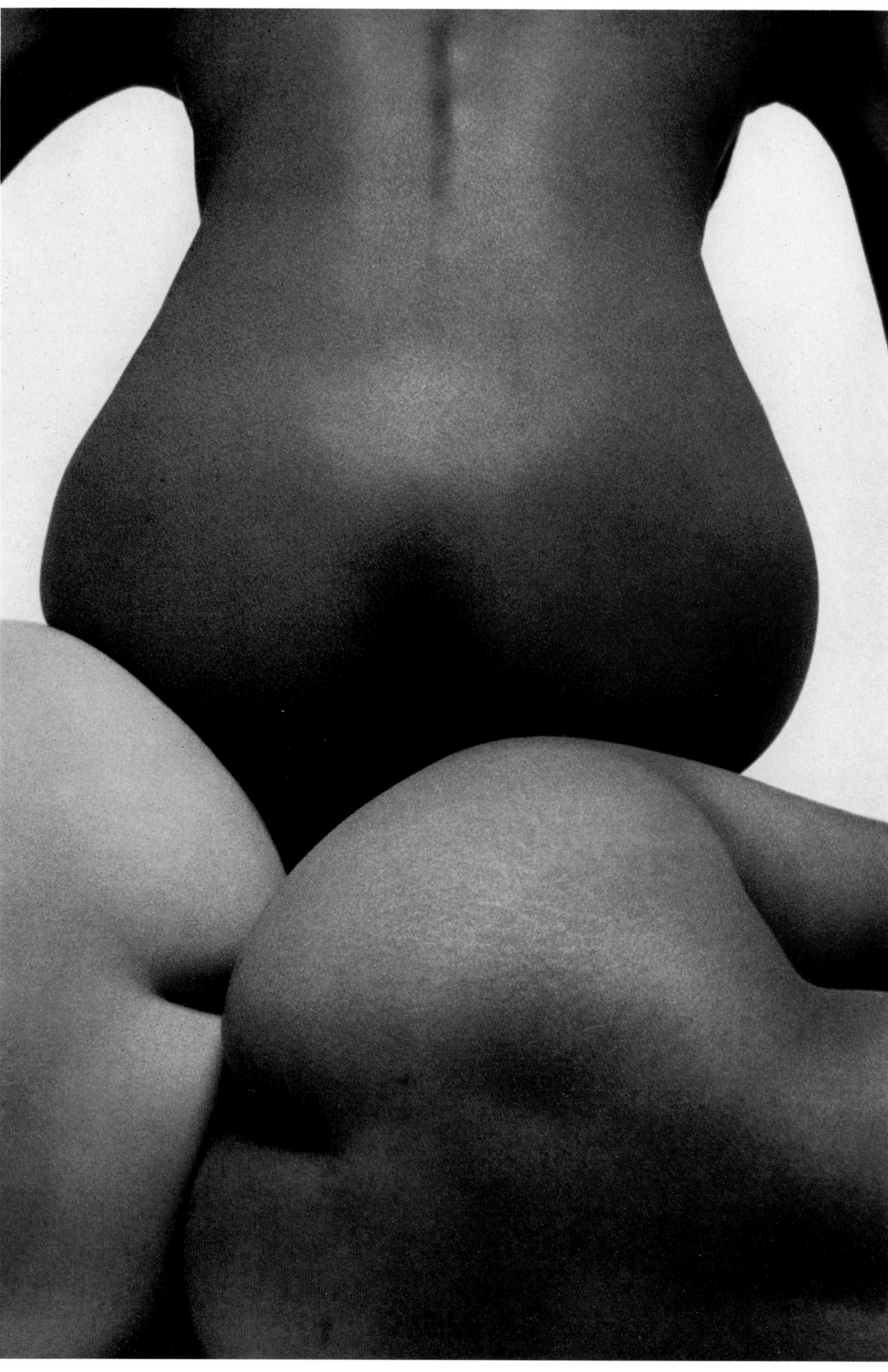

Akira Sato, 1974

Japan

Pierre Cordier, 1976

Belgien/*Belgium*

Lucien Clergue, 1975
Frankreich/*France*

Franco Fontana, 1972
Italien/*Italy*

Beppe Buccafusca, 1976
Italien/*Italy*

Piet van Leeuwen, 1970
Niederlande/*The Netherlands*

Horst H. Baumann, 1974
Deutschland/*Germany*

Sonja Bullaty, 1970
USA

Ruth Orkin, 1971
USA

Yoichi Midorikawa, 1972
Japan

Kishin Shinoyama, 1975
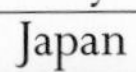
Japan

Thomas Höpker, 1976
Deutschland/*Germany*

Michael Kostiuk, 1975
USA

Pit Ludwig, 1972
Deutschland/*Germany*

Stephen Shore, 1974
USA

Stephen Shore, 1975
USA

Laurence LeGuay, 1972
Australien/*Australia*

Burt Glinn, 1971
USA

Stephan Whealton, 1970

USA

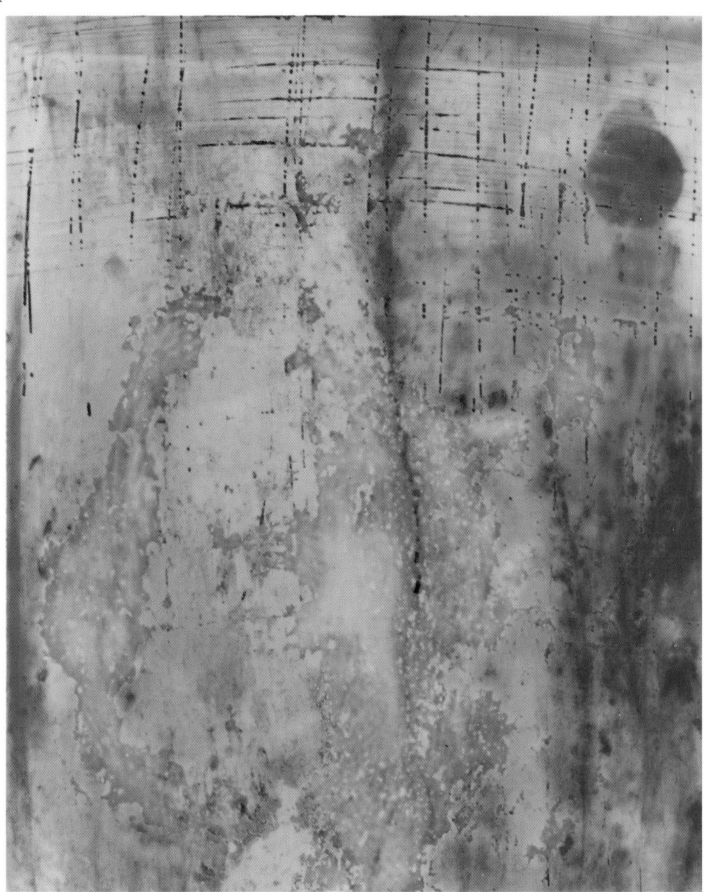

Harry Bowers, 1969
USA

1976-1986

Sally Eauclaire

In der Geschichte der Farbfotografie markiert das Jahr 1976 einen Wendepunkt: John Szarkowski vom Museum of Modern Art in New York zeigte und publizierte die umstrittenen Fotografien von William Eggleston. Damit hatte eine radikal neue fotografische Sichtweise ihre Premiere, die sich dann als Kunstform etablierte. Die Pioniere auf diesem Gebiet wie Stephen Shore, Joel Meyerowitz und andere, zeigten neue Möglichkeiten der Farbfotografie auf und animierten zahlreiche weitere Fotografen, in Farbe zu arbeiten. Gegen Ende der 70er Jahre kam der Farbe innerhalb der zeitgenössischen Fotografie bereits die tragende Rolle zu.

Dieser Aufschwung des Interesses kam so überraschend wie plötzlich. Nur wenige Jahre zuvor hatten viele empfindsame Kunstliebhaber zugestimmt, als Walker Evans die Farbe als "vulgär" denunzierte oder Edward Steichen beklagte, sie sei "zu bunt". Wenige stellten Robert Franks kompromißlose Position in Frage, Schwarz und Weiß seien die Farben der Fotografie. Obwohl viele junge Farbfotografen in den 70er Jahren Arbeiten produzierten, die diese Ansichten widerlegten, stimmten sie doch mit Evans, Steichen und Frank darin überein, daß die Farbfotografie, wie sie aus der Werbung, Amateurschnappschüssen, Fotojournalismus, Reise- und Naturfotografie bekannt war, solches Urteil verdiene. Gegen diese Vorläufer sich absetzend, wählten sie die Begründung einer neuen Kunstform, die in bezug auf Form und Inhalt in der Tradition steht der Fotografien von Eugène Atget, Walker Evans, Robert Frank, Garry Winogrand, Lee Friedlander und anderen.

Aber natürlich lieferte die Schwarzweißfotografie keine Anleitungen für den Gebrauch der Farbe. Entscheidend für die Entwicklung der neuen Farbfotografie in den 70er Jahren war die Erkenntnis der Farbfotografen, daß sie außerhalb der kontrollierbaren Studiosituation nie in der Lage sein würden, traditionelle hierarchische Kompositionen auf der Grundlage von passivem und aktivem Raum zu meistern. Vierzig Jahre farbfotografische Praxis hatten Laszlo Moholy-Nagys Feststellung bestätigt, daß Farbfotografen, die Naturalismus anstreben, wieder da wären, wo die Maler des Realismus in der Renaissance anfingen – bei der Imitation der Natur mit unzureichenden Mitteln.

In Anerkenntnis dieses Defizits beschlossen die neuen Farbfotografen, sich stattdessen die Prinzipen der modernen Malerei seit dem Impressionismus zu eigen zu machen, nämlich die Autonomie der Farbe. Statt die Aufmerksamkeit auf einen zentralen Punkt zu lenken, bemühten sie sich, die Oberfläche des ganzen Bildes vibrieren zu lassen. Der strukturelle Gebrauch der Farbe in der modernen Malerei – artikuliert von dem Maler Hans Hofmann in seinem Konzept von Farben, die gegen die Bildläche "drücken und schieben" – erwies sich als entscheidend für die Reifung der direkten (die Realität abbildenden – *d. Übers.*) Farbfotografie zur Kunstform. Diese neue Betrachtungsweise machte es möglich, farbliche übertreibungen zu antizipieren und in Anspruch zu nehmen, und so die Nachteile der früheren Farbfotografien in Vorzüge zu verwandeln.

Das soll aber nicht heißen, die neuen Farbfotografen der 70er und 80er Jahre würden die moderne Malerei imitieren. Im Gegenteil, die Prämissen ihrer Kunst sind rein fotografische Sachverhalte und

In the history of color photography 1976 stands as a landmark year. John Szarkowski of the Museum of Modern Art, New York, exhibited and published the controversial photographs of William Eggleston, thus premiering a radical new vision that would establish color photography as an art form. Pioneering work by Stephen Shore, Joel Meyerowitz, and others offered alternative possibilities and spurred scores of photographers to take up color. By the late 1970s color had become the foremost issue in contemporary photography.

This explosion of interest was both surprising and sudden. Only a few years before many sensitive art lovers had agreed when Walker Evans dismissed color photography as "vulgar" and Edward Steichen complained that it was "too coloriferous". Few argued with Robert Frank's uncompromising position that the colors of photography were black and white. Although many of the color photographers emerging in the 1970s produced works which rebut these views, they largely agreed with Evans, Steichen, and Frank that earlier color photography (as known through advertising, snap-shooting, photo-journalism, travel, and nature photography) deserved such opprobium. Rejecting such precedents, they chose instead to forge a new art form whose form and content owes a substantial debt to the black-and-white photographs of Eugene Atget, Walker Evans, Gary Winogrand, and Lee Friedlander, among many others.

Black-and-white photography, of course, offered no lessons in the use of color. Crucial to the development of the new color photography of the 1970s was the acknowledegment by color photographers that outside controlled studio environments, they would never be able to master traditional hierarchical compositions based upon passive and active space. Forty years of color photography had verified Laszlo Moholy Nagy's observation that color photographers attempting naturalism were "back where realistic painters started in the Renaissance – the "imitation of nature with inadequate means".

Given this deficiency, the new color photographers chose instead to assimilate the principles of modern painting from the Impressionists emancipation of color onward. Rather than focus on a central point of interest, they sought to make the picture surface reverberate from edge to edge. The structural use of color in modern painting – articulated by painter Hans Hofman with his concept of colors "pushing and pulling" against the picture plane – proved crucial to the maturation of straight color photography as an art form. This new way of seeing made it possible to anticipate and enlist color photography's inherent hue exaggerations, thus turning the deficiencies that had stymied earlier color photographers into assets.

This is not to say that the new color photographers of the 1970s and 1980s imitate modern paintings. To the contrary, their art is premised on issues and effects that are tenaciously photographic. Unlike color photographers who photograph painted patterns, peeling billboards, and other 'art-like' subjects, the best of the new color photographers understand that their photographs should carry two interdependent contexts – a descriptive illusion of three-dimensional space and a design of lines, tones, shapes, colors and textures upon the picture surface.

Ergebnisse. Im Unterschied zu Farbfotografen, die gemalte Muster, abblätternde Plakatwände oder andere 'künstlerische' Motive fotografierten, geht es den besten unter den neuen Farb fotografen in ihren Aufnahmen um zwei einander bedingende Faktoren – um die Darstellung des dreidimensionalen Raumes in der Fläche und um die Gestaltung von Linien, Tonwerten, Umrissen, Farben und Texturen.

Ihre Arbeiten sind fotografisch, gerade auch in ihrer zeitweisen Einbeziehung von fotografischen 'Schnappschuß'-Effekten. Hier trifft das Diktum des Kunstkritikers Clement Greenberg zu, daß sich jede Kunst "durch ihre spezifische Form des Handlens bestimmt, durch Ergebnisse, die spezifisch und ausschließlich in ihr möglich sind". Wie die in Schwarzweiß arbeitenden Verfechter der Schnappschuß-ästhetik, nehmen auch die zeitgenössischen Farbfotografen jene visuellen Eigenheiten des Mediums in Anspruch, die fähige Berufsfotografen einst beharrlich vermieden. Diese Fotografen erkannten, daß 'unachtsame' Ausschnitte, 'unsaubere' Belichtungen und 'falsche' Filme für die gegebenen Lichtverhältnisse auch zu überzeugenden Ergebnissen führen können, wenn sie intelligent genutzt werden. Obwohl die Schnappschuß-Effekte viele Betrachter wütend machen, weil sie meinen, die neuen Farbfotografen würden das Publikum mit Arbeiten, die sich wenig von jenen Fotos unterscheid, die Onkel Otto beim Fotohändler reklamiert, zum Narren halten, haben diese Fotos tatsächlich soviel Gemeinsamkeiten mit dem Amateurschnappschuß, wie abstrakte expressionistische Gemälde mit Ölflecken.

Solche Fotografien unterscheiden sich aber ebenso radikal von photorealistischen Gemälden wie denen von Ralph Goings, Robert Bechtle und anderen, die peinlich genau mundane Schnappschüsse kopieren, um die Aufmerksamkeit des Betrachters auf die Rolle des gewöhnlichen Schnappschusses als kulturelles Ikon zu lenken. Die Ziele der neuen Farbfotografen sind ganz andere. Indem sie die visuellen und konzeptuellen Möglichkeiten der Farbfotografie ausschöpfen, benutzen sie das Medium im Sinne einer eigenständigen Kunstform.

Eggleston, Shore und Meyerowitz – sowie die bedeutenden jüngeren Talente wie Mitch Epstein, Len Jenshel, Roger Mertin, John Pfahl, Joel Sternfeld und viele andere, deren Werk nach und nach in die Museen kommt – kombinieren in ihren Fotografien formale, dokumentarische und metaphorische Bedeutungen; die Intertation kann so reichhaltig und ambigue sein, wie das Leben selbst.

Weniger umstritten sind die konstruierten Farbfotografien, die sich in den späten 70er Jahren im Kampf um die museale Anerkennung zu den direkten (die Realität abbildenden – *d. Übers.*) Farbfotografien hinzugesellten. Jan Groover, Barbara Kasten, David Haxton und andere begaben sich in ihre Studios, um Stilleben aufzubauen, wobei sie schöpferisch mit Kunstrichtungen wie Kubismus, Konstruktivismus, abstrakter Expressionismus, umgingen, während Bernard Faucon, Sandy Skoglund, Boyd Webb, William Wegman und andere Tableaus inszenierten, die mit dem Absurden spielen. Lucas Samaras verfolgte weiterhin seine Interessen, die auf die 60er Jahre zurückgehen, als er einer der ersten war, der Polaroid Sofortbildmaterialien für seine narzistischen, exhibitionistischen und fetischistischen Zwecke einsetzte. Vergleichbar führte auch Robert

Their work is photographic as well in its frequent embrace of peculiarly photographic 'snapshot' effects. Art critic Clement Greenberg's dictate that each art ought to "determine through the operations peculiar to itself, the effects peculiar and exclusive to itself", applies. Like black-and-white proponents of the snapshot aesthetic, contemporary color photographers imaginatively enlist the visual peculiarities of the medium that capable professionals once assiduously avoided. These photographers recognize that 'careless' cropping, 'improper' exposures, and films 'wrong' for given lighting conditions can be intelligently exploited to serve potent pictorial ends. Although snapshot effects infuriate many viewers, who claim the new color photographers are 'conning the public' with works that differ little from the rejects that Uncle Harry takes back to Fotomat, these photographs in fact bear as much realtionship to snapshots as Abstract Expressionist paintings do to oil spills.

Such photographs also differ radically from Photo-Realist paintings by Ralph Goings, Robert Bechtle, and others who meticulously copy mundane snapshots to draw the viewer's attention to the ordinary color snapshot's role as a cultural icon. The new color photographers' aims are far different. Mining color photography's visual and conceptual potential, they regard the medium as a means to a distinct new art form.

The photographs of Eggleston, Shore, and Meyerowitz – and those of major new talents such as Mitch Epstein, Len Jenshel, Roger Mertin, John Pfahl, Joel Sternfeld, and many others whose work subsequently appeared in museums – combine formal, documentary, and metaphorical meanings. Interpretation can be as rich and ambiguous as life itself.

Less controversial are the fabricated color photographs that by the late 1970s had joined straight color photography in the battle for museum recognition. Jan Groover, Barbara Kasten, David Haxton, and others repaired to their studios to set up still lifes that inventively drew upon the precedents of Cubism, Constructivism, Abstract Expressionism, and other art movements, while Bernard Faucon, Sandy Skoglund, Boyd Webb, William Wegman, and others directed tableaus toying with the absurd. Lucas Samaras pursued concerns he had initiated in the 1960's when he pioneered the use of Polaroid self-developing materials for his own narcissistic, exhibitionist, and fetishistic ends. Similarly, Robert Heinecken continued his long-standing obsession with appropriated images from the popular media environment of magazines, billboards, television, film, and posters. By the mid-1980s David Hockney was the best known of many photographers to explore the Cubist potential of color photographs employed in collaged or modular compositions. Size, too, sets these photographs apart, for these photographers blow up their prints or combine many photographs into a monumental whole to compete in an art world that values scale and impact.

Clearly, the range of color photography produced during the past decade offers proof that color has sky-rocketed from medium to phenomenon. Such language, however, belies an important truth. Color photography today is no longer newsworthy. On the contrary, in the worlds of both photography and art its legitimacy finally lies unquestioned.

Heinecken seine lange währende Obsession für entsprechende Fotos aus den populären Medien wie Magazinen, Reklametafeln, Fernsehen, Film und Plakat fort. In der Mitte der 80er Jahre war David Hockney der bekannteste unter jenen Fotografen, die das kubistische Potential von Farbfotografien erkunden, realisiert in collageartigen oder ähnlichen Kompositionen. Auch ihre Größe stellt diese Fotografien heraus, weil die Fotografen ihre Abzüge aufblasen oder viele Fotografien zu einem monumentalen Ganzen kombinieren, um in der Kunstszene, die große Formate und Effekte zu würdigen weiß, konkurrenzfähig zu sein.

Offensichtlich bestätigt die Bandbreite der während des letzten Jahrzehnts produzierten Farbfotografien, daß die Farbe vom Medium zum Phänomen aufstieg. Diese Ausdrucksweise täuscht allerdings über eine wichtige Tatsache hinweg. Die Farbfotografie ist heute keine Schlagzeile mehr wert. Im Gegenteil, in der Fotografieszene und in der Kunstwelt ist ihre Legitimität endlich unbestritten.

AUTONOMIE DER FARBE

AUTONOMY OF COLOR

Klaus Honnef

Die Geschichte wiederholt sich nicht, und Vergleiche hinken häufig. Dennoch spricht manches dafür, daß sich in der Fotografie am Ende des 20. Jahrhunderts eine Entwicklung wiederholt, von der die traditionellen Bildkünste 100 Jahre zuvor erfaßt wurden. Damals herausgefordert durch das Aufkommen des neuen technischen Mediums: der Fotografie. Sie übernahm gleichsam die Alltagsfunktion, das Geschäft, das bislang zahlreiche Porträt- und Landschaftmaler sowie im Pressewesen die Kommentatoren mit der Lithografenkreide besorgt hatten. Der Streit zwischen den Künstlern im Rückzugsgefecht und den Fotografen auf dem Vormarsch ist hinlänglich bekannt. Die Künstler der Avantgarde begrüßten den Prozeß, formulierten das Konzept einer Kunst, die nur noch den eigenen Gesetzen gehorchte und ledig war aller anderen gesellschaftlichen Verpflichtungen.

Die elektronischen Bildmedien haben 100 Jahre später die Fotografie in eine ähnliche Lage gebracht und beackern mit immer noch wachsendem Erfolg Terrains, die von der Fotografie lange Zeit als ureigene Felder betrachtet wurden. Entsprechend sind die Fotografen wie dereinst die Künstler auf der Suche nach einem neuen Selbstverständnis, zugleich nach einer Ästhetik, die das künstlerische Element betont, ohne das spezifisch fotografische aufzugeben. Allerdings gilt es von vornherein, eines zu beachten: Fotografie ist nicht Fotografie. Von allen diesen Vorgängen unbeeindruckt zeigt sich die Massenfotografie der Amateure.

Vor dem Hintergrund des dramatischen Paradigmenwechsels in der Fotografie fiel der Farbe eine besondere Rolle zu. Und das in zweierlei Hinsicht. Einerseits "emanzipierte" sie sich zum hauptsächlichen Ausdrucksträger der Bewegung, andererseits fungierte sie als eine Art Lackmuspapier, dessen "Verfärbung" den tiefgreifenden Wandel signalisiert. Verändert hat sich allerdings weniger die Farbe an sich als vielmehr ihre Position im "Verbundsystem" des fotografischen Bildes. Messen die Hersteller ihr die Aufgabe zu, die naturalistischen Eigenschaften des Mediums Fotografie zu stärken, was die Heerschar der Amateure lebhaft begrüßte, begann die Farbe sich zugleich in der Sphäre der künstlerisch ambitionierten Fotografie unter dem Einfluß der allmählichen Veränderung des fotografischen Selbstverständnisses zu verselbständigen. Es waren vornehmlich die Künstler, die den künstlichen Charakter der Farbe in der Fotografie erkannten und als eigenständiges ästhetisches Mittel verwendeten.

In der Mode- und Werbefotografie hatte sich die Farbe verhältnismäßig rasch durchgesetzt, in der Reportage und Dokumentarfotografie blieb sie bis heute – von Ausnahmen abgesehen – verpönt. Hat die Fotografie unsere Sehgewohnheiten schon dermaßen geprägt, daß wir unsere Wirklichkeit im künstlichen Licht der Schwarz-Weiß-Schilderung als "realistischer", wirklichkeitsgetreuer empfinden denn in der "naturalistischeren" Version der Farbfotografie? Niemand käme auf die Idee, einem in Schwarz und Weiß getauchten Gemälde einen höheren Grad an Realitätsnähe zuzubilligen als einem in Farbe. Bei der Fotografie ist es offenbar umgekehrt. Die Mode- und Werbefotografen schildern die Welt nicht so, wie sie augenscheinlich ist oder wie sie sich in unserem Bewußtsein spiegelt, sondern im Lichte unserer Vorstellungen, unserer Wünsche und mitunter unserer Träume. Insofern nutzt diese Form von Fotografie auf säkulare Weise

History does not repeat itself and comparisons are of little value. However there is a certain repetition of a development in photography at the end of the twentieth century which was first realised in traditional Art 100 years before. At that time it was challenged by the arrival of a new technical medium: photography. It took over the daily functions, the tasks which up to that time had been conducted by innumerous portrait and landscape artists and by reporters using lithographs in the Press. The battle between artists in retreat and photographers in advance is sufficiently well-documented. The avant-garde artist embraced the processes and formulated a concept of art which only obeyed its own laws and was exempt from all other social restrictions.

The electronic picture medium has brought photography into a similar position 100 years later and cultivates areas with ever increasing success which for a long time were regarded by photography as its own inherent fields. Accordingly, photographers, like the artists before them, started to search for a new self-awareness and, at the same time, for an aesthetic element which embodies the artistic without embodying a specific photographic pose. In any case, one thing was of primary importance: photography is not photography. Mass amateur photography remains uninfluenced by all these processes.

Color played a special part in the background of this dramatic paradigmic change in photography. On two fronts. On the one hand it 'emancipated' itself as the most important form of expression in the movement and on the other hand, it acted as a sort of litmus paper whose 'color change' signalled a far-reaching transformation. In fact, color itself did not change as such but rather its position in the 'combined system' of the photographic picture. The inventors gave it the task of strengthening the natural characteristics of the photographic medium which the host of amateurs animatedly greeted; color began to distinguish itself at the same time in the sphere of artistically-motivated photography under the influence of the gradual change in photographic self-awareness. It was primarily the artists who recognised the artistic character of color in photography and used it as an individual aesthetic medium.

In fashion and advertising photography, color proportionately made itself invaluable very quickly; in reporting and documentary photography it remains up to the present – excluding some exceptions – taboo. Has photography impragnated our ability to see in such measures that we see our reality in the artistic light of black-white pictures as 'more realistic'; do those seeking the truth find a 'more natural' version in color photography? No-one thought to view a black and white painting as being closer to the truth than one in color. With photography this is obviously the other way around. Fashion and advertising photography does not portray the world as it obviously is or how it reflects in our conscience but in the light of our imagination, our desires and our dreams. Insofar this form of photography uses, in a secular manner, the capital massed by the art of the era, which ended with the dawn of the avant garde. However, with this difference: that the art of reality has always transcended and not deluded.

das Kapital der Kunst der Zeit, die mit dem Aufbruch der Avantgarde beendet wurde. Mit dem Unterschied jedoch, daß die Kunst die Wirklichkeit stets transzendiert und nicht verblendet hat.

Schneller als die herkömmliche Farbfotografie erregte die Polaroid-Fotografie die Aufmerksamkeit der Künstlerschaft, die dann über das technische Verfahren des Sofortbildes in den Entwicklungsgang der Farbfotografie immer stärker eingriff. Vor allem die besonderen Farben der SX-70 faszinierte zahlreiche Künstlerinnen und Künstler dank ihrer außergewöhnlichen Künstlichkeit. Das Sofortbild war die adäquate Antwort auf die glitzernde, so flüchtige wie hedonistische, oberflächliche und scheinhafte Großstandtkultur unserer Megalopolis mit ihrer Atemlosigkeit und sinnlichen Verführungskraft.

In der Sofortbildfotografie verdichtete sich jenes schwankende Lebensgefühl, das unserer Zeit seinen Stempel aufgedrückt hat. In diesem Lebensgefühl nimmt die Welt im abrupten Wechsel mal traumhafte, mal monströse, mal paradiesische, mal gigantische und mal niedliche Züge an, verzerrte und häufig fiktive, selten solche, die Ausfluß empirischer Erfahrung sind. Die Sofortbildfotografie verdichtete dieses Lebensgefühl und verlieh ihm gleichwohl nur eine flüchtige Substanz. Dabei errang die Farbe die Funktion eines Leitsterns und potenzierte das Gefühl, daß unsere Wirklichkeit nicht (mehr) von dieser Welt sei. Jüngere Fotografen, aufgewachsen in der künstlichen Wirklichkeit der Medienwelt, die erste echte Fernsehgeneration, erprobten die Qualität der Farbe auch in der herkömmlichen Fotografie, wo sie inzwischen dazu dient, das Fiktive unserer Welt kraft Verdoppelung zu demonstrieren. Wo dem 'natürlichen' Voyeurismus des Fotografen/Künstlers der selbstverständliche Exhibitionismus der Darsteller begegnet, wie in unserer Welt allgemeiner 'Stimulation' (Baudrillard), produziert der dokumentarische Gestus der Fotografie nichts als 'Theater' – höchste Authentizität ist zum Synonym für größtmögliche Fiktion geworden. In der zeitgenössischen Farbfotografie verwandelt sich das dreidimensionale Erscheinungsbild der Wirklichkeit in pure Flächenwerte fotografischer Aufnahmen. Damit vollzieht sich eine Metamorphose des Seins in den reinen Schein. Im Scheinhaften des fotografischen Bildes verdoppelt sich die 'fiktive' (simulierte) Wirklichkeit und kristallisiert sich zum Schein einer Realitätsfiktion: neuerlich zur Wirklichkeit.

'Inszenierte Fotografie' ist die angemessenste Spielart fotografischer Kunst, angesichts einer Wirklichkeit der simulierten Handlungen und Ereignisse. In einer Zeit, wo der mächtigste Mann der Welt ein Darsteller ist, der mit Bildern virtuos umzugehen weiß, ist es die Farbfotografie, die unsere Sinne zu schärfen vermag für die künstlichen Paradiese, die uns die kommerziellen Medien vorgaukeln, weil die fixieren und mit dem ästhetischen Mittel der Übertreibung pointieren, was diese vor unserem 'zerstreuten Blick' (Benjamin) vorrüberhuschen lassen. Die Farbe akzentuiert und 'dramatisiert', entkleidet das Drama freilich aller tragischen Dimensionen. Dabei werden Fotografen, die sich der Möglichkeiten und Wirkungen ihres Mediums bewußt sind und natürlich des Umstandes, daß dieses Medium unser Weltbild 'verkörpert', beinahe zwangsläufig zu Künstlern; zu Künstlern, die den Bilderberg, unter dem die empirische Wirklichkeit längst verschwunden ist, vielleicht aufzusprengen in der Lange sind.

Polaroid photography roused the attention of the artistic community faster than the original color photography did, and this strengthened it's hold via the technical procedure of instant pictures in the path of development of color photography. Above all, the special colors of the SX-70 material fascinated innumerous artists by virtue of their extraordinary artistic quality. The instant picture was the adequate reply to the glittering, fleeting as well as hedonistic, superficial and illusory Big City Culture of our megalopolis with its breathlessness and sensual seduction.

Every precarious feeling in life which has printed its stamp on our era, is condensed in instant photography. In this feeling in life, the world takes on aspects in abrupt succession, sometimes dreamy, sometimes monstrous, sometimes paradise-like, sometimes gigantic and sometimes elegant, distorted and often fictitious, seldom as a result of empirical experience. Instant photography condenses this feeling in life and gives it nevertheless a fleeting substance. Thus, color fulfilled the function of a guiding star and gave rise to the feeling that our reality was not (no longer) of this world. Young photographers, brought up in the artistic reality of the media world, the first real TV-generation, also tested the quality of color in the original photography, where, in the meantime, they served to demonstrate the fiction of our world by means of duplication. When the 'natural' voyeurism of the photographers/artists meets the self-aware exhibitionism of the actors, the general 'simulation' (Baudrillard) in our world, the documentary basis of photography produces nothing but 'theatre' – greatest authenticity has become a synonym for largest possible fiction.

In contemporary color photography the three-dimensional illusory picture of reality changes into the pure superficial values of the photographic picture. Thus completing the metamorphosis of being into pure illusion. The 'fictional' (simulated) reality is duplicated in the illusion of the photographic picture and is crystallised into the appearance of real fiction: repeated into reality. 'Staged photography' is the most suitable manner of presenting the photographic art, considering the reality of the simulated actions and events. In a time when the most important man in the world is an actor who is a master in pictures, it is color photography, which is capable of sharpening our senses for the aristic paradise, which leads us to believe the commercial media, because it fixes and points with aesthetic means to the exaggeration, which hurriedly slips past in front of our 'distracted glance' (Benjamin). Color accentuates and 'dramatises', divested of virtually all it's tragic dimensions. Thus photographers who are aware of the difficulties and effects of their media and naturally of the circumstances which this medium 'embodies' of our world view, are almost forced into being artists, artists who are perhaps capable of splitting the mountain of pictures asunder, under which the empirical reality has long disappeared.

Donald C. Landwehrle, 1984
USA

Pete Turner, o.D./*n.d.*
USA

Jürg Andermatt, 1980
Deutschland/*Germany*

Jan Ságl, 1979
CSSR

Robert Glenn Ketchum, 1983
USA

Gerd Schnakenwinkel, 1984
Deutschland/*Germany*

David Mendelsohn, 1981
USA

Richard Misrach, 1984
USA

Angelo Lomeo, 1983
USA

Len Jenshel, 1985
USA

Vadim Gippenreiter, 1975
Sowietunion/*USSR*

Wolfgang Volz, 1983
Deutschland/*Germany*

Dr. Georg Gerster, 1980
Schweiz/*Switzerland*

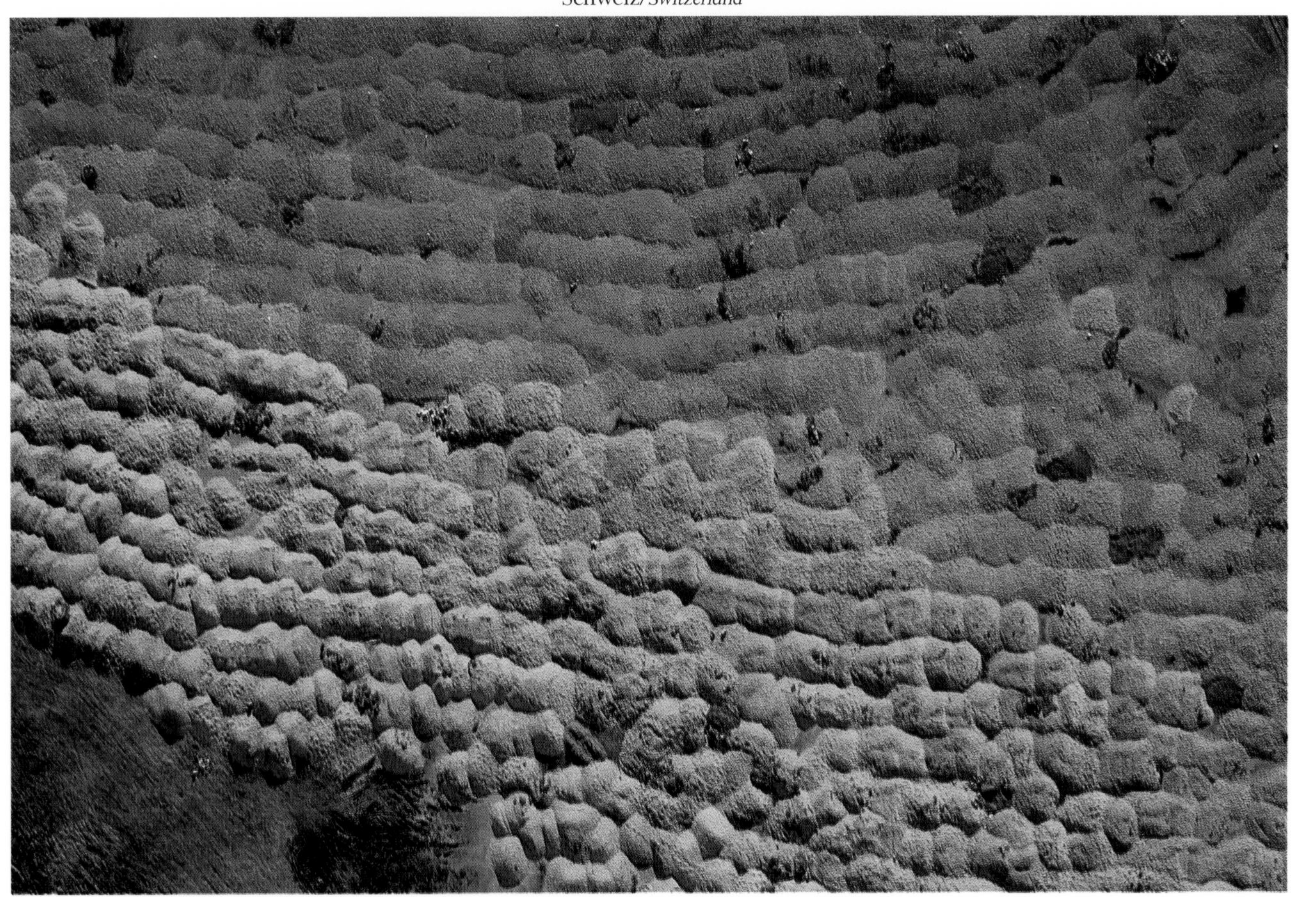

Paul Graham, 1985
Großbritannien/*Great Britain*

Art Sinsabaugh, 1979
USA

Horst Munzig, 1984
Deutschland/*Germany*

Joe Maloney, 1977
USA

Melissa McCord, o.D./*n.d.*
Australien/*Australia*

John Pfahl, 1983
USA

Martin Kers, 1984
Niederlande/*The Netherlands*

Anselm Spring, 1985
Deutschland/*Germany*

Ulrich Mack, 1979

Deutschland/*Germany*

Clinton Smith, 1981

USA

Mark Klett, 1982
USA

Larry Babis, 1980
USA

Wout Berger, 1982
Niederlande/*The Netherlands*

Ulrich Mack, 1979
Deutschland/*Germany*

Dr. Georg Gerster, 1982

Schweiz/*Switzerland*

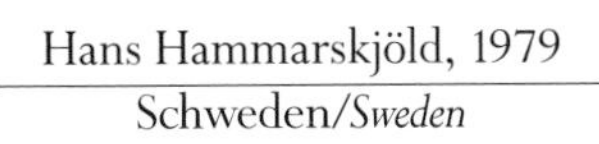

Hans Hammarskjöld, 1979

Schweden/*Sweden*

Jan van Steenwijk, 1986
USA

Raghubir Singh, 1983
Frankreich/*France*

Art Sinsabaugh, 1969

USA

Brian Griffin, 1984

Großbritannien/*Great Britain*

David Hanson, 1985
USA

Len Jenshel, 1978
USA

Joel Sternfeld, 1982
USA

William Christenberry, 1981
USA

William Larson, 1982
USA

Joel Meyerowitz, 1979
USA

THE CANARY CAFE
TAKE AWAY FOODS
MILK BAR FRESH CUT SANDWICHES
MILK BAR
FRESH CUT SANDWICHES
CAFE GRILLS
HAMBURGER BAR
Espresso
HAMBURGER BAR
Roast Chicken
FISH & CHIPS
HOT DOGS
SOUVLAKI
The CANARY CAFE
TAKE AWAY FOODS
CARDIGAN ST
STATE SAVINGS BANK
ESSO

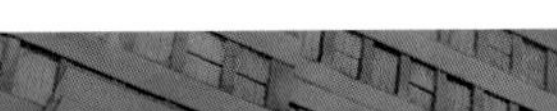

Elizabeth Lennard, 1983
USA

Harry Callahan, 1984
USA

Luigi Ghirri, 1985
Italien/*Italy*

Gabriele Basilico, 1985
Italien/*Italy*

Lajos Keresztes, 1984
Deutschland/*Germany*

Lajos Keresztes, 1982
Deutschland/*Germany*

Guenther Cartwright, 1985
Großbritannien/*Great Britain*

David Graham, 1984

USA

Jay Maisel, o.D./*n.d.*
USA

Jay Maisel, o.D./*n.d.*
USA

Reinhart Wolf, 1979

Deutschland/*Germany*

Michael Ruetz, 1978
Deutschland/*Germany*

John Margolies, 1983
USA

Richard Pare, 1983
USA

Olivio Barbieri, 1982
Italien/*Italy*

Eikoh Hosoe, 1984
Japan

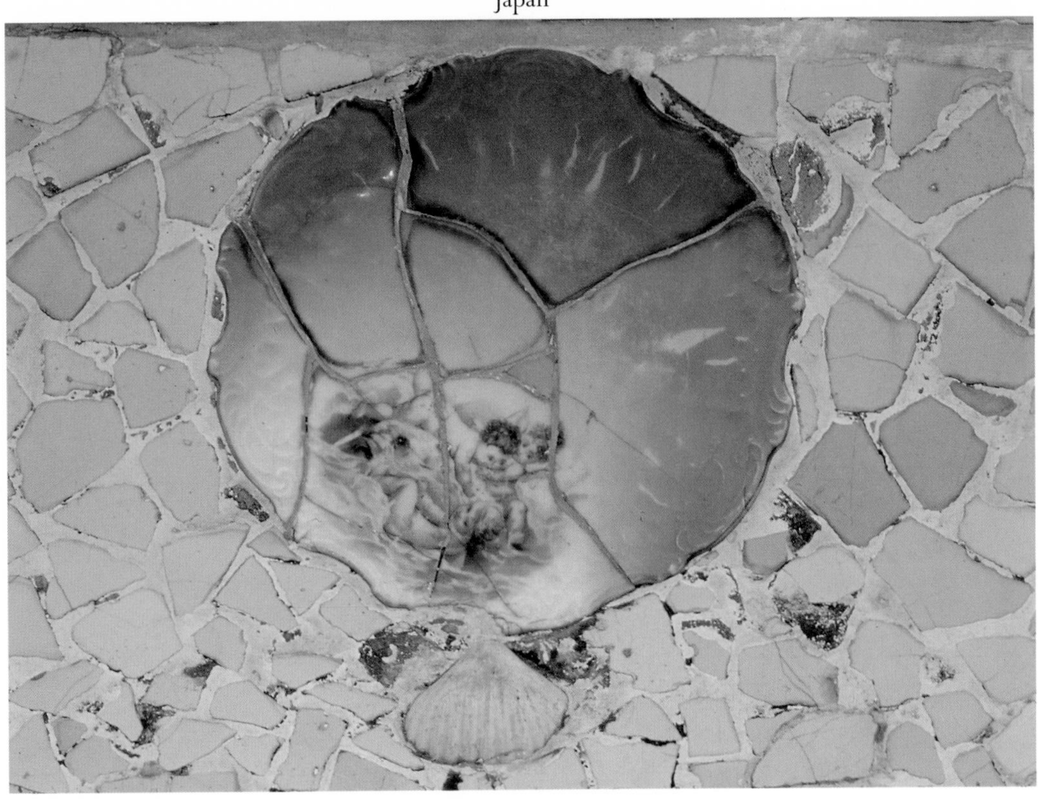

Jay Maisel, 1984
USA

Jan Ságl, 1984
CSSR

Harald Mante, 1986
Deutschland/*Germany*

Len Jenshel, 1985
USA

David Moore, 1982
Australien/*Australia*

Jean Meziere, 1978
USA

Richard Payne, 1985
USA

Stephan Erfurt, 1985
Deutschland/*Germany*

Kazumi Kurigami, 1980
Japan

Anne-Marie Grobet, o.D./*n.d.*
Schweiz/*Switzerland*

Emil Schulthess, 1979

Schweiz/*Switzerland*

Emil Schulthess, 1981

Schweiz/*Switzerland*

Nikolai Rachmanov, 1980
Sowjetunion/*USSR*

John Vink, 1982
Belgien/*Belgium*

Serge Hambourg, 1983
Frankreich/*France*

Guenther Cartwright, 1984
Großbritannien/*Great Britain*

Waclav Nowak, 1976
Polen/*Poland*

Stephan Erfurt, 1985
Deutschland/*Germany*

Wilhelm Schürmann, 1979
Deutschland/*Germany*

Dr. Peter Stepan, 1984
Deutschland/*Germany*

Henry Talbot, o.D./*n.d.*
Australien/*Australia*

Hans Wiesenhofer, 1982
Österreich/*Austria*

Roger Mertin, 1980
USA

Jim Dow, 1982
USA

Jerry Dantzic, 1977
USA

Langdon Clay, 1977
USA

Science and Health with Key to the Scriptures
GUINNESS BOOK OF WORLD RECORDS
A Way of Life
DIVINE PRINCIPLE

Dušan Šimánek, 1979

CSSR

Dieter Leistner, 1981

Deutschland/*Germany*

Vincenzo Castella, 1976

Italien/*Italy*

Elaine Mayes, 1981
USA

Stanley Bowman, 1984
USA

Luigi Ghirri, 1985
Italien/*Italy*

Thomas Lüttge, 1984
Deutschland/*Germany*

Reinhold Ludwig Hilgering, 1985
Deutschland/*Germany*

Phil Bergerson, 1979
Kanada/*Canada*

Pascal Kern, 1985
Frankreich/*France*

Eberhard Grames, 1985
Deutschland/*Germany*

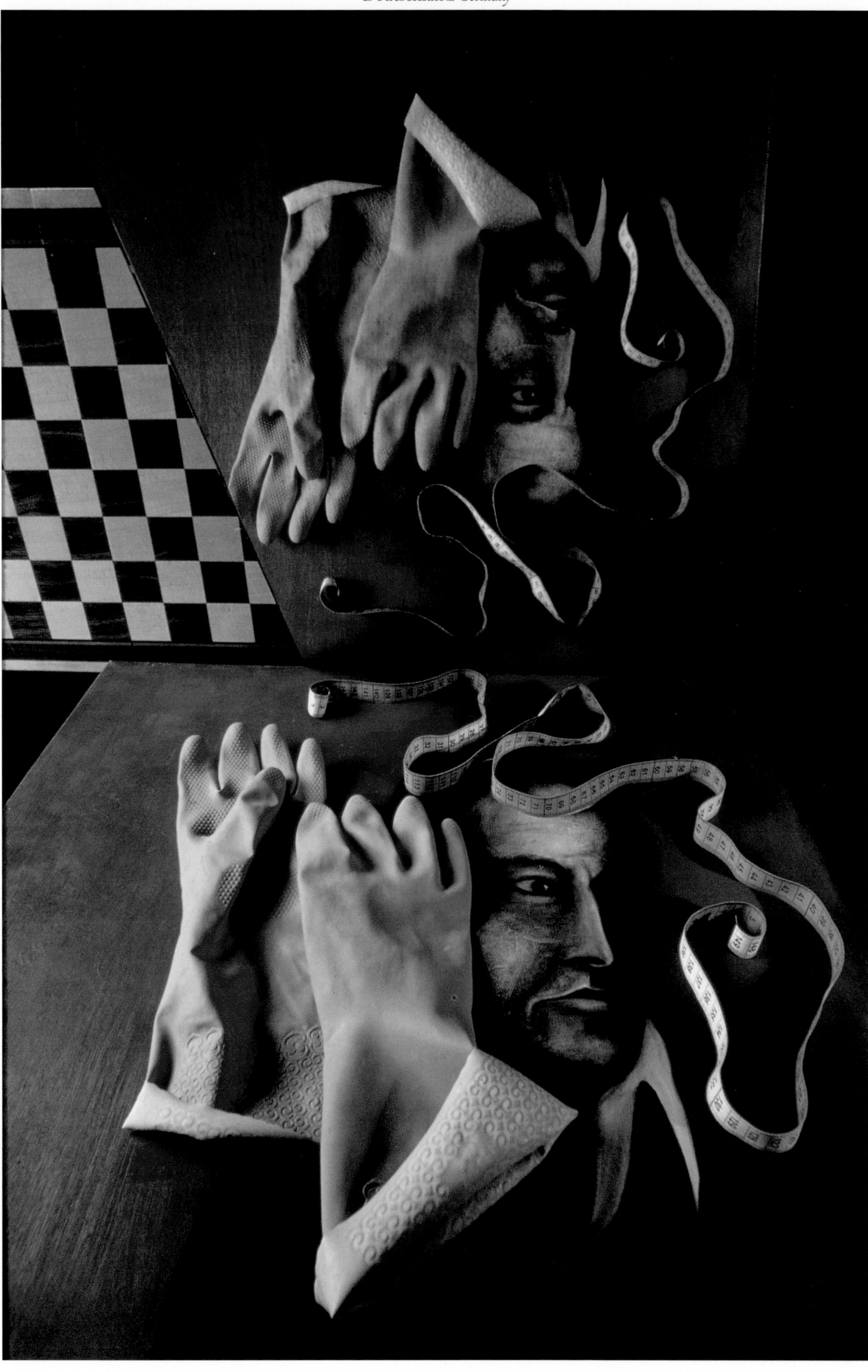

Rommert Boonstra, 1985
Niederlande/*The Netherlands*

Manfred Willmann, 1982
Österreich/*Austria*

Jo Ann Callis, 1985
USA

Henze Boekhout, 1982

Niederlande/*The Netherlands*

Vicki Ragan, 1978
USA

Sandi Fellman, 1980
USA

Peter Ruting, 1982
Niederlande/*The Netherlands*

Olivia Parker, 1979
USA

Jean Dieuzaide, 1980
Frankreich/*France*

Michael Geiger, 1984
USA

Arno Jansen, 1982
Deutschland/*Germany*

Toni Catany, 1983

Spanien/*Spain*

Ed Suister, 1979
Niederlande/*The Netherlands*

Betty Hahn, 1980
USA

Klaus Frahm, 1985
Deutschland/*Germany*

Peter Fraser, 1985
Großbritannien/*Great Britain*

Don Worth, 1984
USA

Jan Groover, 1980
USA

John Batho, 1980
Frankreich/*France*

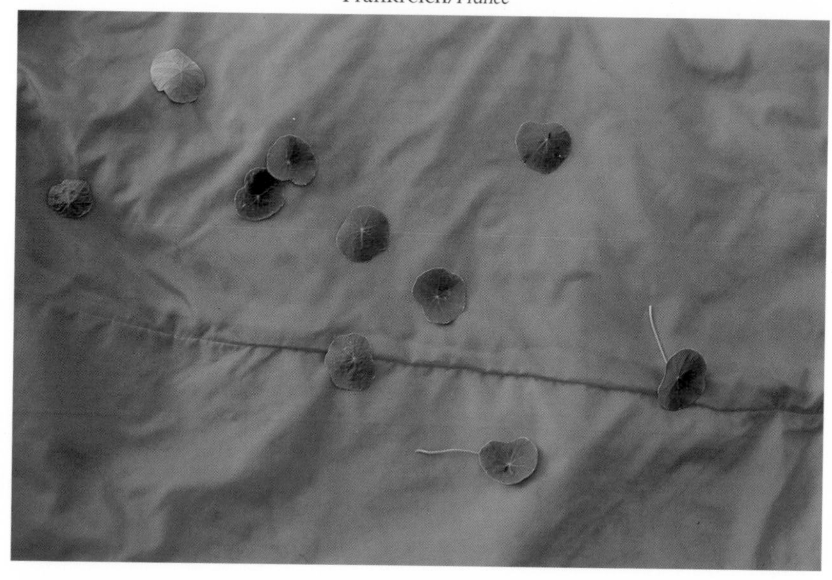

Hans Hansen, 1983
Deutschland/*Germany*

Victor Schraeger, 1980
USA

Paul den Hollander, 1984

Niederlande/*The Netherlands*

Arthur Tress, 1985
USA

Jerry McGrath, 1985
USA

David Haxton, 1979
USA

Rosamond Wolff-Purcell, 1985
USA

Chris Enos, 1980
USA

Chris Enos, 1979
USA

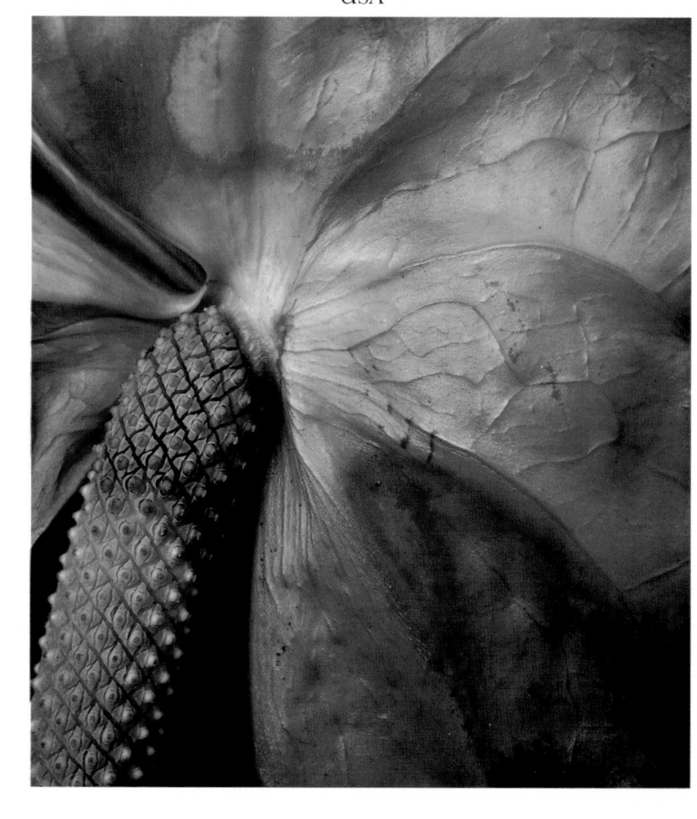

Sandi Fellman, 1979
USA

Michael de Camp, 1979
USA

Markus Rössle, 1985
Deutschland/*Germany*

Beatrice Helg, 1984
Schweiz/*Switzerland*

Michael Grayson Levine, 1981
USA

Joanne Mulberg, 1982
USA

Reed Estabrook, 1985
USA

Robert W. Fichter, 1979

USA

Gottfried Jäger, 1980
Deutschland/*Germany*

Michael Somoroff, 1979

Deutschland/*Germany*

Barbara Kasten, 1983
USA

Hans Vogler, o.D./*n.d.*
Österreich/*Austria*

Alan David Tu, 1985

Niederlande/*The Netherlands*

Patrick Dolique, 1984
Frankreich/*France*

Arthur Tress, 1985
USA

David Em, 1979

USA

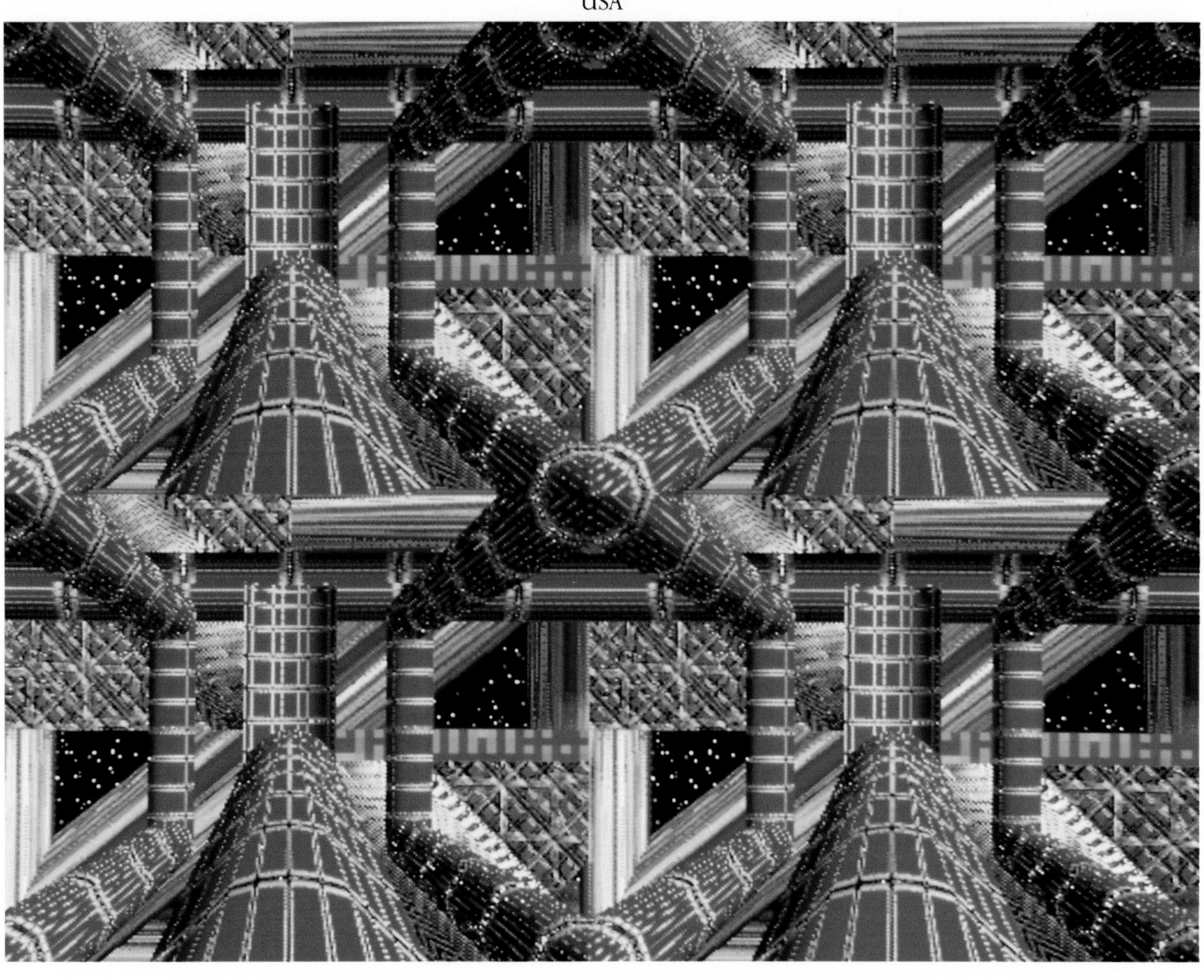

Giorgio Pezzato & Paola Masoero, 1985

Italien/*Italy*

Roberto di Vincenzo, 1983
Italien/*Italy*

Yulla Lipschitz, 1982
USA

Ralph Gibson, 1985
USA

Thomas Walther, 1976
Deutschland/*Germany*

Hans Hansen, 1985

Deutschland/*Germany*

Pavel Baňka, 1981
CSSR

Brian Joseph Quinn, 1984
Niederlande/*The Netherlands*

Jan Saudek, 1979
CSSR

Sam Haskins, 1986
Großbritannien/*Great Britain*

Diana Blok & Marlo Broekmans, 1980
Niederlande/*The Netherlands*

Tana Kaleya, 1976
Frankreich/*France*

Sam Haskins, 1986
Großbritannien/*Great Britain*

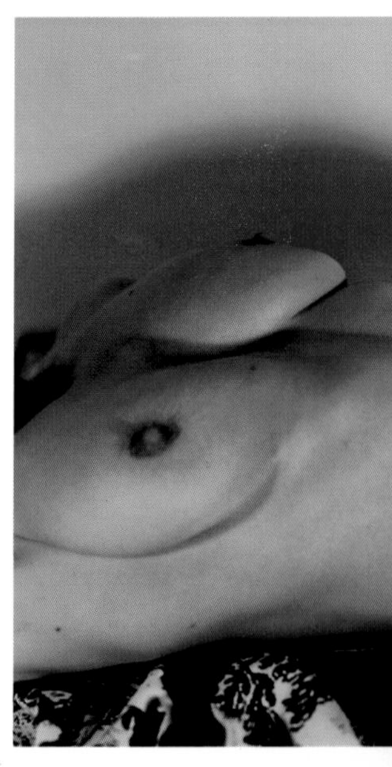

Pietro Privetera, 1980
Italien/*Italy*

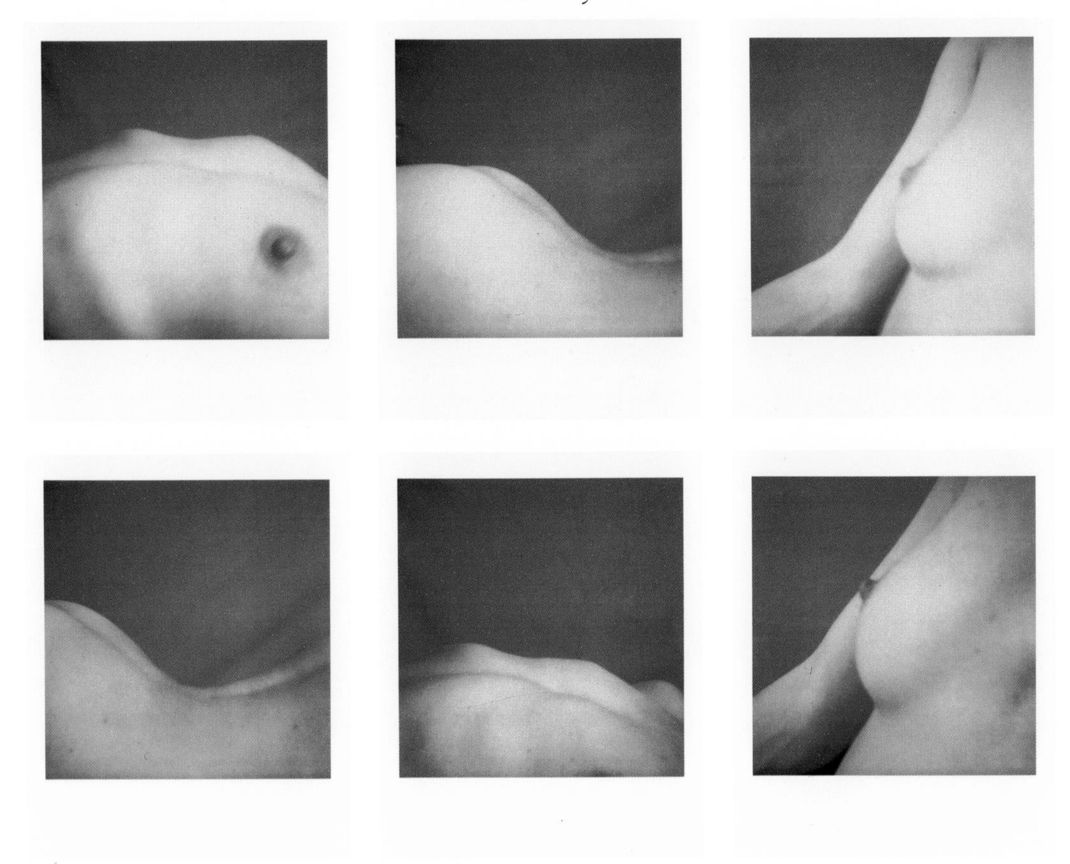

Toto Frima, 1985
Niederlande/*The Netherlands*

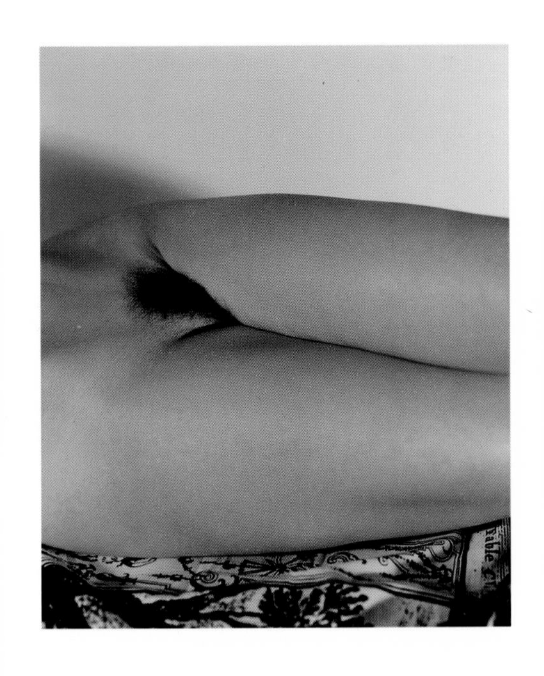

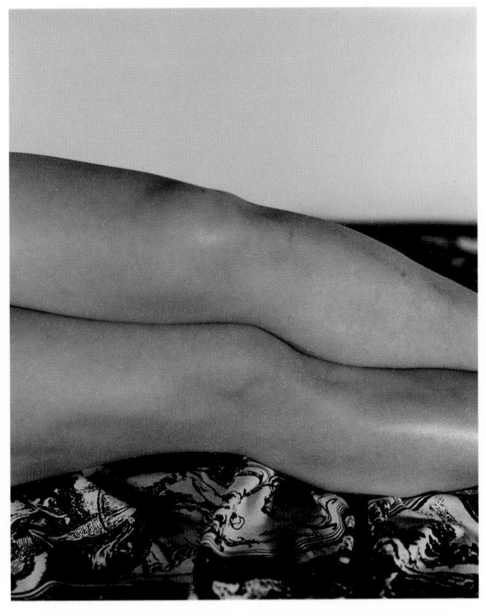

Gunther Sachs, 1982
Deutschland/*Germany*

David Hamilton, 1978
Frankreich/*France*

Tana Kaleya, 1979
Frankreich/*France*

Rainer Griese, 1986
Deutschland/*Germany*

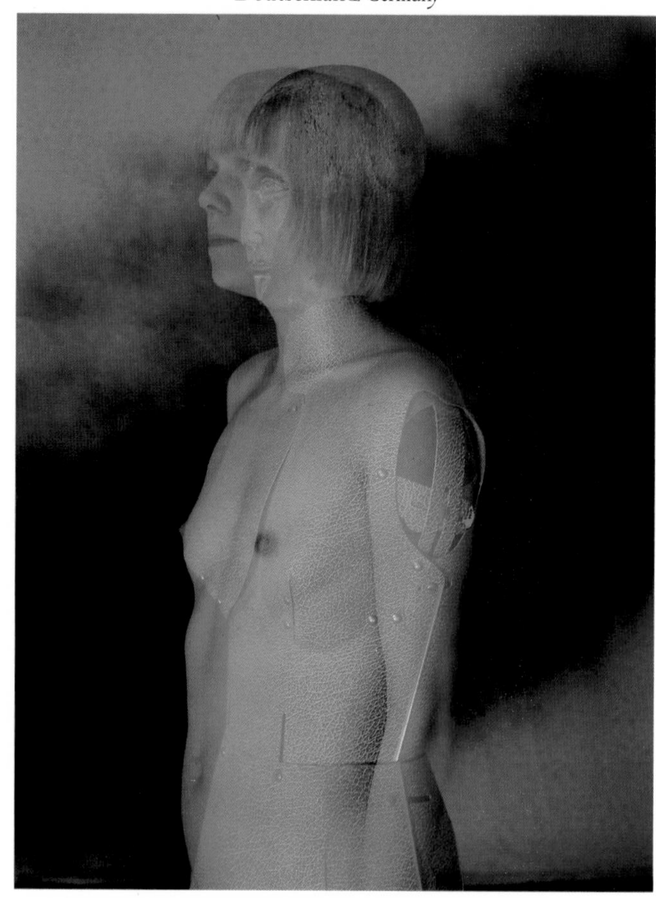

Jeanloup Sieff, 1976
Frankreich/*France*

Joachim Würfel, 1985
Schweiz/*Switzerland*

Frank Horvat, 1982
Frankreich/*France*

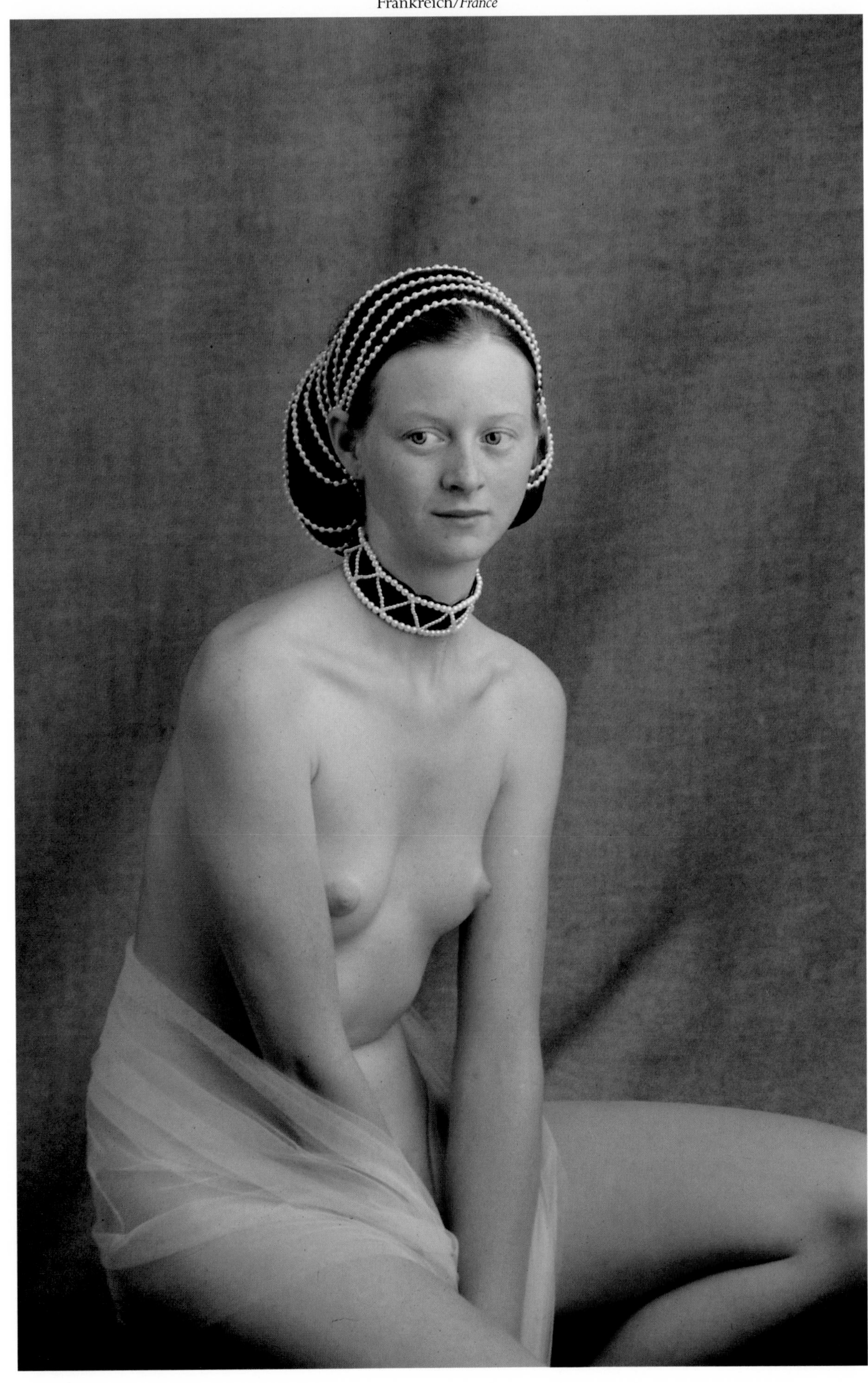

David van 't Veen, 1985

Niederlande/*The Netherlands*

Guy Bourdin, 1979
Frankreich/*France*

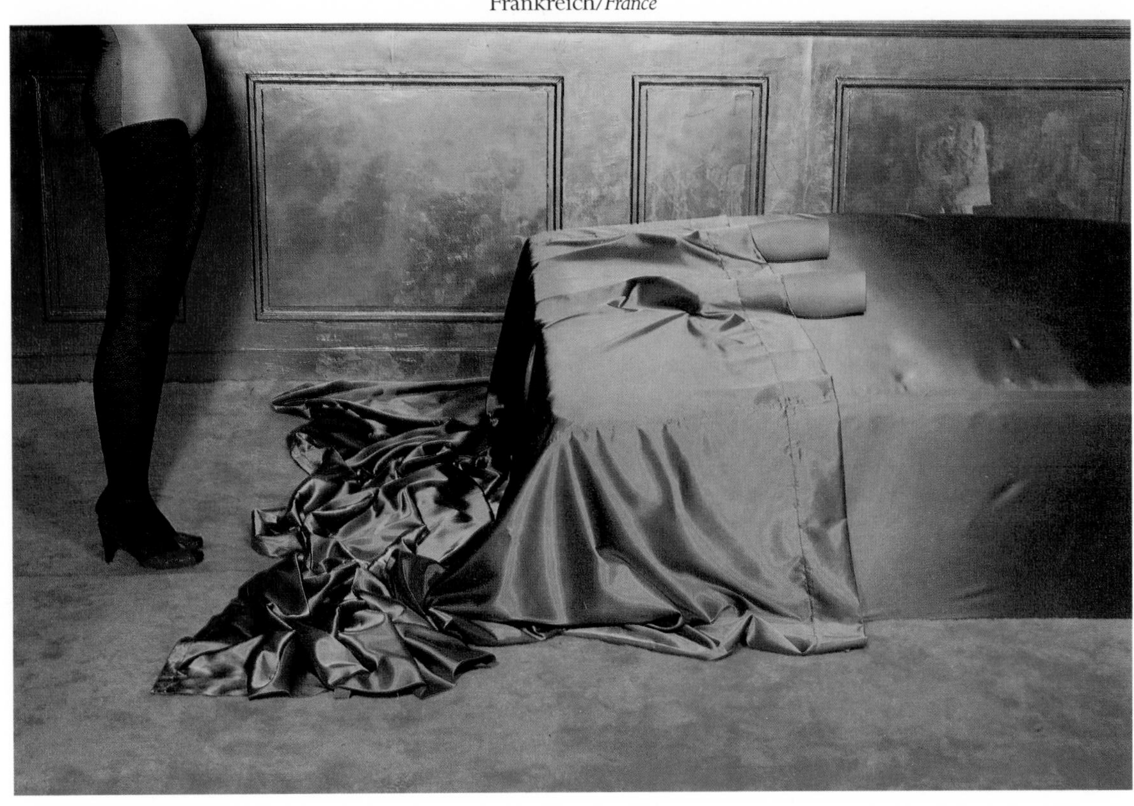

Helmut Newton, 1982
Monaco

Karin Székessy, o.D./*n.d.*
Deutschland/*Germany*

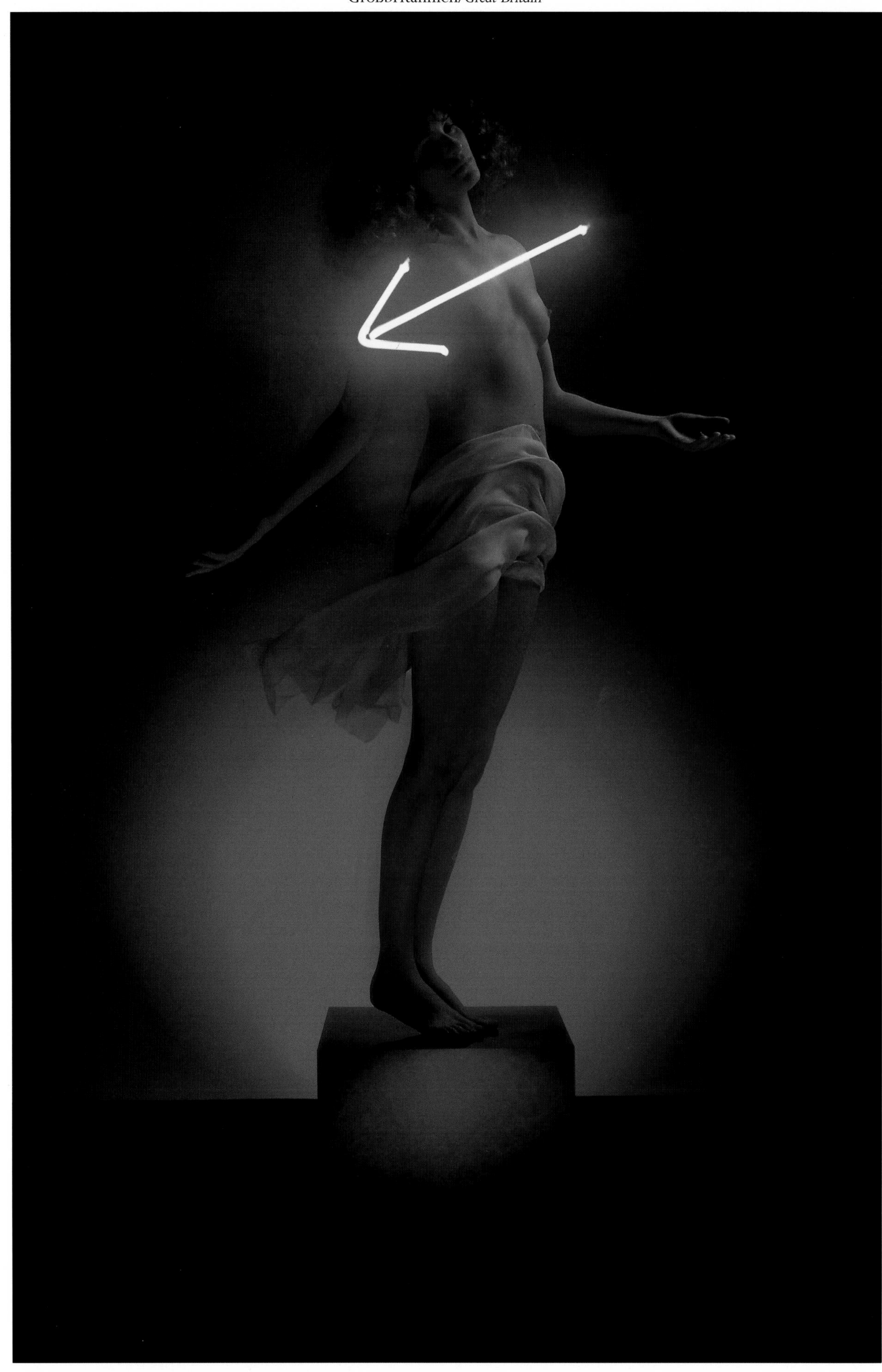

Luciano Franchi de Alfaro III, 1983
USA

William Wegman, 1982
USA

Chuck Close, 1985
USA

Yousuf Karsh, 1981
Kanada/*Canada*

Manfredi Bellati, 1985
Italien/*Italy*

Cindy Sherman, 1983
USA

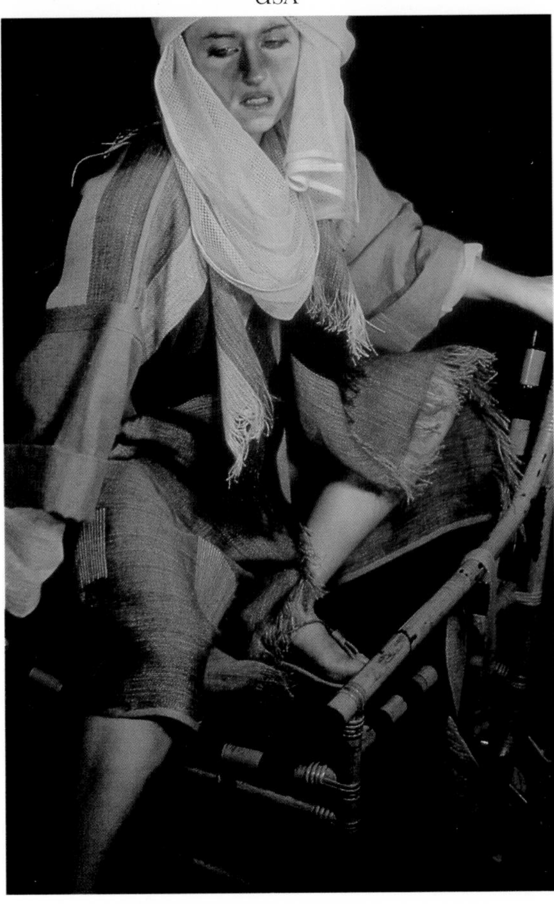

Werner Pawlok, 1985
Deutschland/*Germany*

Barbara Bordnik, 1978
USA

Cindy Sherman, 1982
USA

Andy Warhol, 1978
USA

Andy Warhol, 1978
USA

William Klein, 1980
USA

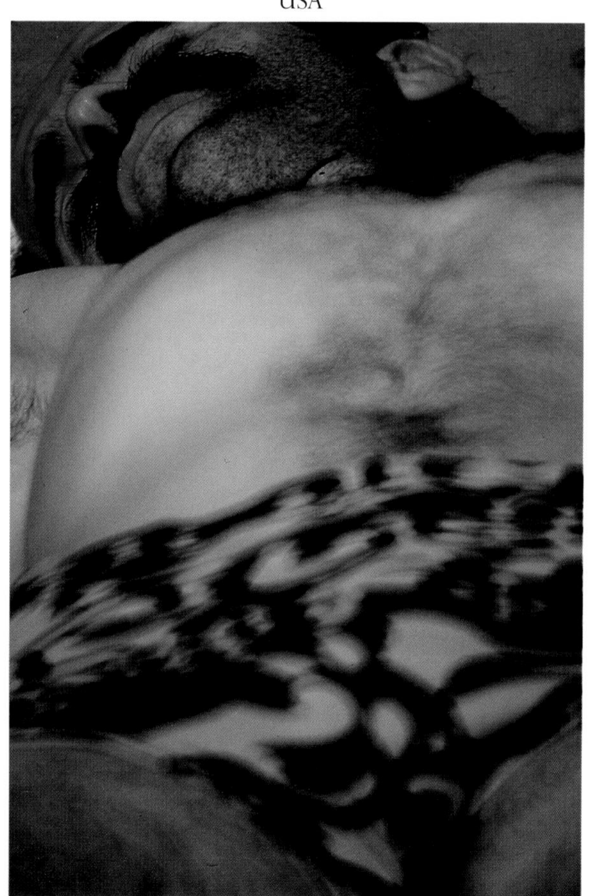

Serge Cohen, 1985
Frankreich/*France*

Snowdon, 1980

Großbritannien/*Great Britain*

Krzysztof Pruszkowski, 1984

Frankreich/*France*

Neal Slavin, 1985
USA

Marco Saroldi, o.D./*n.d.*
Italien/*Italy*

Marco Saroldi, o.D./*n.d.*
Italien/*Italy*

Alex Webb, o.D./*n.d.*
USA

Bob Mazzer, 1985
Großbritannien/*Great Britain*

Carolina Haggstrom-Wells, 1978
Australien/*Australia*

Monique Jacot, 1986
Schweiz/*Switzerland*

Alain Bizos, 1982
Frankreich/*France*

Mark Cohen, 1977
USA

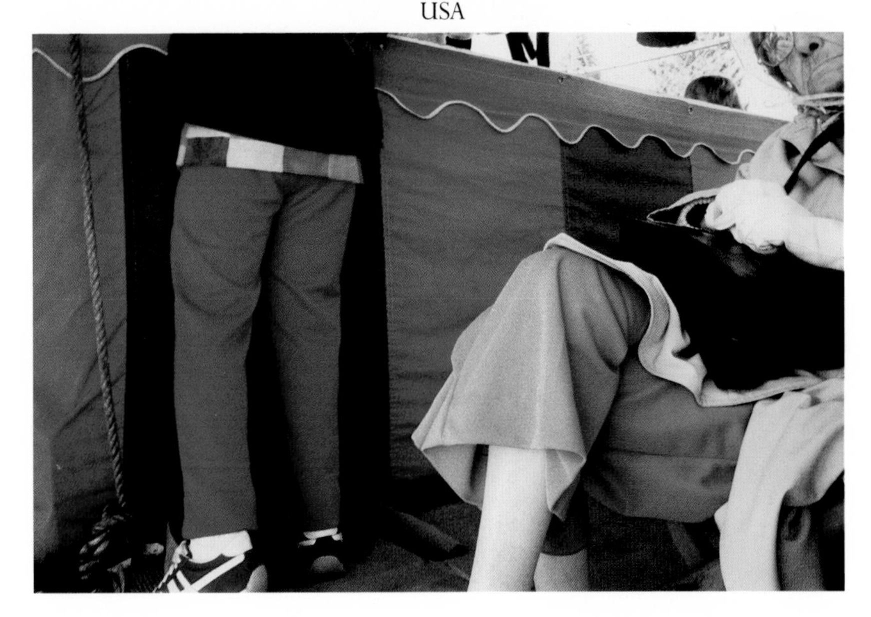

Dan Williams, o.D./*n.d.*
USA

Fulvio Roiter, 1980
Italien/*Italy*

Pedro Meyer, o.D./*n.d.*
Mexiko/*Mexico*

Abbas, 1979
Frankreich/*France*

Robert Azzi, 1981
USA

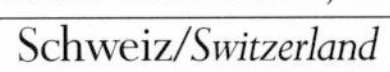

Adriano Heitmann, 1981
Schweiz/*Switzerland*

Mary Ellen Mark, o.D./*n.d.*
USA

Alex Webb, o.D./*n.d.*
USA

Francisco Hidalgo, 1978
Frankreich/*France*

Francisco Hidalgo, 1978
Frankreich/*France*

Kikuji Kawada, 1978
Japan

Co Rentmeester, o.D./*n.d.*
USA

Pablo Pérez-Mínguez, 1984
Spanien/*Spain*

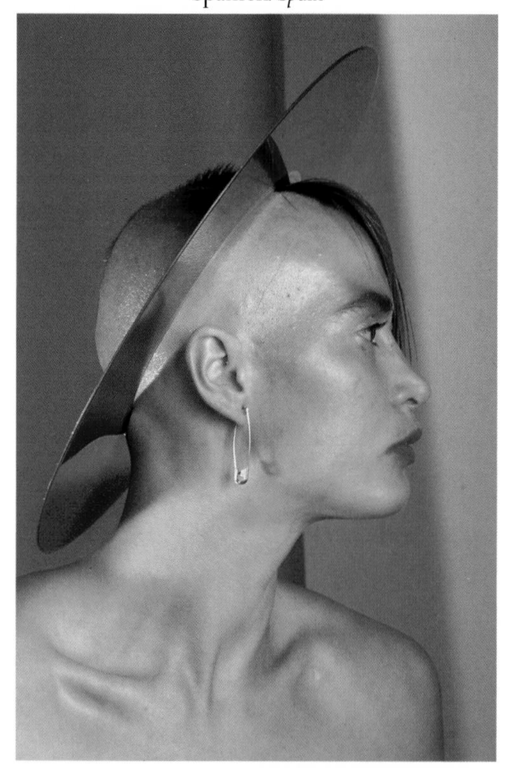

Hans-Jürgen Gerke, 1984
Deutschland/*Germany*

Bill Ravanesi, 1983
USA

Susan Meiselas, 1981
USA

Susan Meiselas, 1981
USA

Miguel Rio Branco, 1979
Brasilien/*Brazil*

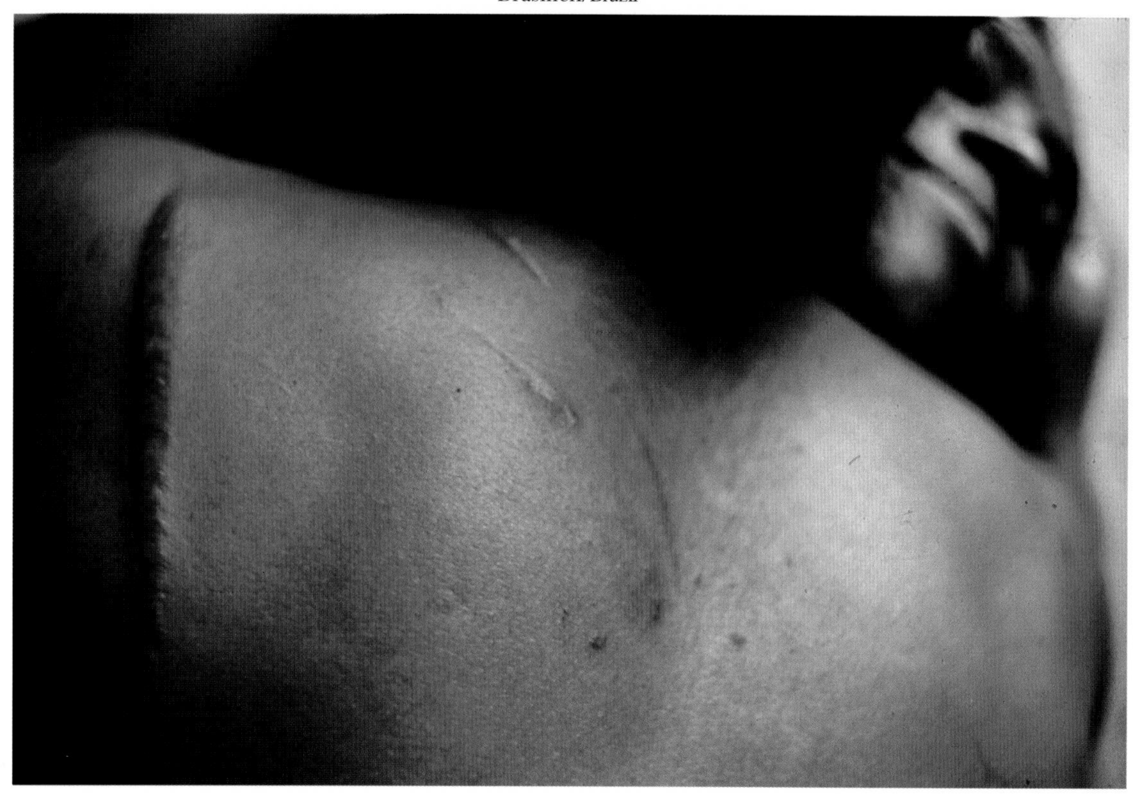

Catherine Leroy, 1984
Frankreich/*France*

Joel Sternfeld, 1978
USA

Michael Bishop, 1979
USA

Kenneth McGowan, 1976
USA

Wolfgang Zurborn, 1985
Deutschland/*Germany*

Marta Sentís, 1984
Spanien/*Spain*

Martin Parr, 1985
Großbritannien/*Great Britain*

Heinz-Jürgen Gerke, 1984
Deutschland/*Germany*

Karl Müller, 1982
Deutschland/*Germany*

Peter Hensch, 1985
Deutschland/*Germany*

Hans Siwik, 1982
Deutschland/*Germany*

Burkhard von Harder, 1985
Deutschland/*Germany*

Carolyn Johns, o.D./*n.d.*
Australien/*Australia*

Mitch Epstein, 1981
USA

Burkhard von Harder, 1985
Deutschland/*Germany*

Olivio Barbieri, 1982

Italien/*Italy*

Boudewijn Neuteboom, 1986

Niederlande/*The Netherlands*

Joachim Bonnemaison, 1985
Frankreich/*France*

Bill Thompson, 1982
USA

Cecilia Schneider, 1985
Deutschland/*Germany*

Martine Franck, 1984
Frankreich/*France*

Kenda North, 1985
USA

Coca-Cola
MEE BOTT. MARCHI REG.

L.J.A.D. Creyghton, 1985
Niederlande/*The Netherlands*

Jan van der Horn, 1985
Niederlande/*The Netherlands*

Jacques Schumacher, 1985
Deutschland/*Germany*

Anthony Browell, 1985
Australien/*Australia*

Luigi Ghirri, 1985
Italien/*Italy*

Milan Horaček, o.D./*n.d.*
Deutschland/*Germany*

Geert Kooiman, 1984

Niederlande/*The Netherlands*

Holger Trültsch/Vera von Lehndorff, 1979

Deutschland/*Germany*

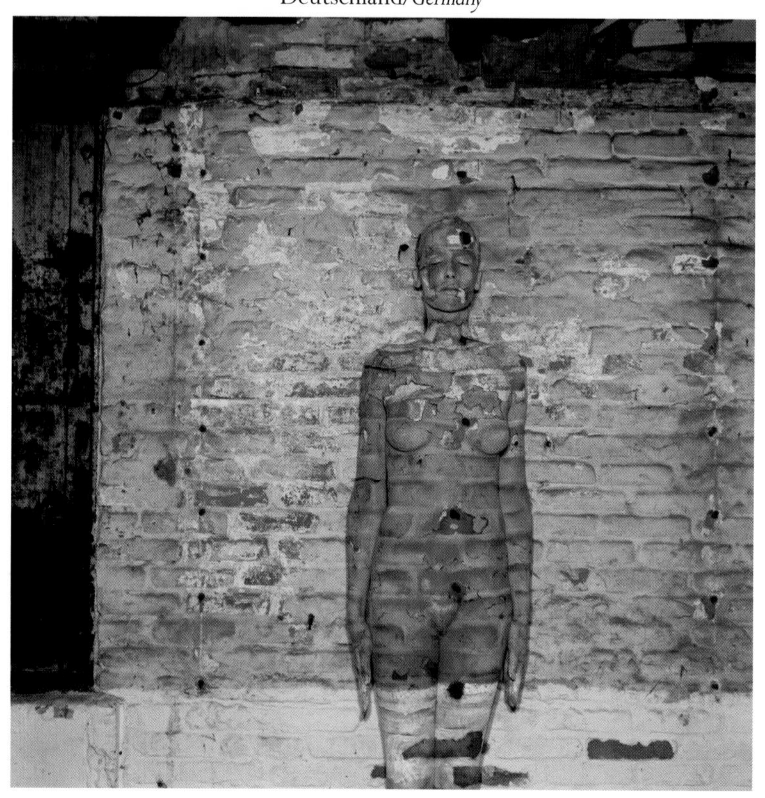

Stefan Richter, 1984

Deutschland/*Germany*

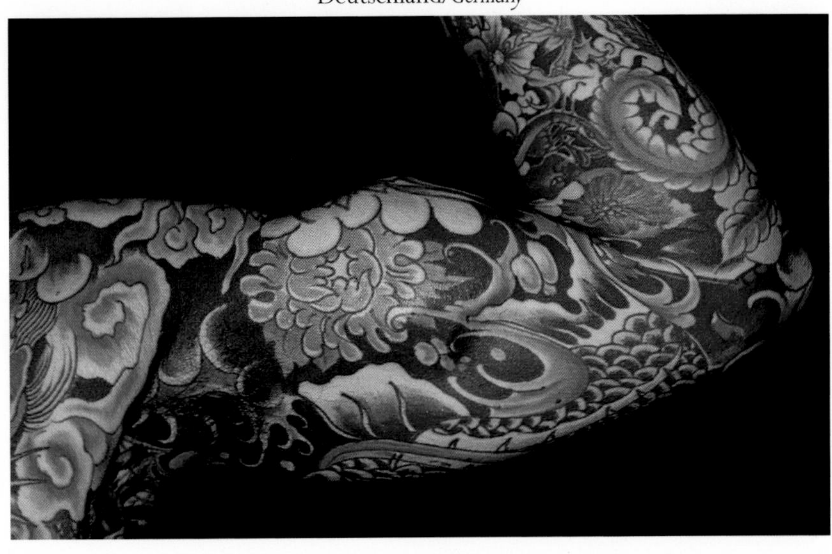

Todd Merrill, 1985

USA

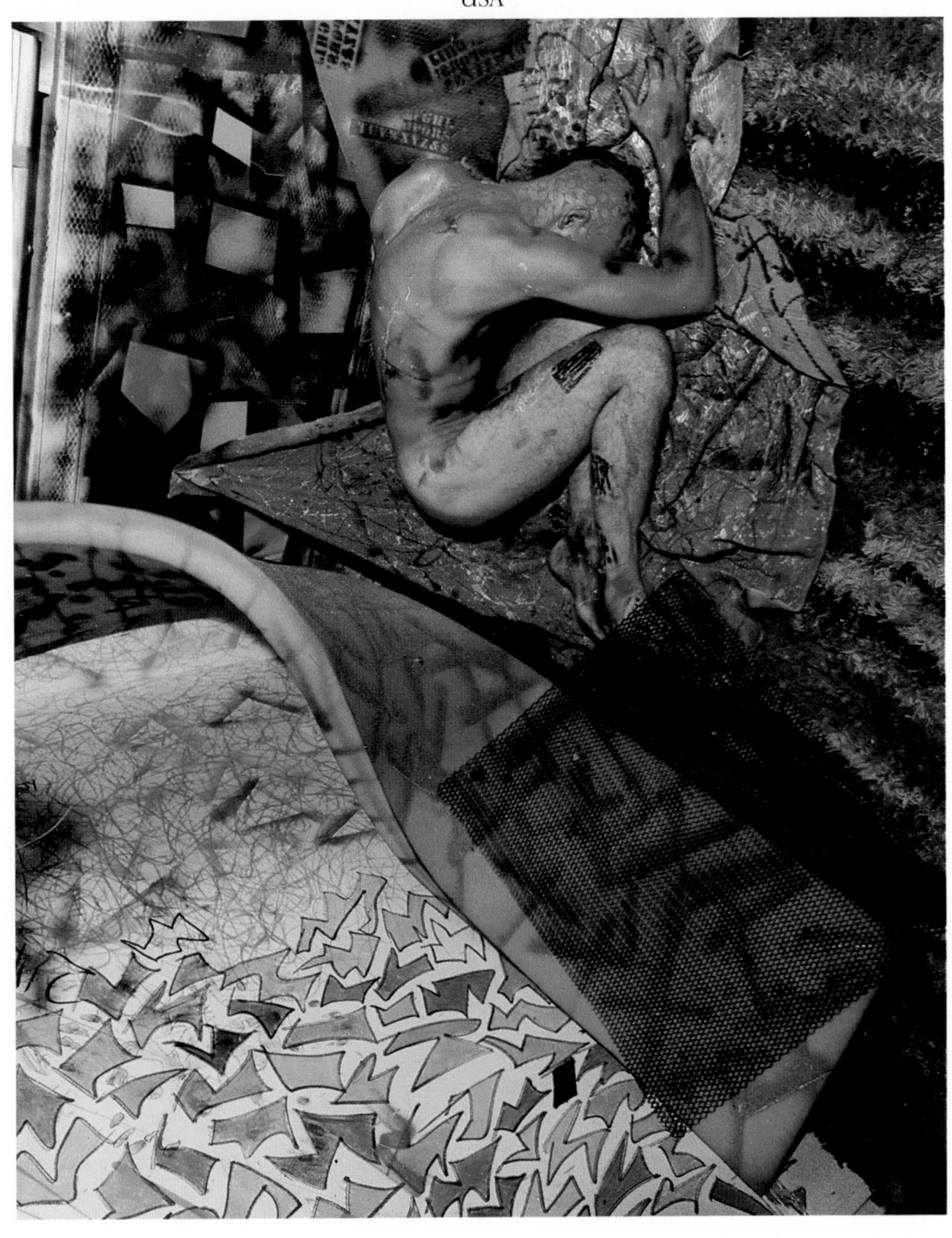

Marvin Gasoi, 1982

USA

Hartmut Helm, 1985

Deutschland/*Germany*

Bernard Faucon, 1980
Frankreich/*France*

Francoise Hugier, 1985
Frankreich/*France*

Occhiomagico, 1983
Italien/*Italy*

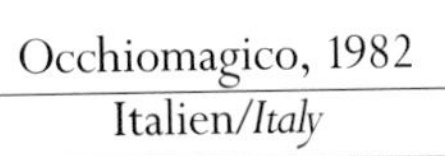

Occhiomagico, 1982
Italien/*Italy*

Audrey Flack, 1979
USA

Oliviero Toscani, 1985
Italien/*Italy*

Tim Simmons, 1985
Großbritannien/*Great Britain*

Horst Wackerbarth, 1983
Deutschland/*Germany*

Thomas Simpfendörfer, 1984
Deutschland/*Germany*

Reza Khatir, 1985
Schweiz/*Switzerland*

Evon Streetman, 1984
USA

9130

Patric Nagatani/Andree Tracey, 1985
USA

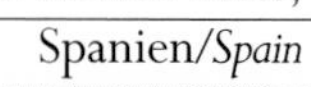

Juan Ramón Yuste, 1985
Spanien/*Spain*

Maarten Chris, 1984
Schweiz/*Switzerland*

Les Krims, o.D./*n.d.*
USA

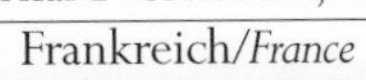

Gerhard Vormwald, 1984
Frankreich/*France*

Ben Oyne, o.D./*n.d.*
Frankreich/*France*

Shoji Ueda, 1984
Japan

Elliott Erwitt, 1977
USA

Charlotte March, 1985
Deutschland/*Germany*

David Buckland, 1985
Großbritannien/*Great Britain*

Evergon, 1984
Kanada/*Canada*

Hubertus Mall, 1976
Deutschland/*Germany*

Gladys, 1984

Frankreich/*France*

Bill Ravanesi, 1980

USA

David Graham, 1983

USA

Sandy Skoglund, 1981
USA

Andreas Horlitz, 1985

Deutschland/*Germany*

Boyd Webb, 1984

Großbritannien/*Great Britain*

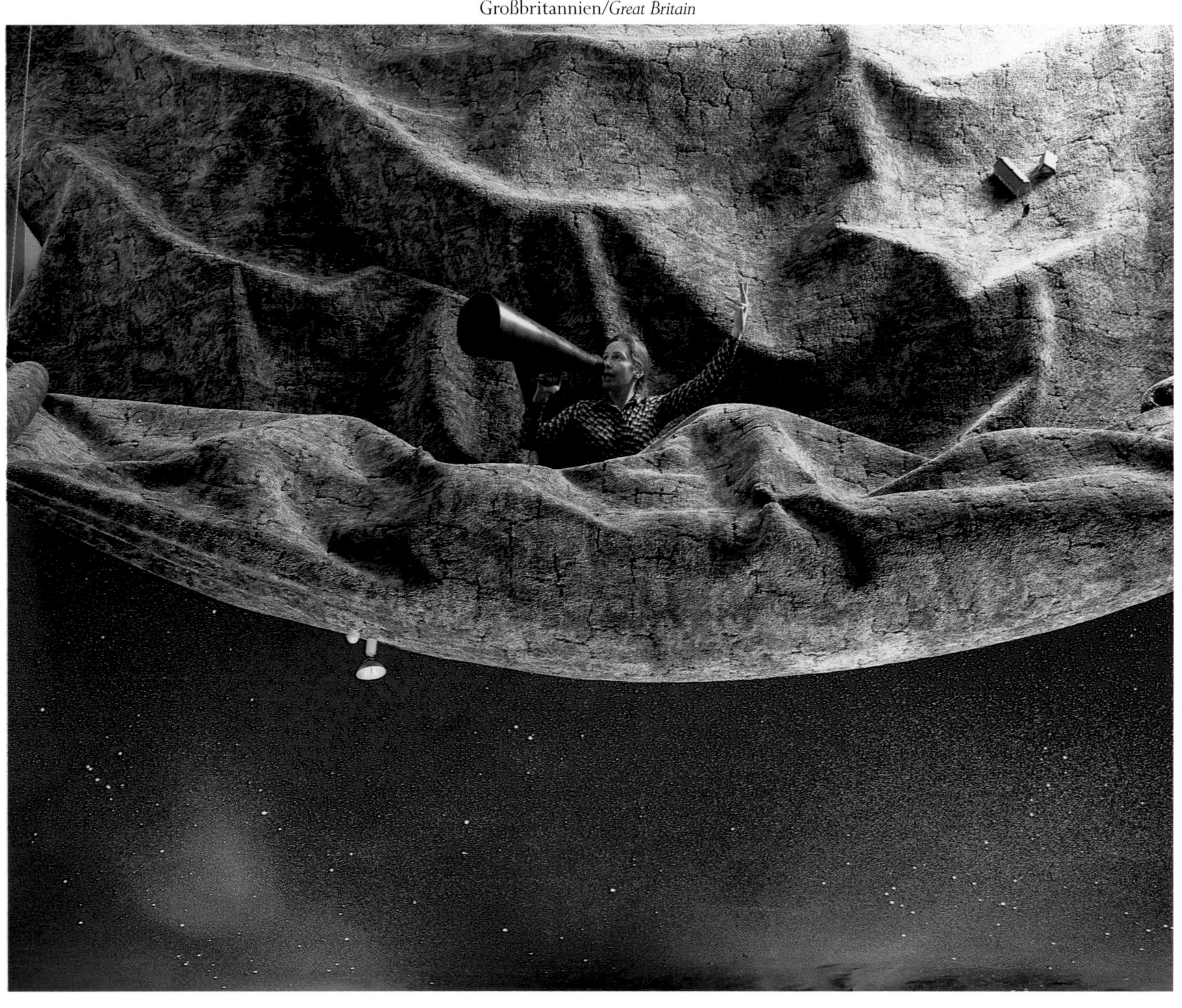

Paolo Gioli, 1978

Italien/*Italy*

Peter van der Velde, o.D./*n.d.*
Niederlande/*The Netherlands*

Van Deren Coke, 1984
USA

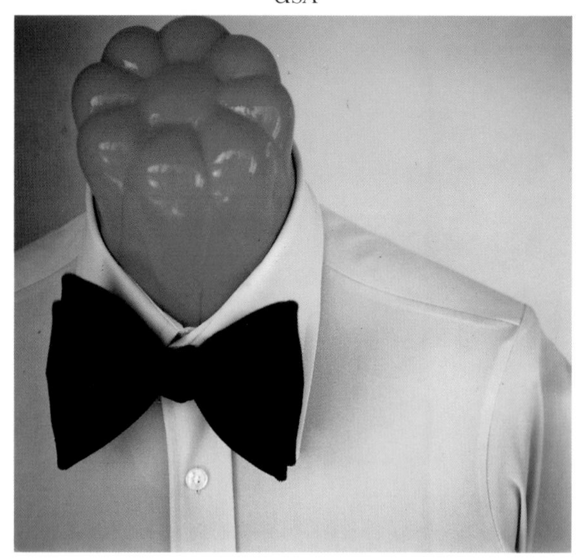

Joe Gantz, 1983
USA

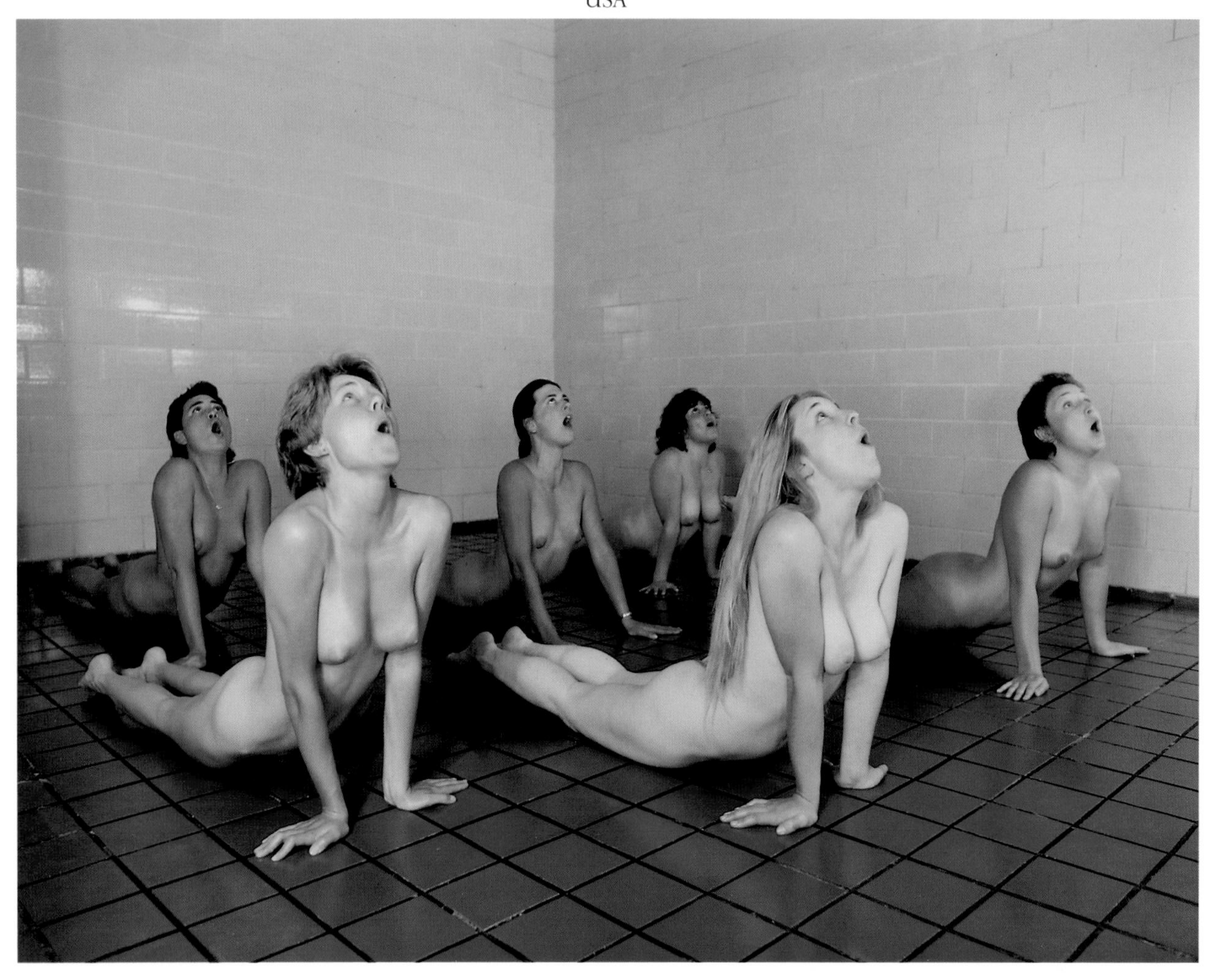

Al Souza, 1978
USA

Sorel Cohen, 1986
Kanada/*Canada*

Damien Hustinx, 1985

Belgien/*Belgium*

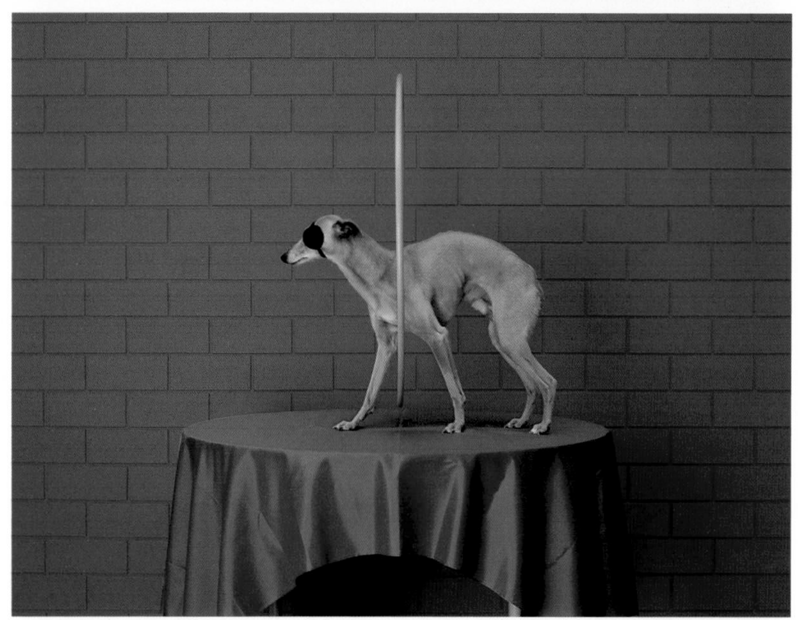

Jeff Millikan, 1985
USA

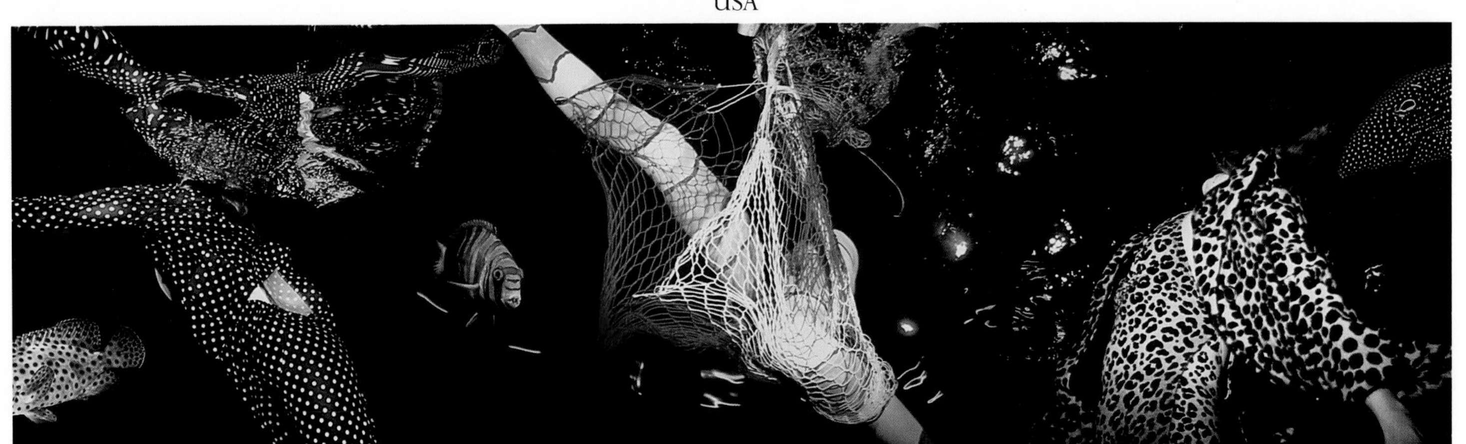

Lucas Samaras, 1985
USA

Paul de Nooijer, 1976
Niederlande/*The Netherlands*

Silvio Wolf, 1983
Italien/*Italy*

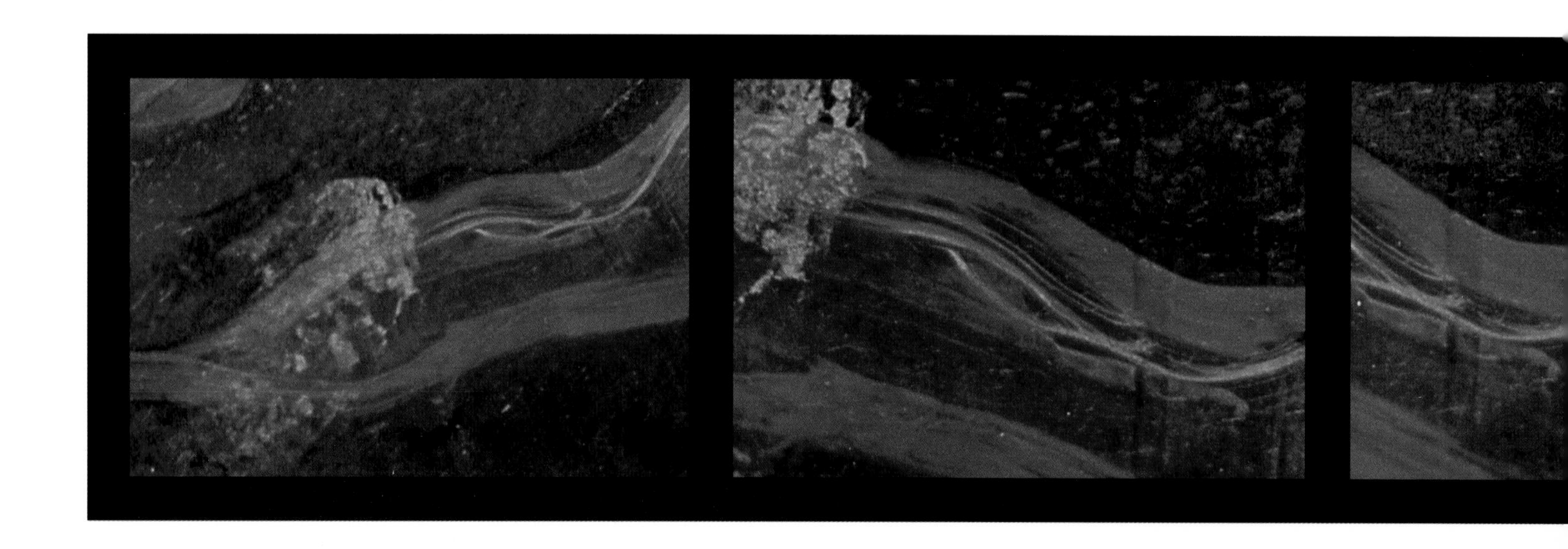

Rudolf Herz, 1986
Deutschland/*Germany*

Verena von Gagern, o.D./*n.d.*
Deutschland/*Germany*

Kristi Eisenberg, o.D./*n.d.*
USA

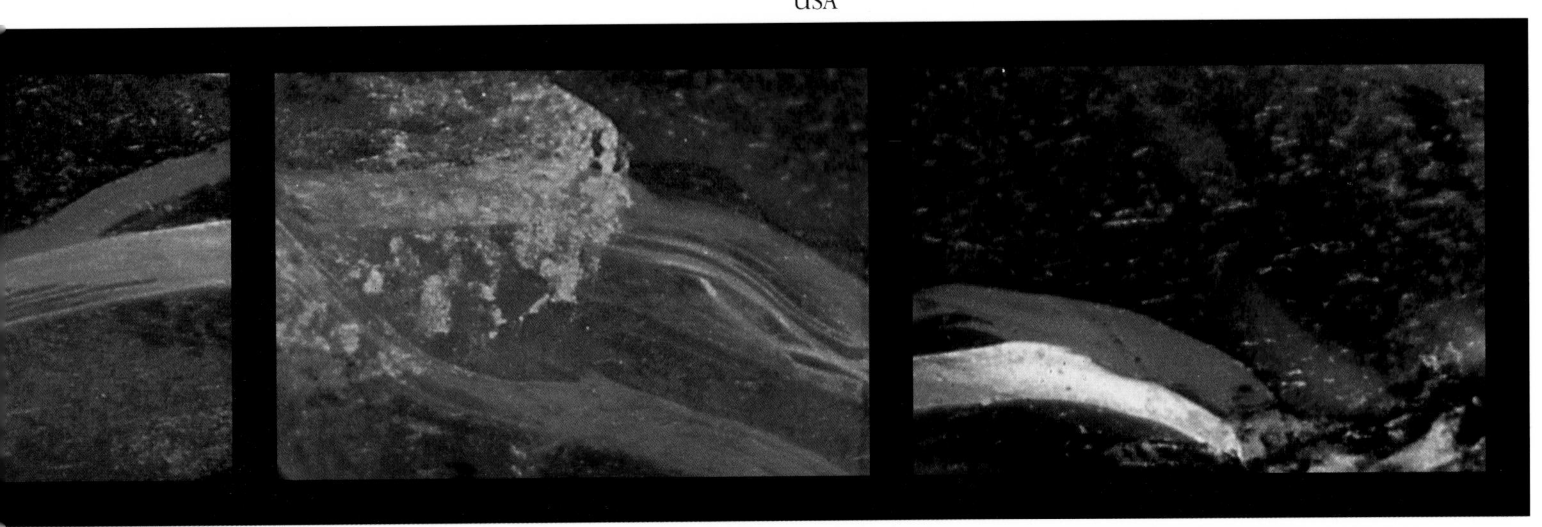

Jerry Uelsman, 1984
USA

David Hockney, 1982

Großbritannien/*Great Britain*

Robert Heinecken, 1983

USA

Frederic Karikese, 1985

Belgien/*Belgium*

Ulay/Abramovic, 1981

Niederlande/*The Netherlands*

Juan Ramon Yuste, 1984

Spanien/*Spain*

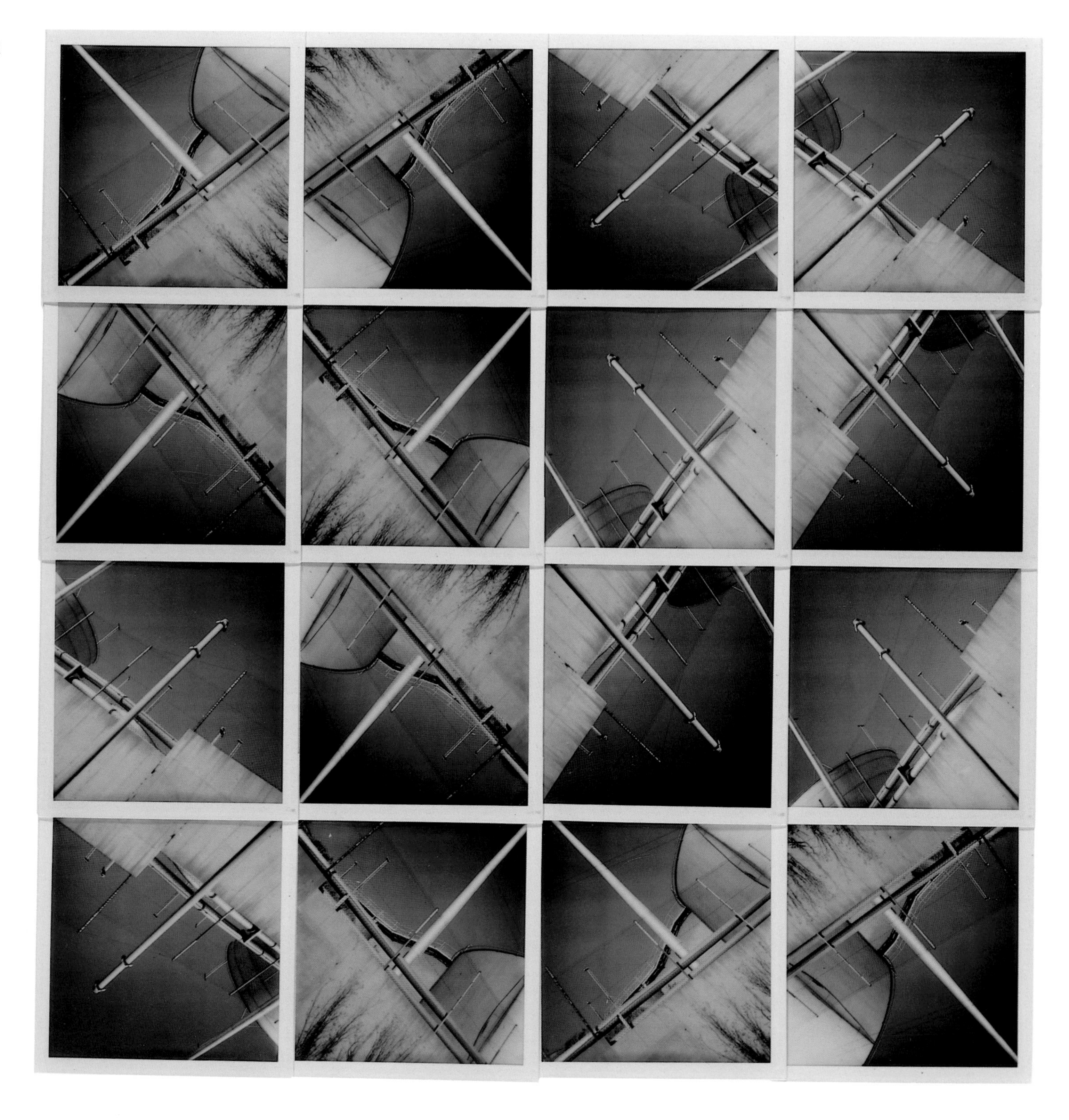

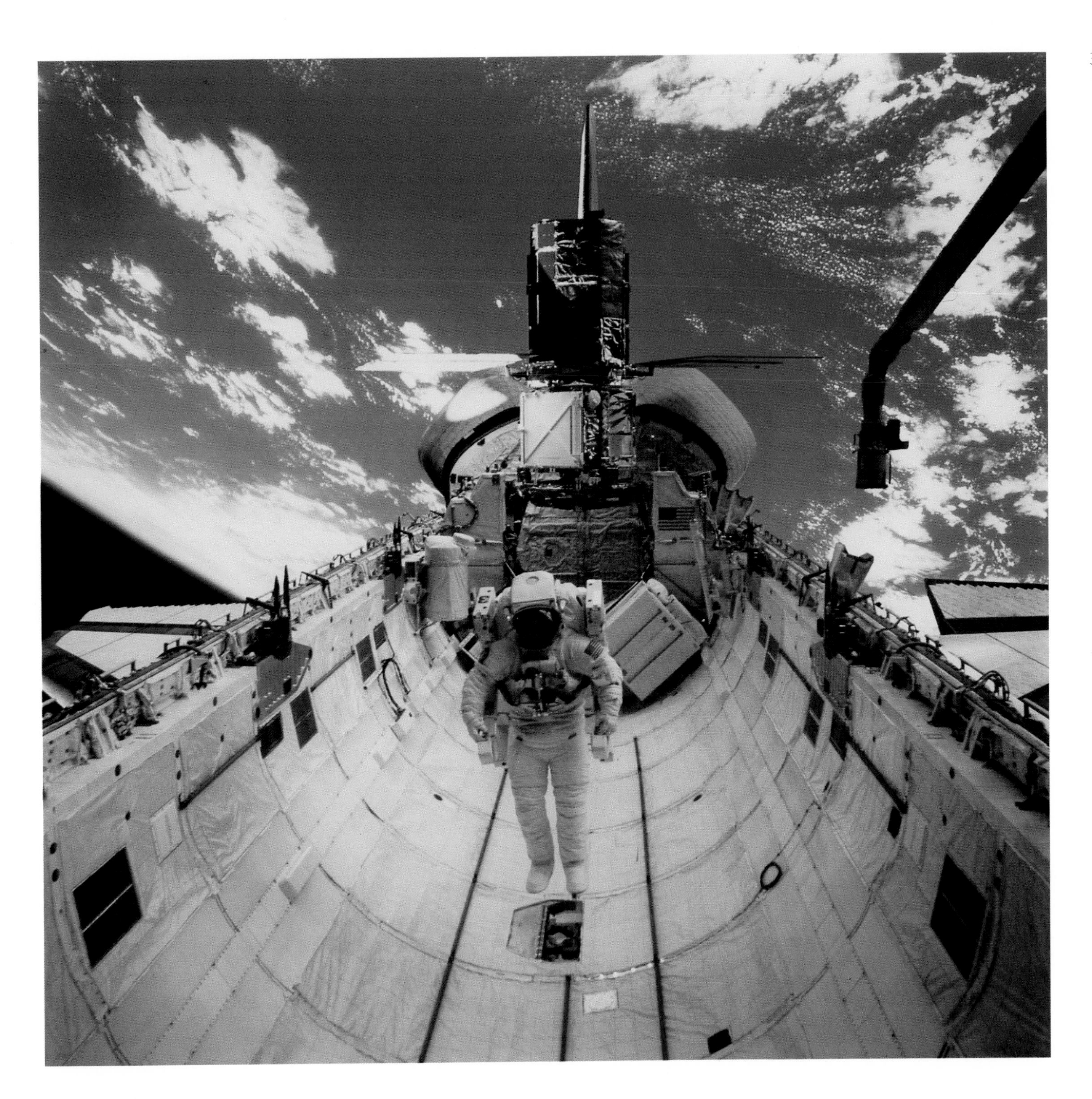

LEIHGEBER DER ORIGINALE
ORIGINALS ON LOAN FROM

Land/Country	Leihgeber/Lender	Fotografen/Photographers
Australien/*Australia*	**Photo Publishing Company** GPO Box 606, Sydney, NSW 2001	Anthony Browell, Carolina Haggstrom-Wells, Carolyn Johns, Laurence LeGuay, Melissa McCord, David Moore, Henry Talbot
Deutschland/*Germany*	**Fotografie Forum Frankfurt** Weckmarkt 17, 6000 Frankfurt 1	Rainer Griese, Jan Saudek, Douglas Holleley
	The Image Bank Prinzregentenstraße 89, 8000 München 80	Michael de Camp, Paul Fusco, Francisco Hidalgo, Donald C. Landwehrle, Jay Maisel, Co Rentmeester, Fulvio Roiter, Pete Turner
	Rudolf Kicken Galerie Albertusstraße 1, 5000 Köln 1	Joel Meyerowitz, Richard Pare, Edward Steichen, Thomas Walther
	Kodak Archiv Postfach 600345, 7000 Stuttgart 60	George Sheedy, Toni Frissell, John Rawlings, Anton F. Baumann, Erich Bauer, Ivan Dmitri, Helmut & Erna Blenck, Martin Munkacsi, Harald Mante
	PPS Galerie Feldstraße, Hochhaus 1, 2000 Hamburg 4	F.C. Gundlach, Erwin Blumenfeld
Frankreich/*France*	**Galerie Michèle Chomette** 24, rue Beaubourg, 75003 Paris	Joachim Bonnemaison, Paolo Gioli
	Magnum Photos, Inc. 20, rue des Grands Augustins, 75006 Paris	Abbas, René Burri, Martine Franck
	Sipa Press 14, rue Roquépine, 75008 Paris	Catherine Leroy
	VU Agence de Photographes 9, rue Christiani, 75899 Paris	Alain Bizos, Bernard Faucon, Françoise Huguier, John Vink
	Galerie Zabriskie 37, rue Quincampoix, 75004 Paris	John Batho, Pascal Kern
Großbritannien/*Great Britain*	**The Photographers' Gallery** Halina House, 5 Great Newport Street, London, WC2H 7HY	Paul Graham, Peter Fraser, Brian Griffin, Snowdon, Bob Mazzer
Japan	**Goro International Press** 1103, 2-33-8 Jingumae Shibuya-Ku, 150 Tokyo	Hideki Fujii, Osamu Hayasaki, Yasukiro Ishimoto, Kikuji Kawada, Kazumi Kurigami, Shinzo Maeda, Yiochi Midorikawa, Ikko Narahara, Akira Sato, Kishin Shinoyama, Shoji Ueda, Ruiko Yoshida
Niederlande/*The Netherlands*	**Torch Gallery** Prinsengracht 218, 1016 HD Amsterdam	Henze Boekhout, Piet van Leeuwen, Alan David Tu
USA	**Amon Carter Museum** P.O. Box 2365, Fort Worth, TX 76101	Laura Gilpin
	Aperture Foundation/Paul Strand Archiv 20 East 23 Street, New York, N.Y. 10010	Paul Strand
	Benteler Galleries, Inc. 2409 Rice Boulevard, Houston, TX 77005	Serge Hambourg
	The Condé Nast Publications, Inc. 350 Madison Avenue, New York, N.Y. 10017	Serge Balkin, Cecil Beaton, Erwin Blumenfeld, Clifford Coffin, Horst P. Horst, Constantin Joffé, André Kertész, Alexander Liberman, Frances McLaughlin-Gill, Gjon Mili, Norman Parkinson, Irving Penn, John Rawlings, Richard Rutledge, Guy Bourdin, Charlotte March

306

USA	**Louise Dahl-Wolfe Trust** **Christopher E. Green** 73 Washington Avenue, Brooklyn, N.Y. 11205	Louise Dahl-Wolfe
	Fotomann, Inc. 42 East 76th Street, New York, N.Y. 10021	NASA, Robert Glenn Ketchum, Yulla Lipchitz
	Fraenkel Gallery 55 Grant Avenue, San Francisco, CA 94108	Richard Misrach
	Ursula Gropper Associates 10, Laurel Lane, Savsolito, CA 94965	Richard Misrach
	G. Ray Hawkins Gallery, Inc., 7224 Melrose Avenue, Los Angeles, CA 90046	Harry Bowers, Wynn Bullock, Ruth Orkin, Max Yavno
	Edwynn Houk Gallery 200 West Superiorstreet, Suite 306, Chicago, IL 60610	Arthur Siegel
	Jan Kesner Fine Arts 1240½ La Jolla, Los Angeles, CA 90035	Jo Ann Callis, Michael Levine, Jerry McGrath
	Pearl Korn 25 Knolls Crescent, Riverdale, N.Y. 10463	David Graham
	Laguna Beach Museum of Art 307 Cliff Drive, Laguna Beach, CA 92651	Paul Outerbridge
	Janet Lehr Inc. 891 Park Avenue, New York, N.Y. 10021	Audrey Flack, Reed Estabrook, David Graham
	Light Gallery 724 Fifth Avenue, New York, N.Y. 10019	William Larson, Jack Delano, Russel Lee, Marion Post Wolcott, John Vachon
	Lunn Ltd. 42 East 76th Street, New York, N.Y. 10021	Manuel Alvarez-Bravo, Gisèle Freund, Yousuf Karsh, Ansel Adams, Martin Bruehl, Walker Evans
	Magnum Photos, Inc. 251 Park Avenue South, New York, N.Y. 10010	Elliot Erwitt, Burt Glinn, Susan Meiselas, Eli Reed, Alex Webb
	Middendorf Gallery 2009 Columbia Road N.W., Washington D.C. 20009	William Eggleston
	Laurence Miller Gallery, Inc. 138 Spring Steet, New York, N.Y. 10012	Jeff Millikan
	Robert Miller 41 East 57th Street, New York, N.Y. 10022	Jan Groover, Robert Mapplethorpe
	Moody Gallery 2815 Colquitt, Houston, TX 77098	Manual
	Pace/MacGill 11 East 57th Street, New York, N.Y. 10022	Harry Callahan, Harold Edgerton, Mark Klett, Raghubir Singh, Stephen Shore, Lucas Samaras
	The Polaroid Collection 549 Technology Square, Cambridge, MA 02132	Beppe Buccafusca, Chuck Close, Jean Dieuzaide, Chris Enos, Evergon, Robert W. Fichter, Luciano Franci de Alfaro III, Betty Hahn, Robert Heinecken, David Hockney, Barbara Kasten, Sahin Kaygun, Reza Khatir, Patrick Nagatani/Andree Tracey, Kenda North, Olivia Parker, Richard Payne, Pietro Privetera, Ulay/Abramovic, Rosamond Wolff-Purcell, Neal Slavin, Jan van Steenwijk, Evon Streetman, Jerry Uelsmann, Andy Warhol, William Wegman, Joachim Würfel
	The Viking Press, Inc. 625 Madison Avenue, New York, N.Y. 10017	Eliot Elisofon
	The Weston Gallery Inc. Box 655, Carmel, CA 93921	Clinton Smith, Cole Weston, Don Worth
	Daniel Wolf, Inc. 30 West 57th Street, New York, N.Y. 10019	Helen Levitt, John Margolies, Sheila Metzner, Arnold Newman, Eliot Porter, Art Sinsabaugh, Joel Sternfeld, Michael Geiger
	Zabriskie Gallery 724 Fifth Avenue, New York, N.Y. 10019	William Klein
	Private Collections	Cees van Gelder, Ansel Adams, Jeanloup Sieff, Robert Häusser, Michael Kostiuk, Auke Bergsma, Chris von Wangenheim, Holger Trültzsch/Vera von Lehndorff, Diana Blok & Marlo Broekmans, Paul de Nooijer, Toto Frima, Les Krims, Ernst Haas, Man Ray

BIOGRAFIEN
BIOGRAPHIES

Abbas
*1944, Iran

Abbas absolvierte 1962 eine Lehre bei einer algerischen Tageszeitung. 1968/69 war er Fotograf des Olympischen Komitees in Mexiko. Während seiner Tätigkeit als Fotojournalist für die Agentur *Sipa* in Paris von 1971 bis 1973, hielt er sich für fünf Monate in Vietnam auf. 1975 wechselte Abbas zu *Gamma* und berichtete 1978 über Südafrika, 1978-80 über die Revolution im Iran. Seit 1981 ist er Mitglied bei *Magnum*, der berühmten Fotoagentur, in Paris.

In 1962 Abbas was an apprentice to a newspaper in Algeria. By 1968/69 he photographed for the Olympic Committee in Mexico. During 1971 to 1973 he worked for *Sipa* Press, Paris, which included a five month stay in Vietnam. He joined *Gamma* Agency in 1975, reported on South Africa in 1978 and covered the Iranian Revolution during 1978-80. Since 1981 he has been a member of the famous *Magnum* agency, Paris.

Adams, Ansel
*1902, USA, † 1984, USA

Der spätere Meister der *Straight Photography* machte seine ersten Fotos als Vierzehnjähriger. 1927 begann er dann seine legendäre Laufbahn als Fotograf. Die High Sierra und Yosemite Valley waren die bevorzugten Motive seiner weltberümten schwarzweißen Landschaftsaufnahmen. Weniger bekannt ist, daß Adams 1949 Berater der Polaroid wurde und zahlreiche Aufträge für Kodak ausführte, u.a. bedeutende Colorama Aufnahmen. Adams erhielt alle Ehren und Preise, die ein Fotograf bekommen kann; er war ein Mann von großem Einfluß auf die Entwicklung der Fotografie. In über 60 Büchern wurden seine Fotografien und das von ihm entwickelte Zonen-System publiziert.

The master of *Straight Photography* took his first pictures at the age of fourteen and in 1927 he started his legendary career as a photographer. The black-and-white landscape photographs of his beloved High Sierra and Yosemite Valley have become world famous. Less known is that in 1949 Adams became adviser to the Polaroid Corporation and also did a lot of commercial work for Kodak, including important Colorama photographs. Adams was awarded every honor, every prize a photographer could possibly receive; he has been a major influence in the development of photography, More than 60 books on Adam's work and the Zone System invented by him, have been published.

Alvarez Bravo, Manuel
*1902, Mexiko

Espiritu Santo 83
Coyoacán, 04330 Mexico
Mexico

1924 kaufte er seine erste Kamera und begann unter der Anleitung des deutschen Fotografen Hugo Brehme seine fotografische Laufbahn. 1927 lernte er Tina Modotti kennen, die als sie 1930 Mexiko verlassen mußte, ihm ihre 8x10 inch Kamera hinterließ. Er traf mit den mexikanischen Muralisten zusammen und wurde Kameraman bei Sergei Eisensteins Film *Que Viva México*. 1931 beschloß er, von der Fotografie und dem Fotounterricht zu leben. 1934 drehte er den Film *Tehuantepec*. 1938 traf er André Breton, der im Jahr darauf Fotos von Alvarez Bravo auf einer Ausstellung der Surrealisten in Paris zeigte. 1959 gründete er mit anderen 'El Fondo Editorial de la Plástica Mexicana' und wurde ihr Chef-Fotograf. Eine Monografie über seine fotografische Arbeit erschien 1980 in Londen.

In 1924 Alvarez Bravo purchased his first camera and began his photographic career initially under the guidance of the German photographer, Hugo Brehme. Three years later he was introduced to Tina Modotti and when she had to leave Mexico in 1930, she left with him her 8x10 view camera. Alvarez Bravo met Mexico's muralists and worked as a cameraman on Sergei Eisenstein's film *Que Viva México*. In 1931 he decided to become a freelance photographer and simultaneously started teaching. In 1938 he made the movie, *Tehuantepec*. That same year he met up with Andre Breton, who in 1939 showed photos by Alvarez Bravo at an exhibition of the surrealists in Paris. In 1959, in collaboration with others, he began 'El Fondo Editorial de la Plastica Mexicana', where he was chief photographer. A monograph of his photographic work was published in 1980 by Travelling Light in London.

Andermatt, Jürg
*1944, Schweiz

Hohenmoor 55
2811 Asendorf
West-Germany

Nach der Physiklaborantenlehre arbeitete Andermatt in der Chemischen Industrie in Basel. 1968 machte er in Japan seine ersten Aufnahmen, und er lebte dann drei Jahre lang in Kyoto. Zum Abschluß seines Japan-Aufenthaltes erschien dort 1972 sein erstes Fotobuch. 1973 ließ er sich in der Nähe von Bremen als Foto-Designer nieder und fotografierte in Niedersachsen für seine Bücher *Teufelsmoor, Bremerhaven, Inseln im Licht* und *Bremen*. Andermatt arbeitet auch weiterhin an Landschafts- und Städtebildbänden.

Jürg Andermatt did an apprenticeship at a physics laboratory to then work in the chemical industry in Basle. In 1968 he travelled to Japan, where he took his first photographs. He lived in Kyoto for three years and at the end of his stay in Japan, his first photo book was published. In 1973 he settled near Bremen, Germany as a photo-designer and started to photograph the German North Sea Coast, which resulted in the books *Teufelsmoor, Bremerhaven, Inseln im Licht* and his recent title, *Bremen*. Andermatt continues to produce books on landscapes and cityscapes.

Azzi, Robert
*1943, USA

Azzi studierte Architektur und arbeitet seit 1968 als Fotograf. Bis 1976 lebte er in Beirut, von wo aus er über die Palästinenser, Jordanien, Pakistan, die Zypern Krise, den Libanon Konflikt und die Entwicklung der arabischen Ölstaaten berichtete. Er arbeitet seitdem als kommerzieller Fotograf in New York, beendete gerade eine Porträtserie über die noch lebenden Söhne von Ibn Saud, dem Begründer des Saudi Arabischen Staates, mit dem Polaroid 50x60cm System und begann in diesem Jahr an dem Projekt *Amerikanische Helden* zu arbeiten.

Robert Azzi studied architecture and has been working as a photographer since 1968, when he was based in Beirut until 1976, covering the Palestinian, Jordanian, Pakistani, Cypriot and Lebanese civil wars, and the development of the Arab States. Azzi now lives in New York City, working as a commerical photographer. He has just finished a portrait series on the surviving sons of Saudi Arabia's founding King, Ibn Saud, using the Polaroid 20x24″ system. In 1986 he started a project, entitled *American Heroes*.

Babis, Larry
*1949, USA

410 Stephens Avenue, apt. Nr. 3
Missoula, Montana 59801
USA

Während des Studiums an der Cooper Union, das er 1975 mit einem B.F.A. abschloß, hatte Babis angefangen zu fotografieren. In der Tradition des dokumentarischen Stils von →Walker Evans und ermutigt von →Joel Meyerowitz und Tod Papageorge, wandte er sich der Abbildung von Doppelhäusern und Vorgärten in den Wohngebieten von New York zu. Nachdem er zwei Jahre lang in den Stadtteilen Brooklyn und Queens fotografiert hatte, fuhr er an die Küste von New Jersey, nach Philadelphia und Chicago. 1976 trampte er durch das ganze Land, dann bereiste er Neu-Schottland (Kanada), Neufundland, Mexiko, Ägypten, Italien und Australien.

Babis began photographing while still a student at Cooper Union, where he received his B.F.A. in 1975. Following the tradition of the documentary style of →Walker Evans and encouraged by →Joel Meyerowitz and Tod Papageorge, he began photographing the double houses and mini gardens of New York City's residential areas. After exploring Brooklyn and Queens for two years, he traveled to the New Jersey coast, Philadelphia and Chicago. In 1976 he hiked all over America and later visited Nova Scotia, Newfoundland, Mexico, Egypt, Italy and Australia.

Balkin, Serge
*c.1905, Rußland

Serge Balkin ging in Deutschland zur Schule und absolvierte eine Ingenieursausbildung. Er reiste dann als Fotograf durch Europa und fotografierte für *Die Woche, Koralle* und andere Illustrierte, 1940 ging er in die USA und zwei Jahre später erschienen seine Fotos erstmals in *Vogue*. 1945 wurde er Vertragsfotograf der Condé Nast Publikationen und fotografierte Landschaften und Menschen in Europa und den USA in Farbe.

Serge Balkin was educated in Germany and trained as an engineer. He then travelled around Europa as a photo-journalist and had his work published in *Die Woche, Koralle* and other publications. In 1940 he arrived in the States; two years later his photographs began to appear in *Vogue*, and in 1945 he joined the staff of the Condé Nast Publications. On his trips to Europe and across the States, he did several color pictures of people and landscapes.

Baňka, Pavel
*1941, Tschechoslowakei

Benice 8
Prague 10
Czechoslovakia

Ursprünglich als Ingenieur tätig, begann Pavel Baňka 1977 ernsthaft zu fotografieren. Seit 1979 arbeitet er hauptsächlich als Werbefotograf, fotografiert aber auch Außen- und Innenarchitektur für verschiedene Magazine. Baňkas freie Arbeiten sind oft von seinen kommerziellen inspiriert. Auf der Suche nach neuen Möglichkeiten bei Farbe und Form, zeigen seine Fotografien den speziellen Manierismus der postmodernen Periode.

Initially employed as an engineer, Pavel Baňka started to photograph seriously in 1977 and since 1979 he mainly has been working as an advertising photographer, but he also photographs architecture and interior design on commission by several magazines. Often Baňka's personal works are inspired by his commercial assignments. Looking for new possiblities in the field of color and form, his photographs illustrate the special mannerism of the post-modern period.

Barbieri, Olivio
*1954, Italien

Via M. Buonarroti 2
41012 Carpi-MO
Italy

Barbieri besuchte in Modena die Schule und studierte dann Philosophie an der Universität von Bologna. Dort besuchte er die von →Paolo Monti geleiteten Kurse in Fotogeschichte und Fototechnik. 1971 nahm Barbieri zum ersten Mal an einer Gruppenausstellung teil. 1973 reiste er nach Paris, heiratete und gab das Studium auf. Seitdem kehrt er jedes Jahr nach Frankreich zurück, um dort Landschaftsaufnahmen zu machen. Seit 1978 betrachtet er sich selbst als ernsthaften Fotografen. Obwohl er die Technik der Schwarzweißfotografie perfekt beherrscht, zieht er es vor, in Farbe zu fotografieren.

Olivio Barbieri was educated in Modena an studied philosophy at the University of Bologna. There he also attended the classes of →Paolo Monti on the history of photography and photo techniques. In 1971 Barbieri participated in a group exhibition for the first time. He travelled to Paris in 1973, married and abandoned his studies. Since then he has returned every year to France to photograph landscapes. He has considered himself a serious photographer since 1978. A fine technician in black-&-white photography, he prefers to work in color.

Basilico, Gabriele
*1944, Italien

Piazza Tricolore 4
20129 Milano
Italy

1969, auf einer Reise nach Schottland, fotografierte Gabriele Basilico eine Reportage über Glasgow. Im Jahr darauf hatte er in der Galerie Il Diaframma in Mailand seine erste Einzelausstellung und er beschloß, als Fotograf zu arbeiten. Seit 1975 fotografiert er für die Architekturzeitschriften *Domus* und *Abitare*, sowie für Industriefirmen und Institutionen. Seit 1976 hat er überdies zahlreiche Länderreportagen fotografiert. 1983 entstand die Serie *Contact* mit Unterstützung von Polaroid Italien. Seit 1984 arbeitet Basilico u.a. in der Mission DATAR in Frankreich. Die Farbe benutzt er auschließlich für seine kommerziellen Arbeiten.

In 1969 Gabriele Basilico covered Glasgow on a journey through Scotland. The following year he held his first solo exhibition in Gallery Il Diaframma in Milan, and decided to become a photographer. Since 1975 he collaborated with the architectural magazines *Domus* and *Abitare*, while working for companies and institutions. Besides architecture he has photographed several travel reportages since 1976. In 1983 he did the series *Contact* with the help of Polaroid Italy. In 1984 he joined the Mission DATAR in France. Basilico uses color only for his commercial work.

Batho, John
*1939, Frankreich

5, rue des Minimes
75003 Paris
France

Batho, ein ausgebildeter Buchkonservator und Restaurator, begann 1961 zu fotografieren, seit 1963 arbeitet er ausschließlich in Farbe. Im selben Jahr heiratete er die Fotografin Claude Batho (1935-1981). Über seine Fotografien, die er 1977 erstmals öffentlich zeigte, sagt er: "Sie erzählen nichts, sie dokumentieren nichts, und sie sind nicht kommerziell." Da bei ihm die Farbe selbst zum Gegenstand der Aufnahme wird, legt er besonderen Wert auf die Ausarbeitung, welche vorzugsweise von Michel Fresson durchgeführt wird, dessen Verfahren, der Carbon Prozess, eine größmögliche Lichtbeständigkeit der Abzüge garantiert. 1981 begann Batho auch selbst Abzüge auf Cibachrome herzustellen.

Trained in the conservation of old books and the restoration of paintings, John Batho's involvement with photography began in 1961 and since 1963 he has worked exclusively in color. That same year he married the photographer, Claude Batho (1935-1981). Referring to his photographs, which he first presented to the public in 1977, Batho states: 'They tell nothing, they document nothing, nor are they commercial'. Because in his work, color itself is the subject, the printing has to be perfect. Batho therefore collaborates with the printer, Michel Fresson, whose method, known as the Carbon process, guarantees the best possible preservation of color. In 1981 Batho started to do his own printing on Cibachrome paper.

Bauer, Erich
*1908, Deutschland
† 1984, Deutschland

Bauer Fotostudio GmbH
Klammweg 1
7500 Karlsruhe 31
West-Germany

Erich Bauer besuchte die Fotoschule in Dresden und München und erhielt 1932 seinen Meisterbrief. Er arbeitete dann in dem heute seit über 100 Jahren bestehenden Porträtatelier seiner Familie in Karlsruhe. Bauer fotografierte schon in den 30er Jahren in Farbe und er gehörte noch zu jenen kommerziellen Fotografen, die auf unterschiedlichen Gebieten erfolgreich waren: Er fotografierte für die Presse, machte Landschaftsaufnahmen, Mädchenfotos und vor allem Modefotos und Markenartikelwerbung. So fotografierte er z.B. in den USA für Levis Jeans aber auch für Versandhauskataloge in der BRD.

Bauer learned his craft at photographic schools in Dresden and Munich. In 1932 he received his 'Meister' degree and then went to work in his family's portrait studio, which in the meantime has existed for more than 100 years in Karlsruhe. Erich Bauer's involvement with color photography began in the 1930's and he belonged to a generation of commercial photographers, who were successful in a number of fields. Bauer did press photography, landscapes and pictures of girls, but above all worked as a fashion and advertising photographer. He was commissioned by Levis Jeans in the USA but also photographed for mail order catalogues.

Baumann, Anton F.
*1901, Deutschland,
† 1939, USA

Begann 1915 bei den Leitz Werken eine Ausbildung zum Feinmechaniker und arbeitete später im Konstruktionsbüro, wo er sich auch mit der Mikrofotografie befaßte. Durch seine Begeisterung für die von Oskar Barnack entwickelte Kleinbildfotografie kam er in die Leica-Werbeabteilung, für die er Lichtbildvorträge ausarbeitete und abhielt. Im Sommer 1936 begann er als einer der ersten mit dem Kodachromefilm zu fotografieren. 1937 veröffentlichte er ein Buch mit farbigen Aufnahmen. Bei der Arbeit an einem Auftrag für *Life* über amerikanische Pferdezüchter kam Baumann 1939 ums Leben.

In 1915 Anton Baumann began his training in precision mechanics at the Leitz factory, where he later worked in the construction department and got involved with microphotography. Because of his obvious enthusiasm about 35 mm photography, invented by Oskar Barnack, Baumann was taken into Leica's promotion department, where he produced and presented photographic shows. In the summer of 1936 he was one of the first to use Kodachrome films and a year later he published a book of color photographs. While shooting a reportage on American horse breeding for *Life* in 1939, Anton Baumann died.

Baumann, Horst H.
*1934, Deutschland

Baumann studierte an der Technischen Hochschule in Aachen. 1956 erhielt er seine erste Auszeichnung durch die *photokina*, deren Jugendwettbewerb er auch 1958 und 1960 wieder gewann. 1957 gab er das Studium auf und arbeitete als Presse- und Werbefotograf. Sehr schnell wurde er für seine avantgardistischen Farbfotografien bekannt. 1960 dehnte er sein Arbeitsgebiet auf das Grafikdesign aus und 1966 gründete er in Düsseldorf Communication Design Baumann, ein Studio für visuelle Kommunikation, Planung und Design. Seit 1968 arbeitet Horst H. Baumann hauptsächlich mit Laser- und Videotechnik.

Horst H. Baumann studied at the Technical College in Aachen and was awarded the *photokina* 'Young Photographers Prize' in 1956, 1958 and 1960. In 1957 he gave up his studies in favour of working as a photo-journalist and advertising photographer. Soon he became known for his avant-garde style in color photography. In 1960 he extended his field of activity to graphic design and in 1966 established the 'Communication Design Baumann', a studio for visual-communication, planning and design in Düsseldorf. Since 1968 he has mainly been working with laser and video technology.

Beaton, Sir Cecil
*1904, Großbritannien,
† 1980, Großbritannien

Beaton begann schon früh zu fotografieren, ab 1926 dann berufsmäßig. Berühmt wurde er für seine Porträts und Modefotos, so gehörte er z.B. zwischen 1928 und 1950 zu den Stammfotografen von *Vogue*. 1938 wurde er zum Hoffotografen ernannt und während des Krieges reiste er im Auftrag des Informationsministeriums nach Indien, China, Afrika und fotografierte auch das zerstörte London. Ab 1945 entstanden dann wieder Modeaufnahmen und zusätzlich wurde Beaton in London und Hollywood als Kostümbilder und Filmausstatter aktiv; er erhielt zweimal den *Oscar*. 1972 wurde er geadelt und zwei Jahre später erlitt er einen Schlaganfall, der es ihm jahrelang unmöglich machte, zu fotografieren. 1977 ging sein komplettes Archiv in den Besitz von Sothebys über.

Cecil Beaton began to photograph early in life and since 1926, professionally. He became famous for his portrait and fashion photography and served as staff photographer for *Vogue* from 1928-1950. In 1938 he was appointed court photographer and during the war years he worked for the Ministry of Information in India, China, Africa and he also photographed the bombardment of London. After the war, Beaton once again turned to fashion photography and in London and Hollywood he became a costume and set designer, as well. The latter won him two Academy Awards. Further honors were awarded him and in 1972 he was knighted. In 1974 Sir Cecil Beaton suffered a stroke and for many years thereafter, he could not photograph. His entire archives were purchased by Sotheby's in 1977.

Bellati, Manfredi
*1937, Italien

Via S. Crose 4
20122 Milano
Italy

Wuchs in Venedig auf und studierte dort Architektur, beschäftigte sich aber gleichzeitig auch mit Skulptur und Malerei. Nach der Fortsetzung seines Studiums in Leeds, England, arbeitete er in Venedig als Innenarchitekt. Zuerst fotografierte er nur um seine Arbeit zu dokumentieren, dann verselbständigte sich die fotografische Tätigkeit. In *Vogue* veröffentlichte er Porträts, kam dann zur Modefotografie, der er sich seit 1965 hauptsächlich widmet. Hinzu kamen in jüngerer Zeit die Reportage- und Werbefotografie.

Bellati grew up and studied architecture in Venice, painting and sculpturing at the same time. He continued his studies in Leeds, England and then worked in Venice as an interior architect. Manfred Bellati first used photography simply as a means to document his work, but later in its own right. His portraits were published in *Vogue* and subsequently he went into fashion photography, to which he has devoted himself almost entirely since 1965. Lately his work includes reportages and advertising photography.

Benser, Walther
*1912, Deutschland

Zefa GmbH
Schanzenstr. 20
4000 Düsseldorf 11
West-Germany

Benser absolvierte bei der Firma Leitz eine Lehre als fototechnischer Kaufmann und begann dort Anfang der 30er Jahre Vorträge über die Kleinbildfotografie mit der Leica zu halten. Befreundet mit →Paul Wolff, benutzte Benser schon ab 1937 dessen und eigene Farbdias für seine Vorträge. Er nahm als PK-Mann am Zweiten Weltkrieg teil, setzte dann in den 50er und 60er Jahren seine Vorträge fort und veröffentlichte auch Anleitungsbücher wie *Farbiges Fotografieren in der Praxis erlebt* von 1954, das auch ins Englisch übersetzt wurde. 1959 gründete Benser in Düsseldorf die Zentrale Farbbildagentur, in der er heute noch tätig ist.

Benser did an apprenticeship with the Leitz company as a phototechnical salesman and began to lecture for them on 35 mm photography with the Leica at the beginning of the Thrities. Already in 1937, Benser began to use his and also his friend, →Paul Wolff's color slides for his lectures. He went into World War II and afterwards in the Fifties and Sixties continued his lectures and published instruction manuals on color photography which were also translated into English, such as *35 mm Color Magic* (1956). In 1959 Benser established a color photo agency in Düsseldorf, in which he still works today.

Berger, Wout
*1941, Niederlande

Uitdammerdijk 51
1154 PT Uitdam
The Netherlands

Berger erhielt seine Ausbildung an der Fotoschule in Den Haag. Er arbeitet als Fotograf für Illustrierte wie z.B. *Avenue*, schreibt aber auch Filmdrehbücher und regissiert Filme. Er ist ein anerkannter Landschaftfotograf und beendete gerade ein Fotoprojekt über die Schöpfungsgeschichte.

Wout Berger studied at the Dutch School for Photography in The Hague. As a photographer he has worked on assignments of magazines such as *Avenue*, but also wrote film-scripts and has worked as a filmmaker. A reknown landscape photographer, he just finished his series on the genesis.

Bergerson, Phil
*1947, Kanada

70, Wintermute Blvd.
Agincourt, Ontario M1W 3P8
Canada

Bergerson erhielt seine Ausbildung an der York University und am Ryerson Institute in Toronto, wo er 1970 ein Diplom in Fotografie erhielt und seit 1972 selbst unterrichtet. Er organisierte u.a. 1983 ein internationales Symposium über Fototheorie. Während der letzten Jahre befaßte er sich mit sehr unterschiedlichen Gegenstandsbereichen und Techniken in diversen Medien.
1983 begann er dann, Tableaus von 24 Aufnahmen eines Motivs zusammenzustellen. Diese Wiederholungen erzeugen sowohl einen formalen wie farblichen Rhythmus.

Educated at York University, Phil Bergerson graduated in photography from Ryerson Institute, Toronto, in 1970. He has been teaching there since 1972. He organized an International Symposium on Photographic Theory in 1983. For the past ten years, he explored a wide range of subject matter, ideas and techniques using a variety of media. In 1983 he chose a grid system of 24 exposures for each photograph, to present his subject. This repetition leads both to a structural rhythm and a rhythm of color.

Bergsma, Auke
*1950, Niederlande

Van Hogendorplaan 172a
3135 CL Vlaardingen
The Netherlands

Bergsma besuchte die Fotovakschool in Apeldoorn, dann die Modefotoschule von Hans Götze in Haarlem. Seit 1980 arbeitet er freiberuflich, produziert von seinen Fotos Postkarten und Poster. 1982 entstand der zehnminütige Videofilm "Gentlemen take Polaroids" über die Arbeit mit der 50x60 Kamera. 1982 brachte Bergsma Fotopostkarten in Farbe heraus.

Auke Bergsma studied at the Photographic Technical College in Apeldoorn and he attended the fashion photo school of Hans Götze in Haarlem. Since 1980 Bergsma has been freelancing, producing postcards and posters of his photographs. In 1982 he produced the video film 'Gentlemen take Polaroids' about a day at work with the 50x60 camera. In 1982 Bergsma published postcards in color for the first time.

Berko, Ferenc
*1916, Ungarn

P.O. Box 360
Aspen, Colorado 81611
USA

1921 kam Berko nach Deutschland, wo er in Dresden 1927 zu fotografieren begann. 1932 emigrierte er nach England, arbeitete als freier Dokumentarfotograf in Paris und London, wurde dann Chefkameramann bei der Bhavani Filmproduktion in Bombay und produzierte auch Fotoessays für die London Film Produktion von 1938 bis 1949. Er unterhielt sogar ein eigenes Studio für Werbung und Porträt in Bombay. 1947 ging er in die USA, wo er für die Container Corporation of America arbeitete. Ab 1952 wirkte er freiberuflich als Fotograf und Filmemacher. Seine fast abstrakten Farbaufnahmen sowie seine Farbreportagen über Länder wie Marokko, Mexiko, Japan, die er in den 50er Jahren machte, brachten ihm erst jetzt die Anerkennung als einer der führenden Farbfotografen.

In 1921 Berko moved to Germany, where he began photographing in 1927 in Dresden. In 1932 he emigrated to England and worked as a freelance documentary photographer in Paris and London. He was director of photography with Bhavani Film Productions in Bombay and between 1938 and 1949 he also produced photo essays for London Film Productions. Berko maintained his own commercial and portrait studio in Bombay until shortly before he emigrated to the United States in 1947, where he went to work for the Container Corporation of America. Since 1952 he has been an independent photographer and film maker. His almost abstract color photography and his reportages of countries like Morocco, Mexico and Japan, done in the Fifties, have only lately earned him a reputation as one of the masters of color photography.

Bing, Ilse
*1899, Deutschland

210 Riverside Drive
New York, N.Y. 10025
USA

Studierte 1920-29 Mathematik und Kunstgeschichte in Frankfurt und Wien. 1929 kaufte sie sich eine Leica und fotografierte Künstler und Avantgarde Architektur, sowie Reportagen für *Das Illustrierte Blatt*. 1930 emigrierte sie nach Paris und 1931 holte Van Loon sie für zwei Jahre nach Holland. Mitte der 30er Jahren entstanden Modefotos und 1941 ging sie nach New York, wo sie weiterhin als Fotografin arbeitete. Ab 1957 fotografierte sie nur noch in Farbe, entwickelte und vergrößerte ihre Farbarbeiten auch selbst. 1959 gab sie die Fotografie zugunsten anderer Kunstformen auf. 1976 wurde sie als Fotografin vom Museum of Modern Art in New York wiederentdeckt.

Ilse Bing studied mathematics and art history at the universities of Frankfurt and Vienna, 1920-29. She bought a Leica in 1929 and photographed artists and avantgarde architecture, as well as reportages for *Das Illustrierte Blatt*. In 1930 she emigrated to Paris and in 1931, Van Loon brought her over to Holland for two years. In the mid Thirties, she produced fashion photographs and in 1941 left for New York, to freelance. From 1957 onwards she photographed exclusively in color, doing her own developing and printing. In 1959 she abandoned photography in favor of other art forms. As a photographer, Ilse Bing was rediscovered in 1979 by the Museum of Modern Art in New York.

Bischof, Werner
*1916, Schweiz, † 1954, Peru

Bischof studierte 1932-36 an der Kunstgewerbeschule in Zürich, wo er am Fotounterricht von Hans Finsler teilnahm. 1942 hatte er in der Schweizer Illustrierten *DU* seine erste größere Veröffentlichung und er arbeitete dort auch redaktionell mit. 1944 fotografierte er in Farbe eine Serie über Invaliden, 1946 die vom Krieg zerstörten Städte in Europa. Ab Ende der 40er Jahre arbeitete er für die Zeitschriften *Life, Picture Post, Epoca*; 1949 trat er der Agentur *Magnum* bei. Aus einem tiefen Mitgefühl für die Menschen im Elend fotografierte er in Indien, Indochina und Korea. 1954, während einer Reportage in Südamerika, kam er bei einem Autounfall in den Anden ums Leben.

Werner Bischof studied at the school of Arts and Crafts in Zurich, where he attended photography courses with Hans Finsler. In 1942 the Swiss magazine, *DU* gave him his first major publicity, and Bischof then worked for them as editorial consultant. In 1944 he did a series of color photographs on invalides and in 1946 covered European countries, ravaged by war. In the late 1940's he collaborated with *Life, Picture Post, Epoca* and other magazines. Bischof joined the *Magnum* agency in 1949. Prompted by his intense sympathy for human misery, he reported from India, Indo-China and Korea. In 1954, while on a reportage on South America, Bischof died in a car accident in the Andes mountains in Peru.

Bishop, Michael
*1946, USA

P.O. Box Nr. 10
Jackson, CA 95642
USA

Studierte Fotografie bei Henry Holmes Smith und Kunst am San Francisco State College, erhielt 1971 seinen Master of Arts. Seitdem ist er freier Fotograf und unterrichtet Fotografie. 1971-72 entstand die Serie *Space/Technology* in schwarzweiß, bei der Bishop ein Negativ zweimal belichtete, indem er jeweils die Hälfte des Kameraobjektivs maskierte. Über das Tonen der Abzüge (1972-75) kam er zum Vergrößern von Schwarzweißnegativen auf Farbfotopapier und schließlich, 1974 begann er Farbfilm zu verwenden.

Michael Bishop studied photography with Henry Holmes Smith and art at San Francisco State College. He received his M.A. in 1971. Since that time he has been a freelance photographer and he also teaches photography. Between 1971-72 he worked on a black-and-white series, *Space/Technology*. By masking half of the lens, he made double prints on one negative. From b/w print toning, he moved on to produce enlargements of b/w negatives on color paper and finally began using color film in 1974.

Bizos, Alain
*1948, Frankreich

4, rue René Villermé
75011 Paris
France

Bizos besuchte von 1968 bis 1970 die *Ecole des beaux arts* in Paris und arbeitete dann fünf Jahre lang als Assistent des Malers und Bildhauers Arman in den Vereinigten Staaten. 1975-80 setzte sich diese Zusammerarbeit in Europa und den USA fort. 1976 erhielt Bizos von Arman seine erste Kamera. Im Auftrag des französischen Journals *Actuel* fotografierte er 1979 in den USA seine ersten Reportagen und im gleichen Jahr entstand auch eine Fotoserie über Nina Hagen. Seit 1979 arbeitet Bizos als Reportagefotograf, illustriert aber auch Buch- und Plattenhüllen, sowie Plakate.

Alain Bizos attended painting classes at the *Ecole des beaux arts* in Paris, 1968-70. The following five years he worked as assistant to the painter and sculptor, Arman in the USA and continued this collaboration during 1975 to 1980 in Europe and the States. In 1976 Arman presented him his first camera. Commissioned by the French journal, *Actuel*, Bizos photographed his first reportages in 1979 in the USA. That same year he did a series on the singer Nina Hagen. Since 1979 he has been working as a photo-journalist and an illustrator of record and book covers and posters.

Blazer, Carel
*1911, Niederlande
† 1980, Niederlande

1933 machte Blazer die Fotografie zu seinem Beruf und besuchte im folgenden Jahr den Unterricht von Hans Finsler in Zürich. 1937 war er als Fotojournalist bei den republikanischen Regierungstruppen im Spanischen Bürgerkrieg. In Holland gehörte er zur zunächst illegallen Fotografengruppe *De Ondergedoken Camera*, die ab 1944 das Vorgehen der deutschen Besatzer, die Aktivitäten des Widerstandes und die Hungersnot documentierte. 1946 war er der Mitbegründer von GKf, einer Gruppe von politisch engagierten Fotografen und Künstlern. Blazers Buch *Rome* von 1950 zeigt dann bereits den Übergang von der sozialdokumentarischen zu einer mehr "Subjektiven Fotografie". Carel Blazer machte später Industrie- und journalistische Reportagen, Kalender und war Spezialist für Großvergrößerungen.

Carl Blazer started to work in the field of photography in 1933 and took lessons with Hans Finsler in Zurich the following year. in 1937 he covered the civil war in Spain, working with the Republican troops. In Holland he became a member of the forbidden group of photographers, *De Ondergedoken Camera*, which was founded in 1944 with the purpose of recording the German occupation, the activities of the resistance movement and the starvation in the country. In 1946 Blazer became the co-founder of the GfK, an important national group of politically engaged artists and photographers. Carel Blazer's book, *Rome* which appeared in 1950, already marked his shift from social-documentarial to a more 'subjective' style of photography. Later Blazer did industrial and journalistic reportages and calendars and specialized in large format prints.

Blenck, Helmut und Erna

Die Blencks waren bereits vor der Zweiten Weltkrieg bekannte Reisejournalisten, die insbesondere das damals sehr populäre Genre 'Reisen mit dem Auto' abdeckten. So berichteten sie über ihre Amerikareisen, eine Leistungsfahrt im Auto rund um die Welt und über eine Afrikadurchquerung. Ihr Buch *Afrika in Farben*, das 1941 erschien, war das erste nach Farbdias gedruckte Fotobuch. Auf 120 ganzseitigen Farbfotos werden darin die ehemaligen deutschen Kolonien Ost- und Südwestafrika gezeigt. Nach dem Krieg setzte das Ehepaar seine Reiseberichte fort: 1952 erschien das Buch *Farbenfrohes Finnland*, 1954 *Südafrika heute* und ein weiteres Buch über Südwestafrika kam 1956 heraus.

Even before World War II, Helmut and Erna Blenck were known as travel journalists, specialized in the former popular genre of 'travels by car'. They reported on their journeys in America, a car race around the world and a criss-cross through Africa. Their book, *Afrika in Farben* appeared in 1941, and was the first German photo book printed from color transparencies. The 120 plates depict the former German colonies, East and South-West Africa. The Blencks continued their travel reports after the war. In 1952 the book, *Farbenfrohes Finnland* (Colorful Finland) was published and followed by *Südafrika Heute* (South Africa Today) in 1954. In 1956 they published another book on South Africa.

Blok, Diana &
Marlo Broekmans
*1952, Uruguay
*1953, Niederlande

1e Sweelinckstraat 22III,
Amsterdam
The Netherlands

Diana Blok studierte zunächst in Mexiko, dann ab 1975 Kunstgeschichte in Amsterdam. 1976 gab sie ihr Studium auf, in der Absicht Fotografin zu werden. 1979 traf sie die Fotografin Marlo Broekmans und durch ein staatliches Stipendium konnten sich beide der gemeinsamen kreativen Arbeit widmen. Die Publikation ihrer inszenierten Sebstbildnisse in Fotozeitschriften und auf Ausstellungen in Europa, den USA und Japan machten sie sehr schnell international bekannt. 1981 gaben sie ihre Zusammenarbeit auf, reisten dann aber 1983 gemeinsam für längere Zeit nach Indien.

Diana Blok studied in Mexico, before coming to Amsterdam in 1975 to study art history. She abandoned her studies in 1976 and decided to become a photographer. A grant from the Dutch Government enabled her to devote herself to the creative collaboration with the Dutch photographer Marlo Broekmans. Through the publication of their staged self-portraits in photo magazines and the numerous exhibitions in Europe, the States and Japan, they soon became known internationally. In 1981 their partnership broke up, but in 1983 they went to India together for a long period.

Blumenfeld, Erwin
*1897, Deutschland
† 1969, Italien

K. & H. Blumenfeld
33 Feverie
91190 Gif-sur-Yvette
France

Nach dem Ersten Weltkrieg ging Blumenfield nach Amsterdam, wo er unter dem Einfluß der Dadaisten erste Collagen und Fotografien anfertigte. Zwischen 1922 und 1936 betrieb er einen Lederwarenhandel, nach dessen Konkurs er sich entschloß, als Fotograf zu arbeiten. Seine von Dada und Surrealismus inspirierten Fotos wurden zuerst in *Verve* veröffentlicht und 1938 wurde er dann Fotograf bei *Vogue* in Paris. Aus einem Internierungslager in Frankreich flüchtete er nach New York. Bis 1965 gehörte er dort zu den bestbezahlten Fotografen; spezialisiert auf Mode fotografierte er für *Vogue* und *Harper's Bazaar*, für *Look* und *Life*. Nicht zuletzt er verhalf der Farbfotografie in den USA zum Durchbruch.

Following World War I, Erwin Blumenfeld moved to Amsterdam where under the influence of the Dada movement he created his first collages and photographs. Between 1922 and 1936 he traded leather goods out when that failed he decided to work as a photographer. His pictures, inspired by Dada and Surrealism, were first published in *Verve* and in 1938 Blumenfeld became staff photographer to *Vogue*, Paris. Later he managed to escape from a concentration camp in France – to New York, where he soon became one of the best paid photographers, specializing in fashion. He worked for *Vogue, Harper's Bazaar, Look* and *Life*. Last but not least, Blumenfeld greatly contributed to the break-through of color photography in the U.S.

Boekhout, Henze
*1947, Niederlande

Oranjeboomstraat 160
2013 WC Haarlem
The Netherlands

Bevor er zu seinem heutigen Stil fand, hatte Henze Boekhout schon mehrere Jahre lang als freier Fotograf gearbeitet. Während dieser Zeit machte er unter anderem Reisereportagen, die auch auf Ausstellungen gezeigt wurden. Heute interessiert es ihn viel mehr "wie die Fotografie die Welt abbildet, als das, was auf den Fotos zu sehen ist". Um daran zu arbeiten, sagt er, waren weite Reisen nicht mehr nötig. Der unmittelbare Umgang mit der eigenen Umgebung, mit Licht und Farben wurden sein Ausgangspunkt.

Henze Boekhout had several years experience as a freelance photographer doing travel reportages which were shown at exhibitions, before he found his personal style. Today he is more interested in how photography pictures the world than in the things shown in the photographs. To work on that concept he no longer needs to travel far away. The daily and direct contact with his surroundings, as well as with light and colors became his focal point.

Boje, Walter
*1905, Deutschland

Johannisberg 41
5653 Leichlingen 1
Germany

Nach dem Studium der Volkswirtschaftslehre, das er 1930 mit der Promotion abschloß, arbeitete er auf diesem Gebiet, bis er nach dem Krieg als Standfotograf zum Film ging. Ab 1949, als das Agfacolor Positiv-Negativ-Verfahren den Berufsfotografen zur Verfügung stand, fotografiert er, zunächst als Fotojournalist in Hamburg, Ballett- und Theaterszenen in Farbe. Die anfangs notwendigen langen Belichtungszeiten brachten es mit sich, daß er Bewegungsabläufe durch Unschärfen im Foto festhielt, wobei er dann die Farbe gezielt als Ausdrucksmittel einsetzte und dies zu seinem persönlichen Stilmittel machte. Boje hat seine meisterliche Beherrschung der Farbe auch in zahlreichen Lehrbüchen zu vermitteln gesucht.

Walter Boje studied economics, graduating in 1930 and working in this field until the end of the war, when he was taken into the film industry as a still photographer. In 1949 the Agfacolor positive/negative process became available to professional photographers and Bojo used it to cover ballet and theater performances in Hamburg, where he worked as a photo journalist. The initially long exposure time was responsible for the way he captured movement in a picture by blurring it, thereby using color as a means of expression and adopting this as his own personal style. Boje attempted to illustrate his masterly command of color in the numerous text books he had published.

Bonnemaison, Joachim
*1943, Frankreich

Nach dem Abitur absolvierte Bonnemaison eine Ausbildung zum Agraringenieur. 1970 war er verantwortlich für die Öffentlichkeitsarbeit eines Büros für urbane Studien und begann in diesem Zusammenhang die Fotografie einzusetzen. 1974 etablierte er sich dann als Werbetexter und Fotograf. Seitdem arbeitet er für Architekten, Stadtverwaltungen und die Industrie. Seine freien, farbigen Landschaftsaufnahmen fotografiert Bonnemaison mit selbst konstruierten, rotierenden Panoramakameras, die Fotografien stellt er meist zu Triptychen zusammen.

After his final school examination, Joachim Bonnemaison underwent a training as an agrarian engineer. In 1970 he was made responsible for the public relations of an office for urban studies and it was in this context that he first used photography. In 1974 he then established himself both as a textwriter and a photographer. Since then he has been working for architects, municipalities and industry. For his private projects, mostly landscape photography, Bonnemaison uses self-constructed, rotating slit scan cameras, often combining his prints into triptychs.

Boonstra, Rommert
*1942, Niederlande

Schietbaanlaan 126 A
3021 LP Rotterdam
The Netherlands

1968-70 schrieb er Kunstkritiken für die Zeitung *Nieuwsblad van het Noorden*, dann leitete er zwei Jahre lang das Theater in Assen. 1972-78 arbeitete er dann als Koordinator am 'De Lanteren' Theater in Rotterdam. Seit 1978 ist er freiberuflich tätig: Er schreibt Artikel über die Kunstszene und Reiseberichte für *Elseviers Magazine* und andere Zeitschriften. Er veröffentlicht auch Gedichte und schreibt Texte für Herman Brood. Seine Fotografien wurden von verschiedenen Zeitschriften gedruckt. 1984 brachte er eine Serie von farbigen 'table top'- Landschaften heraus.

Boonstra worked as an arts critic for a Dutch daily newspaper from 1986-70. During the following two years he directed the theater of Assen and in 1972 became coordinator at the 'De Lanteren' theater in Rotterdam. He started his freelance activities in 1978, which include writing articles on the art scene, as well as travel reportages for *Elseviers Magazine* and other periodicals. He also publishes poems and writes lyrics for the Dutch singer, Herman Brood. His photographs are published in various magazines and in 1984 he exhibited a series of 'table-top' landscapes.

Bordnick, Barbara
*1945, USA

39 E 19 Street
New York, N.Y. 10003, USA

Bordnick studierte am Pratt Institute, um Modezeichnerin zu werden, aber stattdessen wurde sie Mode- und Werbefotografin. Anfang der 70er Jahre begann sie ihre Karriere bei *Harper's Bazaar* in Paris, dann in New York. Sie war damals die jüngste Fotografin, die für diese Zeitschrift arbeitete. 1977 konnte sie eine Beilage der *Sunday Times* zum Thema 'Mode unserer Zeit' selbst konzipieren und illustrieren. 1979 war sie eine der Ersten, die Modefotos direkt auf Polaroid Material realisierte. Ihre 50 x 60 cm Sofortbilder wurden damals von der holländischen Zeitschrift *Avenue* publiziert.

Barbara Bordnick studied at Pratt Institute, intending to become a fashion designer, but instead she established herself as a fashion and advertising photographer. In the early 70's she started her career, working for *Harper's Bazaar* in Paris, then in New York. At the time she was the youngest women photographer working for that magazine. In 1977 she got the opportunity to create and illustrate a *Sunday Times* supplement on contemporary fashion. In 1979 she was one of the first to produce fashion photos directly on Polaroid 20 x 24" material which were published by the Dutch magazine, *Avenue.*

Bourdin, Guy
*1933, Frankreich

Seit gut 25 Jahren ist der Name Guy Bourdin ein Markenzeichen für Mode- und Farbfotografie. Er fotografiert seit 1955 Mode- und Kosmetikreportagen für *Vogue* und wurde insbesondere durch seine aufregend, ausgefallenen Werbefotos für die Schuhfirma Charles Jourdan bekannt, für die er ab 1965 arbeitete. Bourdin arbeitet immer mit dem gleichen Team, er ist für seine Detailbesessenheit bekannt.

For more than 25 years the name Guy Bourdin is a trademark for fashion and color photography. Bourdin has done reportages for *Vogue* (fashion and beauty) since 1955, but he especially became known for his execiting and extraordinary shoe advertisements, photographed on assignment for Charles Jourdan, with whom he started his collaboration in 1965. Bourdin always works with the same team and he is known as being fanatical about details.

Bowman, Stanley
*1934, USA

204 Willard Way
Ithaca, N.Y. 14850
USA

Machte einen Abschluß 1959 in Soziologie und 1964 in Architektur. Während er gleichzeitig als Architekt arbeitete, begann er 1966 eine Zusatzausbildung als Fotograf, die er 1973 mit dem Master of Fine Arts von der University of New Mexico, wo er Assistent von →Van Deren Coke war, abschloß. Seit 1973 ist er erst Assistenzprofessor, dan ab 1979 Professor an der Cornell University in Ithaca und leitet den Fotounterricht sowohl im Architektur als auch im Kunst Fachbereich. Mit einer Großbildkamera fotografiert er in konstruktivistischer Manier zusammengefügte Assemblagen. Die Abzüge zeigen die Objekte im Maßstab 1:1.

Stanley Bowman graduated in sociology in 1959 and in architecture in 1964. While working as an architect, he began further studies in photography. In 1973 he received his M.F.A. form the University of New Mexico, where he became →Van Deren Coke's special assistant. Bowman has been teaching photography at Cornell University, Itaça, N.Y., in both the architecture and art faculties. He was promoted to Associate Professor in 1979. He photographs assemblages in constructivist style with a 4x5 view camera. The final prints present all objects in a 1:1 ratio.

Browell, Anthony
*1945, Großbritannien

Studierte Anfang der 60er Jahre Fotografie an der Brighton Art School und an der Ealing School und arbeitete dann zwei Jahre lang als Assistent. 1966-69 fotografierte er freiberuflich für die London Times und wanderte dann nach Sydney aus. Seit 1969 arbeitet er für Werbeagenturen, Firmen und Illustrierte. Seine Tätigkeit als kommerzieller Fotograf in Sydney unterbrach er 1978 mit einer längeren Reise durch Amerika und Europa und von 1980 bis 1985 als er einen Schaufelraddampfer auf dem Murray River betrieb. Seit 1985 unterhält er ein Studio.

Browell studied photography at Brighton Art School and Ealing School 1961-64, then worked as a photographic assistant for two years. In 1966 he started to freelance for the London Times and emigrated to Sydney in 1969. In Sydney he established himself as journalistic, corporate and commercial photographer. Twice he interrupted his career: In 1978 he toured America and Europe and from 1980 to 1985 built and operated a paddlesteamer on Murray River. He maintains a studio since 1985.

312

Bruehl, Anton
*1900, Australien

2175 South Ocean Blv.
Delray, Florida 33444
USA

Begann in Melbourne eine Ausbildung zum Elektro-Ingenieur, emigrierte 1919 in die USA, wo er 1940 die Staatsbürgerschaft erhielt, und wandte sich 1924 der Fotografie zu, nachdem er zwei Jahre lang als Ingenieur tätig war. Nach einer kurzen Ausbildung bei Clarence White machte er sich 1926 als Mode- und Werbefotograf selbständig und gründete im Jahr darauf ein Studio, das bis 1966 existierte und zu den angesehendsten in New York zählte. Bekannt für seine werblichen Stilleben, fotografierte er für *Vogue* auch Prominenz und Mode. 1932 publizierte *Vogue* die erste Farbaufnahme, die Bruehl in Zusammenarbeit mit dem Techniker Fernand Bourges produziert hatte. Der Bruehl-Bourges-Prozeß setzte neue Maßstäbe für die Farbeproduktion und Bruehl wurde in den 30er Jahren Chef der Farbfotografie bei Condé Nast.

Bruehl studied electrical engineering at Melbourne, emigrated to the United States in 1919 (naturalized 1940) and turned to photography in 1924 after working as an engineer for two years. After a brief training with Clarence White, he started as a freelance fashion and advertising photographer in 1926. The following year he founded the 'Anton Bruehl Studio', which became one of the most reputed studios in New York. Bruehl's reputation extended beyond commercial still lifes; he also did celebrity portraiture and fashion photography for *Vogue*. In 1932 *Vogue* published the first of the color photographs Bruehl produced in collaboration with the color technician Fernand Bourges. The Bruehl-Bourges process set new standards for color reproduction and Bruehl became chief of color photography for Condé Nast Publications in the 1930's.

Bruehl, Martin
*Australien

Martin Bruehl kam 1923 zusammen mit seinem Bruder →Anton Bruehl aus Australien in die USA. 1927 eröffneten sie zusammen in New York ein Fotostudio, spezialisiert auf Werbefotografie und Illustration. Beide hatten zuvor von 1924 bis 1926 die Fotoschule von Clarence White besucht.

Martin Bruehl and his brother →Anton Bruehl emigrated to the United States from Australia in 1923. The Bruehl brothers opened a commercial photography studio in New York in 1927 where they specialized in commercial photography and illustrations. Both Anton and Martin Bruehl were students at the Clarence White Photographic School from 1924-26.

Buccafusca, Beppe
*1953, Italien

Corso Buenos Aires 66
20124 Milano
Italy

Begann 1976 als Assistent von Modefotografen in Mailand zu arbeiten. Seit 1978 hat er sich auf Stilleben und Mode für Werbung und Illustrierte spezialisiert. Seine ersten Erfahrungen mit Polaroid-Material sammelte er 1979. Die neusten Arbeiten nennt er *Colaroid*; es sind Fotos, in denen er seine Vorliebe für die Farbe Rot und durch eine Symbol dargestellte Empfindungen zum Ausdruck bringt.

Beppe Buccafusca started as an assistant to a number of fashion photographers in 1976. From 1978 on he specialized in still-life and fashion photography for promotion purposes and magazines. In 1979 he had his first experience with Polaroid material. He calls his latest work, *Colaroid*. These are pictures in which Buccafusca expresses his passion for the color red and hidden emotions, which are represented by a symbol.

Buckland, David
*1949, Großbritannien

239 Royal College Street
Londen NW1
Great Britain

Buckland studierte von 1967 bis 1970 Fotografie am London College of Printing. 1971 erhielt er ein zweijähriges Stipendium. Er beschäftigte sich Anfang der 80er Jahre mit dem Erstellen von Tableaus, bestehend aus Platinabzügen, die sein Interesse für die Malerei der Renaissance widerspiegeln. Seine neueren Farbporträts entstanden aus der Liebe zum Theater. Buckland arbeitet als Lehrer am Harrow College of Technology and Art.

David Buckland studied photography at London College of Printing during 1967–70. In 1971 he received a two year bursary. In the early 1980's Buckland created tableaus of platinum prints reflecting his interest in Renaissance paintings. His more recent color portrait photography emerged from his passion for the theatre. He is a lecturer at Harrow College of Technology and Art.

Bullaty, Sonia
*1923, Tschechoslowakei

336 Central Park West
New York, N.Y. 10025
USA

1937 mußte Sonia Bullaty die Schule verlassen und erhielt von ihrem Vater zum Trost eine Kamera, ihre erste. Nach der jahrelangen Internierung in Konzentrationslagern kehrte sie 1945 nach Prag zurück und wurde die Assistentin des berühmten Fotografen Josef Sudek. Bald aber ging sie nach Paris, dann nach New York, wo sie den Fotografen →Angelo Lomeo traf, mit dem sie seitdem zusammenarbeit und den sie 1951 heiratete. Oft fotografierte Sonia Bullaty in der Tschechoslowakei, unter andem auch 1968 den Einmarsch der sowjetischen Truppen. Neben Reportagen fotografiert sie vor allem Landschaften, Natur und New York. Unter den vielen Büchern mit ihren Fotos sind hervorzuheben: *Vermont in All Weathers* von 1973 und *Circle of Seasons – Central Park Celebrated* von 1984.

By 1937 Sonia Bullaty was obliged to leave school and as consolation her father gave her her first camera. After being interned in various concentration camps, she returned to Prague in 1945 and became the assistant of the famous photographer Josef Sudek. Later she went to Paris, then emigrated to New York where she met and started to collaborate with the photographer →Angelo Lomeo whom she married in 1951. Sonia Bullaty often photographed in Czechoslovakia, where she also covered the invasion by the Soviet Union in 1968. Besides reportages she photographes landscapes, nature, the City of New York. Among her published books are *Vermont in all Weathers,* 1973, and *Circle of Seasons – Central Park Celebrated*, 1984.

Bullock, Wynn
*1902, USA, † 1975, USA

Ursprünglich mit Sprachstudien und Musik befaßt – Wynn Bullock trat in den 20er Jahren als Sänger in Revuen auf – wurde er später zu einem international geachteten Fotokünstler. Seine Aufnahmen von Bäumen, fließenden Gewässern und die Aktstudien in der Natur sind bedeutende Beispiele der 'Straight Photography'. In den frühen 60er Jahren perfektionierte Bullock die Technik seiner mit Licht gestalteten farbigen Abstraktionen. Er war aber nicht nur als Fotograf, sondern auch als Lehrer tätig. In seinen Schriften legte er seine Auffassung von Fotografie und visueller Perzeption im Rahmen eines philosophischen Systems vor. Wynn Bullock starb im November 1975 an den Folgen eines Krebsleidens.

Initially involved in language studies and music, Wynn Bullock worked as a singer in music revues in the Twenties, to later became one of the most respected photo artists of our time. His photographs of trees, nudes in nature and moving water are striking examples of Straight Photography. In the early Sixties, Bullock perfected his technique in producing color light abstractions. As well as a skilled photographer, he was a teacher and writer. He attempted to formulate his ideas about photography and visual perception into a philosophical system. He died of cancer in November 1975.

Burri, René
*1933, Schweiz

Wegackergasse 7
8041 Zürich
Switzerland

Burri studierte Film sowie Fotografie bei Hans Finsler an der Kunstgewerbeschule in Zürich. Finsler machte ihn mit →Werner Bischof bekannt, der Burris Fähigkeiten als Fotograf erkannte und ihn bei *Magnum* einführte. Ab 1956 fotografierte er für *Magnum*, und seine Reportagen erschienen in allen führenden Magazinen. 1962 erschien in Paris und Zürich sein Buch *Die Deutschen*, das 1985 in München wieder aufgelegt wurde. Burri heiratete 1963 Rosellina Bischof und berichtete im selben Jahr über die Eskalation des Vietnam Krieges. Zuvor hatte er einen Foto-Essay in Farbe über das Heilige Land für *Paris Match* fotografiert. Im ürbrigen machte er seine bekanntesten Reportagen für die schweizerische Zeitschrift *DU*. In den letzten Jahren hat sich Burri auf die Produktion von Industriefilmen und die Arbeit für das britische und deutsche Fernsehen konzentriert.

René Burri studied photography under Hans Finsler and film-making at the school of Arts and Crafts in Zurich. Through Finsler he met →Werner Bischof, who recognized Burri's abilities as a photographer and introduced him to *Magnum* agency. Burri started his collaboration with *Magnum* in 1956 and his reportages have been published in all major magazines. In 1962 his book *Die Deutschen* (The Germans) was published in Paris and Zurich (And Edition Munich 1985). He did a color essay on the Holy Land for *Paris Match*. Burri married Rosellina Bischof in 1963 and that year reported on the escalation of the Vietnam war. His best-known reportages were done for the Swiss magazine *DU*. Burri nowadays concentrates almost exclusively on movie work, and produces industrial films as well as programs for BBC and for German TV.

Callahan, Harry
*1912, USA

Studierte Ingenieurwesen und arbeitete bis 1944 für Chrysler Motors. Seine ersten Aufnahmen entstanden 1938, 1941 besuchte er einen Workshop von →Ansel Adams, der ihn animierte, sich ganz der Fotografie zu widmen. Seine Frau Eleanor, die er 1936 geheiratet hatte, wurde das bevorzugte Modell seiner schwarzweißen Fotografien. Die ersten Farbaufnahmen entstanden zwar schon 1942, sie wurden aber zunächst wenig bekannt. Seit 1977 arbeitet Callahan fast nur noch in Farbe; 1980 erschien in New York *Harry Callahan: Color.* Bis 1967 wirkte Callahan vor allem als Lehrer: am Institute of Design in Chicago lehrte er ab 1946, 1961 wurde er Leiter der Fotografie-Abteilung an der Rhode Island School of Design.

Harry Callahan studied engineering and worked for Chrysler Motors from 1934-44. He took his first amateur photographs in 1938 and became totally committed to photography in 1941 after attending a workshop held by →Ansel Adams. His wife Eleanor Knapp, whom he married in 1936, became the favourite model for his black & white photographs. Callahan took his first color pictures way back in 1942 but at first they drew little attention. Since 1977 he has worked almost exclusively in color. In 1980 the book, *Harry Callahan: Color* was published in New York. Looking back on his career, we find that until 1967 Callahan was primarily known as a teacher: he taught at the Institute of Design in Chicago since 1946. Then in 1961 he was appointed Head of the Photographic Department of the Rhode Island School of Design.

Callis, Jo Ann
*1940, USA

5129 Westwood Blvd.
Culver City, CA 90230
USA

Nachdem sie schon verschiedene Künstlerische techniken erprobt hatte, kam sie 1973 zur Fotografie als sie an der University of California in Los Angeles bei →Robert Heinecken studierte. 1977 schloß sie mit dem M.F.A. ihre studien ab und begann in Farbe zu fotografieren.
Ihre Farbfotos handeln, wie sie selbst sagt, von Schönheit und Empfindsamkeit, zur gleichen Zeit aber ach von Angst und Gefahr.
Sie setzt die Farbe sehr emotional ein, ihre Aufnahmen sind keine Untersuchungen über Farbe, sondern diese wird benutzt, um ein suggestives Element hinzuzufügen.

Having explored various media, Jo Ann Callis finally took up photography in 1973 while studying at the University of California, Los Angeles with →Robert Heinecken. In 1977 she received her M.F.A. degree and started using color film. Her color pictures are about 'beauty and sensuality, while at the same time one senses anxiety and fear', as Callis puts it. She uses color in an emotional way, her photographs being not only about color: 'instead color is used to add another suggestive element'.

Camp, Michael de
*1928, USA

417 S. Broad Street
Edenton, NC 27932
USA

Michael de Camp studierte an der Universität Princeton und arbeitete als Unterwasserfotograf in der Antarktis. Er leitete Expeditionen auf der Suche nach und bei der Identifizierung von Schiffswracks vor der amerikanischen Küste. Er hält auch Dia-Vorträge über seine Unterwassererkundungen. Bei seiner freien fotografischen Arbeit befaßt sich de Camp mit Skulptur und er produziert surreale, abstrakte oder sehr geometrische Fotografien.

Michael de Camp is a graduate of Princeton University. He has been an underwater photographer in the Antarctic, and an expedition leader in the search for and identification of hundreds of shipwrecks off the coast of the United States. De Camp also lectures on his underwater explorations. In his private photographic assignments, de Camp combines sculpture and photography, producing work that is surrealistic, abstract or geometric.

Cartwright, Guenther

Village Farm
Main Street Heslington
York YO1 5 EQ
Great Britain

Cartwright ist Assistenzprofessor für Fotografie am Rochester Institute of Technology. Gegenwärtig lebt er für zwei Jahre in der Grafschaft York in England, um dort zu fotografieren. Seine Farbfotografien, die er zuvor in Nordamerika und Kanada aufnahm, stellen eher unauffällige, alltägliche Gegenden und Objekte heraus, wobei er durch den formalen Gebrauch der Farbe Schönheit in das Chaos einer Industrielandschaft bringt.

Guenther Cartwright is assistant professor of photography at Rochester Institute of Technology. Presently he is on a two-year sabbatical living in York, England, to photograph there. His color pictures which he previously took in North America and Canada, present spaces or objects that one sees everyday but perhaps does not record. Using color in formalist tradition, Cartwright manages to bring beauty to the apparent chaos of an industrial landscape.

Castella, Vincenzo
*1952, Italien

Vicolo delle Palle 29
00186 Roma
Italy

Er studierte Literatur und Kunstgeschichte an der Universität in Rom und begann 1975 zu fotografieren, von Anfang an in Farbe. 1976 fotografierte er im Süden der Vereinigten Staaten und setzte sich dort insbesondere mit der schwarzen Bevölkerung und der Architektur auseinander. 1978 und 1980 reiste er wiederum in die Südstaaten der USA, in der Zwischenzeit entstanden Landschaftaufnahmen in Italien. 1981 wurde er freier Mitarbeiter der *Neuen Züricher Zeitung* und bei anderen Zeitschriften in Europa. Castella zählt heute zu Italiens bekanntesten Landschafts- und Reportagefotografen.

Vincenzo Castella studied literature and art history at the University in Rome. In 1975 he started to photograph, using color film from the beginning. The following year he covered the South of the U.S., concentrating primarily on architecture and the black population. He again travelled the Southern States in 1978 and 1980, while doing landscape work in Italy. In 1981 he began to work for the *Neuen Züricher Zeitung* as well as for other journals in Europe as a freelance photographer. Castella today is one of Italy's foremost landscape photographers and photo journalist.

Catany, Toni
*1942, Spanien

Carrer nou de la Rambla 34
pral
Barcelona 1
Spain

Begann 1954 als Amateur zu fotografieren, studierte dann Chemie und ließ sich 1967 als freiberuflicher Fotograf in Barcelona nieder. 1968 reiste er durch Ägypten und Israel im Auftrag von *Destino*, es wurden 10 Reportagen veröffentlicht. 1974 begann er Tänzer in Farbe zu fotografieren, seitdem arbeitet er mit Verlagen zusammen, illustriert Schallplattencover, macht Mode- und Porträtfotos. Als freie Arbeiten entstanden ab 1976 Aufnahmen im Kalotypieverfahren mit der Großbildkamera. 1980 begann er seine Stilllebenserie in Schwarzweiß, ab 1982 in Farbe.

Toni Catany began amateur photography in 1954, then studied chemistry and in 1967 established himself as a freelance photographer in Barcelona. In 1968 the magazine *Destino* commissioned him to cover Egypt and Israel; 10 reportages were published. In 1974 he began to photograph dancers in color. Since then he works with publishers, illustrating record covers and doing fashion and portrait photography. Since 1976 his personal work includes a series of calotype pictures taken with an old view camera. In 1980 Catany began his black & white still-life series, which he has continued in color since 1982.

Chris, Maarten
*1958, Niederlande

Avenue du Grey 51
1018 Lausanne
Switzerland

Nach dem Abitur absolvierte Chris von 1979 bis 1983 eine Fotografenausbildung an der *Ecole d'Arts Appliqués* in Vervey in der Schweiz. Seitdem ist er als freier Werbefotograf tätig. Für seine freien Arbeiten beschreibt er Zeit und Raum als die wesentlichen Elemente. Die Farbe steht bei ihm für die Gegenwart, den Augenblick, Schwarzweiß fur die Ewigkeit, das Unendliche. Es sind 'innere Bilder', die er unter dem Motto *Presence - Absence* fotografiert.

After finishing his final school examinations, Maarten Chris attended the photographic faculty of the *Ecole d'Arts Appliqués,* Vervey, Switzerland from 1979-1983. Since then he has been working as a freelance advertising photographer. The essential elements of his personal work, are time and space. For him color symbolizes the presence, the moment; black & white represents eternity, the infinite. These are introspective images, which Maarten Chris photographs under the title, *Presence - Absence*.

Christenberry, William
*1936, USA

2739 Macomb Street N.W.
Washington D.C. 20008
USA

1959 beendete Christenberry sein Studium and der Universität von Alabama und machte mit einer Box-Kamera Farbfotos, die er als Skizzen für seine Gemälde und Zeichnungen ansah. Erst 1962 wurde er durch →Walker Evans ermutigt, die Fotografien als eigenständige Werke zu akzeptieren. Mit Evans gemeinsam hatte er die Leidenschaft für alte Reklameschilder, die beide sammelten und fotografierten.
Christenberry arbeitet nach wie vor als Künstler, er malt, zeichnet, stellt Skulpturen her und fotografiert. 1983 erschien in den USA ein Buch mit seinen Farbfotografien, die er im Verlauf von zwanzig Jahren in Hale Country aufgenommen hatte.

In 1959, the year he finished his studies at the University of Alabama, William Christenberry loaded a box camera and took color shots which he used as sketches for his paintings and drawings. In 1962 →Walker Evans convinced him to accept these photographs as original works. Evans and Christenberry shared a common passion for collecting old placards and signboards, which they both sometimes also photographed. Christenberry still works as an artist in various media such as painting, drawing, sculpture and photography. In 1983 a book was published in the USA, portraying his color photographs taken in Hale Country in the course of 20 years.

Clay, Langdon
*1949, USA

42 West 28th Street
New York, N.Y. 10001
USA

Clay arbeitet seit 1972 freiberuflich als kommerzieller Fotograf in New York. Er brachte sich das Fotografieren auf der Highschool selbst bei und benutzt seit 1975 Farbmaterial. Sein Portfolio *Cars* wurde 1978 die erste, vom Viktoria und Albert Museum in London veranstaltete Farbfotoausstellung. Nach *Cars* wechselte Clay vom Kleinbilddia zur Großformatkamera und Negativfilm, weil er meint: "Je mehr Informationseinheiten pro Quadratmillimeter, desto besser die Fotografie."

Since 1972 Langdon Clay has worked as a freelance commercial photographer in New York City. He taught himself photography at high school and has worked in color since 1975. Clay's portfolio *Cars* resulted in the first exhibition of color photographs at the Victoria and Albert Museum, London, in 1978. Following the *Cars* series, Clay switched from 35 mm slide film to a view camera and negative film which he has used ever since, because: "the more bits of sharp undiffused information per square millimeter, the better the photograph".

Clergue, Lucien
*1934, Frankreich

17, rue Aristide Briand
13632 Arles
France

Wie ihm sein Freund Picasso vorausgesagt hatte, wurde Clergue zuerst durch seine Aufnahmen von im Wasser oder im Sand liegenden Frauenkörpen bekannt, bevor seine anderen Arbeiten Beachtung fanden. Die überwiegend in seiner provenzialischen Heimat angesiedelten fotografischen Themas kreisen oft um die Extreme Leben und Tod. So wie die Akte und das Meer Symbole des Lebens sind, so fotografierte Clergue den Stierkampf, den Friedhof von Montmajour und Tierkadaver als Symbole des Todes. Darüberhinaus entstanden Landschaftsaufnahmen, die in mehreren Bildbänden veröffentlicht wurden. 1970 gründete Clergue in Arles die "Rencontres internationales de la photographie", deren künstlerischer Leiter er 15 Jahre lang war.

As his friend, Picasso predicted, Lucien Clergue was to became known in the first instance for his pictures of female bodies spread out in water or on the sand – before the rest of his work would be recognized. Most of his photography was done in the countryside where he was raised, and the themes often touch on the extemities of life and death. As the nudes and the sea symbolize life, so Clergue photographed bull-fights, the cemetry of Montmajour and animal carcasses as symbols of death. Furthermore he did landscape photography, which has been published in numerous albums. In 1970 Clerque founded the 'Rencontres internationales de la photographie' in Arles, where he filled the post of creative director for 15 years.

Close, Chuck
*1940, USA

Chuck Close studierte Kunst an der Universität in Washington und in Yale. Ab 1967 lehrte er selbst an der School of Visual Arts in New York und ab 1970 an der New York University. Close gilt als einer der bedeutendsten Vertreter der Kunstrichtung des Hyperrealismus. Er malt riesige Porträts, die alle Details der Gesichtshaut zeigen. Dafür benutzte er großformatige Fotografien als Vorlagen. Inzwischen haben die von ihm selbst aufgenommen Porträts ihren eigenen Stellenwert innerhalb seines künstlerischen Gesamtwerkes.

Chuck Close studied art at the University of Washington and at Yale University. From 1967 he lectured at the School of Visual Arts, New York, and since 1970 he has been teaching at New York University. Close has been considered one of the most important exponents of the art trend of Hyper-realism. His gigantic painted portraits show all details of the facial skin. For these paintings Close initially used large format photographs, but in the meantime these portraits have become an important part of his artistic work in their own right.

Coffin, Clifford
*c.1915, USA

Nach dem Studium an der Universität in Los Angeles arbeitete Coffin im Hotelgewerbe, bei einer Werbeagentur, bei MGM und der Texas Ölgesellschaft bevor er Fotograf wurde. 1944 erhielt er von *Vogue* seine ersten Auftrag als Berufsfotograf. Er wurde Vertragsfotograf der Condé Nast Publikationen und lebte in London und Paris, fotografierte Mode und Porträts aber ebenso in Rom, Honululu, Havanna und Stockholm.

Following his studies at U.C.L.A., Clifford Coffin jobbed in the hotel branch, in advertising, at M.G.M., and at the Texas Oil Company, before his involvement with photography began. *Vogue* in 1944 gave him his first professional photographic assignment. Since then as a staff member of the Condé Nast Publications, he has lived and photographed in London and Paris, but he has also done fashion and portraits in Rome, Honululu, Havana and Stockholm.

Cohen, Mark
*1943, USA

32 West South Street
Wilkes-Barre, PA 18702
USA

Cohen ist in Wilkes-Barre geboren, aufgewachsen, zur Schule gegangen, hat dort studiert und unterrichtet am dortigen Kings College. Fotograf ist er seit 1956 und er betreibt in diesem Ort ein kleines, kommerzielles Studio. Mit seinen freien Arbeiten zählt er seit den 70er Jahren zu den prominentesten Vertretern der sog. Schnappschußfotografie. Mit einer Kleinbildkamera und einem kleinen, in der Hand gehaltenen Blitz geht er auf die Straße und fotografiert Fragmente bewegter Szenen. Durch die künstliche Beleuchtung und die kurze Belichtungszeit zeigen seine Fotografien Momente, die mit bloßen Auge so nicht sichtbar wären. Seit 1975 macht Cohen seine künstlerischen Schnappschüsse auch in Farbe.

Mark Cohen was born, raised and educated in Wilkes-Barre, where he also studied and nowadays teaches photography at Kings College. He has worked as a photographer from 1956, maintaining a small commercial studio. Since the 1970's Cohen has became one of the best known street photographers. With the use of a 35mm camera and a small hand-held flash he captures fragments of moving persons and street scenes. Through the artificial lighting and the short exposure time, his photographs bring to life moments, which otherwise would not be visible to the human eye. In 1975 Mark Cohen started to use color film for his artistic snapshots.

Cohen, Serge
*1951, Frankreich

17, rue du Banquier
75013 Paris
France

Cohen begann während seiner einjährigen Assistenzzeit bei Daniel Frasnay in Paris zu fotografieren. Ab 1971 wohnte er mehrere Jahre lang in Köln, ohne aber von seiner fotografischen Tätigkeit leben zu können. Dies änderte sich erst 1982, als ihm das *Frankfurter Allgemeine Magazin* eine Chance gab. Seitdem arbeitet Cohen hauptsächlich für das *FAZ Magazin* und ist für seine Foto-Essays mit dem Schwerpunkt Porträt ständig unterwegs.

Serge Cohen's involvement with photography started in 1970 when he became assistant to Daniel Frasnay in Paris. From 1971 on he resided in Cologne, Germany for some years, but could not make a living from his photography. The turning point of his career came in 1982, when the *Frankfurter Allgemeine Magazin* gave him a chance. Since that time Cohen has been working mainly on commission for this magazine. He travels extensively to produce his photo-essays, which primarily feature portraits.

Cohen, Sorel
*1936, Kanada

631 Lansdowne Avenue
Montréal, Québec H34 2V7
Canada

Studierte an den Universitäten McGill und Concordia in Montreal, wo sie 1979 den M.F.A. mit einer Arbeit über die feministische Kunst der 70er Jahre erhielt. Ihre fotografische Arbeit entsteht, wie sie selbst schreibt, "aus dem Interesse am Bühnenereignis für die Kamera – der Foto-Performance", bei der sie oft innerhalb eines autobiografischen Kontextes agiert und bei der dann die Fotos gleichzeitig Referenzen enthalten an die zeitgenössische Malerei. In *an extended and continuous metaphor* ist sie ihr eigenes Subjekt, Objekt, sowie Betrachter und Publikum ihrer eigenen Aktionen.

Sorel Cohen studied at McGill and Concordia Universities in Montreal, received her M.F.A. in 1979 with a thesis on Feminist Art in the 70's. Her work evolved, as she states, through her 'continuing interest in the staged event for the still camera – the photo-performance, in which I often performed within an autobiographical context, and where the photographs made references to contemporary painterly aesthetics.' In *an extended and continuous metaphor* she is her own subject, object, as well as spectator and audience of her own actions.

Coke, Van Deren
USA

Dept. of Photography
San Francisco Museum of Modern Art
401 Van Ness Ave.
San Francisco, CA 94102
USA

Van Deren Coke fotografiert seit 1936, er wurde allerdings eher als ein sich für die Fotografie einsetzender Kunsthistoriker bekannt, denn als Fotograf. An der Universität von New Mexico in Albuquerque war er Professor und Leiter des Kunstmuseums, 1970-72 leitete er das Internationale Museum für Fotografie am George Eastman House in Rochester und seit 1979 leitet er das Department of Photography am San Francisco Museum of Modern Art. Er ist der Autor des bekannten Buches *The Painter and the Photograph: From Delacroix to Warhol*, Albuquerque 1974. Seit 1980 fotografiert Van Deren Coke ausschließlich in Farbe.

Van Deren Coke has been photographing since 1936, but he is less known as a photographer than as an art historian engaged in photography. He has been professor of art and director of the Art Museum at the University of New Mexico, Albuquerque. He directed the International Museum of Photography at George Eastman House in Rochester during 1970-72. Since 1979 he is director of the department of photography at San Francisco Museum of Modern Art. He is the author of several books, his most famous probably being *The Painter and the Photograph: From Delacroix to Warhol*, Albuquerque 1974. Since 1980 Coke photographs exclusively in color.

Cordier, Pierre
*1933, Belgien

20, rue Reigersvliet
1040 Bruxelles
Belgium

Begann um 1955 mit ersten fotografischen Experimenten und entwickelte 1956 das 'Chemigramm', bei dem ohne Kamera, nur durch die Einwirkung von Chemikalien auf ein lichtempfindliches Material, ein Bild erzeugt wird. 1963 begann Cordier Fotos oder Gemälde als Ausgangspunkt für seine Chemigramme zu verwenden, so entstand z.B. um 1975 die Serie *Hommage à Marey.* Seit 1965 lehrt er an der *Ecole nationale supérieure des arts visuels,* La Cambre, und entwickelt immer neue Varianten der kameralosen Bilderzeugung.

Pierre Cordier started his first photographic experiments about 1955 and in 1965 developed the 'Chemigram' which creates an image by means of localized action of chemical substances on a photo sensitive surface, without the aid of a camera. Since 1953 he also uses photos or drawings as a basis for his chemigrams, including his *Hommage à Marey*-series, which he produced in the mid-seventies. Since 1965 he has been teaching at the *Ecole nationale supérieure des arts visuels,* La Cambre, and continues to invent new variations of 'camera-less' imagery.

Cosindas, Marie
*1925, USA

770 Boylstonstreet
Boston Mass.
USA

Studierte an der Modern School of Fashion Design, Boston, und an der Boston Museum School. von 1945 bis 1960 arbeitete sie als Illustratorin und Designerin, dann fing sie an zu fotografieren und nahm einem Workshop über Studiofotografie von →Ansel Adams teil, aber in den dort entstehenden Schwarzweißfotos vermißte sie immer die Farbe. 1962 bekam sie von Polaroid deren neuen Farbfilm Polacolor zu Testzwecken und sie war dann der erste künstlerisch arbeitende Fotograf, der erfolgreich mit dieser Technik experimentierte. 1978 erschien *Marie Cosindas: Color Photographs* in Boston. Sie fotografiert bis heute vorzugsweise Stilleben und Porträts, die durch das von ihr getroffene Arrangement wie Stilleben wirken.

Marie Cosindas studied at the Modern School of Fashion Design, Boston and at Boston Museum School. 1945-60 she made a living as a commercial artist, doing illustrations and designs.Then she took up photography in 1961 and went to study with →Ansel Adams in his studio workshop, which was geared for black & white photography only and she soon found she missed color. In 1962 Polaroid offered her their new color film, Polacor for testing and she became the first creative photographer to successfully experiment with this technique. In 1978 the book, *Marie Cosindas: Color Photographs* was published in Boston. Right up until today she prefers to photograph still lifes and portraits.

Creyghton, L.J.A.D.
*1954, Niederlande

Gasstraat 5
5041 AL Tilburg
The Netherlands

Creyghton studierte von 1979 bis 1984 an der St. Joost Akademie der Bildenden Künste in Breda Fotografie und audiovisuelles Design. Seitdem arbeitet er als freiberuflichter Fotograf. 1986 erhielt er ein Stipendium des holländischen Kulturministeriums.

Creyghton studied at the Academy of Fine Arts St. Joost in Breda during 1979 to 1984. Since that period he has been working as a freelance photographer. In 1986 he received a grant from the Dutch Ministry of cultural affairs.

Dahl-Wolfe, Louise
*1895, USA

48 Broad Street
Flemington, N.J. 08822
USA

Sie studierte Design und Farbtheorie bei Rudolf Schaeffer, bevor sie 1921 anfing zu fotografieren. In New York unterhielt Louise Dahl-Wolfe von 1933 bis 1960 ein eigenes Studio. Bekannt wurde sie in erster Linie als Modefotografin, sie hat aber auch Porträts und Landschaften fotografiert. 1936 bis 1958 arbeitete sie unter Carmel Snow als festangestellte Fotografin bei *Harper's Bazaar*, anschließend für kurze Zeit erst für *Vogue*, dann für *Sports Illustrated*. Da ihr aber die Magazine nicht mehr die kreative Freiheit ließen, die sie in den 22 Jahren bei Harper's Bazaar hatte, gab sie die Fotografie 1960 ganz auf.

Louise Dahl-Wolfe studied design and color theory under Rudolf Schaeffer. In 1921 she got involved with photography and had her own studio in New York from 1933 until 1960. Primarily known as a fashion photographer, she also did portrait and landscape work. During the period 1936-1958 she was a member of the *Harper's Bazaar* staff, under the editorship of Carmel Snow. For a short period of time she then worked for *Vogue* and for *Sports Illustrated*. Since the magazines no longer allow her the creative freedom she had enjoyed at Harper's Bazaar for 22 years, Louise Dahl-Wolfe gave up photography altogether in 1960.

Dantzic, Jerry
*1925, USA

910 President Street
Brooklyn, N.Y. 11215
USA

1953-54 studierte Jerry Dantzic bei Alexey Brodovitch an der New School in New York und ab 1954 arbeitete er hauptberuflich als Fotojournalist und Illustrator. Er unterrichtet seit 1968 Fotografie an der Long Island University. Anfang der 70er Jahre erwarb er eine Cirkut Panoramakamera, die um 1895 in den USA hergestellt wurde. Mit ihr ist ein Bildwinkel von bis zu 360 Grad erreichbar, wobei die Kamera durch ein Federwerk gedreht und der Film zur Belichtung an einem Schlitz vorbeigezogen wird. Von besonderem Reiz ist es für Dantzic, diese Kamera aus der Ära der Schwarzweißfotografie mit modernem Farbfilm zu laden.

During 1953-54 Jerry Dantzic studied with Alexey Brodovitch at the New School in New York, and since 1954 he has worked professionally as a photo-journalist and illustrator. Since 1968 he has taught photography at Long Island University. At the beginning of the Seventies, Dantzic acquired a turn-of-the-century Cirkut camera. It has a capability of up to 360 degrees, because the camera rotates on a spring, while the film is gradually exposed as it is pulled past a slot. Dantzic is particularly fascinated by the results he achieves from loading this camera, which belongs to the era of black & white photography, with modern color film.

D'Arazien, Arthur

Arthur d'Arazien begann seine Laufbahn als Assistent eines berühmten Theaterfotografen am Broadway. Nach dem Krieg spezialisierte er sich auf Industriefotografie, ein Gebiet auf dem er zur Weltspitze zählt. Er fotografiert im Auftrag von großen Konzernen und ist bekannt für seine dramatischen Nachtaufnahmen von Industrieanlagen und die Aufnahmen von riesigen Innenräumen. Außer als Fotograf betätigt sich D'Arazien auch als Maler und er stellt Metallskulpturen her.

Arthur d'Arazien began his career in photography by working as an assistant to a famous theatrical photographer doing Broadway shows. After WW II he turned to industrial photography, a field in which he earned an outstanding reputation. He has carried out assignments for numerous major coporations and is particularly known for his dramatic portrayal of industrial night scenes and huge interiors. He is an accomplished painter and metal sculptor as well.

Dater, Judy
*1941, USA

P.O. Box 709
San Anselmo, CA 94960
USA

Nachdem sie das Kunststudium 1962 abgeschlossen hatte, besuchte Judy Dater ihren ersten Fotokurs bei Jack Welpott, der dann 1970 ihr Mann wurde. 1964 arbeitete sie bei Imogen Cunningham, über die sie später ein Buch schrieb. Judy Dater begann Fotografie zu unterrichten und 1967 mit der Aktfotografie, die, neben Porträts und Selbstporträts, zum bekanntesten Teil ihres fotografischen Werkes wurde. Nach diesen Arbeiten in Schwarzweiß entstehen seit 1982/83 großformatige Cibachromeprints, bei denen sie zum Teil die Ästhetik von Werbefotos ironisiert.

Following her art studies, Judy Dater in 1962 attended her first photography course under Jack Welpott, who became her husband in 1970. In 1965 she worked with Imogen Cunningham, and later on wrote a book about her. Besides teaching, Dater started to do nude studies in 1967, for which she became especially known, but her portraits and self-portraits in black & white are equally popular. Since 1982/83 she produces large format Cibachrome prints, in which she sometimes displays irony about the esthetics of advertising photography.

Delano, Jack
(Jack Ovcharov)
*1914, Sowjetunion

1923 emigrierte seine Familie in die USA. 1936, im letzten Jahr seines Studiums an der Kunstakademie, reiste Delano durch Europa und machte mit einer Speed Graphic seine ersten Fotos. Für ein Federal Arts Projekt fotografierte er 1938 die Anthrazit-Minen in Pennsylvania. Im Jahr darauf folgten Aufträge von der Farm Security Administration, für die er bis 1943 arbeitete, zuletzt sporadisch auch in Farbe. 1946 ging er nach Puerto Rico, dort gründete Delano die Abteilung für Volksbildung innerhalb des Erziehungsministeriums. Im Vordergrund seiner Arbeit standen seitdem die Realisation von Bildungsprogrammen für Funk und Fernsehen.

In 1923 Jack Delano's family emigrated to the States. One year before graduating from the art academy, Delano travelled through Europe and with a Speed Graphic he took his first photos. He did a documentation on the anthracite mines in Pennsylvania for a Federal Arts Project in 1938. The following year his involvement with the Farm Security Administration began. Shortly before the FSA project ended, Delano did some photography in color. In 1946 he settled in Puerto Rico, where he founded the Division of Community Education in the Department of Education. Delano since then concentrates on the realization of educational programs for radio and TV.

Dieuzaide, Jean
*1921, Frankreich

7, rue Erasme
31400 Toulouse
France

Jean Dieuzaide ist nicht nur ein sehr vielseitiger und außergewöhnlicher Fotograf, er ist auch ein Kämpfer für die Fotografie. So eröffnete er 1974 das "Chateau d'Eau", eine städtische Galerie für Fotografie und ebenfalls in Toulouse, 1976 die Galerie "Jean Dieuzaide". Seine Karriere als Fotograf begann 1944 mit einem Porträt von General de Gaulle. Schon immer interessierten ihn die kleine Dinge, seien es die Menschen und Landschaften seiner Region oder die wie Stilleben präsentierten organischen Objekte und Gebilde, wie sie auf der *photokina* 1982 zu sehen waren. Neben vielen anderen Auszeichnungen war Jean Dieuzaide 1975 der erste Fotograf, der zum offziellen "Maler der Marine" ernannt wurde.

Jean Dieuzaide is not only a versatile and extraordinary photographer, he is also a promoter of this medium. In 1974 he opened the 'Chateau d'Eau', a municipal gallery, devoted to photography, and also in Toulose he founded the photo gallery 'Jean Dieuzaide' in 1976. His career as a photographer started back in 1944 with a portrait of General de Gaulle. Dieuzaide was always interested in daily details of life; he photographed the landscapes and people of his home region as well as organic objects, presented like stilllife-pictures which were shown at the *photokina* exhibition in 1982. Besides several other great honors, Dieuzaide was the first photographer appointed as official 'Painter of the Navy' in 1975.

Dmitri, Ivan
(Levon West)
*1900, USA, †1968, USA

Levon West, der sich in den 20er Jahren in den USA durch seine Radierungen einen Namen gemacht hatte, benutzte als Fotograf das Pseudonym Ivan Dmitri. Während der Weltwirtschaftskrise entdeckte er den 'Zauber der Kamera' und nachdem er zuerst in Schwarzweiß gearbeitet hatte, schuf er dann viele bedeutende Dokumente der modernen Farbfotografie. So stammte der erste Farbtitel nach einem Kodachrome Dia auf der *Saturday Evening Post* von ihm, sowie zahlreiche weitere Titelfotos auf *Vogue* und *House and Garden*. 1940 schrieb er das erste englischsprachige Lehrbuch über den neuen Farbfilm *Kodachrome and how to use it* und 1944 erschien der Bestseller *Flight to Everywhere*, ein Farbbericht über Einsätze der amerikanischen Luftwaffe.

Levon West, a well-known etcher in the 1920's, turned to photography during the depression years and changed his name to Ivan Dmitri. He was 'completely fascinated with the camera' and after starting in black & white, he created several important documents of modern color photography. The first cover in color of the *Saturday Evening Post*, printed from a Kodachrome slide, was one of his photographs, as well as several more covers for *Vogue* and *House & Garden*. In 1940 he wrote the first instructions on the new color film in English entitled *Kodachrome and how to use it*. In 1944 the best-seller *Flight to Everywhere* appeared, a report in color on the American Air Forces.

Dolfo, Ferdinando
*1946, Italien

Via dell'Artigliere 10
37129 Verona
Italy

Studierte in Porderone Chemie, dann Sprachen und Literatur an der Universität von Padova. Nachdem er schon einige Jahre lang in Schwarzweiß fotografiert hatte, wechselte er 1976 zur Farbe. Er ist als Werbefotograf für Agenturen tätig, realisiert aber auch freie Arbeiten, vor allem experimentiert er gerne mit verschiedenen Materialien und Techniken, und da insbesondere mit Polaroid Material, das er seit 1980 benutzt. Zu seinen freien Projekten zählen *Hot Dummies* über Versuchspuppen, das unter dem Titel *Cold Graffiti*, eine Reihe von Porträts, die mit langer Belichtungszeit vom Videoschirm abfotografiert wurden, sowie 48 Aufnahmen von Mathematiklehren.

Ferdinando Dolfo studied Chemistry in Porderone, then languages and literature at Padova University. After several years of experience in black & white, he switched to color in 1976. As a commercial photographer, he collaborates with advertising agencies and also carries out private projects. Above all he enjoys experimenting with techniques and materials, in particular Polaroid material, which he has been using since 1980. These private projects include *Hot Dummies* on (experimental dummies), which is scheduled to be published as a book carrying the title, *Cold Bodies*. There is also a series called *Photo-Graffiti*; a collection of portraits, taken from the video screen with the use of long exposures; and 48 photographs of *Mathematics Teachers*.

Dolique, Patrick
*1949, Frankreich

7, allée des Hêtres verts
Lognes, 77200 Torcy
France

Seine Ausbildung erhielt er an der Ecole Estienne des arts et industries graphiques. Dolique arbeitete als Drucker und entdeckte 1973 das Fotografieren für sich. Besonders beeindruckt war er von den Fotos van Eugène Atget, Robert Frank und →Harry Callahan. 1975 trat er dem renommierten Fotoclub "30x40" bei. Es entstanden Schnappschüsse in Schwarzweiß von Menschen in der Stadt, bei denen er Gesten aus einem Bewegungsablauf isolierte, sowie von Menschen in der Stadtlandschaft. Angezogen von der Möglichkeit, durch Farbe zusätzliche Aktzente zu setzen, realisierte er 1984 zwei Farbserien. 1985-86 wurden seine Aufnahmen für die Biennale International de Paris ausgewählt.

Patrick Dolique was educated at the Ecole Estienne des Arts et Industries graphiques. Working as a printer, he discovered photography in 1973. He was especially impressed with the work of Eugene Atget, →Harry Callahan and Robert Frank. In 1975 he became a member of the renowned '30x40' photo-club. He did black & white shots of people in the city, isolating single gestures in a sequence of movements. Dolique also did photographic studies of people in cityscapes. Intrigued by the possibilities he saw in color for even greater accentuation, he produced two color series in 1984. In 1985-86 his photographs were chosen for the Biennale International de Paris.

Dow, Jim
*1942, USA

95 Clifton
Belmont, MA 02178
USA

Jim Dow studierte Grafik und Fotografie an der Rhode Island School of Design, wo er 1968 seinen M.F.A. erhielt. Durch die Bekanntschaft mit →Walker Evans war er zu dem Entschluß gelangt, Fotograf zu werden und zwischen 1970 und 1972 stellte er für Evans Vergrößerungen her. Seitdem unterrichtet Dow Fotografie an Hochschulen. Auf Architekturfotografie im weitesten Sinne spezialisiert, arbeitete Dow 1976/77 an dem Seagrams Projekt *County Courthouses* (Ländliche Gerichtsgebäude) mit. Er fotografierte dann die Sportstadien in den USA und England und machte u.a. Panoramafotos von Baseballfeldern.

Jim Dow studied photography and graphics at Rhode Island School of Design, where he received his M.F.A. in 1968. The encounter with →Walker Evans led to the decision to become a photographer, and between 1970-72 Dow worked as a printer for Evans. Since that period he has been an instructor in photography at various institutes. Specialized in architectural photography in the broadest sense, Dow worked on the Seagram's project *County Courthouses* in 1976/77. He later photographed sports arenas in the U.S. and England and took panoramic photos of baseball fields.

Edgerton, Harold E.
*1903, USA

Studierte 1921-25 an der Universität von Nebraska und weiter am Massachusetts Institute of Technology, wo er 1931 promoviert, und dort zum Professor für Elektrotechnik berufen wurden. 1931 entwickelte er ein Elektronenblitzverfahren zur Erfassung extrem kurzer Zeiten, bis zu einer millionstel Sekunde. Seine Aufnahmen von in der Luft hängenden Wassertropfen, von Pistolenkugeln im Flug, gingen in die Geschichte der Fotografie ein. Durch die Belichtung mit 100 Blitzen pro Sekunde auf ein Negativ zeigte Edgerton anschaulich Bewegungsabläufe beim Schlagen eines Golf- oder Tennisballes. Er entwickelte unter anderem 1950 eine Unterwasserkamera mit Blitz für große Tiefen.

Harold Edgerton studied at the University of Nebraska from 1921-25, then went on to the Massachusetts Institute of Technology, where he received his D.Sc. in 1931 and became Professor of Electrical Engineering. That year he combined a camera with a stroboscope so that he could make exposures at one-millionth of a second, showing fast moving objects as though they were stationary. His photographs of water drops suspended in mid-air and those of speeding bullets, have become part of the history of photography. With multiple exposures and a hundred flashes per second, he captured the sequence of motion of a golf or tennis ball. In 1950 he also developed an underwater camera with flash for photographing at great depths.

Eggleston, William
*1937, USA

2282 Jefferson
Memphis Tenn. 38104
USA

Eggleston begann 1962 ernsthaft zu fotografieren und seit 1966 arbeitet er ausschließlich in Farbe. Er gehört zu den ersten in seiner Generation künstlerischer Fotografen, die die neuen Farbtechnologien benutzten. 1976 eröffnete das Museum of Modern Art in New York eine Wanderausstellung seiner Farbarbeiten, die durch den Katalog *William Eggleston's Guide* begleitet wurde, und entsprechend schnell wurden seine Fotografien bekannt. Egglestons Motive sind eigentlich ausgesprochen banal, doch er setzt sie technisch wie ästhetisch auf eine Weise um, daß sie zu herausragenden Objekten werden. 1986 erschien sein Buch *Elvis Presley's Graceland*.

William Eggleston started to photograph seriously in 1962 and since 1966 has exclusively been working in color. He was among the first of his generation of creative photographers to make use of modern color technologies. In 1976 the Museum of Modern Art, New York, launched a traveling exhibition of his color photographs, accompanied by the catalogue *William Eggleston's Guide*. In this way his work soon became well known. Eggleston's subjects are rather banal, but technically and aesthetically he manages to transform them into outstanding objects. In 1986 his book *Elvis Presley's Graceland* appeared.

Eisenberg, Kristi
*1944, USA

1585 Tome Highway
Port Deposit, Maryland 21904
USA

Kristi Eisenberg erhielt 1978 den Master of Fine Arts von der University of Delaware und lehrt heute Fotografie am Cecil Community College in Maryland. Seit 1974 entstehen ihre abstrakten Farbfotografien, bei denen es ihr um die Probleme der Perzeption beim kreativen Prozeß geht. "Meine Fotografien zelebrieren den Akt des Sehens", schreibt sie. "Zeit vergeht, die Sonne scheint sich zu bewegen, die Welt erscheint in ständig wechselndem, aufregendem Licht." Ihre Aufnahmen sind oft Nahansichten von realen Gegenständen, aber es geht ihr nicht um die Darstellung von Realität, sondern darum, beim Betrachter Gedanken und Gefühle auszulösen.

Kristi Eisenberg graduated from the University of Delaware with an M.F.A. degree in 1978 and is now professor of photography at Cecil Community College in Maryland. Since 1974 she has done abstract color photography, reflecting the creative process as visual perception. She stated: "My photographs celebrate the act of seeing... Time passes, the sun seems to move, the world is lit differently in infinitesimally exciting ways." Although her photographs are often close-up views of reality, in fact they are intended to stimulate thoughts and feelings in the beholder.

Elisofon, Eliot
*1911, USA, † 1973, USA

Elisofon interessierte sich immer für das Exotische, für das weit Entfernte. 1937 begann er als Fotojournalist zu arbeiten und 1942 wurde er Vertragsfotograf bei *Life*, reiste durch Südamerika, Afrika, Japan und Europa. Von 1964 bis zu seinem Tod war er dann wieder freiberuflich tätig. Seine Aufnahmen sind meist sehr informationshaltig, er zeigte, wie Dinge, Menschen und Tiere aussehen. Elisofon arbeitete auch als Farbberater an einigen Spielfilmen mit.

Eliot Elisofon was interested in the exotic, the 'far away'. He started his career as a magazine photographer in 1937 and joined the staff of *Life Magazine* in 1942, travelling in South America, Africa, Japan and Europe. From 1964 until his death in 1973 he again worked as a freelance photographer. Elisofon's photographs contain a great deal of information: he shows what things, people and animals look like. Elisofon has also been a color-technique consultant for a number of movies.

Em, David
*1952, USA

P.O. Box 827
Siera Madre, C.A. 91024
USA

Nach der Kindheit in Südamerika besuchte er 1970-72 die Pennsylvania Academy of the Fine Arts, wo er Malerei studierte. 1973 stellte er aufwendige Skulpturen her, 1974 begann er in San Francisco mit Video zu arbeiten und zeigte seine erste elektronische Performance. Seit 1975 beschäftigt er sich mit Computergrafik und seit 1978 benutzt er den Computer als sein vorrangiges Künstlerisches Ausdrucksmittel.

David Em grew up in South America. Between 1970 and 1972 he attended Pennsylvania Academy of the Fine Arts, where he studied painting. He executed a series of sculptures in 1973, which required heavy industrial equipment. In 1974 he began working with video in San Francisco, where he staged his first electronic performance. Since 1975 David Em has worked with computer graphic systems and from 1978 onwards he has used computers as the primary vehicle for the expression of his art.

Enos, Chris
*1944, USA

Am San Francisco State College absolvierte sie eine Ausbildung in Bildhauerei. 1969 erhielt sie ihr Diplom und 1971 am San Francisco Art Institute ihren Magister in Kunsterziehung für Fotografie. Sie gründete und leitet das Photographic Resource Center in Boston und unterrichtet Fotografie.

Chris Enos was trained as a sculptor at San Francisco State College. She received a B.A. in 1969 and a M.F.A. in photography from the San Francisco Art Institute in 1971. Founder and president of Boston's Photographic Resource Center, Enos has taught photography in colleges and workshops across the country.

Epstein, Mitch
*1925, USA

424 West 199th Street, Apt. 67
New York, N.Y. 100027
USA

Epstein studierte an der Rhode Island School of Design und erhielt 1974 seinen B.F.A. von der Cooper Union in New York. Er fotografierte auf Jamaica, in Europa, Ägypten, Indien und natürlich in den USA. Mit seinen Farbfotos, die er mit einer handlichen 6x9 Kamera aufnimmt, versucht er, nicht den Klischees der Reisefotografie zu verfallen, sondern dieses Genre zu reflektieren und eine Distanz zum Malerischen zu behalten.

Mitch Epstein studied at Rhode Island School of Design and received his B.F.A. from Cooper Union in 1974. He photographed in Jamaica, Europe, Egypt, India and of course, in the States. For his color photographs he has been using a handy 6x9 cm camera. His intention is not to reproduce the clichés of travel photography but to reflect this genre and to keep pictorialism at a distance.

Erfurt, Stephan
*1958, Deutschland

Dahlhausen 40
5600 Wuppertal 23
West-Germany

Nach dem Abitur 1977 in Wuppertal begann Erfurt 1981 an der Gesamthochschule Essen Kommunikationsdesign bei Inge Osswald zu studieren. Im Oktober 1984 ging er nach New York und arbeitete dort als Assistent von Hans Namuth und Evelyn Hofer. Das *Frankfurter Allgemeine Magazin* veröffentlichte von ihm *Willkommen in Amerika, Fata Morgana Miami* und in Mai 1986 Fotos von *Montauk Beach*. Seit 1985 befinden sich Arbeiten von Erfurt in den Sammlungen des Museum of Modern Art in New York und des Museum Ludwig, Köln.

Stephan Erfurt finished school in 1977 and started to study communication-design with Inge Osswald at the Essen College in 1981. In October 1984 he moved to New York City where he worked as assistant to Hans Namuth and Evelyn Hofer. The *Frankfurter Allgemeine Magazin* in Germany published his photo essays, *Welcome to America, Fata Morgana Miami* and *Montauk Beach*. Since 1985 his photographs are to be found in the collections of the Museum of Modern Art, New York and the Museum Ludwig in Cologne.

Erwitt, Elliott
*1928, Frankreich

Als Kind russischer Eltern wuchs Erwitt in Mailand auf und 1939 emigrierte die Familie in die USA. 1944 entstanden seine ersten Aufnahmen: Porträts und Paßfotos. 1949 arbeitete er als Kameramann in Frankreich, 1950 in einem Fotostudio in New York. Seit 1953 fotografiert Erwitt Mode und für die Werbung, sowie Reportagen für *Magnum Photos*. Der in seinen fotojournalistischen Arbeiten oft vorhandene, dezente Humor zeichnet auch seine Hundefotos aus, die 1974 als Buch erschienen. Außerdem machte Erwitt bemerkenswerte Porträtaufnahmen.

A son of Russian parents, Elliott Erwitt grew up in Italy. In 1939 his family emigrated to the States. In 1944 Erwitt took his first pictures: portraits and passport photos. In 1949 he worked as a cameraman in Paris, and in 1950 he was assistant in a studio back in New York. Since 1953 Erwitt has been a freelance photographer, doing fashion and advertising photography as well as reportages for *Magnum Photos*. Erwitt's photo-journalistic work often includes subtle humor. His witty photographs of dogs, published in a book in 1974 became very popular. Elliott Erwitt furthermore is a skilled portrait photographer.

Evans, Walker
*1903, USA, † 1975, USA

Begann ernsthaft zu fotografieren als er 1927 von Paris, wo er Literatur studiert hatte, nach New York zurück kam. 1933 zeigte das Museum of Modern Art, N.Y. als erste Einzelausstellung eines Fotografen überhaupt seine *Photographs of Nineteenth Century Houses*. Jene Fotografien, die ihn zum Meister des dokumentarischen Stills machten, entstanden zwischen 1935 und 1938 als er im Auftrag der Farm Security Administration (FSA) fotografierte. 1945 ging Evans als Autor und Fotograf zur Illustrierten *Fortune*, für die er, obwohl zunächst ungern, auch in Farbe fotografierte. 1965 erhielt er einen Lehrstuhl an der Yale University, den er bis 1972 inne hatte. Während seiner letzten Jahre arbeitete er bevorzugt mit der Sofortbild-Kamera, weil er bereits abends aus den tags gemachten Fotos seine Auswahl treffen konnte.

Walker Evans started to photograph seriously when he returned to New York in 1927 from Paris, where he had studied literature. The Museum of Modern Art exhibited his *Photographs of Nineteenth Centure Houses* in 1933 as their first one-man photographic show. These images, which gained him recognition as master of the documentary style, were taken by Evans during the period 1935-38 when he was on a photographic assignment for the Farm Security Administration (FSA). In 1945 he was employed by *Fortune* as a writer and photographer. For this magazine he also did color photography, at first rather unwillingly. In 1965, Walker accepted a lectureship at Yale University, which he held until 1972. During his last years he mainly worked with instant photography, which enabled him to examine and edit his work on a daily basis.

Evergon (Al Lunt)
*1946, Kanada

P.O. Box STA.A.
Ottawa KIN 8VZ
Canada

Studierte and der Mount Allison University in New Brunswick, Kanada, und am Rochester Institute of Technology, wo er seinen Master of Fine Arts erhielt. Evergon arbeitet u.a. mit großmatigen Polaroids, in die manuelle Eingriffe erfolgen, sowie mit der Kombination von SX-70 Prints. Er nahm bischer an über 40 Gruppen- und Einzelausstellungen teil und seine Arbeiten befinden sich in kanadischen, amerikanischen und europäischen Sammlungen.

Evergon studied at Mount Allison University in New Brunswick, Canada, and holds a Master of Fine Arts degree from Rochester Institute of Technology. Evergon's recent work ranges form large format Polaroids which he alters by hand to the combination of SX-70 prints. He already has had over 40 one-man group exhibits and his work is in collections in Canada, USA and Europe.

Faucon, Bernhard
*1950, Frankreich

16, rue de la Goutte d'Or
75018 Paris
France

Während der Schulzeit begann Faucon zu malen und setzte dies auch während des Philosophiestudiums an der Sorbonne fort. 1967 waren seine ersten fotos entstanden, seit 1976 arbeitet er als freischaffender Fotograf. Faucon begann damals damit, Szenen zu konstruieren, die er mit lebensgroßen Puppen bevölkert. Inzwischen bewahrt er ungefähr 200 dieser Mannequins im Haus seiner Eltern auf, in dessen Umgebung er auch seine Szenen aufbaut, um sie dann abzufotografieren. Die bis 1981 entstandenen Aufnahmen wurden in dem Buch *Les Grandes Vacances* veröffentlicht. Seit 1978 arbeitet Faucon auch mit Magazinen zusammen.

During his schooling Bernhard Faucon started to paint and continued to do so while studing philosophy at the Sorbonne. In 1967 he took his first photographs and since 1976 Faucon has worked as a freelance photographer and began to construct scenes with life size dolls; in the meantime he has collected over 200 mannequins, storing them in his parents' house in the region of Lubéron, where he also build up the settings for his photographs. His work up to 1981 was published in a book entitled *Les Grandes Vacances* (Summer Holidays). Since 1978 Bernard Faucon has been collaborating with several magazines.

Fellman, Sandi
*1952, USA

548 Broadway
Studio 4 E
New York, N.Y. 10012
USA

1976 schloß sie ihre Ausbildung an der Universität von Wisconsin mit einem Master of Fine Arts ab. Als Fotografin wurde Sandi Fellman bekannt mit sehr sublimen, aus oft um ein Modell drapierten Stoffen und sehr weiblichen Utensilien gestalteten Aufnahmen. 1981 begann sie mit der 50x60 Kamera von Polaroid zu arbeiten und im Jahr darauf entstanden mit dieser Kamera in Tokio die ersten Fotos von den der Geheimgesellschaft "Irezumi" angehörenden, stark tätowierten Japanern. An diesem Projekt arbeitete Sandi Fellman über einen Zeitraum von drei Jahren, es erscheint im Herbst 1986 als Buch unter dem Titel *The Japanese Tattoo*.

In 1976 Sandi Fellman received her M.F.A. degree in art from the University of Wisconsin. As a photographer she became known for her pictures which are intended to be both sublime and subliminal, often created with fabrics and other feminine accessories, draped around a model. In 1981 she began working with the 20x24" Polaroid camera which she used for a series of photographs, made in Tokyo of the 'Irezumi', a secret society of heavily tattooed Japanese. Fellman worked on this project over the next three years and the photographs will be published in a book entitled *The Japanese Tattoo* in Fall 1986.

Ferretti, Alfredo Libero
*1919, Italien

Via Gallia 2
00183 Roma
Italy

Als Jugendlicher sammelte er seine ersten fotografischen Erfahrungen im *Studio Luxardo* in Rom. 1939-41 war er Assistent in der Abteilung für Optik am Centro Sperimentale di Cinematografia in Rom. Er wurde auf dem Gebiet der Modefotografie aktiv und vertiefte dann seine Technik der Farbfotografie 1952-55 bei der Kodak Graphic Arts Division in Londen und Horrow, sowie bei Pathé-Kodak in Frankreich. Freiberuflich fotografierte er für Zeitungen. 1957 stellte er eine Serie von Porträts aus, die römische Kunstler in ihrer Arbeitsumgebung zeigt. Er drehte dann einen Farbfilm und wandte sich in den 60er Jahren wissenschaflich-kunstlerischen fotografischen Experimenten zu.

In his youth, Ferretti gained his first photographic experience at *Studio Luxardo* in Rome. Between 1939 and 1941 he worked as an assistant in the optical department of the Centro Sperimentale di Cinematografia, Rome. He became active as a fashion photographer and between 1952-55 developed his color photography technique at Kodak Graphic Arts Division in Londen and Harrow, and at Kodak-Pathé, France. On a freelance basis he worked for news publications in Italy. In 1957 he presented a series of portraits, showing Roman artists in their working environment. In 1958 Ferretti shot a color movie and in the Sixties he turned to scientific-artistic experiments in photography.

Fichter, Robert W.
*1939, USA

Fichter studierte an der Universität von Florida, bei dem Fotografen →Jerry N. Uelsmann, dann bei Henry Holmes Smith an der Indiana University. Seit 1966 arbeitete er als freier Fotograf und war gleichzeitig bis 1968 Assistenzkurator für Austellungen am George Eastman House in Rochester. Fichter lehrt seit 1967 und 1982 zeigte er Cibachrome Abzüge zu politischen und ökologischen Themen. 1983 erschien das Katalogbuch *Robert Fichter – Photography and Other Questions*.

Robert W. Fichter studied at the University of Florida, with the photographer →Jerry N. Uelsmann and with Henry Holmes Smith at Indiana University. Since 1966 Fichter has been working as a freelance photographer and during 1966-68 in addition he was assistant curator of exhibitions at the George Eastman House in Rochester. From 1967 onwards he has been instructing photography and in 1982 he exhibited his Cibachrome prints on political and ecological themes. In 1983 the catalogue *Robert Fichter – Photography and Other Questions* appeared.

Fieger, Erwin
*1928, Tschechoslowakei

Via La Lama, Casa le Mura
52020 Castelfranco di Sopra
Italy

Fieger emigrierte nach Deutschland und studierte in Stuttgart von 1951 bis 1955 Grafik und Typografie. 1960 wechselte er zur Fotografie über und er pendelt seitdem zwischen Deutschland und Italien. Seit 1962 fotografiert er mit großer Ausschließlichkeit in Farbe, reist viel und sucht sich die Themen seiner Fotofeatures stets selbst. Auftragsarbeiten lehnt er ab, und es gibt nur wenige Illustrierte, denen er seine Fotos anvertraut, da er das Buch als die adäquate Publikationsform seiner Arbeiten ansieht. Seit 1971 macht Fieger auch Sportfotos und 1974 hatte er seine erste Einzelausstellung auf der *photokina* in Köln. Seitdem produziert er weiterhin Farbfotos für Bücher, Kalender, Werbung, sowie Sportaufnahmen.

Erwin Fieger emigrated to West Germany and studied graphics and typography in Stuttgart. He turned to photography in 1960 and since then has been operating between Germany and Italy. Since 1962 Fieger concentrates almost exclusively on color photography. He has travelled widely and always chooses his own themes for photo features. He never accepted commissions and there are only few magazines to which he entrusts his photos, because he considers books the only adequate verhicles for his work. Since 1971 Fieger has produced sports pictures and in 1974 he held his first solo exhibition at *photokina* in Cologne. Since then he has continued to photograph for books, calendars, advertising purposes and he still does sport photography.

Flack, Audrey
*1931, USA

1951 beendete Audrey Flack ihre Ausbildung an der Cooper Union zwei Jahre später die am Institute of Fine Arts, beide in New York. Sie ist eine bekannte und erfolgreiche, im Stil des Photorealismus malende Künstlerin. Sie benutzte u.a. Zeitungsfotos für ihre Arbeit, aber sie komponiert auch Stilleben, die sie dann selbst abfotografiert. Insbesondere verbinden sich mit ihrem Namen Bilder über den trivialen, nutzlosen Ramsch der Konsumgesellschaft. Sie lenkt die Aufmerksamkeit auf kitschige, vulgäre Objekte aller Art in morbiden Farben, wobei das Arrangement die westliche Stillebentradition widerspiegelt.

Audrey Flack graduated from Cooper Union in 1951 and from the Institute of Fine Arts in New York in 1953. A successful and well known photo-realistic painter she has used news photographs for her work, but has also taken to composing with her camera, in particular striking still lifes made from trivial and useless oddments from the consumer society. Attention is focused on trashy, vulgar, brashly-colored objects of all kinds; the formal arrangement echoing the Western tradition of the still life.

Fontana, Franco
*1933, Italien

Via R. Benzi 40
41010 Cognento, Modena
Italy

Begann als Innenausstatter 1961 in Amateurclubs zu fotografieren. Nach ersten Ausstellungserfolgen in Italien erschien 1971 sein erstes Buch *Modena una Città*. Fontanas ungewöhnliche Auffassung der natürlichen Landschaft, die er ohne technische Manipulationen, sondern nur durch Ausschnitt, Belichtungszeit und Blende auf farbgeometrische Strukturen reduziert, brachten ihm internationale Anerkennung und eine Vielzahl von Ausstellungen ein. Anfang der 80er Jahre rückte er von der abstrakten Landschaft ab und wandte sich dem Fotografieren von Menschen zu. Die Serie *Gente* (Leute) entsteht auf seinen zahlreichen Reisen. Sein Stil, der ihn zu einem der bekanntesten Farbfotografen machte, bleibt auch hier unverkennbar.

Franco Fontana became a member of amateur photography clubs in 1961, while earning his living as an interior decorator. After his first successful exhibitions in Italy, his book, *Modena una Città* appeared in 1971. Fontana's unusual vision of natural landscapes, without any technical manipulation, and reduced to geometrical structures simply by maneouvering the framing, exposure length and aperture, earned him international recognition. At the beginning of the Eighties he abondoned his abstract landscape work and began to photograph people. His series, *Gente* (people) stems from his extensive travels and the style, which has made him one of the most famous color photographers, is quite unmistakable in this work.

Frahm, Klaus
*1953, Deutschland

Boernsener Str. 26
2050 Boernsen
West-Germany

Nachdem er an seinem neunten Geburtstag die erste Kamera erhalten hatte, fotografierte er mit Leidenschaft Vögel. Mit 15 machte er Aufnahmen für die örtliche Tageszeitung. 1976 gab er das Studium auf und jobbte bei den US-Streitkräften in Mainz als "Darkroom Supervisor". 1980 begann er dann schließlich als freier Fotograf zu arbeiten. Für den Hamburger Verkehrsverbund fotografierte er die Backsteinarchitektur der Stadt und 1983 publizierte er *Bahnhofswelt*. Frahm Fotografiert seit 1981 in Farbe und zwar mit einer 4x5 Inch Großbildkamera sowie mit der Polaroid Museumskamera. Seine freien Projekte finanziert er durch die Arbeit als Architekturfotograf.

His first camera, received on his 9th birthday, led to Frahm's passion for photographing birds. At the age of 15 he took pictures for a local newspaper. He quit his studies in 1976 and went to work as a darkroom supervisor with the US-Forces in Mainz. In 1980 he finally started operating as a freelance photographer. He got a commission to produce a portfolio on red-brick architecture for the Hamburg public transport association. In 1983 he published a project on railway stations entitled *Bahnhofswelt*. Frahm has worked in color since 1981, using a 4x5" view-camera as well as the Polaroid Museum Camera. To support his personal photography he also works on commercial projects, mainly photographing architecture.

Franchi de Alfaro III, Luciano
*1945, Kuba

P.O. Box 14846
Chicago, IL 60614
USA

Erhielt den Doktortitel in Kunstgeschichte von der Universität in Chicago. Zuvor hatte er Fotografie und Skulptur/Keramik studiert und diese Fächer mit dem Magister abgeschlossen. Seine mit der Polaroid Museumskamera aufgenommenen Torsi unterzieht er einer Nachbehandlung: Durch das Perforieren der Oberfläche an ausgewählten Stellen oder durch das Eintragen grafischer Raster und Zeichen.

Franchi De Alfaro III received his Ph.D. in art history from the University of Chicago. Before then he had studied photography and sculpture/ceramics and already held a Master of Fine Arts degree. With the Polaroid Museum camera, he took photographs of torsos, which he subsequently perforated at certain points of the print's surface or painted with graphic rasters and signs.

Franck, Martine
*1938, Belgien

1963 begann Martine Franck in China, Japan und Indien zu fotografieren. Im Jahr darauf arbeitete sie im Fotolabor von Time-Life in Paris und war die Assistentin von →Eliot Elisofon und →Gjon Mili. Ab 1965 arbeitete sie als Fotojournalistin für *Life, Fortune, Sports Illustrated, New York Times* und *Vogue*, sowie für das Theatre du Soleil. Es entstanden auch erste Kurzfilme. 1970 heiratete sie Henri Cartier-Bresson und wurde Mitglied der Fotoagentur *VU*. Zwei Jahre später war sie die Mitbegründerin der Agentur *VIVA* und seit 1980 ist sie außerordentliches Mitglied von *Magnum*.

In 1963 Martine Franck started to photograph in China, Japan and India. During the following year she worked in the Time-Life laboratory and as assistant to →Eliot Elisofon and →Gjon Mili. She established herself as a photojournalist in 1965, working for *Life, Fortune, Sports Illustrated, New York Times* and *Vogue*. She also cooperated with the Theatre du Soleil and produced her first short films. In 1970 Martine Franck married Henri Cartier-Bresson and joined the *VU* photo agency. Two years later she became co-founder of *VIVA* agency and she has been an associate member of Magnum Photos since 1980.

Fraser, Peter
*1953, Großbritannien

17 Victoria Walk Cotham
Bristol
Great Britain

Studierte 1972-76 am Manchester Polytechnic, wo er ein Diplom in Fotografie erhielt. Seine erster Einzelausstellung hatte er 1982 in der Impressions Gallery in York. Im Frühjahr 1986 eröffnete die Photographers Gallery in London eine Wandersausstellung, in der Frasers neueste Serie von Farbfotografien *Everyday Icons* gezeigt wird. Er machte Fotografien in und außerhalb von Kirchen and der Strecke von der Kathedrale in Bristol bis nach Gladstonebury. Ihm lag daran, eine Pilgerreise zu illustrieren, in der Kirchliches und Weltliches ununterscheidbar wird.

Peter Fraser studied at Manchester Polytechnic 1972-76, where he took his diploma in Photography. His first one-man exhibition was held at the Impressions Gallery, York, in 1982. In Spring 1986 the Photographers Gallery in London launched a touring exhibition of color photographs by Fraser, entitled, *Everyday Icons*. He took photographs in and around churches along the route from Bristol Cathedral to Gladstonebury. His aim was to illustrate a pilgrimage in which the sacred and the profane were indistinguishable.

Freund, Gisèle
*1912, Deutschland

12, rue Lalande
75014 Paris
France

Studierte Soziologie in Frankfurt, mußte 1933 vor den Nazis nach Paris fliehen und beendete ihr Studium an der Sorbonne. 1936 wurde ihre Doktorarbeit in Paris veröffentlicht, die in einer erweiterten Fassung in Deutschland unter dem Titel *Photographie und Gesellschaft* erschien. Nach dem Studium wurde das Fotografieren zu ihrem Beruf. Ohne Auftrag entstanden die Porträts berühmter Literaten wie Joyce, Virginia Woolf oder Colette; die meisten Aufnahmen machte sie auf Farbdiamaterial. Als freiberufliche Fotoreporterin arbeitete sie für *Life, Look, Time, Paris Match* und andere Illustrierte. 1947 wurde sie das erste weibliche Mitglied von Magnum Photos; bei der Agentur blieb sie sieben jahre lang. Ihre Aufnahmen erschienen in zahlreichen Bildbänden, zuletzt 1985 in München *Gisèle Freund – Photographien*.

Gisèle Freund studied sociology in Frankfurt, West Germany; fled the Nazis in 1933 to Paris, where she finished her studies at the Sorbonne. In 1936 her famous thesis, *La Photographie en France au 19eme Siècle* was published in Paris. Out of necessity she became a photographer instead of a sociologist. Uncommissioned she did portraits of famous writers like Joyce, Virginia Woolf and Colette. Most of the portraits are color transparencies. She worked as a freelance photo journalist for *Time, Life, Look, Paris Match* and others. In 1947 she became the first woman photographer on the staff of Magnum Photos and she stayed with this agency for seven years. Her pictures have appeared in a great many photographic albums.

Frima, Toto
*1953, Niederlande

Kuinderstraat 28
1079 DC Amsterdam
The Netherlands

Als Autodidaktin fotografiert Toto Frima ausschließlich mit der Sofortbildkamera und exklusiv sich selbst. Die Fotografie ist für sie ein Mittel zur Selbsterfahrung. Nachdem sie anfänglich Einzelfotos aufgenommen hatte, arbeitet sie seit längerem in Serien zu fünf bis sieben SX-70 Polaroid-Fotos. Ihre Fotografien wurden häufig publiziert und in zahlreichen Ausstellungen gezeigt.

As self-taught photographer, Toto Frima has worked exclusively with the Polaroid system. She always photographs herself, using photography as a means of self-experience. Initially she produced single instant images, but some years ago she switched to the creation of series and sequences of five to seven SX-70 Polaroid photographs. Her work has been extensively published and shown in numerous exhibitions.

Frissel, Toni
*1907, USA

77 Harbour Road
St. James, Long Island
N.Y. 11780
USA

Mit der Serie *Beauties at Newport* über ihre Freunde in den Sommerferien startete die Autodidaktin 1931 eine Karriere als Modefotografin. Bis 1942 gehörte sie zum Stab der *Vogue* Fotografen. Damals neu war, daß sie die Modelle stets draußen und nicht im Studio aufnahm. Ab den 40er Jahren arbeitete sie freiberuflich und nach dem Krieg fotografierte sie statt Mode Menschen und Ereignisse. Sie trat insbesondere als Sportfotografin hervor, dokumentierte aber ebenso das Leben Familie und Freunde. Für sie war die Kamera ein Paß zur Welt des Glamour, der Action und des Sports.

Toni Frissel's career in fashion photography began by chance with a series of pictures she took of her friends on holiday in the summer of 1931, which she called *Beauties at Newport*. Until 1942 Frissel was a staff photographer for *Vogue*; she worked out-of-doors with the models, instead of inside studio: an approach which was very new for those times. From the Forties on, she worked freelance and after the war, instead of fashion, she photographed people and events. She specially made a name for herself as a sports photographer, but at the same time documented the lives of her family and friends. She saw her camera as her passport to the world of glamour, action and sport.

Fujii, Hideki
*1934, Japan

Nr. 402 Kuro Kawa Bldg.,
Studio F
6-34-14 Jingumae shibuya-ku,
Tokyo 150
Japan

Studierte Fotografie an der Nihon Universität in Tokio und begann schon während seines Studiums eine Assistenztätigkeit bei dem kommerziellen Fotografen Shotaro Akiyama. Nach drei Jahren ging er zu einem Zeitschriftenverlag und fotografierte Mode für das Magazin *Fukuzo*, dann arbeitete er wiederum drei Jahre lang für das Nihon Design Center, eine Werbeagentur. Seit Mitte der 60er Jahre hat Fujii ein Studio in Tokio, seinen ersten großen Auftrag als Selbständiger erhielt er von der Kosmetikfirma Max Factor. Bekannt wurde er nicht zuletzt durch seine Aufnahmen von seinem Modell Hironi Oka: Durch das maskenhafte der Gesichts- und Körperbemalungen sind sie der japanischen Tradition verpflichtet, sie sind aber auch modern im westlichen Sinne.

Hideki Fujii studied photography at Nihon University, Tokyo, and during that time he already started to assist the commercial photographer, Shotaro Akiyama. After three years as an assistant he joined a publishing house, photographing fashion for the magazine, *Fukuzo*. Therafter for a three year period he worked with the Nihon Design Center, an advertising agency. Since the mid-Sixties Fujii maintains his own studio in Tokyo. His first big commission came from Max Factor. Also well known are Fujii's photographs of his model Hironi Oka; While they follow true Japanese tradition as regards the facial and body paintings, they are also certainly modern in a Western sense.

Fusco, Paul
*1930, USA

Paul Fusco studierte Fotojournalismus an der Ohio University und wurde unmittelbar nach dem Studium Fotograf bei *Look*, wo er von 1957 bis 1971 arbeitete. Seit 1974 ist Fusco Mitglied von *Magnum Photos* und für seine Reportagen reist er in alle Teile der Welt. Hauptsächlich publiziert er in *Life, Time, Newsweek* and *Psychology Today*. Er arbeitet außerdem für Industriefirmen wie General Motors oder Yamaha.

Paul Fusco received his B.F.A. degree in photo-journalism from Ohio University and went directly to *Look* magazine as a staff photographer, where he worked from 1957 to 1971. Fusco joined *Magnum Photos* in 1974, where his fine photo-journalism continues to take him to all corners of the world. His photographs are mainly published in *Life, Time, Newsweek* and *Psychology Today*. His list of corporate clients include General Motors and Yamaha.

Gagern, Verena von
*1946, Deutschland

Genterstr. 13b
8000 München 40
West-Germany

Studierte 1966-72 Architektur in Aachen und München, die beiden letzten Jahre bis zum Abschluß in den USA, wo sie mit der Fotografie in Berührung kam. 1975 erhielt sie in Arles auf den Rencontres International den Preis für junge Fotografen, der ihr den Durchbruch als künstlerische Fotografin brachte. Bekannt wurde sie durch Schwarzweißfotos aus dem familiären Umkreis. Parallel zu ihrem letzten abgeschlossenen Projekt "Die Braut" (1980-84) entstanden in Farbe "Die Lehren der Natur", eine Zusammenstellung von Sofortbildern und Texten, sowie eine Serie von Fotos aus dem fahrenden Zug, von denen einige in Farbe sind.

Verena von Gagern studied architecture in Aachen and Munich, then for two years in the USA, where she graduated and came into touch with photography. In 1975 she received the Young Photographers Award at the festival in Arles, which provided her breakthrough as an artistic photographer. Best known are her black & white pictures taken in the late seventies of the people and things around her. While working on her latest project, 'The Bride' (1980-84) she did a color series 'The Lectures of Nature', a combination of Polaroid pictures and text, and a series of pictures from the train window, of which were some in color.

Gasoi, Marvin
*1949, Kanada

45 West 39th Street
New York, N.Y. 10018
USA

1971 schloß Marvin Gasoi seine Ausbildung mit einem Bachelor of Arts ab. 1976 arbeitete er ein Jahr lang am Optica Center for Contemporary Art und entschied sich dort, seine volle Zeit der eigenen fotografischen Tätigkeit zu widmen. Bis 1981 fotografierte er die Straßen und Stadtlandschaften von Montreal und New York, wo er 1978 hingezogen war. Seitdem arbeitet er im Studio, wo er seine Farb- und Lichtstudien noch intensiver betreiben kann. Die Studioarbeiten haben eine stärkere Ähnlichkeit zu Malerei, Zeichnung und Collage als zur konventionellen Fotografie.

Marvin Gasoi took his B.A. in 1971. For a year in 1976 he worked at Optica Center for Contemporary Art and it was there that he decided to dedicate himself full-time to his photography. He photographed the streets and urban landscapes of Montreal and New York until 1981 when he retreated to his studio in New York, where he could further develop his color and light studies. These studies more closely resemble painting, drawing and collage, than conventional photography.

Geiger, Michael
*1944, Deutschland

Geiger studierte an der Ulmer Hochschule für Gestaltung und ging dann in die USA, um als Assistent für Richard Avedon zu arbeiten. Nach zwei Jahren machte er sich selbständig und wurde ein erfolgreicher Werbefotograf. Gut zehn Jahre später schloß er sein Studio, um sich der künstlerischen Stillebenfotografie zu widmen. Sein bevorzugtes Motiv sind Blumen, die er zum Teil selbst aufzieht. Selbst ein Gourmet, fotografiert Geiger auch weiterhin 'Food' für das *New York Times Sunday Magazine* und stellte auch ein Kochbuch mit eigenen Rezepten und eigenen Illustrationen zusammen.

A graduate of the School for Design in Ulm, Germany, Michael Geiger came to the U.S. as an assistant to Richard Avedon. He retained that position for two years, at which time he made himself independent and soon became a successful advertising photographer. After more than a decade, Geiger recently closed his commercial studio to pursue artistic still life photography, choosing flowers as his subject, Geiger, a gardener and gourmet, continues food photography for the *New York Times Sunday Magazine*, and he has also compiled a cookbook with his own recipes illustrated by his own photographs.

Gerke, Heinz-Jürgen
*1949, Deutschland

Schlöterborgstr. 13
2804 Lilienthal
West-Germany

Nach der Schulzeit in Münster nahm er 1972 das Studium der Fotografie bei →Arno Jansen in Köln auf, setzte es dann fort in Bielefeld bei →Gottfried Jäger und Jörg Boström. 1975 machte er sein Examen und studierte anschließend Kunstpädagogik an der Universität Bremen bis zum Abschluß 1981. Gerke realisierte bisher diverse Reisefotoessays, u.a. hielt er sich 1983 sechs Wochen in der Apache Reservation in Arizona auf, um die Situation der Indianer zu Fotografieren. 1983 erschienen seine Farbaufnahmen von Zirkusleuten, außerdem entstanden die Serien *Strandkörbe – Deutsche an der See, Lebenszeichen, Flugbilder*, und *Fliegende Bauten*.

After finishing school in Münster, Germany, Heinz-Jürgen Gerke took up photographic studies in Cologne under →Arno Jansen, to then continue with →Gottfried Jäger and Jörg Boström in Bielefeld. He graduated in 1975 and then studied Art Education at the University of Bremen until graduation in 1981. Gerke has produced various travel reportages, amongst which a series on the living conditions of Indians, which he did during a 6 week stay at the Apache Reservation in Arizona in 1983. That same year his color photographs of circus people were published. He has also done other photographic series, e.g. *Beach-Chairs – Germans at the Seaside, Signs of Life* and *Flying Buildings*.

Gerster, Georg
*1928, Schweiz

Tobelhuberstr. 24
8126 Zumikon-Zürich
Switzerland

Promovierte 1953 an der Universität Zürich im Fach Germanistik. 1950-56 war er als Wissenschaftsredakteur tätig für die *Weltwoche*, Zürich. Spezialisiert auf wissenschaftliche Reportagen schreibt und fotografiert er seit 1956 für die *Neue Züricher Zeitung*, das *National Geographic Magazine*, das *Sunday Times Magazine, GEO* u.a. Außerdem ist er seit 1960 unter Vertrag bei der Werbeabteilung der Swissair. Gerster ist bekannt für seine Luftaufnahmen, die farbige Muster zeigen, es jedoch auch ermöglichen, einzelne Objekte und Details zu indentifizieren. Seine Aufnahmen wurden in einer Vielzahl von Büchern veröffentlicht.

Georg Gerster received a Ph.D. in German literature and philology from Zurich University in 1953. From 1950-56 he was Science Editor of the weekly magazine, *Weltwoche*. Since then he has been freelancing as a writer-photographer, specialized in science reporting. He contributes to the *Neue Züricher Zeitung, National Geographic Magazine*, the *Sunday Times Magazine, GEO*, etc. He is also contracted to Swissair's advertising department. Gerster is particularly reknowned for his aerial photography, which show colorful patterns in which certain objects and details are identifiable, making his work not totally abstract. His photographs have been published in numerous books.

Ghirri, Luigi
*1943, Italien

Via San Giacomo 38
41100 Modena
Italy

Sein Interesse an der Fotografie begann 1970 und bereits 1973 hatte Luigi Ghirri seine erste Einzelausstellung. Er fotografiert in Farbe und seine Aufnahmen nehmen eine Mittelstellung ein zwischen der Konzept-Fotografie auf der einen Seite und einer eher spontanen, emotionalen Fotografie auf der anderen Seite. In seinem Buch *Kodachrome* (Modena und Paris 1978) sind seine "Stilleben" enthalten, an denen er auch weiterhin arbeitet. Dabei handelt es um Aufnahmen, die wiederum ein Bild oder ein Foto zeigen. Die Serie *Colazione sull'erba* dagegen zeigt formal sehr klar gegliederte Landschaften außerhalb der Stadtzentren, wobei auch hier, wie typisch für Ghirris Fotografien, Künstliches und Authentisches schwer zu unterscheiden ist.

Luigi Ghirri's interest in photography started in 1970 and already by 1973 he held his first solo exhibition. He photographs in color, his work balancing between concept art and a more spontaneous, emotional photography. His book, *Kodachrome* (published in Modena and Paris, 1978) includes his 'still-lifes' which are photographs showing either a painting or a photograph; he is still working on this series. The series, *Colazione sull'erba* is about the natural landscape on the outskirts of towns, presented in clear, well-designed images. As is so often typical of Ghirri's work, here again it is difficult to define whether the composition of these photographs is artificial or authentic.

Gibson, Ralph
*1939, USA

331 West Broadway
New York, N.Y. 10013
USA

Gibson erlernte das Fotografieren in der U.S. Marine und als Assistent von Dorothea Lange. In den 60er Jahren arbeitete er an zwei Filmen von Robert Frank mit, zog nach New York und eröffnete dort 1969 ein Studio. Er fotografierte Mode für *Look* und Fotoessays für die Zeitschrift *New York*. Gleichzeitig gründete er 1969 seinen Verlag *Lustrum Press*, in dem er seine eigenen Bildbände *The Somnambulist, Déjà-vu* und *Days at Sea* veröffentlichte, mit denen er in den 70er Jahren zu einer Leitfigur der künstlerischen Schwarzweißfotografie wurde, sowie 1983 *Syntax*. Gibson tendiert zum Surrealismus und zur Abstraktion, entsprechend auch bei seinen ab Ende der 70er Jahre entstandenen Farbfotografien.

Ralph Gibson studied photography while serving in the U.S. Navy and has been assistant to Dorothea Lange. In the Sixties he cooperated on two of Robert Frank's films and then he moved to New York City and set up a studio in 1969. He took fashion pictures for *Look* and did photo essays for the magazine *New York*. At that same time he founded *Lustrum Press*, where he published his own triology of books *The Somnambulist, Déjà-vu, Days at Sea* (and *Syntax* in 1983), which earned him a leading role in creative black & white photography. Tending towards surrealism and abstraction, Gibson's color work, done since the end of the 70's is of an equally abstract nature.

Gill, Leslie
*1908, Rhode Island
† 1959, USA

Er studierte zunächst bei dem Maler Charles Hawthorne und dann an der Rhode Island School of Design, die er 1929 abschloß. 1932 nahm er die Stelle eines Art Directors bei *House Beautiful* an. Bald begann er zur Lösung redaktioneller Probleme die Fotografie einzusetzen und 1935 machte er sich mit einem Studio selbständig. Seine Fähigkeit, immer den perfekten Gegenstand zur Hand zu haben, sein Gefühl für Eleganz und Klarheit machen seine Stilleben so außergewöhnlich und modern. In erster Linie arbeitete Gill für *Harper's Bazaar* und "man kann", schrieb P. Thomas 1980 "seinen Einfluß auf die eigene und die folgende Fotografengeneration gar nicht überbewerten. Sein Stil ist der Stil schlechthin."

Gill studied painting with Charles Hawthorne and graduated from the Rhode Island School of Design in 1929. In 1932 he took a job as art director of *House Beautiful* magazine. Soon he began using photographs to solve editorial problems and by 1935 he left and opened his own studio. His ability to spot the perfect object and his eye for elegance and clarity, make his still lifes exceptional and quite modern. He mainly worked for *Harper's Bazaar.* "It is difficult to over-estimate his influence both on his own generation of photographers and of those who followed him. The Gill style is simply 'the style' (P. Thomas, 1980)

Gilpin, Laura
*1891, USA, † 1979, USA

1910 machte Laura Gilpin ihr erstes Farbfoto im damals neuen Autochrome Verfahren. Schon vor dem Krieg arbeitete sie auch mit dem Dye Transfer Verfahren, bekannt aber wurde sie in erster Linie für ihre selbsthergestellten Platinabzüge. 60 Jahre lang widmete sie sich der Dokumentation der Landschaft im Südwesten der USA und ihren Ureinwohnern, den Pueblo und Navajo Indianern. Ihre Landschafts-Architektur und Menschenaufnahmen gelten heute als klassisch. In ihren Büchern, insbesondere in *The Enduring Navajo* von 1968 stellte sie ihre außergewöhnlichen Fähigkeiten als Bild- und Textautorin unter Beweis.

In 1910 Laura Gilpin took her first color photo, using the then new autochrome process. Even before the war, she had begun to do dye-transfer work, but in the first place she became known as an excellent platinum printer. For almost 60 years she devoted herself to the documentation of the landscapes and the native cultures of the American Southwest, and most particularly to the Pueblo and Navojo people. Her landscape, architectural and portrait photography is now considered classical. In her books, especially in *The Enduring Navajo*, she demonstrated her skill both as a writer and photographer.

Gioli, Paolo
*1942, Italien

Via Don Minzoni 42
45100 Rovigo
Italy

Besuchte die Schule in Rovigo und Venedig. Er befaßte sich mit Malerei, Lithografie und Serigrafie, bis er 1968 anfing als Fotograf und Filmemacher zu arbeiten. Seit 1977 entstehen Polaroid-Fotos in Farbe. Sein Interesse für die Fotografie, wie auch für Film und Video, is ein experimentelles. Es geht ihm um die Erkundung jener durch die moderne Technologie eröffneten kreativen Potentiale.

Paolo Gioli was educated at schools in Rovigo and Venice. He then got involved with painting and lithography until 1968 when he began to work as a photographer and film maker. Since 1977 he has been producing Polaroid pictures in color. His interest in photography as well as in film and video is of an experimental nature. He strives to discover and exploit every creative potential offered by modern technology.

Gippenreiter, Vadim
*1917, Sowjetunion

Leninskij Prospekt 92
Moscow 117415
USSR

Studierte Medizin, brach das Studium aber ab, um an die Kunstakademie zu gehen, wo er die Bildhauer-Klasse besuchte. Dann wurde er schließlich Jäger, mehrere Jahre lang jagte er Bären in Sibirien. Seit den 50er Jahren ist er freiberuflicher Fotograf und fotografiert die Landschaft Sibiriens. Bekannt wurde er in der UdSSR insbesondere für seine Aufnahmen von Vulkanen. Seine Fotos sind in zahlreichen Landschaftsbildbänden enthalten.

Gippenreiter started studying medicine, gave these studies up to attend sculpture classes at an Art Academy, and then decided to become a professional hunter. He chased down bears in Siberia for a number of years and then in the Fifties became a freelance photographer of Siberian landscapes. In the USSR he is particularly famed for his photographs of vulcanoes. His work is included in many photographic albums.

Gladys (Gladys Tison)
*1950, Algerien

154, rue d'Alesia
75014 Paris
France

1961 ließ sich die Familie Tison in Frankreich nieder und 1969 machte Gladys ihr Abitur. Anschließend bereitete sie sich für die Aufnahme an der *École des Arts Décoratifs* vor. Sie fertigte Collagen, lieh sich 1972 eine Kamera und begann Fotos in ihre Collagen einzubeziehen. Im Jahr darauf kaufte sie einen eigenen Fotoapparat und experimentierte mit Mehrfachbelichtungen, fotografierte Landschaften und Farbtableaus. In der Zeit von 1974 bis 1982 beschränkte sie sich ganz auf die Schwarzweißfotografie, doch dann begann sie mit dem Polaroid Verfahren an collageartigen Fotografien zu arbeiten. 1985 benutzte sie erstmals die 50x60 Kamera von Polaroid.

In 1961 the Tison family settled in France and in 1969 Gladys finished school. Thereafter she prepared for the entry examination to the *Ecole des Arts Décoratifs.* She composed collages and in 1972 borrowed a camera from a friend so that she could integrate photograps into her collages. She bought her own camera the following year, experimented with multi-exposures, photographed landscapes and color tableaux. From 1974 to 1982 she restricted herself to black-and-white photography but there upon started to use Polaroid color material, creating collage-type photographs. In 1985 she worked with the Polaroid 50x60 camera for the first time.

Glinn, Burt
*1925, USA

41 Central Park West
New York, N.Y. 10023
USA

Während seines Harvard-Studiums fotografierte Burt Glinn 1946-49 für *Crimson* und lenkte damit die Aufmerksamkeit von *Life* auf sich. Er wurde Assistent bei *Life* und seit 1950 arbeitet er freiberuflich als Reportage-, Industrie-, und Werbefotograf, hauptsächlich in Farbe. Seine Reisereportagen über die Südsee, Japan, Mexiko, Rußland und Kalifornien füllten während der 60er Jahre ganze Ausgaben der Illustrierten *Holiday*; hinzu kamen politische Reportagen. Glinn war Präsident von *Magnum Photos*, New York.

At Harvard Burt Glinn was a photographer for *Crimson* during 1946-49, where he attracted the attention of *Life*, and began as a photographer's assistant to this magazine. Since 1950 he has been freelancing as a reportage, industrial and advertising photographer, mainly working in color. His travel reportages of the South Sea, Japan, Mexico, Russia and California, all done in the Sixties, filled complete issues of *Holiday* magazine. Additionally Glinn did reportages on polititcal subjects. He has been president of *Magnum*, New York.

Graffenried, Michael von
*1957, Schweiz

Junkerngasse 35
3011 Bern
Switzerland

Von Graffenried arbeitete 1979-80 als Assistent in einem Atelier für Werbefotografie, es folgten längere Reisen nach Indien und Kamerun. 1981 begann er seine Tätigkeit als Fotograf am Berner Stadttheater, hielt sich im folgenden Jahr zu Studienzwecken in den USA auf und arbeitet heute als freiberuflicher Fotograf für Zeitschriften im In- und Ausland. 1983 hatte er eine große Arbeit über die Schweiz begonnen, die demnächst als Buch erscheinen soll.

In 1979-80 Michael von Graffenried worked as an assistant in a commercial studio, which was followed by extensive trips to India and Cameroon. He started to work as a stage photographer at the theater in Bern in 1981, went to the U.S. the following year and since then has been working as a freelance photographer for magazines in Switzerland and abroad. Back in 1983 he began a large project on Switzerland, which will result in a book.

Graham, David
*1952, USA

Tyler State Park
Nr. 1 Lane trail, Richboro Rd.
Richboro, P.A. 18954
USA

Wuchs am Stadtrand von Philadelphia auf, in einer Umgebung, die so charakteristisch für den amerikanischen Mittelstand und so durchschnittlich war, daß seine Schwester in der TV-Dokumentation "The Typical Teenager" vorgestellt wurde. Das Soziologiestudium einerseits und die Fotografie andereseits brachten ihn dazu, seine Umgebung genauer und distanzierter zu betrachten. 1980 machte er den Master of Fine Arts in Fotografie an der *Tyler School of Art,* doch schon 1976 hatte er begonnen, die Fotografie als Ausdrucksmittel und zur Dokumentation einzusetzen. Und natürlich ist die amerikanische Kultur der Gegenstand seiner Farbfotografien.

David Graham grew up in the suburbs of Philadelphia, "smack in the middle of middle America". His surroundings were so average that his sister became the subject of a TV documentary, 'The Typical Teenager'. His sociological studies on the one hand and photography on the other, made him look more carefully and yet more objectively at things around him. In 1980 he took his M.F.A. at the *Tyler School of Art,* but already in 1976 he had begun to use photography as a means of expression and documentation. The subject of his color photography is, of course, American culture.

Graham, Paul
*1956, Großbritannien

14 Northwick House
1st Johns Wood Road
London NW 8 8RD
Great Britain

Als Fotograf Autodidakt begann Graham 1977 in Farbe zu fotografieren. Mit den Jahren wurden seine Fotografien zunehmend dokumentarischer. Sein erstes Buch hieß *A1 – The Great North Road* und 1986 erscheinen gleich zwei weitere Bücher von ihm, nämlich *Beyond Caring* über Arbeitslosigkeit in Großbritannien und *Troubled Land* über Nordirland. Zur Zeit arbeitet er an einem Projekt mit dem Titel *New Europe.*

Self taught in photography, Paul Graham started to work in color in 1977. With time his work became more and more documentary. His first monographic book was entitled *A1 – The Great North Road.* In 1986 he will publish two more photo books, *Beyond Caring* on unemployment in Great Britain and *Troubled Land* on Northern Ireland. Presently he is working on a large scale project, titled *New Europe.*

Grames, Eberhard
*1953, Deutschland

Wolfsboss 1
4193 Kranenburg
West-Germany

Studierte 1972-76 Kunstgeschichte und Völkerkunde in Köln, auf ausgedehnten Reisen nach Island, Griechenland und Tunesien entstanden die ersten Fotoessays in Farbe. Mehrfach besuchte er Japan und die USA. Seine Fotografien, die sich oft durch eine streng formale Komposition der Bildelemente auszeichnen, wurden, außer in Büchern, auch in den Illustrierten *Stern, GEO*, dem *Frankfurter Allgemeine Magazin* und anderen publiziert. Neben seinen Landschaftsaufnahmen im traditionellen Sinne wurden vor allem die nachts bei Neonlicht in den USA fotografierten Autos vor Motels und Restaurants bekannt.

Grames studied art history and ethology in Cologne between 1972 and 1976. On his extensive travels to Iceland, Greece and Tunesia, he produced his first photo essays in color. He also frequently visited Japan and the USA. His photographs which are distinguishable by their strong, formal composition, have been published in books and have appeared in magazines like *Stern, GEO*, the *Frankfurter Allgemeine Magazin*, etc. Besides his landscapes in color, photographed in classical style, Grames' images taken in the USA, of motorcars in front of motels and restaurants, photographed at night in neon-light, became particularly well-known.

Griese, Rainer
*1955, Deutschland

Frankfurter Str. 69
5210 Troisdorf
West-Germany

Griese studierte von 1978 bis 1983 Fotografie an der Fachhochschule in Köln, seit dem Examen ist er Meisterschüler von →Arno Jansen und 1986 erhielt er selbst in Köln einen Lehrauftrag. Im Rahmen einer Dozententätigkeit an der VHS Troisdorf gab er 1979 die Fotodokumentation *Troisdorf - Ansichten* einer Stadt heraus. Griese ist auf Stilleben spezialisiert, die er tont und koloriert; seit 1984 fotografiert er Stilleben und Personen meistens parallel in Schwarzweiß und Farbe.

Rainer Griese studied photography at the Technical College in Cologne under →Arno Jansen from 1978-83. He himself started lecturing in Cologne in 1986. Within the framework of a lectureship at the VHS Troisdorf, he published a photographic documentation on his hometown, Troisdorf in 1979. Griese specializes in still-life photography, which he tones and hand-colors. For the last two years he has been photographing still-life scenes and people, simultaneously in color and black-and-white.

Griffin, Brian
*1948, Großbritannien

121/123 Rotherhite Street
Rotherhite
London SE 16
Great Britain

Als ausgebildeter Ingenieur studierte Brian Griffin von 1969 bis 1972 an der *Manchester Polytechnic School of Photography.* Seit 1972 arbeitet er freiberuflich, er fotografierte etliche Punk and New Wave Gruppen für die Musikindustrie, er arbeitet für Werbeagenturen und zahlreiche Illustrierte. 1981 erschien sein zweites Buch *Power* - Porträts von Managern - und im Jahr zuvor hatte er sein eigenes Studio eröffnet, um die Aufnahmesituation noch besser kontrollieren zu können. Griffin zählt zu den meistgefragtesten Berufsfotografen in England; seine Arbeiten zeichnen zich durch die Betonung von Lichteffekten und surreale Anklänge aus.

Trained as a mechnical engineer, Brian Griffin studied photography at *Manchester Polytechnic School of Photography* 1969-72. From then on he worked as a freelance photographer. doing commercial work for the music industry, photographing several punk and new wave groups, and magazine work. In 1981 *Power*, Griffin's second book, was published in London. The year before he had established his own studio in order to gain even more control over the photographic setting. Griffin is one of the most popular professional photographers in England. His work demonstrates a feeling for lighting effects and he has a surrealistic touch.

Grignani, Franco
*1908, Italien

via B. di Savoia
20123 Milano
Italy

Seit 1932 ist Franco Grignani in Mailand tätig als Maler, Designer, Grafiker und Fotograf. Zwischen 1949 und 1964 arbeitete er als Art Direktor für Alfieri & Lacroix, den Verlag, der das Magazin *Bellezza d'Italia* herausgibt, und seit 1964 ist er Art Direktor der Editions Publicità in Mailand. Zu Beginn seiner fotografischen Tätigkeit befaßte sich Grignani mit Bewegungsunschärfen, dann folgte eine Periode von Untersuchungen zu optischen Verzerrungen. Später dann wandte sich Grignani Untersuchungen über die Spannung zwischen Form und Raum zu.

Since 1932 Franco Grignani has been active as a painter, designer, graphic artist and photographer in Milan. During 1948 to 1964 he served as the art director of the magazine *Bellezza d'Italia*, published by Alfieri & Lacroix. Since 1964 he has been art director for Editions Publicità in Milan. His work as a photographer started with the production of images with blurred effects, followed by a period of research on distortion. Later Grignani turned towards research into the tensions between form and space.

Grobet, Anne-Marie
*1943, Schweiz

311, route du Maudement
1281 Russin
Switzerland

1967, ein Jahr vor ihrem Studienabschluß in Kunstgeschichte, begann Anne-Marie Grobet in Farbe zu fotografieren. Bis 1972 setzte sie ihre Studien am *Institut des Hautes Etudes Internationales* in Genf fort, realisierte aber parallel Reisereportagen und arbeitete auch von Zeit zu Zeit als Assistentin von →Ernst Haas. 1972-77 fotografierte sie eine Dokumentation über verschiedene Schweizer Kantone für eine Publikationsreihe. Seit 1977 hat sie zahlreiche Reportagen für *GEO* und *Merian* fotografiert. Ihre Aufnahmen erschienen aber nicht nur in vielen in- und ausländischen Zeitschriften, sie wurden auch mit großem Erfolg auf Ausstellungen gezeigt.

In 1967, one year before Anne-Marie Grobet graduated in art history, she took up color Photography. She continued her studies at the *Institut des Hautes Etudes Internationales* in Geneva until 1972, but simultaneously did travel reportages and from time to time worked as an assistant to →Ernst Haas. Besides her reportages which she successfully continued, she did a documentation on various Swiss cantons for a series of publications. Since 1977 she has photographed many reportages for the German magazines *GEO* and *Merian*. Her work also appears in various Swiss and foreign magazines and her color photographs have been exhibited and well received.

Groover, Jan
*1943, USA

Jan Groover studierte Malerei am Pratt Institute und an der Ohio State University, wo sie 1970 den M.F.A. erhielt. Als Fotografin arbeitet sie seit 1971 und 1973 begann sie in Farbe zu fotografieren, wobei sie ihre Farbabzüge selbst anfertigt. Ihre Diptychen und Triptychen beschäftigen sich mit formalen und farblichen Veränderungen, hervorgerufen durch den zeitlichen Abstand zwischen den Aufnahmen. Nach dieser konzeptionellen Fotografie wandte sich Jan Groover dem Einzelfoto zu: Im Studio baut sie Stilleben auf, die mit der Großformatkamera abgelichtet werden.

Jan Groover studied painting at Pratt Institute and at Ohio State University, where she received her M.F.A. in 1970. Since 1971 she has been working as a freelance photographer. She started to use color Film in 1973 and from 1975 has done color printing herself. Her diptychs and triptychs are about changes in form and color generated by the time between the exposures. Following this conceptual work she switched to single image still lifes taken in her studio with a view camera.

Gundlach, F.C.
*1926, Deutschland

Feldstr. / Hochhaus 1
2000 Hamburg 4
West-Germany

F.C. Gundlach besuchte für zwei Jahre die Fotoschule Nehrdich in Kassel, anschließend absolvierte er seine Assistenzzeit in verschiedenen Studios. 1952 begann er mit der journalistschen Fotografie für Illustrierte mit dem Schwerpunkt Theater, Film und Starfotos. 1954 gründete er sein erste Studio und fotografierte Mode für *Film und Frau*. 1956 ließ er sich in Hamburg nieder und wurde ständiger Mitarbeiter verschiedener Modezeitschriften, vor allem arbeitet er nach wie vor für *Brigitte.* 1967 gründete er das 'Creative Color Labor' und 1975 die PPS Galerie. Im Frühjahr 1986 wurde in Bonn die Wanderausstellung *ModeWelten - F.C. Gundlach – Photographien 1950 bis heute* eröffnet. Zu dieser ersten Retrospektive auf Gundlachs Schaffen erschien ein gleichnamiges Buch.

Gundlach attended the Fotoschule Nehrdich in Kassel for two years. Then he worked as an assistant in various studios. In 1952 he started to work as a photo-journalist, mainly covering theater, film and star portraiture. In 1954 he founded his own studio and began to specialize in fashion, doing editorial work for *Film und Frau*. He settled in Hamburg in 1956 and became a regular contributor to various fashion magazines; nowadays he mainly works for *Brigitte*. He established the 'Creative Color Labor' in 1967 and 'PPS', a photo-gallery in 1975. In spring 1986 the touring exhibition *ModeWelten - F.C. Gundlach - Photographien 1950 bis heute* was opened in Bonn. This first major retrospective on Gundlach's work was published in book form.

Haas, Ernst
*1921, Österreich

857 Seventh Avenue
New York, N.Y. 10019
USA

Ursprünglich hatte Haas Medizin studiert, doch sich bald den visuellen Künsten verschrieben. Zwischen 1948 und 1950 arbeitete er als freier Fotograf in Paris und New York, begegnete Robert Capa, der ihn aufforderte, *Magnum* beizutreten. Bei einem Auftrag in der Wüste von Neu-Mexico fand Hans zu seiner Berufung: zur Farbe. Zur Zeit als noch kaum Farbseiten in Illustrierten erschienen, druckte *Life* auf 24 Seiten *Magic Images of New York* von Ernst Haas. Seine Bücher *Die Schöpfung* (1971), *In Amerika* (1975), *In Deutschland* (1976) erschienen stets in mehreren Ländern gleichzeitig.

Ernst Haas initially studied medicine, but switched to the visual arts in 1943. During 1948 to 1950 he worked as a freelance photographer in Paris and New York and duly met Robert Capa, who asked him to join *Magnum Photos.* Photographing on assignment in the New Mexico desert, Haas encountered the purpose of his life: color. At a time when color spreads hardly were to be seen in magazines, *Life* printed 24 pages of Haas's *Magic Images of New York*. His books *The Creation* (1971), *In America* (1975), *In Germany* (1976) (to name only his best known) were always published simultaneously in different countries.

Haggstrom-Wells, Carolina
*1956, Schweden

32 Florence St.
Annerley 4103, QLD
Australia

Ihre fotografische Ausbildung erhielt sie 1979-80 am Seven Hills College in Brisbane. Sie wurde dann Fotografin am La Boite Theater und seit 1981 arbeitet sie freiberuflich in Australien und Schweden. Die von ihr ausgestellte Arbeit ist Teil eines Projektes, bei dem sie von 1983 bis 1984 in verschiedenen australischen Regionen ihre persönlichen Eindrücke vom heutigen Leben der australischen Ureinwohner fotografisch festhielt.

Carolina Haggstrom-Wells studied photography at Seven Hills Art College in Brisbane from 1979 to 1980. Thereupon she became the house photographer of La Boit Theatre and since 1981 she has freelanced between Australia and Sweden. Her exhibited work is part of a project she realized during '83 and '84. She travelled around certain parts of Australia to record her personal impressions of the contemporary life of the Aboriginals with her camera.

Hahn, Betty
*1940, USA

Art Department
University of New Mexico
Albuquerque
New Mexico 87131
USA

1966 legte Betty Hahn ihren M.F.A. in Fotografie ab und besuchte dann den Unterricht von Nathan Lyons in Rochester. Seit 1976 ist sie Professor an der Universität in Albuquerque. Betty Hahn benutzte schon immer sehr unterschiedliche fotografische Techniken. Als ein roter Faden zieht sich durch ihre Arbeit das Interesse am amateurhaften Gebrauch von Fotografie, dem Fetischcharakter von Familienschnapp-schüssen. In ihren farbigen Edeldrucken und übermalten Fotografien sind Blumen das zweite wiederkehrende Thema. So auch in der Sofortbildserie *Botanical Layouts*, wo sie die Tradition von japanischen Drucken und naturwissenschaftlichen Pflanzendarstellungen reflektiert.

Betty Hahn received her M.F.A. in photography in 1966 and then attended the classes of Nathan Lyons in Rochester. Since 1976 she has been Professor of Photography at the University of Albuquerque. Betty Hahn always used a wide range of photographic processes and techniques. Her work remains coherent because of her interest in the amateur use of photography: the fetish character of family snapshots. In her large blue-and-brown prints painted excessively, flowers are the second recurring theme of her work. In her series of Polaroid-prints, *Botanical Layouts*, she reflects both the tradition of Japanese prints and botanical drawings.

Hambourg, Serge
*1936, Frankreich

Von 1959 bis 1978 arbeitete Hambourg als Fotograf in Paris: 1966-69 war er Redaktionsfotograf beim *Nouvel Observateur*, 1972-78 angestellt bei der Zeitung *Le Figaro*, zwischenzeitlich war er in der Werbung aktiv. Seit 1978 arbeitet er freiberuflich in New York. Als gemeinsames Element seiner freien Arbeiten zeigt sich die Freude, gewönliche Dinge auf ungewöhnliche Weise zu sehen. Mit seinem Gefühl für Licht gelingt es ihm, die seltsame Atmosphäre herauszuarbeiten, die auf sonst stark belebten Plätzen herrscht, wenn gerade keine Menschen anwesend sind.

From 1959 until 1978 Hambourg worked in Paris. He was staff photographer for the *Nouvel Observateur* 1966-69 and for *Le Figaro* 1972-78. In between he got involved with advertising photography and produced TV-spots. Since 1978 he lives and works as an independent photographer in New York. Consistent in his work is his sense of pleasure in seeing ordinary things in usual ways. His special feeling for light enhances the desolate atmospheres of busy places at very quite times. The absence of people is a very important element in Hambourg's photographs.

Hamilton, David
*1933, Großbritannien

Hamilton absolvierte bei der Zeitschrift *Elle* in Paris eine Ausbildung zum Grafiker und Typografen. In London wurde er Art Direktor von *Queen* und arbeitete dann, wieder in Paris, bei dem Warenhaus Printemps. 1966 etablierte er sich als Berufsfotograf in Paris und publizierte Aufnahmen in *Twen, Réalités, Vogue, Playboy, Esquire* usw. In den 70er Jahren wurde Hamilton weltweit bekannt als Fotograf gesofteter Aufnahmen sehr junger Mädchen. Diese Fotos fanden Verbreitung in Büchern, auf Postkarten und Postern. Im gleichen Stil drehte er auch zwei Filme (*Bilitis* und *Laura Moore*). Etwas weniger populär wurden seine Stilleben-Fotografien.

David Hamilton underwent a training in graphic design and typography with the magazine *Elle* in Paris. Back in London he served as art director to *Queen* magazine, and later in Paris again, he worked for the department store, Printemps. He established himself as a freelance photographer in Paris in 1966 and since then his pictures have been published in various magazines such as *Twen, Réalités, Vogue, Playboy, Esquire*. In the 70's Hamilton became famous for his softened color photographs of very young girls; these images were printed in books, on postcards and posters. In the same style he also photographed two motion pictures (*Bilitis* and *Laura Moore*). Less known than his photographs of girls, are Hamilton's still lifes.

Hammarskjöld, Hans
*1925, Schweden

7 Östermalmsgatan
11424 Stockholm
Sweden

1950 begann Hammarskjöld seine Karriere als freier Fotograf, indem er Mode und Fotossays für schwedische Illustrierte fotografierte. 1955-56 gehörte er zum Fotografenstab von *Vogue* und *House and Garden* in London. Wieder in Schweden wurde er 1958, im Jahr der Gründung, Mitglied der Gruppe *Tio*. Zu dieser Zeit war Hammarskjöld bekannt für seine strengen Schwarzweißaufnahmen im Sinne der "Subjektive Fotografie", er fotografierte aber auch weiterhin, bis 1968, Fotoessays, Food und Stillife, Porträts und Industrieaufnahmen. 1968 stellte er seine erste Audiovisonsschau zusammen und begann auch in Farbe zu fotografieren, hauptsächlich Natur. Diese Aufnahmen verwendet er wiederum in seinen Diashows, die er nach wie vor zusammenstellt.

Hammarskjöld started his career as a freelance photographer in 1950, photographing fashion and picture stories for Swedish magazines. During 1955-56 he was on the staff of *Vogue* and *House and Garden* in London. Back in Sweden he joined the group *Tio* when it was founded in 1958. At that time Hammarskjöld was known for his black-and-white photographs of graphic strength, which were part of the 'Subjektive Fotografie' exhibitions, but he also continued to do photo essays, food-shots, still-life, and portrait and industrial photography until 1968, when he presented his first audio-visual show. At the end of the 1960's he also started to work in color, mainly studies of nature. These photographs are to be seen in the slide shows he continues to produce.

Hansen, Hans
*1940, Deutschland

Winckelmannstr. 2
2000 Hamburg 52
West-Germany

Nach einer Lithografenlehre absolvierte Hans Hansen bei Walter Breker an der Düsseldorfer Kunstakademie eine Ausbildung zum Grafiker. Seit 1962 ist er als Fotodesigner selbständig und seit 1967 hat er im Hamburg ein Atelier. Er machte sich einen Namen für seine Aufnahmen von Autos, die er heute nur noch selten fotografiert. Seine Kunden sind Firmen mit einheitlichen Produktlinien und für den *Stern* fotografiert er auch Mode oder "Food". Hansen ist nicht nur ein Lichtbildner, er ist auch Virtuose im Umgang mit dem Licht.

Following an apprenticeship as a lithographer, Hans Hansen studied graphics under Walter Breker at the Art Academy in Düsseldorf. Since 1962 he has been working as a photo-designer and has had a studio in Hamburg since 1967. He is well-known for his photographs of cars, which he nowadays seldom does. His clients are corporations with unique product lines. For the Magazine *Stern* he also does fashion and food photography. Hansen is a true master in his use of light.

Hanson, David T.
*1948, USA

Hanson schloß 1970 sein Englisch-Studium an der Stanford Universität ab und studierte dan bis 1983 Fotografie an der Rhode Island School of Design. Bevor er seine Colstrip Serie begann, fotografierte er in der Wildnis und bewegte sich immer näher an den Rand der Zivilisation. Bei der Colstrip Serie befaßte er sich erstmals mit sozialen Zusammenhängen und der menschlichen Unwelt.

David Taverner Hanson received his B.A. in English literature from Stanford University, (1970) and his M.F.A. in Photography from the Rhode Island School of Design, Rhode Island (1983). Prior to beginning the Colstrip series, Hanson produced wilderness photographs and gradually moved closer and closer to the edge of civilization. At Colstrip he discovered for the first time a way to address larger social and environmental issues.

Harder, Burkhard von
*1954, Deutschland

Mittelweg 31 c
2000 Hamburg 13
West-Germany

Harder fotografiert seit seinem achten Lebensjahr und erhielt bereits als Elfjähriger seine erste Auszeichnung. 1969 war er der jüngste Bundessieger beim Deutschen Jugendfotopreis und 1973 hatte er die erste Veröffentlichung in dem Jahrbuch *Das Deutsche Lichtbild*. Nach dem Abitur reiste er sechs Monate lang durch Asien, absolvierte dann ein soziales Jahr in den USA. Nach Ausflügen zum Film und zum Theater hörte er bei Willy Fleckhaus und arbeitet nun seit 1984 als freier Fotograf.

Burkhard von Harder took his first photographs at the age of eight and when he was eleven years old, he won his first award. In 1969 he was the youngest winner of the photokina competition for young photographers and he had his first promotion in *The German Photo Annual* in 1973. After his final school examination he travelled through Africa for six months and thereafter spent a year in the United States. Following a period of working experience in film and theater, Harder attended the lectures of Willy Fleckhaus and finally started to work as a freelance photographer in 1984.

Haskins, Sam
*Süd-Afrika

9A Calonne Road
London SW 19
Great-Britain

Studierte Grafik an der Technischen Hochschule in Johannesburg. 1947-50 folgte eine Ausbildung in Fotografie an der Bolt Court School in London. Seitdem arbeitet er als freiberuflicher Buch-, Mode- und Werbefotograf in London, wo er Haskins Studio und Haskins Press gründete. 1962 erschien sein erstes Buch mit Aktfotografien (*Five Girls*), sein zweites, *Cowboy Kate* (1964) war das erste Fotobuch, das eine erotische Bildergeschichte enthielt. Es folgten *African Image* (1966), in dem er alte Idole mit dem Leben der eingeborenen Südafrikaner kontrastiert, *Haskins Posters* (1972) und *Photographics* (1980).

Sam Haskins studied graphic art at the Technical College in Johannesburg and photography at Bolt Court School, London, 1947-50. Since then he has been involved in freelance publishing and fashion and advertising photography in London, where he established Haskins Studio and Haskins Press. His first book of nude studies, titled *Five Girls* appeared in 1962 followed by *Cowboy Kate* (1964), the first erotic photographic story book. *African Image* published in 1966 is a portrait of ancient idols in sharp contrast with the lives of black South African natives. Particularly popular were *Haskins Posters* (1972) and *Photographics* (1980).

Häusser, Robert
*1924, Deutschland

Ladenburgerstr. 23
6800 Mannheim 31
West-Germany

Besuchte 1941-42 die Grafische Fachschule in Stuttgart. Nach dem Krieg lebte er bis 1952 auf dem Bauernhof seiner Eltern in der Mark Brandenburg und fotografierte dort das Leben der Landbevölkerung. 1950 machte er seine Meisterprüfung an der Meisterschule für Handwerk und Kunst in Weimar bei →Walter Hege. 1952 übersiedelte er nach Mannheim, wo er ein Fotostudio gründete. Er veröffentlichte Bücher, das erste 1957 über Mannheim, und unternahm ab 1964 zahlreiche Reisen als Fotojournalist. 1972 gab er sein Studio weitgehend auf, um sich intensiver seiner freien künstlerischen Arbeit widmen zu können. Seine kontrastreichen, grafischen Prinzipien folgenden Aufnahmen machten ihn zu einem Klassiker der modernen Fotografie in Deutschland.

Robert Häusser attended the Graphic Technical College in Stuttgart, 1941-42. After the war he lived on his parent's farm and photographed the life of the country folk. In 1950 he received a degree from the Meisterschule für Handwerk und Kunst in Weimar under →Walter Hege. In 1952 he moved to Mannheim, established a studio and started to publish books. From 1964 on he travelled extensively as a photo-reporter. Then in 1972 he more or less abandoned commercial work to concentrate on his artistic photography. His contrasting, graphic style of photography, makes him one of the classicists of modern German photography.

Haxton, David
*1943, USA

Schon als Junge erlernte Haxton die Technik der Farbfotografie von seinem Vater, einem Berufsfotografen. Als kreative Tätigkeit verstand er die Fotografie jedoch erst, nachdem er 1969 von der Malerei zum Film gewechselt hatte. Seine Filme wurden u.a. im Museum of Modern Art und in der Sonnabend Galerie in New York gezeigt. Die Fotografien entstehen auf den Sets der Filme, bei geringer Beleuchtung, wodurch bei der Großformatkamera lange Belichtungszeiten notwendig werden, die wiederum eine hohe Farbsättigung hervorrufen.

As a boy, David Haxton was taught the technical aspects of color photography by his father, a commercial photographer. Haxton did not understand photography as a creative process, until after he switched from painting to film-making in 1969. His films have been screened in the Museum of Modern Art and the Sonnabend Gallery, both in New York City. Haxton's photographs are derived from the sets and decorations left over from his films. His photos were primarily shot in low light situations, which necessitated a long exposure time resulting in high color saturation.

Hayasaki, Osamu
*1933, Japan

Iikura Central Bldg. 5F
3-1-2-Azabudai, Minato-ku
Tokyo 106
Japan

Gewann bereits 1955 einen Preis auf dem World Student Photo Festival in Warschau und beendete im folgenden Jahr das Studium and der Ritsumeikan Universität. 1957 wurde er Fotograf bei der Light Publicity Company, bei der er bis 1964 arbeitete. 1965 gründete er ein eigenes Studio und seit 1973 leitete er zahlreiche Kampagnen als Art Direktor. 1975 publizierte er sein Buch *Wie man Werbefotos macht*. Gegenwärtig lehrt er an der Aichi Kunsthochschule.

Osamu Hayasaki won a Grand Prix at the Student Photo Festival in Warsaw in 1955 and graduated from Ritsumeikan University the following year. In 1957 he joined the Light Publicity Company, where he worked until 1964. He established his own studio in 1965 and since 1973 he has been the Art Director of a great many campaigns. His book on how to take advertising photographs was published in 1975 and presently he is teaching at the Aichi Art College.

Hege, Walter
*1893, Deutschland
† 1955, DDR

Hege erlernte die Porträtfotografie bei Hugo Erfurth in Dresden und besuchte dann dort die Kunstgewerbeschule. Ab 1923 arbeitete er als Fotograf und spezialisierte sich auf die Abbildung von Plastiken und Architekturfotografie. 1942 erschien sein Bildband über den Naumburger Dom und 1926 das Buch über den Dom in Bamberg. In Auftrag des Metropolitan Museums in New York fotografierte Hege 1928 die Akropolis und ihre Tempel. 1930 bis 1935 war er Professor an der Kunstschule in Weimar, anschließend realisierte er zahlreiche bedeutende Kulturfilme und experimentierte außerdem mit der Farbfotografie.

Walter Hege studied portrait photography with Hugo Erfurth and attended the School of Arts and Crafts in Dresden. In 1923 Hege started his career as a photographer, specializing both in the reproduction of sculptures and architectural photography. In 1924 his picture book on the Naumburger Dom appeared, followed in 1926 by his book on the cathedral in Bamberg. Commissioned by the Metropolitan Museum, New York, Hege photographed the Acropolis and its temple in 1928. During 1930 to 1935 he was a professor at the art school in Weimar. Following that period he produced a number of important cultural films and he also experimented with color photography.

Heinecken, Robert
*1913, USA

Seit Robert Heinecken 1960 sein Studium abschloß, ist er Professor am Fachbereich Kunst der Universität in Los Angeles. In den 60er Jahren benutzte Heinecken Fotos aus Illustrierten als Ausgangsmaterial, in der Mitte der 70er Jahre dann Softpornofotografien, die er übermalte, vervielfachte oder übereinanderkopierte. Erst gegen Ende der 70er Jahre begann er selbst zu fotografieren und stellte SX-70 Polaroid fotos her, die er mit Texten versah und ähnlich wie italienische Fotoromane zusammenstellte. Heinecken arbeitet weiterhin an seinen Untersuchungen über die Grenze zwischen dem Realen und dem Bild.

Since Robert Heinecken graduated from University in 1960 he has been Professor at the art department of Los Angeles University. In the Sixties Heinecken used magazine photos as the basis for his work. In the mid-Seventies he switched to soft-pornographic photographs on which he painted, used in collage, copied and overprinted. By the end of the 70's he started to do photography himself, producing a series of SX-70 prints, accompanied by short texts and arranged like Italian photo novels. Heinecken still continues his research based on the frontier between the real thing and the image.

Heitmann, Adriano
*1951, Schweiz

Case Postale 59
6855 Stabio
Switzerland

Heitmann begann 1971 als Autodidakt zu fotografieren. Da er sich für Bewegung interessiert, fotografierte er Sportereignisse, insbesondere Ski- und Autorennen. 1974 gelang es ihm, als Amateur in die auflangenstärkste Illustrierte der Schweiz, *L'Illustré*, zu kommen und zwar mit Fotos von der Ski-Weltmeisterschaft in St. Moritz. Seitdem arbeitet Heitmann sehr erfolgreich als Reportagefotograf. 1980 realisierte er das erste freie Projekt: Er fuhr nach Mexiko, auf der Suche nach surrealen Motiven für seine Farbfotografien. 1985, nach mehreren weiteren Aufenthalten dort, erschien dann *Le Mexique Aujourd'hui* in der Schweiz als Buch. 1986 war er schon wieder in Mexiko: Er fotografierte die Fußballweltmeisterschaft.

In 1971 Adriano Heitmann began to teach himself photography. Because he likes movement, he photographs sports events, particularly skiing and car races. In 1974 he switched from an amateur to a professional photographer by selling his pictures taken at the World Skiing Campionships in St. Moritz to *L'Illustré*, the best-selling Swiss magazine. Heitmann worked successfully as a photo journalist and in 1980 started his first personal project, travelling to Mexico in search of subject matter for his color photography. He visited this country frequently and finally in 1985 the book *Le Mexique Aujourd'hui* was published in Switzerland. In 1986 he again visited Mexico to cover the FIFA World Cup 1986.

Helg, Beatrice
*1956, Schweiz

19, rue Général – Dufour
1204 Geneva
Switzerland

Beatrice Helg studierte Fotografie in den USA und 1978 fotografierte sie auf dem First Festival of American Mime in Milwaukee. Sie arbeitete dann in den Abteilungen für Ausstellungen und Unterricht am International Center of Photography (ICP) in New York, für die *Venezia '79 – la Fotografia* und bei Robert Delpire in Paris. 1980 richtete sie in Genf ein Studio ein. Nach längeren Untersuchungen zu menschlichen Gesichtsausdrücken, beschäftigt sie sich nun mit dem Stilleben. Dafür benutzt sie auch Polaroid Material oder fertigt ihre Cibachrome-Abzüge selbst an.

Beatrice Helg studied photography in the States and in 1978 she photographed the first Festival of Mime in Milwaukee. During an internship at the ICP in New York she worked in the exhibition and education departments. She also worked for the international biennial *Venezia '79 – la Fotografia* in Venice, Italy, and with Robert Delpire in Paris, France. In 1980 she settled in Geneva where she installed her studio. After several years of research on human facial expressions, she is now involved with still life photography, using Polaroid color film or doing Cibachrome printing herself.

Helm, Hartmut
*1954, Deutschland

Ottostr. 7a
8600 Bamberg
West-Germany

Der angehende Zahnmediziner Hartmut Helm ist als Fotograf Autodidakt. 1970 fing er an, ernsthaft zu fotografieren und er benutzte von Anfang an Farbfilm. Spezialisiert hat er sich auf Sportfotografie und da wiederum auf Formel 1 Autorennen. Es geht ihm weniger um die aktuelle Berichterstattung, als vielmehr um die Darstellung der Dynamik des Motorsports, um die Ästhetik des Technischen.

Hartmut Helm, who is about to become a dentist, taught himself photography. He began to photograph seriously in 1970, using color material right from the start. He specializes in sports and is especially interested in Formula 1 car rallies. He is less concerned with actual news reporting than with the dynamics of motor sports and technical aesthetics.

Helmer-Petersen, Keld
*1920, Dänemark

Kristianiagade 14
2100 Kopenhagen
Denmark

Studierte 1938-39 Englisch am Trinity College in Cambridge und machte dort seine ersten Fotos. 1940 folgten die ersten Aufnahmen in Farbe. Bereits 1949 publizierte er in Kopenhagen ein Buch mit 122 Farbaufnahmen, aus dem *Life* sechs Seiten abdruckte. 1950-51 besuchte er den Fotounterricht von →Harry Callahan in Chicago. Mit seinen streng grafischen Schwarzweißfotos nahm er 1955 an der von Otto Steinert in Saarbrücken organisierten Ausstellung *Subjektive Fotografie 2* teil. Auch für seine Farbfotografien wählt er selbst die Begriffe "puristisch" und "formalistisch". Seit 1964 lehrt er im Bereich Visuelle Kommunikation an der Königlichen Kunstakademie in Kopenhagen.

Keld Helmer-Petersen studied English at Trinity College Cambridge and it was there that he took his first photographs. In 1940 he started working in color and by 1949 he published a book, *122 Color Photographs*, from which *Life* printed six pages. From 1950-51 he studied with →Harry Callahan in Chicago. With his severely graphic black & white work he participated in the exhibition, *Subjective Fotografie 2* curated by Otto Steinert in 1955 in Saarbrücken. Also his color photographs were, as he himself put it, 'puristic' and 'formalistic'. Since 1964 Helmer-Petersen has been teaching at the Department of Visual Communication of the Royal Academy of Arts in Copenhagen.

Henle, Fritz
*1909, Deutschland

P.O. Box 723
Christiansted, St. Croix.
US Virgin Islands 00820
USA

Erhielt 1931 sein Diplom als Fotograf nach einer einjährigen Ausbildung bei Hanna Seewald in München. 1931-33 fotografierte er die Landschaft und Architektur Italiens, hauptsächlich die von Florenz. Als Werbefotograf für eine italienische Schiffahrtslinie reiste er nach Indien, China und Japan. 1936 emigrierte er in die USA (wurde 1942 naturalisiert) und arbeitete bis 1941 im Auftrag von *Life*. Nach dem Krieg fotografierte er für *Harper's Bazaar*, war dann 1952-59 unter Vertrag bei der City Service Oil Company, New York, und ließ sich schließlich mit einem eigenen Studio auf den Virgin Islands nieder. Henle publizierte eine ganze Reihe von Büchern, darunter viele über Rollei Kameras, was ihm den Spitznamen "Mr. Rolleiflex" einbrachte.

Henle Studied briefly with Hanna Seewald in Munich and received his diploma as a photographer in 1931. 1931-33 he photographed the landscape and architecture of Italy, mainly of Florence. Hired as a promotion photographer by an Italian shipping line, this job led him to India, China and Japan. In 1936 he emigrated to U.S. (naturalized in 1941) and was commissioned by *Life* until he left in 1941. After WW II he photographed for *Harper's Bazaar*. During 1952 to 59 he joined the photographers of the City Service Oil Company, New York. Finally he established himself as a freelance photographer and studio owner on the Virgin Islands. He published a lot of books, including several ones on Rollei Cameras, which earned him the nickname 'Mr. Rolleiflex'.

Hennig, Alfred
*1905, Schlesien

Postfach 120 142
5300 Bonn 12
West-Germany

Hennig war zehn Jahre lang, bis 1945, als technischer Leiter bei der Agfa in Berlin für die Farbentwicklung zuständig. Als Bonn 1949 zur Bundeshauptstadt erklärt wurde, zog Hennig dorthin und wurde "Adenauers Fotograf". Er setzte, als Pionier auf diesem Gebiet, die Farbfotografie für Pressezwecke ein und gründete eine Color Umkehr- und Kopieranstalt, der er die "Color Press", einen Farbpressedienst, angliederte. Seit den 50er Jahren hat Alfred Hennig die politische Ereignisse in Bonn in Farbfotografien dokumentiert.

For a decade, until 1945, Alfred Henning was technical director, responsible for the development of color film with Agfa in Berlin. When Bonn became the capital of West-Germany in 1949, he moved to that city and became 'Adenauer's photographer'. He was a pioneer in the field of color photography for press and public relations purposes. He established a color laboratory and thereupon the 'Color Press', an color photo press service. Since the 1950's Alfred Hennig has documented political happenings in Bonn in Color photography.

Hensch, Peter
*1956, Deutschland

Ludwig-Richter-Str. 11b
5300 Bonn 1
West-Germany

Machte nach der Realschule eine Lehre als Bauzeichner und arbeitet heute als Bautechniker bei einer Behörde in Bonn. Seit 1980 ist er Hobbyfotograf. 1981 gründete er mit anderen Amateuren den Fotoclub *Fotoforum Bonn*, der sich 1985 wieder auflöste, und wurde Mitglied im VDAV. Hensch, der vorzugsweise Menschen und Landschaften in Schwarzweiß und Farbe fotografiert, gewann mit seinen Aufnahmen bereits mehrere Auszeichnungen, u.a. bei der "Blende 82", "Blende 84" und den ersten Preis bei der "Blende 85".

Peter Hensch finished his schooling and then did a training in construction design and up until the present day still works as a construction technician with the Bonn authorities. He became a hobby photographer in 1981 and together with other amateurs started the *Fotoforum Bonn* which existed until 1985. Hensch, who is primarily involved with people and landscapes and photographs in black & white and color, has already been awarded a number of prizes at contests like 'Blende 82', 'Blende 84' as well as the first prize at 'Blende 85'.

Herz, Rudolf ("Waggi")
*1954, Deutschland

Kiliansplatz 6
8000 München 2
West-Germany

Der bisher unter dem Namen Waggi Herz ausstellende Künstler studierte 1975 bis 1980 an der Akademie der Bildenden Künste in München. 1980 legte er das Staatsexamen für das Lehramt ab, 1981 erhielt er sein Bildhauer-Diplom. Zwischen 1977 und 1981 zeigte er in München verschiedene Installationen. In seine inszenierten Farbfotografien bezieht er sein Interesse an der plastischen Gestaltung ein. Mit Dirk Halfbrodt gab er das Buch *München 1918-1919 – Novemberrevolution und Räterepublik in Dokumentarfotografien* heraus.

The artist, who in the past exhibit under the name of Waggi Herz, attended the academy of fine arts in Munich form 1975-80. In 1980 he passed his examination as a teacher and in 1981 he received a diploma as a sculptor. Between 1977 and 1981 he exhibited various installations in Munich. His staged color photographs obviously refer to his interest in sculpture. He was the co-publisher of a book of documentary photographs of the November Revolution in Munich 1918/19.

Hidalgo, Francisco
*1929, Spanien

Hidalgo wollte eigentlich Maler werden, scheiterte aber an seinem Perfektionismus und ging 1953 nach Paris, wo er zehn Jahre lang als Kameramann beim Fernsehen arbeitete. Er unternahm dann selbstfinanzierte Fotoreisen. Seine Fotos aus drei Kontinenten hatten auf Anhieb Erfolg, denn sie sind ungewöhnlich: Bei der Aufnahme selbst erzeugt Hidalgo Verwischungen und Farbeffekte, die seinen Eindruck von dem Motiv, meist sind es Stadtlandschaften, wiedergeben sollen.

Francisco Hidalgo intended to become a painter, but failed because of his own perfectionism. Instead he went to Paris in 1953 and worked as a TV-cameraman for a decade. He then undertook photo travels, financed by himself. His pictures, taken on three continents, were successful from the start, because they are so unusual. During exposure, Hidalgo creates blurrs and color effects, which reflect his impression of the subject, mainly being cityscapes.

Hilgering, Reinhold Ludwig
*1942, Deutschland

Weissenburger Str. 12
8000 München 80
West-Germany

Nach dem Abitur und einem Industriepraktikum studierte Hilgering von 1964 bis 1969 Industrie-Design an der Folkwangschule in Essen. Danach arbeitete er als Industrie-Designer in München. Während des Studiums hatte Hilgering begonnen, sich mit der Fotografie zu beschäftigen und seit 1969 entstehen freie fotografische Arbeiten, die seit 1979 auf mehreren Ausstellungen gezeigt wurden.

Following his higher education and an industrial-apprenticeship, Reinhold Ludwig Hilgering studied industrial design at the Folkwang-schule in Essen from 1964-69. Thereafter he worked as an industrial designer in Munich. During his studies Hilgering developed his interest in photography and since 1969 he has realized several personal photographic projects, which have been shown in numerous exhibitions.

Hinz, Hans
*1913, Deutschland

Postfach 60
4123 Allschwil 2
Switzerland

Hinz machte schon 1934 erste Versuche zur Herstellung von Dreifarbenfotos auf Papier. Während eines Volontariats als Fotolithograf entstanden dann Farbaufnahmen von Glasfenstern in französischen Kathedralen, die in einem Buch veröffentlicht wurden. Seit 1937 arbeitet Hans Hinz als selbständiger Farbfotograf, zuerst in Zürich, dann in Basel. Er hat sich auf das Fotografieren von Kunstwerken spezialisiert, machte aber auch bis 1977 Werbefotos in seinem 1941 in Basel gegründeten Studio. Hinz arbeitet weiterhin eng mit dem Kunstmuseum in Basel zusammen und fotografiert nach wie vor Kunstwerke im In- und Ausland.

As early as 1934 Hans Hinz started his first experiments in color photography, using carbro and other early printing processes. During his apprenticeship as a photo lithographer, he photographed the lead-glass windows of French cathedrals, which resulted in a book. Since 1937 Hinz has been active as a color photographer, first in Zurich, then in Basle. He specialized in the photographing of works of art, but also did advertising work in the studio he maintained in Basle from 1941-1977. He still continues his close collaboration with the art museum in Basle and photographs works of art in various countries.

Hiro
(Yashuhiro Wakabayashi)
*1930, China

50 Central Park West
New York, N.Y. 10023
USA

Als Sohn japanischer Eltern wuchs Hiro in China und Japan auf. 1949 machte er seinen Abschluß an der Highschool in Tokio und zog dann 1954 nach New York, wo er bald darauf Assistent von Richard Avedon wurde und von 1957 bis 1971 Teilhaber des Avedon Studios war. Hiro arbeitete auch mit Alexey Brodovitch zusammen und begann 1958 für *Harper's Bazaar* zu fotografieren. Zwischen 1966 und 1974 arbeitete er exklusiv für diese Zeitschrift. Seit 1981 ist er unter Vertrag bei Condé Nast. Hiros Mode-, Werbe- und Porträtaufnahmen zeichnen sich durch klares Design und den meisterhaften Einsatz der Farbe aus.

Son of Japanese parents, Hiro grew up in China and Japan. He graduated from High School in Tokyo in 1949 and moved to new York in 1954, where he later worked as an assistant to Richard Avedon and during 1957 to 1971 was a partner in the Avedon Studio. Hiro also worked with Alexey Brodovitch and began photographing for *Harper's Bazaar* in 1958. Between 1966 and 1974 he worked exclusively for that magazine. Hiro has been under contract with Condé Nast publications since 1981. His fashion, still life and portrait work is of serene design and Hiro is a true master of color photography.

Hockney, David
*1937, England

Hockney wurde weltweit bekannt als Maler, Zeichner und für seine Druckgrafiken. Seit Anfang der 60er Jahre verfaßt er aber auch mit der Kamera eine Art Tagebuch. Die Schnappschüsse von Reisen, Freunden, Eltern, dem Atelier, sammelt er in Alben an. Diese Erinnnerungsfotos verraten jedoch deutlich das geschulte Auge des Künstlers und wurden inzwischen weltweit ausgestellt. Zusätzlich benutzt Hockney die Fotografie als künstlerisches Ausdrucksmittel, indem er Motive und Bewegungsabläufe in zahlreichen Einzelfotos festhält und sie anschließend collageartig zusammenfügt. So entstanden z.B. riesige Tableaus aus SX-70 Fotos, deren weißen Ränder das Bild wie mit einem Raster überziehen.

Hockney has earned himself worldwide recognition for his paintings, drawings and lithographs. Since the early Sixties he has kept a photographic diary of his private life. His pictures of friends, his parents, his studio and his travels are collected in albums. These private images, manifest the trained eye of an artist, however, and have already been widely exhibited. Hockney furthermore uses photography as a means of artistic expression, by capturing subjects and movements in numerous single prints and then assembling them. An example of this is the large tableaux he has created from SX-70 prints, the white borders of which seem to form a pattern across the work.

Hoepffner, Marta
*1912, Deutschland

Eichendorfweg 56-58
7993 Kressbronn/Bodensee
West-Germany

Marta Hoepffner studierte von 1929 bis 1933 an der Kunstschule in Frankfurt bei Willi Baumeister. Mit dem Beginn des Naziregimes gab sie die Malerei auf und wandte sich fotografischen Experimenten zu: Sie realisierte Fotogemälde, Mehrfachbelichtungen, Fotogramme, Solarisationen, Stillebenkompositionen und Porträts. 1948 entstanden erste Interferenzbilder in polarisiertem Licht und zehn Jahre später die ersten Farbfotogramme in polarisiertem Licht. Seitdem spezialisierte sich Marta Hoepffner auf kameralose Fotografien und kinetische Objekte. Von 1949 bis 1971 leitete sie in Hofheim/Taunus eine private Fotoschule und seit Anfang der 70er Jahre lebt und arbeitet sie am Bodensee. 1982, zu ihrem 70. Geburtstag, fanden mehrere große Retrospectiven auf ihr Werk statt.

From 1929 to 1933 Marta Hoepffner studied avantgarde art under Willi Baumeister in Frankfurt. Under the Nazi regime she abandoned painting and turned to creative photographic experiments: photo-paintings, multiple exposures, photograms, solarizations, still life composition and portraiture. In 1948 she worked on her first interference photograms employing polarized light. A decade later she created her first color photograms in polarized light and has worked with lensless photography and lightkinetics ever since. During 1949 to 1971 she maintained a private photographic school in Hofheim/Taunus and she has lived and worked at Lake Constance since the early 70's. In 1982 her seventieth birthday was celebrated with several major retrospectives on her work.

Hollander, Paul den
*1950, Niederlande

Haagweg 386
Breda
The Netherlands

Als Dreizehnjähriger kaufte er seine erste Kamera und von 1986 bis 1973 studierte er an der St. Joost Kunstakademie in Breda. 1975/76 unternahm er Reisen in den Nahen und Fernen Osten und ließ sich dann als Fotograf in Breda nieder. Noch im selben Jahr, 1976, hatte er seine erste Einzelausstellung. Bis 1981 entstanden dann die Aufnahmen zu dem Portfolio *Moments in Time*, seit 1982 fotografiert Paul den Hollander in Botanischen Gärten und Zoos. Er erhielt mehrere Einladungen im Ausland zu fotografieren, u.a. nach Neapel, Dubrovnik, Capri und nach Südfrankreich.

Paul den Hollander bought his first camera at the age of thirteen, and studied at St. Joost Fine Arts Academy in Breda 1968-73. Before he set himself up as a photographer in Breda, he travelled the Near and Far East during 1975/76. Between 1977 and 1981 he produced the pictures for the portfolio *Moments in Time*, and since 1982 he has worked on a series photographed in botanical and zoological gardens. He received a number of invitations to photograph abroad, e.g. in Naples, Capri, Dubrovnik and in the South of France.

Holleley, Douglas
*1949, Australien

Rockcorry
Woodford 2778 NSW
Australia

Arbeitete 1969-73 als Fotograf für verschiedene Lehrbuchverlage und machte gleichzeitig 1971 seinen Abschluß in Psychologie an der Macquarie Universität in Sydney. 1974-76 studierte er am Visual Studies Workshop in Rochester, USA. 1978 fotografierte er im Süden und Südwesten der USA und hielt zahlreiche Workshops ab. Seit 1979 fotografiert und lehrt er in Australien.

Douglas Holleley worked as a photographer for various educational publishers between 1970-73 and graduated in Psychology at Macquarie University in Sydney in 1971. He commenced graduate studies at the Visual Studies Workshop, Rochester from 1974 until he received his M.F.A. in 1976. In 1978 he photographed extensively in south and south-west America, lecturing at lots of workshops. Since 1979 he has been photographing and lecturing in Australia.

Höpker, Thomas
*1936, Deutschland

250 East 63rd Street
New York, N.Y. 10021
USA

1950 machte er seine ersten Fotos mit einer alten Plattenkamera, 1956-59 studierte er Kunstgeschichte und Ärcheologie in Göttingen und München. 1960 begann er als Fotoreporter zu arbeiten, zunächst für die *Münchner Illustrierte*, ab 1962 für *Kristall*. Seit 1964 fotografiert er für den *Stern* – Auslands reportagen. 1974 ging er zusammen mit seiner Frau, der Journalistin Eva Höpker-Windmöller, für zwei Jahre als Korrespondent nach Ost-Berlin, 1976 zogen dann beide als Korrespondenten nach New York. 1978 wurde Höpker stellvertretender Chefredakteur (Bild) der amerikanischen Ausgabe von *GEO*, 1981 gab er diese feste Stellung auf, um wieder freiberuflich für den *Stern* und *GEO* zu fotografieren.

Thomas Hopker took his first photographs with an old box camera. From 1956-59 he studied Art History and Archeology in Gottingen and Munich. Then in 1960 he started out as a photo-reporter, first for the *Münchner Illustrierte* and later for *Kristall*. Since 1964 he has been doing foreign reportages for the magazine, *Stern*. Together with his wife, the journalist, Eva Höpker-Windmöller, he moved to East Berlin, where they both worked as correspondents. In 1976 these two journalists went on to New York and two years later Thomas Höpker became Deputy Editor of the U.S. edition of the magazine, *GEO*. Höpker gave up this appointment in 1981, however, preferring to work freelance again for *GEO* and *Stern*.

Horaček, Milan
*1946, Tschechoslowakei

Bornstr. 1
2000 Hamburg 13
West-Germany

Als Chemielaborant im Filmstudio Prag kam Horaček zum ersten Mal mit der Fotografie in Kontakt. 1968 zog er nach Stuttgart und studierte dann 1970-75 Fotografie bei Otto Steinert in Essen. Seit 1976 ist er als freier Fotograf, vor allem für *GEO* und den *Stern, Art, Zeit Magazin* tätig.

While working in the laboratory of a film studio in Prague, Milan Horaček had his first encounter with photography. He moved to Stuttgart, Germany, in 1968 and studied photography under Otto Steinert in Essen, 1970-75. Since 1976 he has been active as a freelance photographer working mainly for *GEO, Stern, Art, Zeit Magazin*.

Horlitz, Andreas
*1955, Deutschland

Hansaring 37
5000 Köln 1
West-Germany

Nach dem Abitur und einem Praktikum in einem Porträtatelier in Hannover begann er 1975 an der Fachhochschule Hannover Grafik zu studieren, wechselte dann aber 1976 an die Gesamthochschule Essen zum Fachbereich Visuelle Kommunikation. 1978 begann er an der Farbserie *Deutsche Feste* zu arbeiten, mit der er 1980 sein Examen machte. 1981 erhielt er für *Amerikareise* den Otto-Steinert-Preis der DGPh. Im gleichen Jahr entstand die Arbeit *Essen im Frühling*, die aus Farbfotomontagen besteht. Es folgten die Fotos von Kindern in Farbe, Schwarzweiß und mit Text. Ab 1983 gab Horlitz zusammen mit Reinhard Matz die Microfiche Edition *Fotonetz* heraus.

Horlitz finished his schooling, did an apprenticeship in a portrait studio in Hannover and then started to study graphics at the Technical College there in 1975. The next year he transferred to the Faculty of Visual Communication at the Gesamthochschule in Essen. In 1978 he began his color series, *Deutsche Feste* (German Festivities) for which he received his diploma in 1980. In 1981 Horlitz was awarded the Otto-Steinert prize from the DGPh for his collection of color photographs entitled, *Amerikareise*. That same year he produced a series of color montages entitled *Essen in Springtime*. He then did a project on children in color, black & white, accompanied by texts. Since 1983, together with Reinhard Matz, Horlitz published the microfiche magazine, *Fotonetz*.

Horn, Jan van der
*1951, Niederlande

Bloemgracht 81
1016 KH Amsterdam
The Netherlands

1973 beendete er die Ausbildung in Fotografie und audio-visuellen Medien an der Gerrit Rietveld Akademie. Seitdem arbeitet er auf dem Gebiet der Public Relations und der Werbung, wobei er sich auf die Produktion von Diashows spezialisiert hat. Auf der Suche nach größmöglicher Perfektion interessiert ihn zunehmend das zweckfreie Foto. Seine Aufnahmen wurden schon von verschiedenen Magazinen gedruckt, und 1987 hat er in Amsterdam, wo er ein Studio unterhält, seine erste Einzelausstellung.

In 1973 Jan van der Horn graduated from Gerrit Rietveld Academy, where he studied photography and audio-visual media. Since then he has been working in public relations and advertising, specializing in the production of slide shows. In his search for perfection, he has become increasingly fascinated by the image itself. His photos have been published in various magazines and in 1987 he will have his first solo exhibition in Amsterdam, where he has his studio.

Horst, Horst P.
*1906, Deutschland

166 East 63rd Street
New York, N.Y. 10021
USA

Studierte 1926-28 Architektur an der Kunstgewerbeschule in Hamburg und arbeitete 1930 im Atelier des Architekten Le Corbusier in Paris. In Paris machte er auch die Bekanntschaft von George Hoyingen-Huene, dessen Assistent im Studio von *Vogue* er dann wurde. 1935 emigrierte Horst in die USA und arbeitete als Fotograf für *Vogue* in den Condé Nast Studios in New York. Berühmt wurde er für seine schwarzweißen Modefotos aus den 30er Jahren, die sein Gefühl für elegante Linienführung und dramatische Beleuchtungseffekte zeigen. Zur gleichen Zeit eintstanden Prominentenporträts, die sehr viel weniger stilisiert wirken und weite Beachtung fanden. Bereits gegen Ende der 30er Jahre wurden von Horst auch farbige Modeaufnahmen in *Vogue* publiziert.

Horst studied architecture at the Kunstgewerbeschule, Hamburg, 1926-28 and in 1930 he worked in the studio of the architect Le Corbusier in Paris. In Paris he met George Hoyningen-Huene, and went to work with him in the *Vogue* studios, Paris, 1932-35. He emigrated to the USA in 1935 and worked in the *Vogue* studios in New York. His now famous fashion photographs of the 1930's prove his knack for elegant lines and dramatic lighting effects. During the 30's Horst furthermore produced his much-acclaimed series of personality portraits, which is far less stylish than his fashion work. Already in the late 1930's *Vogue* published Horst's fashion color photographs.

Horvat, Frank
*1928, Italien

5, rue de l'Ancienne Mairie
92100 Boulongne-Billancourt
France

Nachdem er Zeichenunterricht an der Accademia di Brera in Mailand genommen hatte, arbeitete Frank Horvat 1949-50 in einer Werbeagentur. Dann wurde seine erste Farbfotografie auf dem Titel der Zeitschrift *Epoca* gedruckt und seitdem arbeitet er als Fotograf. Er fotografierte Reportagen für die Agenturen *Rapho* und *Black Star*. 1957 machte er seine ersten Modeaufnahmen und zwar in der gleichen Technik wie er zuvor die Reportagen fotografiert hatte, damals eine Pioniertat. Horvat arbeitete regelmäßig für *Harper's Bazaar, Glamour, Esquire* und andere Magazine. 1978 präsentierte er ein Buch mit Farbfotos von Bäumen. Seit 1968 betriebt er in der Nähe von Paris ein Studio und vor einiger Zeit beendete er eine Porträtserie über Frauen.

Following his studies at the Brera Academy of Fine Arts in Milan, Frank Horvat worked as a graphic designer in a Milanese advertising agency. In 1950 his first color photography was published on the cover of the magazine Epoca and since then Horvat has been working as a professional photographer. He did assignments for the *Rapho* and *Black Star* photo agencies. In 1957 he took his first fashion photographs, using the same technique as for his reportages - a pioneering achievement at that time. He then photographed regularly for *Harper's Bazaar, Glamour, Esquire* and several other magazines. In 1978 he presented a book of color pictures on trees. Horvat maintains a studio not far from Paris since 1968. More recently he finished a portait series on women.

Hosoe, Eiko
*1933, Japan

5 Aizumicho
Shinjuku-ku, Tokyo 160
Japan

Hosoe studierte von 1951 bis 1954 an der Fachschule für Fotografie in Tokio, seitdem ist er als künstlerischer Fotograf aktiv. Fotografie ist für ihn seine Art zu leben, bei der er immer nach Neuem sucht. 1959 war er Mitbegründer der Fotografengruppe VIVO und seit 1975 ist er Professor am Polytechnischen Institut in Tokio. Hosoe wurde für seine Köperdetailstudien und für die oft montierten, symbolträchtigen Aktstudien bekannt. Durch seine zahlreichen Workshops in Europa und den USA wurde er einer der einflußreichsten japanischen Fotografen.

Eikoh Hosoe studied at the Tokyo College of Photography from 1951 to 54. Since then he has been active as an artistic photographer. 'Photography is the way of my life, in which I always seek after anything that is new to me', he stated. In 1959 he was co-founder of the group VIVO and since 1975 Hosoe has been a professor at the Polytechnical Institute Tokyo. He became well known for his studies of body details and for his often montaged, symbolic nude studies. Through his numerous workshops in Europe and the States, he is one of the internationally most influential Japanese photographers.

Hubmann, Hans
*1910, Deutschland

Angersdorf 2
8311 Kröning 1
West-Germany

Begann als Student zu fotografieren und arbeitete dann als Fotojournalist. 1932 druckte die *Münchner Illustrierte* ein Foto von ihm auf dem Titel. 1933 wurde er wegen Anti-Hitler Propaganda inhaftiert. Ab 1935 arbeitete er für die *Berliner Illustrirte Zeitung* (BIZ), seit 1936 fotografiert er bei den Olympischen Spielen. Es entstanden überdies zahlreiche Auslandreportagen, ab 1949 für *Quick* und *Life*. 1963 verließ er *Quick*, setzte sich 1975 zur Ruhe, machte dann aber von 1977 bis 1983 erneut Reportagen für *Quick*. U.a. erschien 1983 das Buch *Augenzeuge 1933-45*.

Hans Hubmann started photography as a student and worked as a photo-journalist. In 1932 one of his pictures was used for the cover of the *Münchner Illustrierte*. The following year Hubmann was arrested for anti-Hitler propaganda. In 1935 he went to work for *Berliner Illustrirte Zeitung* (BIZ) and since 1936 has been photographing the Olympic Games. From 1949 he did numerous reportages abroad for *Quick* and *Life* and in 1975 he retired, only to start work again for *Quick* from 1977-83. That year his book, *Augenzeuge 1933-45* was published.

Huf, Paul
*1924, Niederlande

Hazenstraat 4-10
1016 SP Amsterdam
The Netherlands

Huf arbeitet seit 1942 und ist königlich niederländischer Hoffotograf. Nach seiner ersten Ausstellungsteilnahme an *Foto '48* im Stedelijk Museum, Amsterdam, machte er 1949 die Aufnahmen für den internationalen Farbkalender der KLM. Seit 1957 realisiert er die Anzeigenkampagnen für die Grolsche Bierbrauerei. 1965 gründete er das Film und Ton Studio "Paul Huf Film Associates". 1965 war er der erste Fotograf überhaupt, der die Genehmigung zu Modefotos im Kremlin in Moskau erhielt. In den folgenden Jahren wurde er mehrfach für seine TV-Werbespots ausgezeichnet. Seit Mitte der 70er Jahre nimmt er mit Polacolor Fotos an dem Sofortbild gewidmeten Ausstellungen teil, 1977 erhob ihn Königin Juliana in den Adelstand. 1981 erschien eine Monografie über seine 40jährige fotografische Karriere: *Paul Huf – Leeg Kijken*

Paul Huf started his career in 1942 and is now the court photographer of the Dutch Royal Family. After his first photographic participation in *Foto '48* at the Stedelijk Museum in Amsterdam, he was commissioned to produce the photographs for KLM's international color calendar in 1949. Since 1957 he has been working on advertising campaigns for the Grolsche Brewery. In 1965 he founded the film-and-sound studio, Paul Huf Film Associates. That same year he became the first photographer ever to be allowed to take fashion pictures in Moscow's Kremlin. In the period to come he received numerous distinctions for his TV-commercials. In the mid-Seventies he started to show Polacolor prints in major exhibitions of instant imagery. Queen Juliana made him a Knight of Oranje in 1977 and in 1981 a book, *Paul Huf - Leeg Kijken* was published, covering his 40 years in photography.

Hustinx, Damien
*1954, Belgien

4, rue Renoz
4020 Liége
Belgium

Besuchte 1960-72 die Schule und beschloß dann Fotograf zu werden. Bis 1979 studierte er Fotografie am Institut St. Luce in Liège. 1980 begann er Fotografie zu unterrichten und gleichzeitig die Fortsetzung seiner Studien an der Ecole Nationale Supérieur des Arts Visuels bis 1985. 1982-84 fuhr er nachts die 1348 km belgischer Autobahn ab und machte Landschaftsaufnahmen bei der Beleuchtung durch die Straßenlaternen. In Farbe arbeitet Hustinx vorzugsweise mit dem Polaroid Verfahren.

Hustinx attended school from 1960-72, then decided to go into photography. Until 1979 he studied photography at the Institut St. Luce in Liège. A year later he began teaching photography regularly while continuing his studies at the Ecole Nationale Supérieur des Arts Visuels until 1985. During 1982-84 he travelled the 1348 km stretch of Belgian highways by night, photographing landscapes by street light. For his color work, Hustinx prefers the Polaroid system.

Infante, Francisko
*1943

I Spasonalivkovskij
Per 1711, Str. 2
Moscow 117049
USSR

Sohn eines Spaniers und einer Russin, der in Moskau die Kunstschule besuchte und dort als Künstler lebt. Seit 1962 beschäftigt er sich mit konstruktivistischer Kunst in der Tradition der russischen Avantgarde der 20er Jahre. Es entstanden verschiedene kinetische Konstruktionen. 1970 gründete er ARGO, eine Gruppe von Künstlern und Ingenieuren, die bisher 13 Projekte realisierte. Seit 1976 setzt er von ihm geschaffene Artefakte mit der Natur in Relation; die Fotografien zeigen das Ergebnis dieser künstlerischen Prozesse.

Infante was born from a Spanish father and a Russian mother. He studied art in Moscow and has been living there ever since, working as a freelance artist. From 1962 he became involved in geometric, mobile art in the tradition of Russian avantgarde of the Twenties, designing different types of kinetic constructions. In 1970 he founded ARGO, a creative group of artists and engineers, who have realized 13 projects up to now. Since 1976 Francisco Infante has been creating artefacts in relation to nature. His photographs illustrate the results of this artistic process.

Ishimoto, Yasuhiro
*1921, USA

Nr. 601 Daiya Mansion
6-7-11 Uitashinagawa,
Shinagawa-ku, Tokyo 141
Japan

1948 begann Ishimoto mit Mehrfachbelichtungen zu experimentieren und im selben Jahr fing er an, Fotografie bei →Harry Callahan und Aaron Siskind am Illinois Institute of Technology zu studieren. Als Student gewann er 1950 einen Preis im Wettbewerb für Nachwuchs-fotografen von *Life*. 1953 beauftragte ihn →Edward Steichen, die japanischen Fotografien für die Ausstellung *The Family of Man* auszuwählen. 1961 ging Ishimoto wieder nach Japan, wo er Fotografie unterrichtete und von wo aus er weite Reisen unternimmt, auf denen seine Fotografien entstehen.

In 1948 Yasuhiro Ishimoto began experimenting with multi-exposure photography and enrolled at the Illinois Institute of Technology, where he studied photography under →Harry Callahan and Aaron Siskind until 1952. As a student he won a prize in *Life*'s, Young Photographers Contest and in 1953 →Edward Steichen asked him to choose the Japanese contributions for *The Familiy of Man* exhibition. Ishimoto went back to Japan in 1961, where he taught photography and from where he still travels extensively for his photographic work.

Jacot, Monique
*1934, Schweiz

1098 Epesses
Switzerland

1953-56 besuchte sie den Fotounterricht von Gertrude Fehr an der Ecole des Arts et Métiers, Vevey. Ab 1956 entstanden Reportagen über soziale und kulturelle Themen für Zeitungen, von 1958 bis 1972 u.a. für *Du, Vogue, Queen, Elle, Fémina*. Außerdem erledigte sie redaktionelle Arbeiten für Verlage. 1967-70 war sie für die Weltgesundheits-organisation in verschiedenen Ländern unterwegs. Aus Madrid berichtete sie 1975 über das Ende der Franco-Ära. Seit 1980 entstanden zahlreiche Farbreportage sowie Dokumentationen für das Fernsehen.

From 1953-56 Monique Jacot took photographic lessons at the Ecole des Arts et Métiers, Vevey, with Gertrude Fehr. As a freelance photographer she has done social and cultural reportages for newspapers since 1956; and from 1958 to 1972 has collaborated with *Du, Vogue, Queen, Elle, Fémina* and other magazines. Additionally she did editorial work for publishers. In 1967-70 missions for the World Health Organization took her to various countries. In 1975 she reported on the end of the Franco era from Madrid. Since 1980 she has been doing reportages in color as well as TV documentaries.

Jäger, Gottfried
*1937, Deutschland

Barnhausen 48
4807 Borgholzhausen
West-Germany

Studierte 1958-60, nach einer Fotografenlehre, Photographie in Köln. 1960 wurde er Dozent für Fototechnik, 1973 Professor für Fotografie an der Fachhochschule Bielefeld. Seit 1962 befaßt sich Jäger mit experimenteller Fotografie und Fotografik. 1968 führte er den Begriff "Generative Fotografie" ein für die systematisch-konstruktive Gestaltungsrichtung in der Fotografie. In den beiden Büchern *Apparative Kunst* zus. m. H.W. Franke, Köln 1973, und *Generative Fotografie* zus. m. K.M. Holzhäuser, Ravensburg 1975, legt er seine Theorien dar. Seit 1979 befaßt er sich mit "Visuellen Systemen" nach dem geometrischen Prinzip der Translation, u.a. mit Farbsystemen. In jüngster Zeit entstanden Fotoobjekte und Fotoinstallationen. Seit 1983 Vorsitzender der GDL ist er seit 1986 Präsident der Fotografischen Akademie GDL.

Following his apprenticeship as a photographer, Jäger studied photography in Cologne. In 1960 he started to lecture photo technology and in 1973 he was appointed Professor for Photography at the Technical College in Bielefeld. Since 1962 Jäger dedicated himself to experimental photography and photo graphics. In 1968 he established the term 'Generative Fotografie' indicating a systematic-structural style of photography. He explains his theories in both his books *Apparative Kunst* (together with H.W. Franke), Cologne 1973 and *Generative Fotografie* (together with K.M. Holzhäuser), Ravensburg 1975. Since 1975 he has worked on 'Visual Systems', geometrical systems of translation, including color systems. Recently he has produced photo objects and photo-installations. Since 1983 chairman of the GDL, he became President of the Photographic Academy GDL in 1986.

Jansen, Arno
*1938, Deutschland

Ubierring 40
5000 Köln 1
West-Germany

Studierte 1957-63 an de Folkwangschule in Essen Grafikdesign, sowie Fotografie bei Otto Steinert. Danach arbeitete er als Grafiker und Fotograf in Braunschweig, wo er zugleich an der Hochschule für Bildende Künste Fotografie unterrichtete. 1965 folgte er einer Berufung an die Kölner Werkschulen, heute Fachhochschule, seit 1973 ist er dort Professor für künstlerische Fotografie im Fachbereich Kunst und Design. In den 70er Jahren wurde Jansen für seine morbiden schwarzweißen Stilleben bekannt, zwischen 1980 und 1983 variierte er dieses Thema durch die Einbeziehung der Farbe.

Arno Jansen studied Graphic Design, as well as Photography with Otto Steinert at the Folkwangschule Essen from 1957-63. After he graduated, he took a position as graphic designer and photographer in Braunschweig, where he simultaneously lectured in Photography at the Academy for Fine Arts. In 1965 he was appointed to the Kölner Werkschule, today called the Technical School, where he is professor for artistic photography in the Department for Art and Design. In the seventies Jansen made a name for himself as an artistic photographer, specializing in black & white still-life pictures. Between 1980-83, he expanded his still-life work to color.

Jenshel, Len
*1949, USA

309 West 93rd Street, Nr. 4A
New York, N.Y. 10025
USA

1975 erhielt Len Jenshel seinen B.A. von der Cooper Union, wo er bei →Joel Meyerowitz, Tod Papageorge und Garry Winogrand studierte. Nach seinem Training als sog. Straßenfotograf, reizte es Jenshel, gegen die Vorurteile anzugehen, die in der künstlerischen Fotografie gegenüber Farbe und pittoresken Motiven herrschten. Nachdem er jahrelang gerade die klischeehaften Farbmotive vermieden hatte, fotografierte er schließlich einen Sonnenuntergang. Seine Fotos sind nicht im üblichen Sinne schön, denn er behält Distanz, zeigt z,B. einen Sonnenuntergang weit entfernt über den Hügeln, devor ein Wohngebiet und die ausgebesserte Straße.

Len Jenshel studied photography under →Joel Meyerowitz, Tod Papageorge and Garry Winogrand at Cooper Union, graduating in 1975 (B.A.). Following his training as a street photographer, Jenshel was temped by the idea of covercoming the prejudices against color and picturesque subject matter in creative photography. After years of avoiding subjects which lead to cliches in color photography, he photographed a sunset. His photographs are not beautiful in the common sense, because Jenshel keeps his distance, e.g. by showing a sunset faraway over the hills – with living quarters and a street in a state of repair, in the foreground.

Jiránek, Otakar
*1954, Tschechoslowakei

U Batterie 26
16200 Prague 6
Czechoslovakia

Während seiner Ausbildung zum Werbegrafiker begann sich Jiránek für die Fotografie zu interessieren. 1974 bis 1980 studierte er dann an der Abteilung für künstlerische Fotografie an der Kunstakademie in Prag. Seitdem arbeitet er als freier Fotograf für Werbezwecke, Buchillustrationen usw. Seine freien Landschaftaufnahmen, Porträts und Reisefotos realisiert er seit einiger Zeit in Farbe. Er fotografierte einen Zyklus über die Lichteffekte in gotischen Kathedralen. Zur Zeit bereitet er ein Buch mit seinen Aufnahmen aus Tunesien vor.

During his studies in commercial art, Otakar Jiránek developed a growing interest in photography. From 1974 to 1980 he then studied at the artistic photography department of the Art Academy in Prague. Since that period he has been working freelance in the fields of advertising, book illustrating etc. In recent times he produced his personal landscapes, portraits, and travel photographs in color. He also created a cycle of photographs on the effects of light inside Gothic cathedrals. At present he is preparing a book of his photographs taken in Tunesia in 1985.

Joffé, Constantin
*c.1910, Rußland

Joffé wuchs in Rußland und Deutschland auf und arbeitete bei der UFA in Berlin und dann in Paris als Kameramann. In Paris begann er auch seine Karriere als Modefotograf, die durch den Zweiten Weltkrieg unterbrochen wurde. Als Soldat der französischen Armee kam er in Gefangenschaft, konnte sich befreien und floh in die USA, wo er vom Fleck weg als Fotograf bei den Condé Nast Publikationen eine Anstellung fand. Neben Mode fotografierte Joffé auch Reisereportagen in Farbe.

Constantin Joffé was educated in Russia and Germany, where he worked with UFA, the great german film company at that time, as a cameraman. While in Paris he switched to a career in fashion photography, which was interrupted by the war. As a member of the French Army, Joffé was captured and subsequently escaped from a prisoner-of-war camp to make his way to the States in 1941. Almost from the very first day of his arrival, he worked on the staff of the Condé Nast Publications. Besides fashion, Joffé also did travel reportages in color.

Johns, Carolyn
*1950, Australien

Seit zehn Jahren werden ihre Fotografien von Zeitungen und Illustrierten gedruckt, z.B. von *The Times, The Guardian* sowie *New Society* in London, von *The National Times, Time Magazine* und *Newsweek* in Australien. Mit ihren Aufnahmen gelang es ihr immer wieder, einen Eindruck von der Lebensgeschichte und den Gefühlen der Fotografierten zu vermitteln. In letzter Zeit hat sich Carolyn Johns auf die Standfotografie bei Film und Fernsehen spezialisiert. Sie machte zum Beispiel die Pressefotos zu Filmen wie *Razorback, Rebel* und *Mad Max II*.

During the past ten years, Carolyn John's work has been published in newspapers and magazines such as *The Times, The Guardian* and *New Society* in London, and *The National Times, Time Magazine* and *Newsweek* in Australia. With her photographs she captures and closely documents the lives and emotions of her subjects. Recently she has specialized in publicity stills for film and television. Her work has been used to promote movies like *Razorback, Rebel* and *Mad Max II*.

Kaleya, Tana
*1939, Polen

128 Blvd. Maurice Barrs
92200 Neuilly
France

Tana Kaleya kam im Alter von acht Jahren von Polen nach Österreich, lebte in Berlin und München und begann 1967 in Paris als Modefotografin zu arbeiten. Als erste Fotografin machte sie Aktaufnahmen von Männern, die 1974 in Paris als Buch unter dem Titel *Hommes* erschienen und sie berühmt machten. Sie fotografierte dann *Femmes en liberté*, Akte in sehr weichem, farbigem Licht. Ende der 70er, Anfang der 80er Jahre hielt sie sich in Poona auf, um im Aschram von Bhagwan zu meditieren und Porträts zu fotografieren.

At the age of eight, Tana Kaleya moved from Poland to Austria. She later lived in Germany and in 1967 started to work as a fashion photographer in Paris. She was the first woman photographer to do male nude studies, which appeared in the book *Hommes* published in Paris in 1974, earning her fame. She then worked on *Femmes en liberté*, female nude studies in a very soft colored light. In the late 70's, early 80's she stayed in Poona, meditating and taking portraits in Bhagwan's ashram.

Kane, Art
(Arthur Kanowsky)
*1925, USA

1181 Broadway
New York, N.Y. 10001
USA

Kane studierte Fotografie an der Cooper Union und begann seine berufliche Laufbahn 1950 als Layouter beim Magazin *Esquire*. 1952-56 war er der Art Director des *Seventeen Magazine*. 1957 erhielt er dann seinen ersten Auftrag als Fotograf: für *Esquire* fotografierte er Jazzmusiker. In den 60er Jahre wurde Kane berühmt als Fotograf der Pop-Ära. Er fotografierte Bob Dylan, The Who und illustrierte auch Beatles Songs.Kanes 'poppige' Fotos entstanden oft unter Verwendung von Weitwinkelobjektiven. 1975 eröffnete er ein neues Studio in New York, in dem er bis heute Mode und Werbung fotografiert.

Art Kane studied photography at Cooper Union and began his professional career in 1950 as a layout designer to *Esquire* magazine. During 1952 to 1956 he served as art director of the magazine *Seventeen*. In 1957 he got his first assignment as a photographer, photographing jazz musicians for *Esquire*. In the Sixties, Art Kane became known as the photographer of the pop-era. He portrayed Bob Dylan, The Who and he also illustrated the songs of the Beatles. For his 'pop' photographs Kane often used a wide-angle lens. He opened up a new studio in 1975, where he continues to do fashion and advertising work.

Karikese, Frédéric
*1948, Afrika

147, rue du Mont Falise
5200 Huy
Belgium

In Belgien lebender Musiker, Schriftsteller und Fotograf. Seine ersten Aufnahmen entstanden 1975. 1978 organisierte er in Huy, wo er lebt, das *Festival d'art*, im Jahr darauf die *Rencontres d'art contemporain*. Er eröffnete in Brüssel ein Studio für Mode und Werbung und machte bisher schon Reportagen über die meisten Länder zwischen der Sahelzone in Afrika und dem Nordpol.

Musician, writer and photographer, Frédéric Karikese lives in Belgium. His first photographs date back to 1975. In 1979 he organized the *festival d'art* and the following year, *Rencontres d'art contemporain*, both in Huy where he resides. Later he opened a studio in Brussels, where he does fashion and commercial photography. He also travels extensively as a photo-journalist, covering everything from Central Africa to the North Pole.

Karsh, Yousuf
*1908, Armenien

Chateau Laurier Hotel
Suite 660
Ottawa, Ontario K1N 8S7
Canada

1924 kam Karsch nach Kanada und wurde Assistent im Porträtstudio seines Onkels, bevor er eine Lehre bei dem Porträtfotografen John H. Garo in Boston absolvierte. 1932 gründete er sein inzwischen berühmtes Porträtstudio in Ottawa. Bis zum Ende des Zweiten Weltkrieges fotografierte Karsh vornehmlich Politiker und Militärs. 1941 entstand in einer nur zweiminütigen Sitzung sein weltberühmtes Porträt von Winston Churchill. Nach dem Krieg porträtierte Karsh in seinem bewährt schlichten, aber gleichzeitig sehr persönlichen Stil die Prominenz aus Wissenschaft, Kunst, Industrie, Sport. Karsh ist einer der großen lebenden Meister der Porträtfotografie.

Yousuf Karsh emigrated to Canada in 1924 and assisted in his uncle's portrait studio before he became an apprentice to the portrait photographer John H. Garo in Boston. In 1932 Karsh established his now famous portrait studio in Ottawa. Until the end of WW II, Karsh mainly photographed military and political leaders. In 1941 he did his famous portrait of Churchill; the fruits of a two minute session. After the war ended, Karsh extended his portrait activites to leaders in all fields: science, industry, the arts, sports, etc. As a portraitist, Karsh's style is formal and solid but very personal at the same time. He is one of the greatest, living masters of portrait photography.

Kasten, Barbara
*1936, USA

P.O. Box 4231
Inglewood, CA 90309
USA

Arbeitet als Bildhauerin, Malerin und Fotografin und studierte an der Universität von Arizona und am California College of Arts and Crafts, wo sie 1970 ihren Magister in Plastischer Kunst erhielt. Seit 1975 unterrichtet sie als Associate Professor am Orange Coast College in Kalifornien, wo sie auch die Fotogalerie des Colleges leitet. 1979-81 entstand die Videodokumentation über vier Fotografinnen und 1982 erhielt sie ein Guggenheim Stipendium, um mit dem Polaroid 50x60 System und in 30x40 Cibachrome-Prints zu arbeiten. Ihre für das jeweilige Foto hergestellten Skulpturen stehen in der Tradition des Konstruktivismus.

Kasten, a sculptress, painter and photographer studied at the University of Arizona and the California College of Arts and Crafts, where she received her M.F.A. in 1970. Since 1975 she teaches as Associate Professor at Orange Coast College, California. She also directs the Colleg's Photo Gallery. During 1979 to 81 Kasten received NEA grants for video documentation on four women photographers and in 1982 she received a Guggenheim grant to work with Polaroid's 50x60 photographic system and to begin experimentation with 30x40 Cibachromes. Her sculptures, in the tradition of constructivism, are created only to be photographed.

Kawada, Kikuji
*1933, Japan

3-8-4 Sadoharacho
Shinjuku-ku, Tokyo
Japan

Begann 1955, nach einem Volkswirtschaftsstudium, als Fotograf bei einem Buchverlag zu arbeiten. 1959 Beteiligung an der Fotografengruppe *Vivo* und Beginn der freiberuflichen Tätigkeit. Kawada zeigte seine Fotos auf zahlreichen Ausstellungen, besonders in Tokio. 1966 reiste er in die USA, nach Europa und in der UdSSR; 1969, 1977 und 1981 hielt er sich wiederum in Europa auf. In Deutschland fotografierte er die Schlösser Ludwig II. und publizierte 1979 ein Buch über den Mikrokosmos des Königs. Bekannt wurden zwei weitere Serien von Kawada, nämlich *Sacré Atavism* in Schwarzweiß vom Ende der 60er Jahre und *Los Caprichos*, deren zweiten Teil er in Farbe fotografierte.

After graduating in Economics in 1955, Kawada began work in the capacity of photographer with a book publisher. Subsequently he joined the photographic group, *Vivo* and set out as a freelancer. Kawada exhibited his work on a wide scale, particularly in Tokyo, In 1966 he travelled to the USA, Europe and the USSR, returnig to Europe again in 1981. In Germany he photographed the castles of Ludwig II, publishing a book on the *Microcosmos of Ludwig II* in 1979. His black & white series, *Sacré Atavism*, produced at the end of the Sixties and *Los Caprichos*, the second part of which is in color, is among his best known work.

330

Keetman, Peter
*1916, Deutschland

Seestr. 17
8211 Breitbrunn
West-Germany

Peter Keetmann studierte vor und nach dem Krieg and der Bayerischen Staatslehranstalt für Photographie in München, wo er 1948 seine Meisterprüfung ablegte. Er gehörte zu einer kleinen Fotografengruppe, die sich um Adolf Lazi geschart hatte und aus der dann die Gruppe *fotoform* hervorging, mit Otto Steinert als primus inter pares. Schon als Mitglied von *fotoform* gehörte Keetmann zu den Vertretern einer modernen, später 'subjektiv' genannten Nachkriegsfotografie. Rückblickend läßt sich sein Werk unterteilen in Naturstudien, Lichtpendelarbeiten, Bewegungsstudien, Landschaftaufnahmen und Industriefotografien.

Interrupted by World War II, Peter Keetmann studied at the 'Bayerische Staatslehranstalt für Photographie' in Munich, where he received his 'Meister' degree in 1948. He belonged to the small circle of photographers, surrounding Adolf Lazi which later emerged as the *fotoform* group with Otto Steinert as its primus inter pares. From that time on, Keetmann became an exponent of modern (later called subjective) post-war photography. In retrospect, his work is divided into nature studies, experiments with light, studies of movement, landscapes and industrial photography.

Keppler, Victor
*1904, USA

11 Ferry Lane West
Westport, Conn. 06880
USA

Der Autodidakt Keppler wurde zu einem der erfolgreichsten fotografischen Illustratoren der dreißiger, vierziger und fünfziger Jahre. Ab den 30er Jahren galt er bereits als einer der führenden Farbfotografen in der Werbung. Von Beginn seiner Laufbahn an war Keppler in der Lage, die ästhetischen Trends der künstlerischen Fotografie oder in der bildenden Kunst auf die Werbung zu übertragen. Vom Art Directors Club erhielt er zahlreiche Auszeichnungen und er kannte seinen Wert und bat seine Kunden entsprechend zur Kasse – oft legte er der Rechnung einige Aspirin bei. 1962 gründete er die Famous Photographers School, deren Präsident und Direktor er blieb, bis er in den Ruhestand trat.

A self-taught photographer, Victor Keppler was to become one of the most successful photographic illustrators of the Thirties, Fourties and Fifties. From the 1930's onwards he established a reputation for himself as a leading color photographer in the advertising world. From the beginning of his career he proved adept at extending the trend of artistic photography or fine arts to his commercial work. He won countless awards from the Art Directors Club and knowing his worth, he charged his clients accordingly, often adding some aspirins to his bill. In 1962 Keppler became the founder of the Famous Photographers School, where he served as President and Director until his retirement.

Keresztes, Lajos
*1933, Ungarn

Rudolph Str. 16
8500 Nürnberg 20
West-Germany

1956 zog Keresztes nach Nürnberg, wo er in einem Architekturbüro arbeitete und 1958 begann er ein Architekturstudium, wechselte dann aber 1961 zur Fotografie. 1963 ließ er sich als Fotograf in Nürnberg nieder und arbeitete hauptsächlich für Illustrierte. 1965-73 enstanden in der Mehrzahl Theaterfotos; 1966 erhielt er den photokina-Obelisken für *Essay in Color*. Nach der Konzetration auf Mode- und Werbeaufnahmen produziert er seit 1978 Illustrationen und Audiovisionschauen. Lajos Keresztes ist Autor verschiedener Bücher, einen des letzten hat den Titel *Yoga – Ursprung Indien*.

In 1956 Lajos Keresztes moved to Nuremberg where he worked in an architects' office. He began to study architecture, than changed to photography in 1961.
Het set up as a freelance photographer in Nuremberg in 1963, working mainly for illustrated magazines. During 1965 to 1973 his main works were on theatre events; he received the photokina Obelisk 1966 for his *Essay in Color*. After a period of fashion and advertising work he started to produce illustrations and audiovisuals in 1978 as well as books; recent one is titled *Yoga – Ursprung Indien*.

Kers, Martin
*1944, Niederlande

Prins Bernhardstraat 14
1901 DS Castricum
The Netherlands

Nach einem Kunststudium an der Akademie in Rotterdam begann Kers in einer Werbeagentur zu arbeiten, später ging er dann als Illustrator zu einem Verlag. 1974 entschloß er sich, die Fotografie berufsmaßig zu betreiben. Seine Liebe zur Natur war die beste Voraussetzung, um zu einem vielbeachteten Fotografen der holländischen Landschaft zu werden. Martin Kers hat schon für viele Firmen, Verlage und Zeitschriften wie *Libelle, Grasduinen, Avenue, Holland Herald* gearbeitet.

After his art studies at the Academy of Rotterdam, Martin Kers began working in an advertising agency. Later he joined a publisher in Amsterdam as an illustrator. In 1974 he decided to operate as a freelance photographer. His talent for landscape photography has since developed and he has carried out assignments for a wide range of companies, publishers and magazines such as the dutch *Libelle, Avenue* and *Holland Herald*.

Kertész, André
*1894, Ungarn, † 1985, USA

Begann als Autodidakt zu fotografieren, z.B. machte er als Soldat während des Ersten Weltkrieges Aufnahmen an der Front. 1925-35 lebte er in Paris als freier Fotograf. Seine Fotos aus dieser Zeit, die er deutschen und anderen Illustrierten veröffentlichte, zählen zu den Meisterwerken der künstlerischen Fotografie. 1936 ging er, in Europa erfolgreich und anerkannt, in die USA, wo er zuerst einen Vertrag mit Keystone hatte, dann 1937-62 mit Condé Nast. Während dieser Zeit entstanden auch Farbaufnahmen, die aber nie den Rang seiner frühen schwarzweißen Fotografien erreichten. Nach 1962 arbeitete er nur noch zu seinem Vergnügen, u.a. mit dem SX-70 System. Er erhielt hohe Ehrungen, hatte zahlreiche Ausstellungen und viele Bücher wurden über ihn und sein fotografischen Oeuvre publiziert.

André Kertész started as an amateur and photographed as a soldier during World War I. Between 1925-35 he lived in Paris, working as a freelance photographer; his pictures were published in German and other foreign magazines. During the Twenties and Thirties he produced photographs which now belong among the masterpieces of artistic photography. In 1936, although successful and recognized in Europe, Kertész decided to move to the USA, where he got a contract first with Keystone and then from 1937-62 with Condé Nast. During that period he also photographed in color but his commercial color work never reached the standards of his black & white photography. From 1962 onwards, he photographed for his own pleasure only, working with the Polaroid system. He was awarded many honors, exhibited extensively and a great many books about him and his work have been published.

Ketchum, Robert Glenn
*1947, USA

696 Stone Canyon Road
Los Angeles, CA 90077
USA

Seit 1968 fotografiert Robert Glenn Ketchum in Farbe und 1974 machte er seinen Universitätsabschluß in Fotografie. Anfang der 70er Jahre begann er sich mit Umweltproblemen auseinanderzusetzen und entsprechend wurde die Natur zu seinem Motiv. Dabei beabsichtigt Ketchum, in seinen Aufnahmen ein Gleichgewicht zwischen politischer Aussage und ästhetischem Anspruch zu finden. Zwei Jahre lang arbeitete er an dem Projekt *The Hudson River and the Highlands*, das 1985 bei Aperture als Buch erschien. Er wurde aber nicht nur als künstlerischer Fotograf bekannt, sondern auch als Ausstellungsorganisator, vor allem durch die Herausgabe der Kataloge zu *Paul Outerbridge* (1976) und zu *American Photographers and the National Parks* (1981).

Robert Glenn Ketchum has been working in color since 1968 and he received his M.F.A. degree in photography in 1974. In the early 70's he became concerned with global environmental problems and wanted his work to address issues related to the natural world. His intention is, to find a balance between politics and aesthetics in his work. His two year project *The Hudson River and the Highlands* was published by Aperture in 1985. Besides being a recognized artist, Ketchum served as a curator/publisher of several major exhibitions and catalogues such as *Paul Outerbridge* (1976) and *American Photographers and the National Parks* (1981).

Klein, William
*1928, USA

5, rue Médicis
75006 Paris
France

Klein studierte kurze Zeit bei Fernand Léger in Paris und realisierte dann abstrakte Wandgemälde für italienische Architekten, 1953 auch abstrakte Fotogramme. 1954 kehrte er nach New York zurück und fotografierte diese Stadt. Von 1955 bis 1965 war er unter Vertrag bei *Vogue* und 1958 entstand der erste von inzwischen 22 Filmen. Seine Fotobücher gestaltet er stets selbst: 1956 erschien *New York*, dann *Rome 1958, Moscou* und *Tokyo* 1964. 1963 wurde er auf der *photokina* als einer von 36 großen Fotografen unseres Jahrhunderts vorgestellt. Klein gab 1965 die Fotografie zugunsten des Films auf, fing dann aber Ende der 70er Jahre wieder an zu fotografieren, diesmal in Farbe.

William Klein studied briefly with Fernand Léger in Paris and created abstract mural paintings for Italian architects; in 1953 he did abstract photograms as well. He returned to his native New York in 1954 and photographed this city. During 1955 to 1965 Klein was under contract with *Vogue*. He started film making in 1958, and has produced 22 films up to now. He always did the layout for his photo books, the first of which was on *New York* in 1956, followed by *Rome* 1958, *Moscou* and *Tokyo* 1964. At *photokina* 1963 in Cologne, he was voted one of 34 great photographers of our century. Klein abandoned photography in favor of filmmaking in 1965, but began photographing again in the late Seventies, this time in color.

Klett, Mark
*1952, USA

Mark Klett studierte Fotografie an der State University of New York in Buffalo, wo er 1977 seinen Magister erhielt. Zuvor hatte er schon einen Abschluß in Geologie gemacht und er ist wahrscheinlich der einzige Fotograf, nach dem ein Fossil benannt wurde. 1977 begründete Klett das "Rephotographic Survey Project" (RSP) und arbeitete als Leiter und Cheffotograf. Dabei wurden fotografische Landschaftsansichten des 19. Jahrhunderts nachfotografiert, um z.B. Veränderungen aufzuzeigen. Die Feldarbeit des RSP endete 1979, aber es dauerte noch Jahre, um das Buch darüber fertigzustellen.

Mark Klett studied photography at the State University of New York, Buffalo, receiving his M.F.A. degree in 1977. He graduated in geology before that and he probably is the only photographer with a fossil named after him. In 1977 Klett initiated the 'Rephotographic Survey Project' (RSP) and served as chief photographer. This assignment involved the photographic copying of 19th century landscapes in order to record changes. The fieldwork for the project was completed in 1979, but it took a further few years before the book was ready.

Kooiman, Geert
*1936, Niederlande

Bickersgracht 56a
1013 LG Amsterdam
The Netherlands

Kooiman studierte von 1953 bis 1958 an der Königlichen Akademie für Bildende Künste in Den Haag. 1959 erlernte er die Fotografie bei Aufenthalten in den USA und Kanada. Zwischen 1960 und 1971 arbeitete er als freier Fotograf in Amsterdam und gab 1971 die Fotografie zugunsten der Malerei auf.

Geert Kooiman attended the Royal Academy of Fine Arts in The Hague during 1953 to 1958. He then studied photography in the U.S. and Canada in 1959. Between 1960 and 1971 he worked as a freelance photographer in Amsterdam. In 1971 he abandoned photography in favor of painting.

Krims, Les
*1943, USA

187 Linwoord Ave.
Buffalo, N.Y. 14209
USA

Krims studierte an der Cooper Union und erhielt 1967 seinen Magister in Kunsterziehung am Pratt Institute. Seit 1969 ist er Professor an der State University of New York in Buffalo. Krims Fotos sind ausgefeilt arrangierte, z.T. groteske Tableaus, die Aspekte der amerikanischen Gesellschaft satirisch beleuchten. 1974 entstanden die ersten SX-70 Polaroidfotos, in denen Krims seinen sexuellen Phantasien freien Lauf ließ. Noch komplexer und elaborierter sind die ab 1980 mit der Großformatkamera entstandenen *Idiosyncratic Pictures* und zur Zeit ist Krims von riesengroßen Farbabzügen fasziniert.

Les Krims graduated from Cooper Union and received his Master of Fine Arts degree from Pratt Institute in 1967. Since 1969 he has been a professor at the State University of New York in Buffalo. His staged photographs are often grotesque, satirically highlighting certain aspects of American society. In 1974 Krims did his first SX-70 Polaroid prints, in which he gave free reign to his sexual phantasies. Even more complex and more elaborate are his *Idiosyncratic Pictures* of 1980, done with a view camera. Most recently Krims is fascinated by large size color images.

**Kühne Sabine/
Bernd Bauer**

"die Maske"
Albertusstr. 13-17
5000 Köln
West-Germany

Der ausgebildete Maskenbildner Bernd Bauer gründete 1981 in Köln, zusammen mit der Fotografin Sabine Kühne und dem Frisör und Stylisten Norbert Runda, eine Ateliergemeinschaft mit dem Namen "die Maske". Als freie künstlerische Projekte und für Werbezwecke werden Körper zu Statuen, Steinen, Klaviaturen, Schuhen oder Waschpulververpackungen geschminkt. Der 30jährige Bernd Bauer gilt als Europas bekanntester und bestbezahlter Make-up Künstler. Die 1957 in Offenburg geborene Fotografin Sabine Kühne erhielt 1978-80 ihre Ausbildung bei H.J. Baus in Köln, sie ist für die fotografische Dokumentation der Body-Art zuständig. "die maske" unterhält u.a. in Köln eine Galerie und eine Schminkschule.

In 1981 Bernd Bauer, a trained mask-designer – in collaboration with the photographer, Sabine Kühne and the hairdresser and stylist, Norbert Runda – founded the artists' association, 'die Maske'. As free artistic projects and alDso for advertising purposes, they painted bodies to look like statues, stones, keyboards, shoes or detergent cartons. The 30-year old Bernd Bauer is said to be the best known and best paid make-up artist in Europe. Sabine Kühne, who was born in Offenburg in 1957, did her photographic training with H.J. Baus in Cologne, 1978-80. She is responsible for the documentation of this Body-Art. 'die Maske' maintains a gallery and a make-up school in Cologne.

Kurigami, Kazumi
*1936, Japan

Suzuesohko 5F
1-14-24 Kaigan, Minato-ku
Tokyo 105
Japan

1961 Schloß er die Fachschule für Fotografie in Tokio ab und begann vier Jahre später als freier Werbefotograf zu arbeiten. 1975 hatte er unter dem Titel *Sky Camel* seine erste Einzelausstellung und im gleichen Jahr erhielt er auch erstmals die Auszeichnung des Art Directors Club Tokio, die ihm 1977, 1978 und 1980 widerum zugesprochen wurde. Er veröffentlichte in Japan eine ganze Reihe von Fotobüchern, darunter eines, das 1984 auch in New York erschien, es heißt *Alternates*.

Kurigami graduated from Tokyo College of Photography in 1961 and started his career as a freelance commercial photographer four years later. In 1975 he held his first solo exhibition entitled *Sky Camel* and also won the Tokyo Art Directors Club Award, which he received again in 1977, 1978 and 1980. In Japan he published numerous photo books, including one entitled *Alternates*, which was also published in New York in 1984.

Landwehrle, Donald C.
*1956, USA

9 Hother Lane
Bay Shore, N.Y. 11709
USA

1969, bei einem Familienurlaub in Kalifornien, machte Landwehrle seine ersten Fotos; er studierte dann Foto-Illustration am Rochester Institute of Technology. Er macht viele direkte, unmanipulierte Aufnahmen, von denen er aber dann häufig Teile für seine Mehrfachbelichtungen benutzt. Dabei achtet er sehr auf Farbe, Perspektive und Komposition, um schließlich realistisch wirkende Aufnahmen von strenger grafischer Gestaltung zu erhalten.

Donald Landwehrle took his first photographs on a family vacation to California in 1969, and he then studied photographic illustration at Rochester Institute of Technology. He still shoots many straight photographs, parts of which he uses for his multiple exposures. He is always very aware of color, perspective and composition, for the purpose of producing realistic, strong graphical images.

Larson, William
*1942, USA

152 Heacock Lane
Wyncote, PA 19095
USA

Larson studierte Kunstgeschichte und Fotografie und seit 1968 ist er Professor an der Tyler School of Art in Philadelphia. Larsons frühe Arbeiten beschäftigen sich mit den Raum/Zeit Relationen innerhalb des fotografischen Prozesses, aber außerhalb der menschlichen Wahrnehmung. Ende der 70er Jahre entstanden die *Little Pictures* (SX-70 Polaroids) und die *Big Pictures* (auf 50 x 60 cm Polacolor Material). Seit Anfang der 80er Jahre konzentriert sich Larson auf die Landschaftsfotografie, wobei er ein Gleichgewicht anstrebt zwischen dem authentischen Charakter der Fotografie und der subjektiven Farbauswahl.

William Larson studied art history and photography. Since 1968 he has been a professor at Tyler School of Art, Philadelphia. Larson's early works were about photographic space/time relationships beyond human perception. In the late 70's he created the *Little Pictures* (SX-70 Polaroids) and the *Big Pictures* (on 20 x 24" Polacolor material). Since the early 80's Larson has concentrated on landscape photography, striving for a balance between the authentic character of photography and his personal choice of colors.

Lazi, Franz
*1922, Deutschland

Pischekstr. 41
7000 Stuttgart 1
West-Germany

Der Sohn des Fotografen Adolf Lazi besuchte 1933-39 die Waldorfschule in Stuttgart. Er erlernte bei seinem Vater die Fotografie und eröffnete, ein Jahr nach der Meisterprüfung, 1949 ein Studio für Werbefotogarfie in Stuttgart. In den frühen 50er Jahren begann Lazi für seine Werbeaufnahmen die ersten Colorplanfilm zu verwenden. Später setzte Lazi oft Mehrfachbelichtungen ein, und seit 1965 widmet er sich vorzugsweise dem Filmen. Für seine Naturfilm- und Fotoaufnahmen reist er in die Antarktis, nach Indien, in die USA und viele andere Länder.

Son of a German photographer, Adolf Lazi, Franz Lazi was educated at the Waldorf School in Stuttgart 1933-39. He learnt his craft from his father and in 1949, a year after he graduated, he established a studio for commercial photography in Stuttgart. In the early Fifties he started to use the first large format color sheet film. Later Lazi often worked with multiple exposures and in 1965 he dedicated himself primarily to film making. For his nature films and photographs, he travels in the Antarctic, India, the USA and many other countries.

Lee, Russell
*1903, USA

3110 West Avenue
Austin, Texas 78705
USA

Studierte zunächst Chemie, dann Malerei und hatte kaum angefangen zu fotografieren, da wurde er 1936 von Roy Stryker in den Fotografenstab der Historical Section der Farm Security Administration (FSA) geholt, dem bisher größten und bedeutendsten Dokumentationsprojekt in der Geschichte der Fotografie. Wie einige andere FSA-Fotografen auch, fotografierte Lee gegen Ende der FSA-Zeit in Farbe. Zwischen 1947 und 1965 arbeitete Lee als Industrie- und Illustriertenfotograf, danach nur noch freiberuflich. Bis 1976 unterrichtete er Fotografie in Workshops.

Russel Lee initially studied chemistry, then painting. He had just started to photograph when Roy Stryker took him on to work as a staff photographer for the Historical Section of the Farm Security Administration, (FSA) in 1936. Towards the end of this project, which was to become one of the largest and most important documentations in the history of photography, Russel Lee – together with a few other FSA photographers – started some color work. From 1947-1965 he worked as an industrial and magazine photographer and after that as a freelancer. Until 1976, Lee taught photography at workshops.

Leeuwen, Piet van
*1942, Niederlande

Hagestraat 18
2011 CV Haarlem
The Netherlands

1956 fing Piet van Leeuwen an zu fotografieren. Er arbeitete eine zeitlang im Holzhandel seiner Eltern und nach dem Militärdienst besuchte er dann in Den Haag eine Schule für Fotografie und Fototechnik. Mitte der 60er Jahre arbeitete er in der Fotoredaktion einer Tageszeitung und begann als selbständiger Fotograf tätig zu werden. 1977 eröffnete er die Galerie VAN, die er bis 1981 leitete. Zur Realisation eigenständiger Projekte erhielt er verschiedene Stipendien, zuletzt 1985 eines von der Provinz Nord-Holland.

Piet van Leeuwen took his first photos in 1956, while assisting in his family's timber-trade, and after military service enrolled at a school for photography and photo technics in The Hague. In the Mid-Sixties he worked on the Picture editiorial staff of a newspaper and started his career as a freelance photographer. He opened his own gallery in 1977 and maintained it until 1981. In order to realize personal projects he has received various grants, the latest from the Province of North Holland in 1985.

Le Guay, Laurence
*Australien

Sein Interesse an der Fotografie als Ausdrucks- und Kommunikationsmittel reicht zurück bis in die frühen dreißiger Jahre. Während des Kriegs diente er als Luftbildfotograf im Range eines Offiziers in den Einsatzgebieten Mittlerer Osten und Europa. Wieder zurück in Australien wurde er Fotograf und Kameramann bei der ersten australischen Nachkriegsexpedition in die Antarktis. Seitdem hat er an vielen weiteren Expeditionen teilgenommen, sowie Fotoaufträge für Agenturen und Publikationen in der ganzen Welt ausgeführt. 1946 gründete er die erste unabhängige australische Fotozeitschrift, *Contemporary Photography* die er einige Jahre lang leitete.

Laurence Le Guay's interest in the medium as a means of self-expression and visual communication goes back to the early Thirties. He served during the war as a flying officer-photographer in the Middle East and Europe. On returning to Australia he went as a photographer and cameraman with the first post-war Australian Antarctic expedition. Since then he has taken part in many geographical expeditions and photographic assignments for local and overseas agencies and publications in most of the world. In 1946 he founded the first independent Australian photographic magazine, *Contemporary Photography*, of which he was editor for a number of years.

Leistner, Dieter
*1952, Deutschland

Syburger Dorfstr. 27-29
4600 Dortmund 30
West-Germany

Dieter Leistner absolvierte eine Tischlerlehre und fotografierte nebenbei für Tageszeitungen. 1977 begann er – statt Architektur wie geplant – Fotografie zu studieren. 1982 machte er an der Gesamthochschule in Essen sein Examen mit 40 Farbfotos von *Deutschen Hallenbädern vor 1944.* Seit 1983 unterrichtet Leistner Architekturfotografie an der FH Dortmund und leitet die Sommerakademie für Architekturfotografie in Amiens. Er fotografierte u.a die neuen Museen in Frankfurt und illustrierte das 1986 erschienene Buch über das Gebäude der Kunstsammlung Nordrhein-Westfalen in Düsseldorf.

As carpentry apprentice, Dieter Leistner freelanced for local newpapers. In 1977 he began to study photography instead of architecture and in 1982 graduated from the University in Essen with a series of 40 color photographs on German indoor swimmingbaths before 1914. Since 1983 Leistner has been teaching architectural photography in Dortmund and directed the summer academy in Amiens, France. He documented the new museum buildings in Frankfurt and illustrated a book, published in 1986, on the new building of the Nordrhein-Westfalian art collection, based in Düsseldorf.

Lennard, Elizabeth
*1953, USA

591 West 26th Street
New York, 10001
USA

Elizabeth Lennard, die abwechselnd in Paris und New York lebt, erhielt ihre Ausbildung am San Francisco Art Institute, wo sie damit begann, ihre Schwarzweißfotos zu kolorieren. Sie studierte danach an der Abteilung für Film und Fernsehen der Universität in Los Angeles. Außer als Fotografin arbeitet sie auch als Filmemacherin: Sie dreht Filme für das französische Fernsehen, produziert aber auch selbst. Ihre Fotos von New York soolen demnächst zusammen mit Texten von Wim Wenders als Buch erscheinen.

Elizabeth Lennard, who lives between Paris, France and New York, attended the San Francisco Art Institute where she started to paint her black & white photographs. Subsequently she studied at the Department of Motion Pictures/Television at UCLA. Besides being a photographer, she is a film-maker, producing the films herself or on commission of the French TV. Her photographs of New York accompanied by texts of Wim Wenders will soon be published in a monographic book.

Levine, Michael
*1952, USA

Seit zehn Jahren beschäftigt sich der Künstler Michael Levine mit Fotografie, Malerei und Bildhauerei und zwar sowohl voneinander unabhängig als auch in der Kombination. Zuvor hatte er als freier Fotograf Aufnahmen in Filmkulissen gemacht und dann die Skulpturen und Gemälde anderer Künstler fotografiert. Nun aber befaßt sich Levine mit dem Formenrepertoire der Großstadt und mit der Frage, wie sich dieses in seine eingenen Bilder umsetzen läßt. In den Environments, die er in seinem Studio aufbaut, tauchen Gebäudefassaden, Schornsteine und Telefomasten auf. Nach der Aufnahmen wird das Arrangement zerstört und die Teile zu neuen Kombinationen zusammengefügt.

Michael Levine is an artist who has been working in photography, sculpture and painting separately and combined for the past decade. He first worked as a freelance photographer, doing stills on movie sets and later photographing sculptures and paintings for other artists. Nowadays Levine is concerned with city layouts and forms and how he can transfer them to his own images. Building facades, chimneys and telephone poles appear in these environments which he has actually fabricated in his studio. Once the photograph has been produced, the 'environments' are demolished and turned into new combinations.

Levitt, Helen
*1913, USA

Helen Levitt begann Ende der 30er Jahre zu fotografieren und war u.a. mit →Walker Evans befreundet, dessen Auffassung von Fotografie sie offensichtlich teilt. Seit den 40er Jahren fotografiert sie in jenen Stadtteilen von New York, in denen sich ein Teil des Familienlebens auf der Straße abspielt. Ihre Aufnahmen dokumentieren Alltäglichkeit; sie zeigen Menschen, vor allem Kinder, die in ihrer 'zufälligen' Konstellation eine sinnvolle Bildstruktur ergeben. Mehr als zehn Jahre lang widmete sich Levitt dem Filmen, sie kehrte dann aber um 1959 zur Fotografie zurück und seitdem entstehen ihre Straßenfotografien in Farbe. Ihre Farbfotos sind abgedruckt in einem Katalog, der 1980 in den USA erschien.

Helen Levitt's involvement with photography began in the late 1930's. At the time she was a close associate of →Walker Evans and she obviously shared Evans attitude towards photography. Since the 40's she has been a street photographer in New York City, working in neighbourhoods where people live much of their domestic lives out on the street. Levitt's pictures show people, mostly children, who in their 'coincidental' constellations, somehow form a meaningful photographic composition. For more than a decade Levitt dedicated herself to film making, but she turned back to photography in about 1959, and since that time she has done her street photography in color. A catalogue on her color work was published in 1980.

Liberman, Alexander
*1912, Rußland

173 East 70th Street
New York, N.Y. 10021
USA

Liberman ging in England zur Schule und studierte in Paris, wo er bis 1941 lebte. 1933-36 war er dort Art Direktor, dann Chefredakteur des Magazins *Vu*, anschließend freier Maler. 1941 emigrierte er in die USA, arbeitete als Layouter und wurde 1943 Art Direktor bei *Vogue*, New York. In der Zeit bis 1961 war aber Liberman nicht nur einer der einflußreichsten und bedeutendsten Auftraggeber von Fotografen, er hatte 1949 auch selbst angefangen zu fotografieren, speziell Künstler und ihre Werke. Seit 1962 zeichnet Liberman als Redaktionsleiter der Condé Nast Publications für die Gestaltung einer großen Gruppe von Mode- und Wohnzeitschriften verantwortlich.

Alexander Liberman was educated in England and studied in Paris, where he lived until 1941. From 1933-36 he was an art director, then managing editor of *Vu* magazine, and subsequently a painter. He emigrated to the States in 1941, initially working as a layout artist, and he became art director to *Vogue* in 1943. During the period until 1961 Liberman not only was a very influential and important employer of photographers, but he himself photographed since 1949, specializing in art and artists. Since 1962 Liberman has been editorial director of Condé Nast Publications, responsible for quite a number of fashion and architectural magazines.

Liebling, Jerome
*1924, USA

39 Dana Street
Amherst, MA. 01002
USA

Liebling studierte Kunst am Brooklyn College und machte bei Walter Rosenblum seinen Abschluß in Fotografie. Er trat der Photo-League bei, wo er am Unterricht von Paul Strand teilnahm. 1948 fing er an, als künstlerischer Fotograf und Filmemacher zu arbeiten, im Jahr darauf begann er, sowohl Film als auch Fotografie zu unterrichten. Liebling gehört unter anderem zu den Gründungsmitgliedern der Society of Photographic Education und ist der Herausgeber des Buches *Photography: Current Perspectives* von 1979. Seine Aufnahmen sind sozialdokumentarisch und zugleich auch formal-ästhetisch außergewöhnlich gelungen.

Jerome Liebling studied art at Brooklyn College, majoring in photography under Walter Rosenblum. He became a member of the Photo-League where he attended classes with Paul Strand. In 1948 Liebling became actively involved as both a creative photographer and a film-maker. He began teaching photography and filming in 1949. He is a founding member of the Society of Photographic Education and editor of *Photography: Current Perspectives* (1979). His photographs are social documentaries yet at the same time extraordinary in a formally aesthetic light.

Lipchitz, Yulla
*Deutschland

Vor dem Ersten Weltkrieg als Tochter jüdisch orthodoxer Eltern in Berlin geboren, studierte sie später Mathematik und Physik. Heimlich nahm sie mehrmals in der Woche unterricht in Bildhauerei. 1938 emigrierte sie in die USA, wo sie den Bildhauer Jacques Lipchitz traf, 1947 heiratete und mit ihm in Italien und New York lebte. Als Lipchitz 1973 verstarb, beendete sie seine Arbeiten. 1979 begann Yulla Lipchitz zu fotografieren.

Born in Berlin before World War I into an orthodox Jewish family, Yulla's education focused on mathematics and physics. Secretly she studied sculpture several times a week. In 1938 she emigrated to the USA where she met the sculptor Jacques Lipchitz. In 1947 they married and maintained homes in Italy and New York. When Jacques Lipschitz died in 1973, Yulla completed unfinished works. In 1979 she began to photograph.

List, Herbert
*1903, Deutschland
† 1975, Deutschland

Im Auftrag der väterlichen Kaffee-Importfirma unternahm Herbert List weite Reisen. 1929 begegnete er Andreas Feininger, der ihn mit der Fotografie vertraut machte. Unter dem Einfluß des Surrealismus entstanden Lists 'metaphysische' Fotografien. Gegen Ende der 30er Jahre fotografierte er in Paris für Illustrierte wie *Verve* und *Vogue*. Zwischen 1940 und 1950 entstanden zahlreiche Künstlerporträts und von 1954 bis 1960 wurden Lists Reisereportagen in Farbe hauptsächlich in *DU*, aber auch in anderen Magazinen publiziert. Danach gab List die Fotografie schrittweise auf.

Working in his family's coffee business, Herbert List travelled widely. In 1929 he met Andreas Feininger, who introduced him to photography. List's still life photographs, taken outdoors, were influenced by Surrealism. In Paris, in the late Thirties, List collaborated with the magazines *Verve* and *Vogue*. For several years he then photographed in Greece and in the Forties he did numerous portraits of artists. During 1954 to 1960 his travel reportages in color were mainly published in the Swiss magazine *DU*, but also in other magazines. After that period, List gradually abandoned photography.

Lomeo, Angelo
*1921, Italien

Seit mehr als dreißig Jahren arbeitet Angelo Lomeo zusammen mit seiner Frau →Sonia Bullaty auf dem Gebiet der Reportage in Farbe. Lomeo hatte Malerei und Design studiert, bevor er zur Fotografie kam. Er wurde insbesondere bekannt für seine sehr grafisch wirkenden Naturstudien, die in zahlreichen Bildbänden erschienen. Zusammen mit Sonia Bullaty publizierte er *Vermont in All Weathers* (1973) und *Circle of Seasons – Central Park Celebrated* (1984).

For more than thirty years Angelo Lomeo and his wife →Sonia Bullaty worked together in the field of color reportage. Lomeo studied painting and design before turning to photography. He became particularly known for his nature studies of strong graphic form, published in several picture books. Together with his wife, he published *Vermont in All Weathers* (1973) and *Circle of Seasons* (1984).

Ludwig, Pit
*1916, Deutschland

Kranichsteiner Str. 108
6100 Darmstadt
West-Germany

Pit Ludwig studierte neun Semester lang Medizin und absolvierte dann ein Volontariat bei Sonia Georgi in Berlin. Nachdem er eine Bildberichterstatter-Prüfung abgelegt hatte, wurde er Pressefotograf bei TOBIS-Film. Bis 1948 arbeitete er dann für *Die Mode, Die neue Linie, Silberspiegel* und andere Magazine. 1948 zog er nach Darmstadt und wurde Pressefotograf beim *Darmstädter Echo*. Seit 1951 ist Pit Ludwig Fotograf am Darmstädter Theater; er gehört zu Deutschlands führenden Bühnenfotografen. Sein kürzlich verkauftes Archiv dokumentiert 35 Jahre Theatergeschichte.

Pit Ludwig studied medicine, but switched to photography before his graduation. He was assistant to Sonja Georgi in Berlin, to become later the press photographer for TOBIS-Film. Until 1948 Ludwig contributed to magazines such as *Die Mode, Die neue Linie, Silberspiegel*. He then moved to Darmstadt where he has been working for the local newspaper. In 1951 his involvement with the Darmstadt theater began and Ludwig soon became a leading stage photographer. His recently sold archive, records 35 years of theater history.

Lüttge, Thomas
*1941, Deutschland

Zeltstr. 2
8157 Ascholding
West-Germany

Thomas Lüttge erhielt seine Ausbildung an den Kunstakademien in Hamburg und Karlsruhe, sowie an der Bayerischen Staatslehranstalt für Photographie in München. Seit 1965 ist er als Fotograf selbständig. Seine Beziehung zur Malerei, insbesondere zum Surrealismus und zur Renaissance, beeinflußten zunächst seine fotografische Arbeit. Auf der photokina 1976 zeigte er Aktfotografien bei denen der Farbe als Ausdrucksmittel eine entscheidende Rolle zukam. Seitdem befaßt sich Lüttge mit Industriefotografie, sowie mit freien Projekten, die häufig in Ostasien realisiert werden, so z.B. 1985 *Bangkok Through a Looking Glass*, Fotos, die in Thailand als Wanderausstellung unterwegs sind.

Thomas Lüttge attended art academies in Hamburg and Karlsruhe and studied photography in Munich. In 1965 he established himself as a professional photographer. His special interest in Surrealist and Renaissance painting initially influenced his photographic work. Color as a means of expression played a prominent part in his nude studies, exhibited at photokina in 1976. Since that time, Lüttge has been involved with both industrial photography and personal projects, which he often produced in East Asia, e.g. *Bangkok Through a Looking Glass*, launched as a touring exhibition in Thailand in 1985.

Mack, Ulrich
*1934, Deutschland

Isestr. 111
2000 Hamburg
West-Germany

Von 1956 bis 1962 studierte Mack Grafik und Fotografie an der Hochschule für Bildende Künste in Hamburg. Bis 1967 arbeitete er dann als Fotojournalist für *Quick, Twen* und *DU*. Er war Redaktionsfotograf des *Stern*, bis er 1972 in Hamburg ein eigenes Studio eröffenete. 1975 begann er an der Fachhochschule in Dortmund zu lehren, 1967 wurde er Professor für visuelle Kommunikation. 1978 begann er seine Farbdokumentation über die Bewohner der Nordseeinsel Pellworm. 1984 entstanden Farbaufnahmen an der Küste von North Carolina, USA.

Ulrich Mack studied graphics and photography at the Academy of Fine Arts in Hamburg 1956-62. Thereafter he worked as a photo journalist for the magazines *Quick, Twen* and *DU*. He joined the photographic staff of the magazine *Stern* in 1967 and left in 1972 when he opened up his own studio in Hamburg. Mack started to lecture at the college in Dortmund and has been professor for Visual Communications since 1967. In 1978 he started his color documentary on Pellworm, an island in the North Sea, and its inhabitants. During 1984 he began work on the North Carolina Coast.

Maeda, Shinzo
*1922, Japan

Tankei Co, Ltd.
402 Maison Aoyama 2-7-26
Kita-Aoyama Minato-Ku,
Tokyo
Japan

Maeda arbeitete zunächst 17 Jahre lang bei der Firma Nichimen, bevor er 1976 die Tankei Fotoagentur gründete und seine Laufbahn als Berufsfotograf begann. Er machte sich ab den frühen 70er Jahren einen Namen für seine Naturstudien in Farbe, die in zahlreichen Bildbänden veröffentlicht wurden, 1978 stellte er schon einmal auf der *photokina* aus. 1983 erschien in Japan eine Monografie über sein fotografisches Gesamtwerk.

For 17 years Shinzo Maeda was employed with Nichimen Company, before he founded the Tankei photo agency in 1976 and started his career as a professional photographer. Since the early 70's Maeda is wellknown for his excellent color studies of nature, published in quite a number of photo books. In 1978 he first participated in the *photokina* exhibition. In 1983 a retrospective monograph, entitled *Shinzo Maeda* was published in Japan.

Maisel, Jay
*1931, USA

190 The Bowery
New York, N.Y. 10012
USA

Jay Maisel, der zu den bekanntesten Farbfotografen zählt, studierte u.a. Farbtheorie bei Joseph Albers. Fotokurse belegte er bei Herbert Matter und Alexey Brodovitch. Seit 1954 arbeitet Maisel freiberuflich für Illustrierte, Werbeagenturen und Industriefirmen. Bekannt wurde er nicht zuletzt durch seine farbigen Städtefotos; so fotografierte er für die Buchserie über Großstädte von *Time Life* die Bände über Jerusalem, San Francisco und viele Aufnahmen des New York Bandes. 1986 erschien das von Maisel herausgegebene Buch *The Most Beautiful Place in the World* zu dem er selbst Fotos von New York beisteuerte.

Jay Maisel, a popular color photographer, studied painting at Cooper Union and color theory under Joseph Albers. He also took photographic courses with Herbert Matter and Alexey Brodovitch. Since 1954 he is a freelance photographer for magazines, advertising agencies and corporations. Maisel became especially known for his color photographs of cities. He illustrated the Jerusalem and the San Francisco issues of the *Great City Series* by Time Life and contributed to the New York book. His most recent project is a book, published by himself, called *The Most Beautiful Place in the World* featuring his photographs of his beloved New York City.

Mall, Hubertus

Taubenheimstr. 23
7000 Stuttgart 50
West-Germany

Mall besuchte den Unterricht von Johannes Itten an der Kunstgewerbeschule in Zürich, sowie die Schule für Gebrauchsgrafik in Hamburg. Er arbeitete zunächst als Grafiker und Karikaturist, bis er mitte der 60er Jahre zur Fotografie kam. Von Anfang an befaßte er sich mit der Farbe als Ausdrucksmittel seiner, der experimentellen Fotografie zuzurechnenden Arbeiten. Seine Bildmontagen und Verfremdungen entstehen oft im Auftrag von Verlagen für Buchumschläge oder für Schallplattenhüllen. Mall realisierte aber ebenso Titelseiten für *Das Deutsche Lichtbild* und die Zeitschrift *Epoca*.

Hubertus Mall attended the classes of Johannes Itten at the school of arts and crafts in Zurich, and he also studied commercial design in Hamburg. Initially he worked as a graphic artist an caricaturist until the mid-Sixties when he turned to photography. Right from the start Mall used color as a means of expression in his experimental photo works. His montages and photo compositions are often created on commission by publishers to illustrate book or music record covers. Mall also produced covers for *Das Deutsche Lichtbild* and the magazine *Epoca*.

Maloney, Joe
*1949, USA

1976 schloß Joe Maloney seine Fotografenausbildung am Ramapo College in New Jersey ab. Seit 1977 arbeitet er für Pace Editions. Die Schwarzweißfotografie erlernte Maloney in der Armee und seit 1976 arbeitet er mit einer Großformatkamera in Farbe. Die unnatürliche Farbigkeit seiner Abzüge erreicht er durch die Benutzung von Kunstlichtfilm bei Tageslicht, und durch die zum Teil mehrere Minuten lange Belichtungszeit erscheinen bewegte Objekte im Foto verwischt.

Joe Maloney received his B.A. in photography from Ramapo College, New Jersey, in 1976. Since 1977 he has worked at Pace Editions and moved to New York in 1979. Joe Maloney learned black-and-white photography while in the army and since 1976 he has worked with a 4x5" view camera. The unusual colors in his prints are derived from the use of film for artificial light in daylight and the delayed exposure time, up to several minutes, is responsible for the blurring in Maloney's photographs.

Man Ray
(Emmanuel Rudnitsky)
*1890, USA, † 1976, Paris

Nahm 1913 den Künstlernahmen Man Ray an und ging 1921 nach Paris, wo er der Gruppe der Dadaisten angehörte. In Paris entstanden ab 1922 die ersten Rayografien, Porträts, sowie Modefotos für Paul Poiret. Später fotografierte Man Ray auch für *Vogue*. 1940 schloß er sein Studio in Paris, floh vor den Deutschen nach New York und kehrte 1951 nach Paris zurück. 1963 erschien seine Autobiografie. Sein breitgefächertes künstlerisches Oeuvre umfaßt Gemälde, Objekte, Collagen, Fotografien und Filme.

In 1913 Emmanuel Rudnitsky started to work under the artist's name, Man Ray. He went to Paris in 1921, where he joined the Dadaist group. In Paris he invented the 'Rayographs' in 1922, did a considerable number of portraits and produced fashion photographs for Paul Poiret. Later Man Ray also photographed for *Vogue*. In 1940 he closed his studio, fled from the Germans to New York to return to Paris in 1951. In 1963 his autobiography appeared. His wide range of artistic achievements include paintings, sculptures, collages, photos and films.

Mante, Harald
*1936, Deutschland

Am Kraftwerk 11
4600 Dortmund 50
West-Germany

Mante studierte Malerei in Wiesbaden und begann 1960 als Amateur zu fotografieren. 1964 fotografierte er drei Monate lang in Irland, diese Fotos erschienen dann im *Stern* und in *Twen*. Seitdem widmet sich Harald Mante ganz der Fotografie. Bevorzugt in Reihen und Sequenzen arbeitend, wurde er zum Exponenten einer formalen, sehr grafischen Richtung in der Farbfotografie. Seit 1971 unterrichtet er, seit 1976 als Professor and der Fachhochschule in Dortmund. Er wurde überdies bekannt durch seine in Buchform und in Fotozeitschriften erscheinende Anleitungen zur Farbfotografie.

Harald Mante studied painting in Wiesbaden and in 1960 he started amateur photography. In 1964 he travelled through Ireland for three months, his pictures of Ireland were published by the magazines *Stern* and *Twen* and this lead to his taking up photography as a full-time occupation. Mante became an exponent of a formal, very graphic style of color photography. Since 1971 he has been teaching and from 1976 he has been a professor at the Technical College in Dortmund. Mante also is very well known for his instructional notations published in books and photographic magazines.

Manual (Suzanne Bloom & Ed Hill)
*1943, Suzanne Bloom, USA
*1935, Ed Hill, USA

Bloom, die 1943 in Philadelpia geboren ist, studierte bis 1968 an der Universität von Pennsylvania. Hill, 1935 in Springfield, Massachusetts, geboren studierte bis 1960 Kunst und Architektur in Yale. Beide unterrichten seit 1976 an der Universität von Houston in Texas. Im Jahr zuvor hatten sie begonnen, gemeinsam auszustellen.

Bloom was born in Philadelpia in 1943 and studied at the University of Pennsylvania. Hill (1938) was born in Springfield, Massachusetts and studied Art and Architecture at Yale. Both photographers have been teaching at the University of Houston since 1976. A year before that they started to do joint exhibitions of their work.

Mapplethorpe, Robert
*1946, USA

24 Bond Street
New York, N.Y. 10012
USA

Mapplethorpe studierte 1963-1970 am Pratt Institute in Brooklyn und drehte Underground-Filme. 1968-72 lebte er als freier Künstler zusammen mit der Rocksängerin Patti Smith im Hotel Chelsea. 1971 entstanden dann erste Porträtfotos in Schwarzweiß und im Jahr darauf eröffnete Mapplethorpe ein Studio. Er wurde ab Mitte der 70er Jahre international bekannt durch seine Porträts, *sex pictures* und Blumenstilleben. 1980-82 entstanden u.a. die Fotos von Lisa Lyon, die auch in Deutschland als Buch erschienen. 1981 begann er in Farbe zu fotografieren; und arbeitet für die Magazine *Vogue* und *GEO*.

Robert Mapplethorpe studied at Pratt Institute while producing Underground films at the same time. From 1968-72 he lived together with the rock singer, Patti Smith in the Chelsea Hotel. Mapplethorpe did his first black & white portraits in 1971 and opened up a studio the following year. Since the mid-Seventies he gained international recognition with his portrait work, *sex pictures* and flower still lifes. During 1980-82 he portrayed Lisa Lyon, which later appeared as a book. Mapplethorpe started to work in color in 1981, collaborating with the magazines *Vogue* and *GEO*.

March, Charlotte
* Deutschland

Jarrestr. 80
2000 Hamburg 60
West-Germany

Als in Deutschland geborene Tochter einer russischen Mutter und eines deutschen Vaters aus der Nähe von Shanghei besuchte sie 1950-54 in Hamburg die Kunstschule und arbeitete anschließend als Grafikerin. 1955 entschloß sie sich Fotografin zu werden, und eröffnete 1961 ein eigenes Atelier in Hamburg, in dem sie seitdem für Werbeagenturen und Zeitschriften aus dem In- und Ausland tätig ist. 1978 veröffentlichte sie *Mann, oh Mann*, ein Buch mit erotischen Farbfotografien. Insbesondere bekannt und ausgezeichnet für ihre Modefotos, hat Charlotte March seit 1984 in Mailand eine zweite Dependance.

Born in Germany as the daughter of a Russian mother and a German father, both from the Shaghai-area, Charlotte March attended the art academy in Hamburg between 1950-1954. She first worked as a graphic designer but then decided to become a photographer. Six years later she established her own studio in Hamburg and started to work for advertising agencies and magazines in Germany and abroad. Her erotic color photographs of men were published in 1978, entitled *Mann, oh Mann*. Especially known and awarded for her fashion photographs, Charlotte March operates from a second basis in Milan since 1984.

Margolies, John
*1940, USA

Nachdem er Kunstgeschichte, Publizistik und Fotografie studiert hatte, war Margolies vier Jahre lang stellvertretender Chefredakteur der Zeitschrift *Architectural Record*. Margolies schreibt, lehrt und ist seit 1975 als Fotograf tätig. Sein Interesse gilt insbesondere der typisch amerikanischen Architektur und Alltagskultur. Sein erstes großes Projekt *Resorts of the Catskills* wurde 1979 als Buch publiziert. Für das 1981 erschienene Fotobuch *The End of the Road*, eine Farbserie über vor dem Abriß stehende Gebäude entlang der amerikanischen Highways, machte er über 30.000 Aufnahmen von Gewerbebauten.

Following his studies in art history, journalism and photography John Margolies served as assistant editor of the magazine, *Architectural Record* between 1964-68. He is active as a writer, lecturer and full-time photographer with a special interest in architecture and popular culture since 1975. His first major photographic project, entitled *Resorts of the Catskills* was published in 1979. He then produced 30,000 color photographs of buildings along the American highways, which were about to be demolished. This resulted in the book *The End of the Road: Vanishing Highway Architecture in America*.

Mark, Mary Ellen
*1940, USA

143 Prince Street
New York, N.Y. 10012
USA

Mark studierte Kunstgeschichte und Malerei. 1963 wandte sie sich der Fotografie zu und erhielt 1964 ihren Magister. Ein Fulbright-Stipendium ermöglichte es ihr, 1965-66 in der Türkei zu fotografieren. Seit 1966 arbeitet sie freiberuflich für Magazine in den USA und Europa. 1978-79 fotografierte sie die Prostituierten in Bombay; *Falkland Road* erschien 1981 als Buch. Für ihre nachfolgende Reportage über *Mutter Teresa in Calcutta* erhielt sie mehrere Auszeichnungen.

Mary Ellen Mark studied art history and painting. In 1963 she decided to become a photographer and she received her Master of Fine Arts degree in 1964. She received a Fulbright scolarship to photograph in Turkey 1965-66. Since that time she has been working freelance, collaborating with magazines in the States and Europe. She worked on *Falkland Road*, a series on the prostitutes in Bombay, during 1978-79, which in 1981 resulted in a book. For her subsequent reportage on *Mother Teresa in Calcutta* she received several awards.

Mayes, Elaine
*1938, USA

18 Mercer Street
New York, N.Y. 10013
USA

Elaine Mayes erhielt 1959 ihren B.F.A. von der Stanford University und studierte dann Fotografie. Von 1961 bis 1968 arbeitete sie als kommerzielle Fotografin, hauptsächlich als Fotojournalistin. Seitdem unterrichtet sie, dreht Kurz- und Videofilme und widmet sich der künstlerischen Fotografie. An ihrer Serie *Things On the Ground* (Dinge auf dem Boden) begann sie 1978 zu arbeiten. Sie ist in Farbe, weil ihr dies als deskriptives Element wichtig ist, denn die Farbe der Objekte bestimmt auch die Reaktion auf sie.

After receiving her B.F.A. from Stanford University, Elaine Mayes studied photography. She then did commercial photography, primarily photo-journalism, during 1961 to 1968. Since that period she teaches, makes video and short films and devotes herself to photography as an art form. She has been working on her series, *Things On the Ground* since 1978. 'This series is in color', she says, 'because it is important as a descriptive element. Also, the colors of things affect my responses to them.'

Mazzer, Bob
*1948, Großbritannien

35A Clapham Common
North Side
London SW4 ORW
Great Britain

Mazzer begann sich als Dreizehnjähriger für die Fotografie zu interssieren und studierte 1966-1970 am Hamsey College of Art. Schon während der Schulzeit machte er seine ersten Aufnahmen von Menschen in der Undergrundbahn, damals in Schwarzweiß, ab 1979 auch in Farbe, denn das Thema hat ihn bis heute nicht losgelassen. Seit 1984 arbeitet er aber auch an einem Buch über Exzentriker, machte Werbe- und Plattencoverfotos für Bands wie Dire Straits, sowie Porträts für einen Verlag.

Bob Mazzer became interested in photography at the age of 13. He studied at the Hamsey College of Art between 1966-1970. While still at school he took his first photographs on the Underground, in black & white at that time but since 1976 also in color. From 1984 on he has been working on a book about eccentrics, while doing publicity and album photography for bands such as Dire Straits and portraits for a publishing house. Mazzer still photographs on the Underground.

McBride, Will
*1931, USA

Leipziger Str. 36
6000 Frankfurt 90
West-Germany

McBride studierte zunächst Illustration bei Norman Rockwell, dann Kunstgeschichte und Malerei. 1953-55 diente er als Fotograf in der Armee und war in Würzburg stationiert. Er blieb in Deutschland und von 1956 bis 1972 arbeitete er als freier Fotograf für *Life, Look, Paris Match, Stern*, hauptsächlich aber für das von Willy Fleckhaus gestaltete Magazin *Twen*, das durch seine Farbfotografien wesentlich mitgeprägt wurde. Zwischen 1974 und 1979 organisierte McBride Sommerakademien für Fotostudenten in seinem Haus in der Toskana, seit 1984 hat er ein Studio in Frankfurt. Außer als Fotograf, machte sich McBride auch als bildender Künstler einen Namen.

Will McBride studied illustration with Norman Rockwell as well as art history and painting. 1953-55 he served as a photographer in the U.S. Army, Würzburg. He stayed in Germany, and during 1956 to 1972 worked as a freelance photographer, contributing to *Life, Look, Paris Match, Stern*, but mainly to *Twen*, which was designed by Willy Fleckhaus, and carried a considerable number of McBrides color work. From 1974 to 79 McBride organized summer academies for photo students in his house in the Toscana, Italy. Since 1984 he maintains a studio in Frankfurt. A recognized photographer, Will McBride also became known in the world of fine arts, particularly for his sculptures.

McCord, Melissa
*1961, Australien

McCord entstammt einer Viehzüchter-Familie und begann 1979 intensiv zu fotografieren. Es entstanden Fotos von Theaterschauspielern und Musikern. 1980 zog sie nach Sydney und hielt sich dann länger in Jordanien auf, wo sie Ausgrabungen und einen Beduinenstamm fotografierte. 1982 machte sie Farbfotos in Griechenland und auf Kreta und wurde Büromanager der *Rapport Photo Agency* in Sydney. Sie arbeitet weiterhin als Reportagefotografin und für Werbezwecke, außerdem entstehen Porträts, Landschaftsaufnahmen und Stilleben. 1986 erscheint ihr Buch mit Farbporträts und Interviews über australische *Outback Women*.

Melissa McCord grew up on her family's cattle ranch and took up photography intensively in 1979, portraying actors and musicians. She moved to Sydney in 1980 and spent 1980-81 in Jordania, photographing excavations and tribes of Beduins. The following year, McCord did a great deal of color photography in Greece and Crete and when she arrived back in Sydney, she took up a position as office manager for *Rapport Photo Agency*. She continues with assignments and also pursues personal creative portraits, landscapes and still lifes. In 1986 her book on Australia's *Outback Women*, including interviews and color portraits will be published.

McGowan, Kenneth
*1940, USA

504 La Guardia Place
New York, N.Y. 10012
USA

McGowan machte seinen Magister in Kunsterziehung an der Universität in Los Angeles. Als Autodidakt fing er 1959 an, in Schwarzweiß zu fotografieren, 1967 wechselte er zur Farbe. Als Berufsfotograf produziert er seit Mitte der 60er Jahre Diashows, sowie die Spezialeffekte bei Filmen. Seit 1975 fotografiert er mit der Großbildkamera kalifornische Phänomene vom Filmstar bis zum Bodybuilder, die er auf bizarre und parodistische Weise in extrem farbig präsentiert.

Kenneth McGowan received his Master of Fine Arts degree from the University of California, Los Angeles. He taught himself black & white photography in 1959 and turned to color in 1967. Since the mid-Sixties he has been a professional photographer, doing portraits, slide shows, record album covers and contributing to magazines. He additionally produced special effects for movies. Since 1975 McGowan has been working with a view camera, picturing Californian phenomena from movie stars to body builders, and presenting them in a parodistic and bizare manner in his color-saturated photographs.

McGrath, Jerry
*1954, USA

2314 Blackfoot Ave.
Placentia, CA 92670
USA

McGrath studierte an der State University in Fullerton und machte dort 1979, mit dem Schwerpunkt Fotografie, seinen Magister. Seitdem unterrichtet er als Professor für Fotografie die Fächer Illustration, Design und Farbtheorie. 1977 begann er selbst in Farbe zu fotografieren und heute hat er sich auf "Studio Tableaus" spezialisiert.

Jerry McGrath studied visual arts at California State University, Fullerton, where he received his M.F.A. degree in 1979. Since his graduation he has had a professorship there, teaching photographic illustration, design and color theory. He began to photograph in color himself in 1977 spezializing in 'studio tableaux'.

McLaughlin-Gill, Frances
*USA

454 West 46 Street
New York, N.Y. 10036
USA

Frances McLaughlin begann zu fotografieren, nachdem sie 1941 ihr Kunststudium am Pratt Institute abgeschlossen hatte. Bei *Vogues Prix de Paris* Wettbewerb wurde ihr eine ehrende Anerkennung zuteil und daraufhin erhielt sie die Stelle einer Modekoordinatorin. Sie gab diese Position bald auf, um Assistentin bei einem Fotografen zu werden und 1944 fing sie dann als Fotografin bei Condé Nast an, wo sie bis 1955 für *Vogue, Glamour* und *House & Garden* Aufnahmen machte. Seitdem arbeitet sie freiberuflich und zwischen 1964 und 1973 drehte sie zusätzlich Werbespots für das Fernsehen. Als Fotografin und Autorin gab sie fünf Bücher heraus, das letzte war eine Monografie über ihren verstorbenen Mann, →Leslie Gill, mit dem Titel *A Classical Approach to Photography 1935-1958*.

Frances McLaughlin turned from art school to photography. Upon her graduation from Pratt Institute in 1941 she won an honorable mention in *Vogue's Prix de Paris* contest and then got a job as a fashion coordinator. She soon left to become assistant to a professional photographer and in 1944 started out on her own as a staff photographer for the Condé Nast Publications, Working for *Vogue, Glamour, House & Garden* until 1955. From 1955 onwards she has been working as a freelance photographer and between 1964-73, also produced TV commercials. As a photographer and author she has published five books, the most recent being a monograph on her late husband →Leslie Gill: *A Classical Approach to Photography 1935-1958*, New Orleans 1984.

Meiselas, Susan
*1948, USA

1971 machte Susan Meiselas in Harvard ihren Magister in Pädagogik und entwickelte anschließend pädagogische Programme und Anleitungen für die Verwendung von Fotografie und Film im Schulunterricht. Ihr erstes großes Fotoessay, an dem sie mehrere Jahre lang gearbeitet hatte, war *Carnival Strippers*, das 1976 als Buch erschien. Im selben Jahr wurde sie Mitglied bei *Magnum Photos*. Ihre Reportage über die Feindseligkeiten in Nicaragua wurde weltweit publiziert und 1979 mit der Robert Capa Gold Medaille ausgezeichnet. Anfang der 80er Jahre fotografierte Susan Meiselas in El Salvador und 1983 gab sie das Buch *El Salvador: The Work of Thirty Photographers* heraus.

Susan Meiselas received her Masters degree in education from Harvard University in 1971. She then set up programs for using film and photography in the classroom. Her first major photographic essay, spanning several years, focused on *Carnival Strippers* and was published in bookform in 1976. That same year Meiselas joined *Magnum Photos*. Her coverage of the hostilities in Nicaragua was published throughout the world and earned her the Robert Capa Gold Medal in 1979. More recently she concentrated her photographic reportage work on El Salvador, and published the book *El Salvador: the Work of Thirty Photographers*.

Mendelsohn, David
*1951, Alaska

Sky Farm Rd.
Northwood, NH 03261
USA

Eigentlich wollte er Förster werden, doch dann begann er im Fotolabor der University of New Hampshire zu arbeiten. Heute betreibt er die kreative und kommerzielle Fotografie gleicher maßen, Seine Aufnahmen erschienen in diversen Fotozeitschriften und wurden an verschiedenen Orten der USA ausgestellt.

Originally David Mendelsohn wanted to become a forester but then he began to work in the photo laboratory of the University of New Hampshire and became heavily committed to photography. Today he pursues both commercial and creative photography. His work is published in various photo magazines and has been exhibited throughout the United States.

Merill, Todd B.
*1956, USA

3435 Army, Nr. 211
San Francisco, CA 94110
USA

1974, während des letzten Jahres auf der Highschool begann er sich für Fotografie zu interessieren und knipste seine Kommilitonen mit einer Kodak Instamatic. 1976 beschränkten sich seine fotografischen Aktivitäten im wesentlichen auf Manipulationen in der Dunkelkammer. 1978 entschloß er sich, das Fotografieren etwas ernster zu nehmen und begann 1979 am Art Institute in San Francisco bei Linda Connor und Jerry Burchard zu studieren. Zuvor von der klassischen "Straight Photography" beeinflußt, änderte sich seine Einstellung zur Fotografie nun radikal. Er begann zu malen und machte Graffiti. Seine anarchistischen und dann neo-spiritualistischen Phasen fanden ihren Höhepunkt und Ausdruck in der Arbeit an *New Mythologies*.

In 1974, the last year of high school, Merill became interested in photography and took pictures of his colleagues with a Kodak Instamatic. In 1976 his photographic activities centred primarily around darkroom manipulation. He started taking photography more seriously in 1978 and went to study at the Art Institute of San Francisco with Linda Connor and Jerry Burchard. Where as before he had been influenced by the 'Straight Photography' school, his approach to photography now changed radically. He began painting and creating graffity. His anarchic and later neo-spiritualistic phases are best expressed in his *New Mythologies* work.

Mertin, Roger
*1942, USA

16 Upton Park
Rochester, N.Y. 14607
USA

Als Student am Rochester Institute of Technology begann sich Roger Mertin ernsthaft für die Fotografie zu interessieren. 1972 schloß er sein Studium mit einem M.F.A. ab und seit 1975 ist er Assistenzprofessor an der Universität von Rochester. 1970 machte er seine ersten bedeutsamen Farbfotografien und seit 1976 arbeitet er mit der Großformatkamera in Farbe, mit der er in Amerika allgegenwärtige und typische Motive aufnimmt, wie Apfelbäume und Basketballkörbe.

While a student at Rochester Institute of Technology, Roger Mertin became seriously interested in photography. He received his M.F.A. degree in 1972 and has been assistant professor of fine arts at the University of Rochester since 1975. His first serious work in color he did in 1970 and since 1976 Mertin has worked with the view camera, picturing typical American subjects such as apple trees and basketball hoops.

Metzner, Sheila
*1939, USA

1956-60 studierte sie Visuelle Kommunikation am Pratt Institute, Brooklyn. 1962-65 arbeitete sie als Werbeleiterin beim Fernsehsender CBS. 1965-68 brachten sie Werbeaufträge zusammen mit →Richard Avedon, Bob Richardson, Melvin Sokolsky und Diane Arbus. 1966 richtete sie sich eine Dunkelkammer ein und brachte sich das Fotografieren selbst bei. Ihre ersten Arbeiten waren noch scharf und in Schwarzweiß, aber in 1974 begann sie dann weichgezeichnete Fotos von geringem Kontrast zu machen, einige von Hand koloriert. Seit 1978 fotografiert sie in Farbe, die Negative werden im Fresson-Verfahren vergrößert.

Sheila Metzner studied Visual Communication at Pratt Institute, Brooklyn, 1955-60. She was employed in the capacity of Advertising director by CBS Television from 1962-65. During the next three years she carried out a number of commercial assignments together with →Richard Avedon, Bob Richardson, Melvin Sokolsky and Diane Arbus. She installed a darkroom and taught herself photography in 1966. Her first pictures were in black & white and sharply-focussed but in 1974 she began a series of soft-focussed, low-contrast pictures, some hand painted. Since 1978 she has been working in color, and her negatives are printed in the Fresson process.

Meyer, Pedro
*1935, Spanien

Ortega 20
Coyoacan 04000
Mexico D.F.

1937 gingen seine Eltern nach Mexiko und 1942 wurde Pedro Meyer eingebürgert. Von 1956 bis 1974 war er in der Verwaltung verschiedener Firmen tätig, seit 1974 widmet er sich ganz der Fotografie, die er schon seit 1952 nebenberuflich betrieb. So war er in den 60er Jahren Mitbegründer der *Grupo arte fotográfico* und er hat seitdem aktiv die mexikanische Fotografie im Ausland repräsentiert, sei es durch die Teilnahme an Kolloquien und Tagungen, durch die Organisation von Ausstellungen oder durch die Publikation und Präsentation eigener Arbeiten, die sowohl Reportagen als auch Audiovisionsschauen umfassen.

His parents emigrated to Mexico in 1937 and Pedro Meyer took on Mexican nationality in 1942. Between 1956 and 1974 he worked as an administrator in various companies, but also as a photographer in his free time. He was a founding member of the *Grupo arte fotográfico* in 1963. In 1974 he turned full-time to photography and began to represent Mexican photography abroad. Meyer has participated on the panel of several European photographic manifestations in Latin America, has curated exhibitions and published and exhibited his own work, which includes reportages and audiovisuals.

Meyerowitz, Joel
*1938, USA

817 West End Avenue
New York, N.Y. 10025
USA

Von 1956 bis 1959 studierte Meyerowitz Kunst an der Ohio State University, dann begann er, als Art Director einer Werbeagentur zu arbeiten. 1963 gab er diese Tätigkeit auf, und fing an zu fotografieren. Straßenszenen in New York nahm er zunächst in Schwarzweiß auf, wandte sich dann aber ab 1973 ausschließlich der Farbfotografie zu. Für seine farbigen Landschaftsaufnahmen benutzt er seit Mitte der 70er Jahre eine Großbildkamera, die so alt ist, wie er selbst. 1978 erschien *Cape Light,* sein erstes Buch, 1981 folgte *St. Louis and the Arch* und schließlich 1983 *Wild Flowers.* In jüngster Zeit beschäftigt sich Meyerowitz mit einer Serie von Triptychen, die meisten fotografiert am Strand von Cape Cod. 1985 erschien seine jüngstes Buch *Ein Sommertag*.

Joel Meyerowitz studied art at Ohio State University during 1956 to 1959 and following that period worked as an art director in an advertising agency. He left that job and took up photography in 1963. He initially photographed the street scenes of New York in black & white, but turned exclusively to color in 1973. For his landscape work since the mid-Seventies he has used a field view camera, which is as old as himself. In 1978 the first of his books, entitled *Cape Light* appeared, followed by *St. Louis and the Arch* in 1981 and *Wild Flowers* of 1983. Lately Meyerowitz has been working on a series of triptychs, mostly taken at the beach of Cape Cod. In 1985 his most recent book *A Summer Day'*.

Mézière, Jean
*1946, Frankreich

P.O. Box 140 181
Dallas, Texas 75214
USA

Mézière studierte Ökonomie in Paris, arbeitete in Afrika und kam 1971 in Genf erstmals mit der Fotografie in Kontakt. Es entstanden abstrakte und grafische Schwarzweißfotos. 1977 reiste er in die USA, um sich dort niederzulassen und begann 1978 in Dallas als Modefotograf zu arbeiten. Für seine Fotos erhielt er mehrere Preise, u.a. 1982 ein Stipendium zur Realisation mit der 20 x 24″ Polaroid Farbkamera. 1986 wurde in den USA sein Fotobuch *Echoes* publiziert.

Jean Mézière studied economics in Paris and worked in Africa. He made his first contact with photography in Geneva in 1971, when he produced abstract and graphic black & white photographs. He travelled to the States in 1977 in order to settle there and the following year he established himself as a fashion photographer in Dallas. He received several prizes and awards, including a Polaroid grant for working with 20 x 24″ color material. In 1986 his photo book *Echoes* was published in the U.S.

Midorikawa, Yoichi
*1915, Japan

12-23 Ekimoto-cho
Okayama-shi
Japan

Midorikawa studierte Zahnmedizin und eröffnete 1937 eine Zahnklinik. Zugleich begann er zu fotografieren – 1938 wurden seine Aufnahmen erstmals publiziert. Sein Interesse konzentrierte sich zunehmend auf die Landschaftsfotografie. Seit sich in Japan die Farbfotografie durchsetzte, wird sie von Midorikawa benutzt, da sie seinem Sinn für Design entspricht. Er wird sogar als der "Magier der Farbe" und als "Designer der Landschaft" bezeichnet. Sein Medium für Veröffentlichungen ist der Bildband, es sind inzwischen mehr als 30 Bücher, in denen seine Fotografien erschienen.

Yoichi Midorikawa studied dentistry and opened up a dental clinic in 1937. At the same time he started to photograph, and his photographs were first published in 1938. Midorikawa subsequently concentrated on landscape photography. As soon as color photography became known in Japan, Midorikawa adapted to it because it appealed to his sense of design. He even became known as 'the magician of color' and a 'designer of landscapes'. His medium of publicity basically is the photo-album – Midorikawas pictures have been published in more than 30 books.

Mili, Gjon
*1904, Albanien, † 1984, USA

Mili emigrierte 1923 in die USA und studierte dort bis 1927 Elektroingenieurwesen am Massachusetts Institute of Technology. Als Fotograf Autodidakt, arbeitete er einige Zeit bei →Harold E. Edgerton. Mit ihm zusammen experimentierte er 1938 mit dem Elektronenblitz für extrem kurze Belichtungszeiten. Anfang der 30er Jahre hatte Mili bereits an der Verbesserung der Ausleuchtung für Farbaufnahmen gearbeitet. Ab 1939 fotografierte Mili für *Life* und andere Illustrierte und zwar hauptsächlich Bewegungsabläufe von Tänzern, Sportlern und Theaterschauspielern. Ab 1944 drehte er auch Filme, außerdem entstanden zahlreiche Prominentenporträts.

Gjon Mili emigrated to the States in 1923 and until 1927 studied electrical engineering at Massachusetts Institute of Technology. Self-taught in photography, he worked for some time under →Harold E. Edgerton, with whom he collaborated on a number of experiments with high-speed electronic flash in 1938. Even before that Mili had worked on the perfectioning of lighting for color photography. As a freelance photographer from 1939 on he worked for *Life* and other magazines. He mainly photographed the movements of dancers, sportsmen and stage performers. Mili also was a film-maker and photographed numerous portraits of prominent persons.

Millikan, Jeff
*1952, USA

1605 Elliot Ave.
Minneapolis, MN 55404
USA

Als ausgebildeter Fotograf begann Millikan 1976 Fotografie zu unterrichten. Seine *Fish Dreams* Serie, an der er weiterhin arbeitet, besteht aus Kombinationen von inszenierten Unterwasserfotos und Aufnahmen von tropischen Fischen in Aquarien. Um die im Wasser treibenden Elemente und menschlichen Körper zu fotografieren, sitzt Millikan mit seinen Kameras auf dem Grund eines Schwimmbeckens. In der Dunkelkammer kombiniert er dann zwei Negative mit Hilfe von zwei Vergrößerern auf ein Blatt Cibachromepapier.

Trained as a photographer and print-maker, Jeff Millikan started to lecture photography in 1976. His ongoing series on *Fish Dreams* are composites of staged underwater events and of tropic fish shots taken through aquarium windows. To shoot floating objects and human elements, Millikan sits on the bottom of a pool with his camera. In the darkroom, after selecting a fish/folk duo that appeals to him, Millikan combines the two images on Cibachrome papier, using two enlargers.

Misrach, Richard
*1949, USA

1420, 45th Street
Emeryville, CA 94609
USA

Misrach studierte von 1967 bis 1971 Psychologie in Berkeley und begann dort zu fotografieren. Seine Aufnahmen von der Straßenkultur in Berkeley erschienen 1974 als Buch unter dem Titel *Telegraph 3 A.M.* und brachte ihm den Western Books Preis ein. Seitdem entstanden Nachtaufnahme von der Vegetation in der Mojave Wüste. Durch die langen Belichtungszeiten sieht man die Leuchtspuren der Sterne und durch den Blitz werden Details im Vordergrund aufgehellt. Es folgten großformatige Farbaufnahmen von Bäumen, Pflanzen und Landschaften, ebenfalles nachts und mit Blitz. Z.Zt arbeitet Misrach für die Aufnahmen in seinem neusten Buch *Desert Cantos*.

Richard Misrach studied psychology at Berkeley University during 1967 to 71. He began as a photographer by recording the street life of Berkeley, resulting in the book *Telegraph 3 A.M.*, which won him the Western Book Award. Since then Misrach is known for his nighttime studies of plants in the Mojave Desert. By drawing out the exposure time, the illumination of stars becomes visible and with a strong flash the foreground is brightened. Misrach also did large color photographs of trees, plants and landscapes, also at nighttime and with the use of a flash. Recently he has been working on a series, which will result in the book *Desert Cantos*.

Monti, Paolo
*1908, Italien, † 1982, Italien

Er gilt als die einflußreichste Persönlichkeit in der zeitgenössischen italienischen Fotografie. 1930 machte er in Mailand seinen Abschluß in Politischer Ökonomie und nahm dann in Venedig eine leitende Position in der Industrie ein. Er begann sich der Fotografie zuzuwenden und 1947 gründete er den Fotografenzirkel *La Gondola*. Er war der erste Fotograf in Italien, der die neuen internationalen Tendenzen rezipierte, insbesondere Otto Steinerts "Subjektive Fotografie". Im Alter von 45 Jahren machte er die Fotografie zu seinem Beruf: In Mailand arbeitete er von 1953 bis zu seinem Tod als Architekturfotograf. 1970 erhielt er an der Universität von Bologna den ersten Lehrstuhl für Fotografie in Italien.

Paolo Monti played a key role in the history of contemporary Italian photography. In 1930 he graduated in Political Economy and then started a promising career in industry in the city of Venice. In 1947 he founded the photographic circle *La Gondola*. Monti was the first photographer in Italy to adopt the new, international tendencies, especially German 'subjective photography'. At the age of 45 he became a professional photographer. From 1953 he worked in Milan, specializing in architectural photography and in 1970 the University of Bologna appointed him as the first Professor of Photography in Italy.

Moon, Sarah
*1938, Großbritannien

Villa Adrienne
19, avenue du Général Leclerc
75014 Paris
France

Als Tochter französischer Eltern besuchte Sarah Moon eine Kunstschule, wurde dann aber Fotomodell. 1968 wechselte sie dann hinter die Kamera: Ihre ersten Modeaufnahmen erschienen unter dem Titel *Patchwork* und machten sie gleich in der Branche bekannt. Ihre Aufnahmen wurden seitdem in allen führenden Modemagazinen und Fotozeitschriften veröffentlicht. Bekannt wurde insbesondere ihre Anzeigenkampagne für die Modefirma Cacharel. Eine Auswahl aus ihren getonten schwarzweißen und in pointellistischer Manier gehaltenen Farbfotos präsentiert das Fotobuch *Improbable Memories* von 1981.

The daughter of French parents, Sarah Moon attended art school, but became a photo model instead. In 1968 she switched over to working behind the camera. Her first fashion photographs, entitled *Patchwork* earned her the recognition of the fashion world. Since then her photographs havee been published in leading fashion and photo magazines. Especially known are her advertising pictures for the ready-to-wear firm, Cacharel. A selection of her toned black & white photographs as well as of her color photographs with the characteristic grain-texture effects, was presented in the picture book *Improbable Memories* published in 1981.

Moore, David
*1927, Australien

Arbeitete als Fotojournalist 1951-58 in London. In Europa, Afrika, Asien und den USA war er im Auftrag von Illustrierten und Zeitungen unterwegs, insbesondere für *Life* und *The Observer*. Seit 1960 widmet er sich in erster Linie der Architekturfotografie. In den frühen 70er Jahren entwickelte er zusammen met anderen das Konzept für das australische Zentrum für Fotografie.

David Moore has worked as a photojournalist in London during 1951-58. In Europe, Africa, Asia and the USA he traveled for magazines and newspapers including *Life Magazine* and *The Observer*. Since 1960 architectural photography has been one of his major interests. In the early 1970's he was responsible, together with others, for developing the concept of The Australian Centre for Photography.

338

Morath, Inge
*1923, Österreich

Inge Moraths Eltern waren beide Naturwissenschaftler und sehr kosmopolitisch. Sie studierte Romanistik und machte dann eine Fotografenlehre beim "Vater des Fotojournalismus" Simon Guttman. 1953 wurde Inge Morath Mitglied bei *Magnum*. Neben ihrer eigenen fotografischen Tätigkeit, war sie als "Researcher" für Henri Cartier-Bresson aktiv. 1962 zog sie in die USA und heiratet den Schriftsteller Arthur Miller. Moraths umfangreiche Literatur- und Sprachenkenntnisse waren die besten Voraussetzungen für ihre präzisen fotografischen Situationsschilderungen aus so unterschiedlichen Kulturen wie der des Mittleren Ostens, Südeuropas, Rußlands und Chinas.

Inge Morath's parents were both scientists and rather cosmopolitan. Inge Morath studied Romanic languages and in 1952 she did a photographic apprenticeship with the 'Father of Photo-journalism', Simon Guttman. In 1953 she joined *Magnum* agency. Besides taking her own pictures, she worked with Henri Cartier-Bresson as a researcher. She moved to the States in 1962 and married the playwright, Arthur Miller. Her extensive knowledge of literature and languages was the perfect prerequisite for her accurate photographic rendering of people and places and a diversity of cultures such as that of the Middle East, South Europe, Russia and China.

Mulberg, Joanne
*1954, USA

12 Severin Place
Huntington, N.Y. 11743
USA

Joanne Mulberg studierte Malerei an der Cooper Union und während des letzten Jahres ihres Studiums ging sie oft mit der Kamera auf den Straßen Long Islands spazieren. Innerhalb eines Jahres gab sie dann die Malerei zugungsten der Fotografie auf. Sie fotografierte die Fenster von Banken, die Fronten von Geschäften und Schönheitssalons auf Long Island und in Paris. Danach beschäftigte sie sich mit den, einer ständigen Veränderung unterworfenen Aspekten der visuellen Welt wie Licht, Wetter usw.

Joanne Mulberg received her B.F.A. from Cooper Union. During her final year as a painting student, she often walked the streets of Long Island with a 35 mm camera and within a year she switched from painting to photography. Her first serious work was of windows of banks, storefacades, and beauty salons on Long Island and in Paris. Mulberg's more recent work is preoccupied with light, weather, construction and other facets of the visual world in the state of change.

Müller, Karl
*1952, Deutschland

Untermainkai 34
6000 Frankfurt 1
West-Germany

1977 begann Karl Müller bei Günter Rambow und Floris Neusüss in Kassel Visuelle Kommunikation und Fotografie zu studieren. Von 1980 bis 1982 entstanden die Farbaufnahmen zu dem Thema *Sonntage*, bei dem Müller auf Ausflügen typisch sonntägliche Augenblicke spontan festhielt. In ihrer Präsentation als frei im Raum hängende Riesenpostkarten wird der Betrachter wiederum selbst zum Sonntagsspaziergänger. Seit dem Studienabschluß 1983 arbeitet Müller an neuen freien Projekten, die aber noch nicht abgeschlossen sind, sowie für Werbung und Verlage im Rahmen der 1981 gegründeten Gruppe "Moderne Reklame".

Karl Müller began to study visual communication and photography under Günter Rambow and Floris Neusüss in Kassel in 1977. Between 1980-1982 he produced a color series on *Sundays*; spontaneous photographs of typical Sunday moments, mainly featuring German people on their Sunday outings. Presented as giant postcards suspended in space, the onlooker himself becomes a Sunday-walker. Since his graduation in 1983, Müller has been working on new personal projects, which are still in progress as well as on advertising and publishing assignments within the framework of the 'Moderne Reklame' group, established in 1981.

Munkacsi, Martin
*1896, Ungarn, † 1963, USA

John Munkacsi Hammes
12 Charles Street
New York, N.Y.
USA

Schon mit 18 Jahren arbeitete Munkacsi als Sportfotograf für die Budapester Zeitung *Az Est*. 1927 ging er nach Berlin und erhielt einen Dreijahresvertrag vom Ullstein Verlag. In Deutschland gehörte er mit zu den Begründern des modernen Fotojournalismus. Der dritte Teil seiner Karriere begann 1933, als er in den USA, wohin er 1934 emigrierte, Bademoden für *Harper's Bazaar* fotografierte. Sein über den Strand laufendes Modell war eine Sensation und dieses Foto leitete eine neue Ära der Modefotografie ein. Bei Hearst war Munkacsi bis 1946 unter Vertrag und bis zu seinem Tod 1963 arbeitete er außerdem als Kameramann für das Fernsehen.

At the age of 18, Martin Munkasci started his carreer as a sports-photographer for the Hungarian newspaper, *Az Est*. He moved to Berlin in 1927, where he got a three-year contract with Ullstein. In Germany he was among the pioneers of modern photo journalism. The third part of his career began in 1933 in the States (he immigrated there in 1934), when he photographed bathing suits for *Harper's Bazaar*. His picture of a model running along the beach was a sensation and introduced a new era in fashion photography. He was under contract with Hearst until 1946 and until his death in 1963 he also worked as a lighting cameraman for television.

Munzig, Horst
*1933, Deutschland

Bergwaldstr. 2
8948 Mindelheim
West-Germany

Nachdem er schon in zwei verschiedenen Berufen gearbeitet hatte, wählte er 1960 die Fotografie als seinen dritten. Beraten und unterstützt von →Herbert List, konnte er sich bald als Fotojournalist durchsetzten und wurde bekannt für seine Farbfotoessays, die in *DU, Life, Stern, Camera, Zeitmagazin* und *GEO* erschienen. Nach wie vor ist er viel unterwegs und hauptsächlich ist er an "natürlichen Dingen" interessiert.

After having worked in two different professions, Munzig chose photography as his third in 1960. Advised by →Herbert List he soon established himself as a photo journalist, known for his essays in color which appeard in *DU, Life, Stern, Camera, Zeitmagazin* and *GEO*. He still travels a lot and is mainly interested in "natural things".

Nagatani, Patrick
*1945, USA

3051 Rosslyn Street
Los Angeles, CA 90065
USA

Er studierte bis 1968 an der California State University und erhielt 1980 seinen Master of Fine Arts von der University of California. Seitdem arbeitet er als freier Fotograf und Lehrer für Fotografie. Er war Chefredakteur von *Obscura*, einer vom Los Angeles Center for Photographic Studies herausgegebenen Vierteljahresschrift. Er arbeitete als Illustrator und Art Direktor, außerdem organisierte er zahlreiche Austellungen. Seit 1984 arbeitet er, zusammen mit Andree Tracey, hauptsächlich mit der Polaroid Museumskamera.

Nagatani studied at California State University where he earned a B.A. in 1968 and subsequently his M.F.A. in 1980 at the University of California, Los Angeles. As well as creating photographs, Nagatani teaches photography. He formerly served as the managing editor of *Obscura*, a photographic quarterly published by the Los Angeles Center for Photographic Studies; worked as a technical illustrator and art director, and has curated numerous exhibitions. Since 1984 he mainly uses the Polaroid museum camera, collaborating with Andree Tracey.

Narahara, Ikko
*1931, Japan

Villa Fresca, Nr. 702
2-30-22 Jingumae
shibuya-ku, Tokyo 150
Japan

Ikko, wie er sich lange Zeit nannte, studierte bis 1954 Jura an der Chuo Universität und anschließend bis 1959 Kunstgeschichte an der Waseda Universität. Im selben Jahr schloß er sich mit anderen bekannten Fotografen zur Gruppe VIVO zusammen; er hatte schon 1956 begonnen, ernsthaft zu fotografieren. Sein erstes Buch *Wo die Zeit stehenblieb*, erschien 1967 und das Thema Zeit nahm er wieder auf in *Wo die Zeit verschwand* von 1975. Nicht zuletzt durch seine mehrjährigen Aufenthalte in Europa und den USA zählt Ikko zu den international bekanntesten japanischen Fotografen.

Ikko, as he has been known artistically for several years, graduated from the Faculty of Law, Chuo University in 1954 and he received an M.A. in art history from Waseda University in 1959. That same year he was the co-founder of the group VIVO – having started to photograph seriously back in 1956. His first book, entitled *Where Time has Stopped* appeared in 1967 and the theme reappeared in *Where Time has Vanished*, published in 1975. Ikko stayed in Europe and the States for several years, which helped him to become one of the most internationally known Japanese photographers.

Neuteboom, Boudewijn
*1941, Indonesien

Sloterweg 996
Amsterdam
The Netherlands

1959 bis 1964 studierte er Fotografie an der Akademie St. Joost in Breda. Nach verschiedenen Aufenthalten in anderen europäischen Ländern, eröffnete er schließlich 1967 in Amsterdam ein Studio. Seitdem arbeitet er für die großen holländischen und deutschen Werbeagenturen. Anfang der 70er Jahre begann er für *Avenue* zu fotografieren und er machte Modeaufnahmen auch für andere Illustrierte. Er will vermeiden, auf eine bestimmte Art von Fotografie festgelegt zu werden, er sieht sich als Allroundtalent, und so dehnte er sein Arbeitsgebiet 1985 auf das Produzieren von TV-Werbespots aus.

Boudewijn Neuteboom studied photography at the Art Academy, St. Joost, Breda, 1959-64. He travelled and lived all over Europe to finally establish a studio in Amsterdam in 1967. Since that time he has been working for major advertising agencies in Holland and Germany. In the early 70's he started fashion photography for *Avenue* as well as for other magazines. Neuteboom tries not to specialize in any particular trend of photography and attempts to be an all-round talent. In 1985 he extended his field of activity to TV-commercials.

Newman, Arnold
*1918, USA

39 West 67 Street
New York, N.Y. 10023
USA

Während der Schulzeit in Atlantic City begann er zu malen, nahm zwei Jahre lang Mal- und Zeichenunterricht, mußte diesen aber aus finanziellen Gründen aufgeben und wurde Mitarbeiter in einem Porträtstudio in Philadelphia. 1942 machte er sich als Porträtfotograf selbständig, ging 1946 nach New York und bekam Aufträge von *Harper's Bazaar* und anderen Zeitschriften. Schon bald gehörte Newman zur Porträtfotografenelite. Er fotografiert seine Kunden und Modelle bevorzugt in ihrer gewohnten Umgebung oder, wie er es oft bei Künstlern machte, gestaltet selbst ein Ambiente.

Newman started to paint while at school in Atlantic City. From 1936-38 he took drawing and painting lessons, abandoned this for financial reasons and went to work in a portrait studio in Philadelphia. He has been working as an independent portrait photographer since 1942. He moved to New York in 1946, where he received commissions from *Harper's Bazaar* and other magazines. Within a short while he became a leading portrait photographer. He prefers to photograph his clients and models in their familiar surroundings or, as often in the case of artists, he creates the background himself.

Newton, Helmut
*1920, Deutschland

7, ave. St. Roman
Residence Park
Monte Carlo
Monaco

Besuchte bis 1935 in Berlin die Schule und kaufte sich 1934 seine erste Kamera. 1936-40 machte er eine Fotografenlehre bei der Mode- und Theaterfotografin Else Simon (Yva) in Berlin. Er emigrierte 1940 nach Australien und diente in der dortigen Armee. Seit 1945 arbeitet er als freier Fotograf, spezialisiert auf Mode. In Australien heiratete er die Schauspielerin June Brunell, die ab 1971 als Fotografin unter dem Namen Alice Springs bekannt wurde. 1957 ließ er sich mit seiner Frau in Paris nieder und begann für *Elle, Marie-Claire, Jardin des Modes, Playboy, Nova, Queen,* sowie für alle Länderausgaben von *Vogue* zu arbeiten. 1982 zog er nach Monte Carlo, seitdem publizierte er Bücher und fotografierte für *Vogue* und den *Stern*.

Helmut Newton went to school in Berlin where he bought his first camera in 1934. From 1936 to 1940 he was apprentice to the fashion and theater photographer Else Simon (Yva) in Berlin. He emigrated to Australia in 1940 and served in the Australian Army. Since 1945 Helmut Newton has worked as a freelance fashion photographer. In Australia he married the actrice June Brunell, who in 1971 started working as a photographer under the name Alice Springs. In 1957 they both settled in Paris and Newton began to work for *Elle, Marie-Claire, Jardin des Modes, Playboy, Nova, Queen* and all editions of *Vogue*. In 1982 he moved to Monte Carlo and published several books. He still collaborates with *Vogue* and the German magazine *Stern*.

Nooijer, Paul de
*1934, Niederlande

Postbus 943
5600 AX Eindhoven
The Netherlands

Nachdem er Industrie-Design an der Akademie für industrielle Formgebung in Eindhoven studiert hatte, arbeitete de Nooijer von 1968 bis 1973 als kommerzieller Fotograf auf den Gebieten Werbung und Illustration. Seit 1974 konzentrierte er sich dann auf freie, künstlerische Foto- und Filmprojekte und unterrichtete Fotografie an diversen Instituten. De Nooijers Fotografien stellen eine konstruierte persönliche Welt dar, sie sind aber bei aller Absurdität sehr humorvoll angelegt. Drei Bücher hat er selbst verlegt: *Losing One's Head* 1978, *Losing One's Photos* 1981 und *Home Sweet Home* 1982. Seitdem installiert er Fotowände von etwa drei Meter Höhe und zwanzig Meter Länge.

After finishing his studies in industrial design, Paul de Nooijer worked as a commercial photographer, doing advertising and illustration, from 1968-73. Since 1974 he has concentrated on personal photographic and film projects, while lecturing at various institutes. With his photographs he constructs an intense personal world, both absurd and humorous at the same time. De Nooijer produced three books, all published by himself: *Losing One's Head*, 1978: *Losing One's Photos*, 1981; and *Home Sweet Home*, 1982. Since then he has turned his hand to photographic walls, measuring from three to twenty meters.

Occhiomagico
Italien

Viale Caldara 17
20122 Milano, Italy

Occhiomagico arbeitet seit ca. 15 Jahren für Zeitschriften und Werbeagenturen. Sie realisierten bisher Kampagnen in Italien und dem Ausland für Olivetti, Fiat, Pioneer, Seiko, Wedgwood, Levi's, Nazareno Gabrielli, J&B.

For the past 15 years Occhiomagico has been working for magazines and advertising agencies. They have launched campaigns in Italy and other countries abroad for Olivetti, Fiat, Pioneer, Seiko, Wedgwood, Levi's, Nazareno Gabrielli, J&B, etc.

Orkin, Ruth
*1921, USA, † 1985, USA

65 Central Park West
New York, N.Y. 10023
USA

Ruth Orkin wuchs in Hollywood auf und interessierte sich schon früh für das Kino und die Fotografie. 1944 zog sie dann nach New York, wo sie ihre Laufbahn als Fotojournalistin begann. In den folgenden Jahren erschienen ihre Aufnahmen in vielen bedeutenden Illustrierten und 1959 wurde sie unter die zehn führenden Fotografinnen der USA gewählt. Einen eigenen Teil ihres fotografischen Werkes bilden die Farbaufnahmen aus den Fenstern ihrer Wohnung am Central Park, die entstanden, während sie ihre Kinder großzog. Die Fotos erschienen 1978 in dem wirklich außergewöhnlichen Buch *A World Through My Window*. Über ihre fotojournalistischen Arbeiten erschien 1981 das Buch *A Photo Journal*, aber Ruth Orkin war auch eine anerkannte Filmemacherin.

Ruth Orkin grew up in Hollywood and became interested in movies and photography at an early age, and in 1944 moved to New York to start her career as a photo-journalist. In the years that followed, her work appeared in many major magazines. In 1959 she was voted one of the 'Top Ten Women Photographers in the U.S.'. While raising her children, another aspect of Orkin's work emerged: over a period of years she took color photos from the windows of her home, facing Central Park. This resulted in the magnificent book *A World Through My Window*, published in 1978. A book on her photo-journalistic work, entitled *A Photo Journal* appeared in 1981. Ruth Orkin was also a recognized film maker.

Outerbridge, Paul, Jr.
*1896, USA, † 1958, USA

Outerbridge war schon als Maler und Designer tätig, bevor er 1921/22 die Clarence White School of Photography besuchte. 1922 hatte er seine erste Veröffentlichung in *Vogue* und arbeitete auch für *Vanity Fair* und *Harper's Bazaar*. Seine Zusammenarbeit mit *Vogue* setzte er in Paris fort, wo er sich zwischen 1925 und 1929 aufhielt. Er war außerdem an den Dreharbeiten von Filmen beteiligt und nach seiner Rückkehr nach New York (1929) begann er sich intensiv mit dem äußerst komplizierten Carbro-Farbverfahren zu befassen. Bis 1939 war er mit seinen Farbfotos kommerziel sehr erfolgreich. 1945 eröffnete er ein Porträtstudio in Laguna Beach, Kalifornien. Während seiner letzten zehn Lebensjahre benutzte Outerbridge Kleinbildfilm, um seine Reisen zu dokumentieren.

Paul Outerbridge was a painter and designer before he attented the Clarence White School of Photography 1921-22. In 1922 he had his first coverage in *Vogue* and he also worked for *Vanity Fair* and *Harper's Bazaar*. He continued his collaboration with *Vogue*, during his stay in Paris between 1925-29. Outerbridge also participated in the production of motion pictures and following his return to New York in 1929, his intense occupation with the Carbro process, a long and difficult method of making color prints, started. Until 1939 Outerbridge's color photographs were highly successful in the commercial world. In 1945 he set up a portrait studio in Laguna Beach, California. During the last ten years of his life, Outerbridge used a 35 mm camera to document his travels.

Oyne, Ben
*1938, Schweden

184, rue de l'Université
75007 Paris
France

Ben Oyne besuchte von 1958 bis 1962 die Kunstfachschule in Götenborg und arbeitete dann bis 1973 als Art Direktor in New York, Frankfurt und Hamburg. In New York hatte er ein Filmstudium absolviert und 1974 machte er sich mit einem Studio in Hamburg als Fotograf selbständig. Dort realisiert er außer Werbeaufnahmen auch Werbespots für das Fernsehen. Seine bekanntesten Aufnahmen sind kunstvolle, im Studio konstruierte Szenen, die auf den ersten Blick wie aus dem Leben gegriffen erscheinen. Es sind herausragende Werbefotografien, nicht zuletzt deshalb, weil sie mit Witz und Humor inszeniert wurden.

Ben Oyne attended the art school in Götenborg 1958-62 and during the next decade worked as an art director in New York, Frankfurt and Hamburg. In New York he studied film making and in 1974 he established himself as a studio photographer in Hamburg, doing advertising work as well as TV-commercials. His best known photographs are artificially staged scenes which at first sight seem to be taken from life. This is outstanding commercial work, most of all because it is executed with wit and humour.

Pare, Richard
* Großbritannien

Geboren und aufgewachsen in England ging Richard Pare 1971 in die USA, um am Art Institute of Chicago Fotografie zu studieren. 1974 wurde er zum Leiter des *County Court House* Projektes, einer fotografischen Dokumentation ländlicher Gerichtsgebäude ernannt, die von der Firma Seagrams & Sons initiiert wurde. Seit der Gründung des kanadischen Zentrums für Architektur in Montreal im Jahre 1974 ist Pare dort Kurator für Fotografie. Er zeichnete verantwortlich für die Ausstellung und den Katalog *Photography and Architecture: 1839-1939* von 1982. Als Fotograf hat sich Pare auf Landschaft und Architektur in Farbe spezialisiert. Seine Ägypten-Fotos aus den Jahren 1982-84 wurden u.a. in Köln ausgestellt.

Born and educated in England, Richard Pare went to the U.S. in 1971 to study photography at the Art Institute of Chicago. In 1974 he was appointed editor of the project *County Court House: A Photographic Document* by Seagrams & Sons, Inc., which was published in 1978. He has been curator of photography for the Canadian Centre for Architecture since its inception in 1974. He curated and edited *Photography and Architecture: 1839-1939*, an exhibition and book, launched in 1982. As a photographer Richard Pare specialized in landscape and architectural color photography. His photographs of Egypt, done during 1982-84 were also exhibited in Cologne, Germany, in 1984.

Parker, Olivia
*1941, USA

229 Summer Street
Manchester, MA 01944
USA

Parker beendete 1963 ihr Kunstgeschichtsstudium am Wellesley College. 1971 begann sie zu fotografieren und für ihre Stilleben verwendet heute Muscheln, Federn, Zeichnungen und andere Objekte, die sie seit ihrer Kindheit sammelte. Ihre schwarzweißen, selenium-getonten Fotos erschienen 1978 in dem Buch *Signs of Life*. Im selben Jahr erhielt sie von Polaroid die Möglichkeit, in Farbe mit dem neuen 8 x 10″ Material zu fotografieren. Da bei den Sofortbildern keine Negative entstehen, macht sie meist mehrere Aufnahmen, je nachdem, ob das natürliche Licht konstant bleibt und ob die Konstruktion solange hält. Die Farbfotos wurden 1983 in dem Buch *Under the Looking Glass* veröffentlicht.

Olivia Parker graduated in art history from Wellesley College in 1963. She took up photography in 1971, specializing in still life, because she was a collector of shells, feathers, drawings and other objects since childhood. Her black & white selenium toned prints were reproduced in her monograph *Signs of Life* (1978). That same year Polaroid Corporation gave her the opportunity to work in color, using the new 8 x 10″ material. Because the instant images do not provide a negative, Parker exposes several prints, "depending on whether or not the natural light holds out and whether or not my construction collapses". The color photos were reproduced in her 1983 monograph *Under the Looking Glass*.

Parkinson, Norman
*1913, Großbritannien

Galerie Point
Post Box 242
Scarborough
Tobago, West Indies

Parkinson absolvierte eine Lehre bei den Hoffotografen Speaight & Sons Ltd, in London und eröffnete 1934 sein eigenes Studio. 1935 bis 1940 fotografierte er Mode für die britische Ausgabe von *Harper's Bazaar.* Nach dem Krieg wurde er durch seine Porträts und Modefotos für *Vogue* weltweit berühmt. 1960 wurde er Mitherausgeber des *Queen* Magazins und 1963 zog er nach Tobago auf den Westindischen Inseln. Norman Parkinson, der Fotograf der königlichen Familie, arbeitet weiterhin als Modefotograf für führende Magazine.

Norman Parkinson was an apprentice with the Court Photographers, Speaight & Sons Ltd, in London, establishing his own studio in London in 1934. During 1935 to 1940 he did fashion photography for the British edition of *Harper's Bazaar.* Following World War II Parkinson became famous for his portrait and fashion work, which he carried out for *Vogue*. In 1960 he became associate editor for *Queen* magazine. He moved to Tobago in the West Indies in 1963. Norman Parkinson, photographer of the Britisch Royal Family, still continues his celebrated fashion work for leading magazines.

Parr, Martin
*1952, Großbritannien

30 Egremont Promenade
Wallasey, Merseyside L 448 BQ,
Great Britain

Nach dem Fotografiestudium am Manchester Polytechnikom arbeitete Parr als Fotojournalist für das Manchester Council for Cummunity Relations. Seit 1974 ist er freiberuflich tätig und er fotografierte für Tanz– und Theatergruppen, Illustrierte, sowie freie Projekte aus denen Bücher entstanden wie *Bad Weather* (1982) und *A Fair Day* (1984). Seine Arbeiten, die im Moment in Farbe und mit Blitzlicht entstehen, bezeichnet Parr selbst als 'subjektiv dokumentarisch'. 1985 beendete er eine Serie über den Badeort New Brighton mit dem Titel *The Last Resort*. In diesen Aufnahmen zeigt er ganz unglaublich präzise charakteristische Momente des alltäglichen Lebens.

Following his studies at Manchester Polytechnical College, Martin Parr worked as a photojournalist for the Manchester Council for Community Relations. Since 1974 he has been a freelance photographer, working for dance and theater companies, magazines, as well as pursuing personal projects, which resulted in such books as *Bad Weather* (1982) and *A Fair Day* (1984). Parr himself calls his recent work done in color and with flashlight, "subjective documentary". In 1985 he finished a series on New Brighton, entitled *The Last Resort*, which is unbelievably precise in the way it portrays the characteristic moments of everyday life.

Pawlok, Werner
*1953, Deutschland

Schwabstr. 2
7000 Stuttgart 1
West-Germany

Werner Pawlok arbeitet seit 10 Jahren als selbständiger Fotograf mit eigenem Studio in Stuttgart. Seine Arbeiten wurden in Fotozeitschriften wie *Color Foto, Photo Technik International* oder *Bronica News* vorgestellt, und er realisierte Beiträge für Illustrierte wie den *Stern, Per Lui* oder den *Spiegel*.

Since a decade, Werner Pawlok has been working as a freelance fashion photographer in Stuttgart, where he maintains a studio. His works have been published in photo magazines such as *Color Foto, Photo Technik International* and *Bronica News*, and he carried out editorial work for the magazines *Stern, Der Spiegel, Per Lui*.

Payne, Richard
*1935, USA

2029 Haddon Street
Houston, Texas 77019
USA

Richard Payne arbeitete als Architekt, bevore er 1968 seine Karriere als Architekturfotograf begann. Seine Aufnahmen erscheinen in den bedeutenden Architekturmagazinen in den USA, Deutschland, England und Japan. 1976 begann Payne für Philip Johnson zu arbeiten und fotografierte das Buch *Johnson / Burgee Architecture*. Zwei weitere Bücher befinden sich in Vorbereitung. Ab September 1986 wird sich Payne für sechs Monate im American Center in Paris aufhalten.

Richard Payne worked as an architect before launching his career as an architectural photographer in 1968. His photographs appeared in major architectural publications in the U.S., Germany, England and Japan. In 1976, he began working for Philip Johnson and produced the book *Johnson / Burgee Architecture*, two more books are currently scheduled for publication. In September 1986, Payne will begin a six month sojourn at the American Center, Paris, France.

Penn, Irving
*1917, USA

P.O. Box 934, F.D.R. Station
New York, N.Y. 10150
USA

Penn studierte Design bei Alexey Brodovitch und arbeitete dann als Grafikdesigner in New York. Von *Vogue* wurde er als Ideenliferant für Titelseiten engagiert und im Laufe der Zeit gestaltete und fotografierte er mehr als 100 Titel für dieses Magazin. Seit 1946 arbeitet er als Modefotograf für Condé Nast unter *Vogues* Art Direktor →Alexander Liberman. 1961 hatte Penn seine erste Einzelausstellung im MOMA in New York. Außer für seine Mode- und Werbeaufnahmen wurde Penn für seine Porträts berühmt, die er stets vor neutralgrauem Hintergrund aufnimmt. Das Museum of Modern Art in New York publizierte 1984 eine umfangreiche Monografie über Penns fotografisches Werk.

Irving Penn studied design under Alexey Brodovitch and he worked as a graphic designer in New York, where he was engaged by Vogue as an ideas man for covers, and with Penn created and photographed more than 100 Vogue covers. Since 1946 he has cooperated with →Alexander Liberman, art director of Vogue, while working for Condé Nast publications. In 1961 he held his first one-man show in the Museum of Modern Art, New York. Besides his fashion and advertising work, Penn has gained international recognition for his black & white portraits against familiar grey backgrounds. The MOMA published an extensive monograph on Penn's photographic oeuvre in 1984.

Péréz-Mínguez, Pablo
*1946, Spanien

Monte-Esquinza 14
28010 Madrid
Spain

Péréz-Mínguez gründete und leitete die Zeitschrift für Avantgarde-fotografie *Nueva Lente* von 1971 bis 1975. Heute ist er Leiter des Photocentro und der Photogaleria. Bekannt wurde er denn auch mehr als Fotokritiker und Ideologe, denn als Fotograf. Beruflich fotografiert er Porträts und Mode, seine freien Arbeiten waren jahrelang einem einzigen Thema gewidmet, *Mi vida misma*, seinem Leben, wobei er die Fotografie als autobiografisches Dokumentationsmittel benutzte. Zur Zeit ist er mit dem Aufbau des ersten spanischen Fotomuseums befaßt.

Pablo Péréz-Mínguez founded and edited the photo avantgarde magazine, *Nueva Lente* during 1971 to 75. Today he is the artistic director of the Photocentro and la Photogaleria. Péréz-Mínguez is more known as a photo-critic and an idiologist than as a photographer. For several years he devoted his personal work to a single series, entitled *Mi vida misma* (My Life Itself), which functioned as an autobiographical testimony. As a professional, he is involved with portrait and fashion and presently he is busy establishing the first Spanish photo museum.

Pezzato, Giorgio & Paola Masoero
*1945, Italien
*1940, Italien

G. Pezzato
Via Kennedy 14
32030 Fener di Alano, Belluno
Italy

P. Masoero
Via Arena 19
20123 Milano
Italy

Giorgio Pezzato ist gelernter Architekt, der 1978 von der UNESCO ein Stipendium erhielt, um sich in Paris mit Fotogrammetrie, Kartografie und Mikrofilm zu befassen. Seit 1979 widmet er sich der Didaktik der Fotografie und den visuellen Künsten im allgemeinen, seit 1980 richtet sich sein Interesse insbesondere auf systeme der elektronischen Bilderzeugung.

Paola Masoero beschäftigt sich seit 1978 mit Fotografie. Ihre Aufnahmen erschienen in *Vogue Shopping* und mehreren italienischen Fotozeitschriften. Seit zwei Jahren befaßt sie sich, in Zusammenarbeit mit Giorgio Pezzato, mit der elektronischen Bilderzeugung.

Trained as an architect, Giorgio Pezzato received a UNESCO grant to do research in the field of photogrammetry, earthography and microfilming in Paris. Since 1979 he has dedicated himself to the didactics of photography as well as to the visual arts in general. Since 1980 he has mainly been interested in creating images with the use of electronic media.

Paola Masoero has been involved with photography since 1978. Her photographs appeared in *Vogue Shopping* and various Italian photo magazines. Two years ago her collaboration with Giorgio Pezzato on the use of electronic media, began.

Pfahl, John
*1939, USA

797 Potomac
Buffalo, N.Y. 14209
USA

Pfahl erhielt 1961 den B.F.A. in Grafikdesign und 1968 den Master of Arts in Farbfotografie. 1975 begann er an der Serie *Altered Landscapes* zu arbeiten, die 1981 als Buch erschien. Die Farbaufnahmen zeigen in der Landschaft selbst angebrachte Markierungen, die aber aussehen als wären sie auf den Abzug gemalt. Angeregt wurde Pfahl dazu durch die anamorphotischen Elemente in der Malerei und Zeichnung der frühen Renaissance. 1978 entstand die Serie *Picture Windows* und seit 1981 arbeitet Pfahl an der Serie *Power Places*, für die er Kern- und andere Kraftwerke in der amerikanischen Landschaft fotografiert.

John Pfahl received his B.F.A. in graphic design in 1961 and his M.F.A. in color photography in 1968. He started to work on his *Altered Landscapes* in 1975, a series, which resulted in a book in 1981. For this work he placed materials in the landscape, so that they would appear to be markings on the print itself. He was inspired by the anamorphotic elements in paintings and drawings of the early Renaissance. In 1978 Pfahl photographed *Picture Windows*, and since 1981 he has been working on *Power Places*, a series on nuclear and other power plants in the American landscape.

Porter, Eliot
*1901, USA

Route 4, Box 33
Santa Fe, New Mexico 87501
USA

1913 machte Porter mit einer Box-Kamera die ersten Aufnahmen von Vögeln; nach seiner Promotion zum Dr. med. 1929, kaufte er sich eine Leica und die ersten Naturaufnahmen entstanden. 1939 entschied er sich, als Fotograf zu arbeiten und im Jahr darauf spezialisierte er sich auf Naturfotografie in Farbe. Nach dem Krieg folgten zahllose Reisen und Expeditionen, auf denen er seine vielfach ausgezeichneten Naturaufnahmen fotografierte. Eliot Porters Fotografien erschienen in zahlreichen Bildbänden.

In 1913 Eliot Porter took his first photographs of birds with a box camera. In 1929 he received his M.D. degree and in 1930 he bought a Leica and started nature photography. Nine years later Porter turned full-time to photography and specialized in color. After WW II, he photographed landscapes and nature on countless travels and expeditions. His photographs appeared in books and Eliot Porter has received innumerable awards and honors.

Post Wolcott, Marion
* USA

2265 Broadway
San Francisco, CA 94115
USA

Nachdem sie an der Universität in Wien studiert hatte, kehrte sie 1935 in die USA zurück und nahm Fotounterricht bei Ralph Steiner. Sie arbeitete dann kurze Zeit als Fotografin für *Life, Fortune* und andere Illustrierte und wurde 1938 von Roy Stryker in den Fotografenstab der Farm Security Administration geholt, dem sie bis 1941 angehörte. Während der letzten Monate bei der FSA entstanden einige Dokumentarfotos in Farbe. 1941 heiratete sie Lee Wolcott und reiste dann bis 1968 mit ihrem Mann für den diplomatischen Dienst. Zurück in den USA, begann sie 1975 in Kalifornien wieder ernsthaft zu fotografieren und zwar hauptsächlich in Farbe.

Marion Post Wolcott returned to the United States in 1935 after graduating from Vienna University in 1932. She attended informal photo classes with Ralph Steiner and started to work as a freelance photographer, collaborating with *Life, Fortune* and other magazines. During 1938-41 she was the principal photographer of the Farm Security Administration under Roy Stryker. During the final months with the FSA she did a little color photography. She married Lee Wolcott in 1941 and until 1968 she travelled with her husband for the diplomatic service. Back in the States, she began again to photograph seriously in 1975, mainly in color.

Privetera, Pietro
*1953, Italien

Corso di Porta Ticinese 80
20123 Milano
Italy

Während eines Philosophiestudiums an der Universität in Mailand war Privetera gleichzeitig als Theaterfotograf engagiert und er machte auch Aufnahmen von Avantgardegruppen. 1975-78 entstanden Reportagen für die Architekturzeitschrift *Abitare*. 1977 erwarb er eine Polaroid SX-70 Kamera und begann damit zu experimentieren. 1982 wurde er Redakteur der Zeitschrift *Progresso Fotografico*, beendete eine Stillebenserie und begann für das Modemagazin *Linea Italiana* zu arbeiten.

Already during his philosophical studies at the University in Milan, Pietro Privetera worked as a contract photographer to Milan theaters and did freelance photographing of avant-garde groups. During 1975-78 Privetera photographed reportages for the architectural magazine *Abitare*. He bought a Polaroid SX-70 camera in 1977 and began to experiment with instant photography. In 1982 he became editor of *Progresso Fotografico*, completed his series of still lifes and started his collaboration with the fashion magazine *Linea Italiana*.

Pruskowksi, Krystof
*1943, Polen

2, rue de la Roquette
75011 Paris
France

Pruskowski begann schon 1958 zu malen und zu zeichnen, er studierte dann von 1961 in Warschau Architektur. 1965 reiste er erstmals als Studentendelegierter nach Paris zu einem Architekturkongress. Ab 1966 setzte er mit Unterbrechungen seine Ausbildung in Paris fort und 1968 beschloß er, ganz dort zu bleiben (1975 erhielt er die französische Staatbürgerschaft). 1971 entstanden seine ersten Modefotos für Balmain und verschiedene Konfektionshäuser. Außerdem arbeitet Pruskowski als Reportagefotograf. Mitte der 70er Jahre entstanden die ersten *Fotosynthese* – Porträts, bei denen die Gesichter von berühmten Paaren, Familien oder Teams übereinanderkopiert werden. Diese Serie nennt er *Compressions*, sie wurde 1984 erstmals ausgestellt.

Pruskowski started to paint and draw in 1958 and he studied architecture in Warsaw, 1961-67. As a students' delegate he went to an architectural congress in Paris in 1965. There he continued his studies, with short visits to Paris in between, until 1968 when he decided to stay in Paris (naturalized in 1975). Pruskowski did his first fashion photographs in 1971, when he got commissions from Balmain and various ready-to-wear firms. Besides his fashion work, he did several reportages. In the mid-Seventies he started his composite portraits of famous couples, families, teams, and a series which he called *Compressions*. It was exhibited in 1984 for the first time.

Rachmanov, Nikolaj
*1932, Sowjetunion

2-Ja Pugacovskaja 8
Korpus 5, Mocow B 61
USSR

Studierte Gesang an der Musikhochschule, dann Publizistik an der Universität in Moskau. Er arbeitete dann zunächst bei der Presseagentur *TASS* als Fotoreporter, doch seit 1969 ist er freiberuflich tätig. Bekannt wurde er in der Sowjetunion als Pionier der Farbfotografie. Er illustrierte zehn Bildbände, u.a. über Moskau, Leningrad, alte russische Orte und historische Bauten. Seine Bücher dienen der offiziellen Repräsentation der Sowjetunion im Ausland, aber auch in seinen persönlichen Arbeiten widmet er sich der Architektur des alten Rußland.

Nikolaj Rachmanov studied singing at the School of Music, then journalism at Moscow State University. He worked at *TASS*, the Press Agency of the Soviet Union as a photo reporter until he went into freelance photography in 1969. Rachmanov became known as a pioneer of Soviet color photography and is the author of ten photo albums devoted to Moscow, Leningrad, old Russian towns, historical monuments, etc. His books serve to officially present the Soviet Union abroad but even his own work is deeply devoted to the architecture of old Russia.

Ragan, Vicki
*1951, USA

Vicki Ragan erhielt ihre Ausbildung als Berufsfotografin am Colorado Mountain College und gegen Ende der 70er Jahre machte sie an der Universität von Arizona ihren Magister. Seit 1973 arbeitet sie als kommerzielle Fotografin, realisierte aber auch eigene, freie Arbeiten in Schwarzweiß und Farbe.

Vicki Ragan studied commercial photography at Colorado Mountain College and she received her M.F.A. degree from the University of Arizona in the late 70's. Since 1973 she has been working as a commercial photographer, realizing personal works both in black & white and color.

Ravanesi, Bill
*1942, USA

15 Middle Street
Hadley, MA 01035
USA

Ravanesi studierte zunächts Biologie und machte dann 1978 seinen Abschluß in Fotografie. Sein politisches Engagement hatte ihn dazu geführt, 1974 Aktivisten wie Angela Davies zu fotografieren. Später machte er dann eine Dokumentation über Farmarbeiter, vor allem über philippinische Immigranten in Kalifornien. Seine Aufnahmen bieten eine außergewöhnliche Mischung aus Dokumentation, politischer Stellungnahme und der Anwendung einer formalen Farbästhetik.

Bill Ravanesi graduated in biology and in 1978 he received his Masters degree in photography. In 1974 Ravanesi's political commitment led him to photograph activists like Angela Davies. He later did a documentation on farm workers, mainly on Philippine immigrants in California. His pictures demonstrate an extraordinary combination of documentation, political statement and formal color aesthetic.

Rawlings, John
*1912, USA

Bevor er zur Fotografie kam, arbeitete Rawlings als Schaufensterdekorateur. Gegen Ende der 30er Jahre wurde er Vertragsfotograf von Condé Nast und arbeitete vor dem Zweiten Weltkrieg in den Condé Nast Studios in Paris und London. 1945 richtete sich Rawlings ein Tageslichtstudio ein, wo er Werbefotos ebenso aufnahm, wie Modefotos für *Vogue* und andere Magazine. Etwa ein Drittel seiner redaktionellen Arbeit für *Vogue* waren Porträts von berühmten Leuten aus der Gesellschaft oder aus der Welt des Theaters und Films.

John Rawlings turned from window design to photography. He joined the staff of the Condé Nast Publications in the late 30's and before WW II worked in the company's London and Paris studios. In 1945 he established his own daylight studio where he combined advertising work with his Condé Nast assignments, and did fashion photographs for other magazines. Almost a third of every hundred pages he did for *Vogue*, were portraits of famous people in society or from the world of theater and films.

Reed, Eli
*1946, USA

Reed begann 1970 zu fotografieren und 1978 wurde er Redaktionsfotograf bei der *Detroit News*. 1980 engagierte ihn dann der *Examiner* in San Francisco, für den Reed über Atomkraftgegner, Ghettos und 1982 über Zentralamerika berichtete. Reed erhielt 1981 einen Pulitzer Preis für sein Fotoessay über ein Wohnprojekt für untere Einkommensklassen in San Francisco, sowie zahlreiche weitere Auszeichnungen. Er fotografierte in Beirut, El Salvador, Belize und war u.a. beteiligt an den Projekten *Ein Tag im Leben von Hawaii* und *Ein Tag im Leben von Kanada*.

Eli Reed began photography in 1970; by 1978 he joined the staff of the *Detroit News*. In 1980 he was hired as a staff photographer at the *San Francisco Examiner*, for whom he reported on nuclear blockades, ghetto areas, and Central America. In 1981 Reed was awarded a Pulitzer Prize for his essay *The Pink Palace*, a low income housing project in San Francisco. Reed also covered Beirut, El Salvador, Belize and he took part in the projects *A Day in the Life of Hawaii* and *A Day in the Life of Canada*.

Relang, Regina
*1906, Deutschland

Paganinistr. 49
8000 München 60
West-Germany

Regina Relang studierte an der Kunstakademien in Stuttgart und Berlin. In den 30er Jahren entstanden erste Reisereportagen und 1938 machte sie ihre ersten Modeaufnahmen, die ihr Aufträge von *Vogue* Paris, New York und London einbrachten. Eine ihrer ersten aufsehenregenden Realisationen war das *Handschuhballet*. Während des Krieges fotografierte sie für *Die Dame* und machte Modeaufnahmen in Wien. Nach 1945 entstanden zuerst Reportagen für *Constanze*, *Film und Frau* und bis 1982 für *Madame*. Seit einigen Jahren konzentriert sich Regina Relang auf die Veröffentlichung ihres Lebenswerkes in Büchern und die Kreation freier Fotografien in Farbe.

Regina Relang attended art academies in Stuttgart and Berlin. During the 1930's she did travel reportages and in 1938 took her first fashion photographs, which earned her commissions from *Vogue* Paris, London, New York. One of her first outstanding achievements was the *Ballet of Gloves*. During the war years she worked for the magazine *Die Dame* and did fashion photography in Vienna. After WW II, she continued her fashion work for *Constanze* and *Film und Frau*. Until 1982 she mainly worked for *Madame*. In recent years Regina Relang concentrates on editing and publishing books. She also does free color photography.

Renau, Josep
*1907, Spanien, † 1982 Spanien

Renau befaßte sich speziell mit der sozial-politischen Fotomontage. Während der Franco-Ära lebte er in Ost-Berlin im Exil und seine bemerkendswerte Serie *The American Way of Life* (1952-66) erschien in Spanien erst im Jahre 1976.

Josep Renau became particularly known as a creator of social-political photomontages. During the Franco era he lived in East-Berlin in exile, and his remarkable series *The American Way of Life* (1952-66) did not appear in Spain until 1976.

Retzlaff, Erich
*1899, Deutschland

Eichendorffstr. 17
8918 Dießen/Ammersee
West-Germany

Kam als Autodidakt zur Fotografie und betrieb gegen Ende der 20er Jahre bereits ein gutgehendes Porträtatelier in Düsseldorf. Seinen ersten Bildband *Antlitz des Alters* publizierte er 1930, es folgten *Die von der Scholle* und *Menschen am Werk*, beide 1931. Retzlaff avancierte zum Prominentenfotograf: 1944 entstand eine Porträtserie deutscher Wissenschaftler und Künstler in Farbe: *Das Antlitz des Geistes*. Auch Aufnahmen von Menschen in Trachten vor der Landschaft als Hintergrund entstanden; sie weisen Retzlaff als einen der führenden Farbfotografen seiner Zeit aus. Nach dem zweiten Weltkrieg bearbeitete er auch andere Motivgebiete, doch in erster Linie blieb er Porträtfotograf.

A self-taught photographer, Erich Retzlaff ran a successful portrait studio in Düsseldorf already at the end of the Twenties. In 1930 he published his first photo album, *Das Antlitz des Alters* (Face of Age), and *Menschen am Werk* (People at Work). Retzlaff became a celebrity portraitist and in 1944 did a series of photographs in color on German scientists and artists, *Das Antlitz des Geistes* (Face of the Intellect). His portraits of people in national costume against countryside backgrounds distinguish him as one of the leading color photographers of his time. After the Second World War he also worked in other fields, but above all, he was a portrait photographer.

Richter, Stefan
*1952, Deutschland

Konrad-Adenauer-Str. 21
7401 Reutlingen 1
West-Germany

Richter studierte Biologie in Zürich und Tübingen und arbeitet seit 1983 als Berufsfotograf für Zeitschriften wie z.B. *DU, Vogue, Cosmopolitan, Sunday Express*. 1985 erschien in London sein Buch mit Fotografien von Tatowierungen unter dem Titel *Tattoo*.

Stefan Richter studied biology in Zürich and Tübingen and since 1983 has been working as a professional photographer receiving assignments from such magazines as *DU, Vogue, Cosmopolitan, Sunday Express*. In 1985 his book *Tattoo* was published in London.

Riefenstahl, Leni
*1902, Deutschland

Tengstr. 20
8000 München 40
West-Germany

Nahm Unterricht in klassischem Ballett bei Eduardova in Berlin, dann in modernen Tanz bei Mary Wigman in Dresden. 1923-26 arbeitete sie als Tänzerin, 1926 erhielt sie dann eine Rolle in dem Film *Der heilige Berg*. Weitere Rollen, zumeist unter der Regie von Arnold Fanck, machten sie zu einem bekannten Filmstar. Mit *Das blaue Licht* von 1932 realisierte sie ihren ersten eigenen Film, 1935 entstand *Triumph des Willens* über den Reichsparteitag in Nürnberg. Seit 1962 arbeitet Riefenstahl als Fotografin: 1973 publizierte sie den Bildband *Die Nuba*, seitdem fotografierte sie weiterhin die in totaler Isolation lebenden Nuba von Kau im Sudan, insbesondere zeigt sie auf ihren Fotos deren Körperbemalungen. 1980 hatte sie in Tokio ihre erste Einzelausstellung.

Leni Riefenstahl took lessons in classical ballet with Eduardova in Berlin, then went on to modern dancing with Mary Wigman in Dresden. From 1923-26 she was engaged as a dancer and given a part in the movie, *Der heilige Berg*. She became a popular moviestar, playing mostly under director Arnold Fanck. In 1932 she directed the first of her own films, *Das blaue Licht* and in 1935 *Triumph des Willens* based on the Nuremberg Rally. Since 1962 Leni Riefenstahl has been working as a photographer: in 1973 she published *Die Nuba* and then continued to photograph the Nuba of Kau, a tribe who lives in total isolation in the Sudan. She was especially interested in their body paintings. She gave her first solo exhibition in 1980 in Tokyo.

Rio Branco, Miguel
*1946, Gran Canaria

Als Sohn eines brasilianischen Diplomaten ging Rio Branco in verschiedenen Ländern zur Schule und fing bereits als Dreizehnjähriger an, Kunst zu produzieren. Nach der Beschädigung mit Malerei wurden Ende der 60er Jahre Film und Fotografie zu seinen Hauptinteressen. Er arbeitete als professioneller Mode- und Werbefotograf und war als Kameraman an Filmen beteiligt. Ende 1972 kam er mit *Magnum* in Kontakt und sein Interesse richtete sich zunehmend auf Sozialreportagen in Farbe, bei denen das ästhetisch-formale Element eine wichtige Rolle spielt. 1981 zog er nach Paris und ist seitdem fest bei *Magnum*. Erst kürzlich erschien ein Buch mit seinen Aufnahmen aus Bahia *Dulce Sudor Amargo*.

Son of a Brazilan diplomat, Miguel Rio Branco was educated in several countries and began working with the visual arts at the age of thirteen. Beside his commitment to painting, film and photography became his main interests. He worked professionally in fashion and publicity and also participated in film productions. At the end of 1972 he came into contact with *Magnum* and his interest subsequently turned to social reportages in color with emphasis on the formal esthetic aspects. In 1981 Rio Branco went to stay in Paris and his relationship with *Magnum* became more intense. He recently published a book on his photographs of Bahia, *Dulce Sudor Amargo*.

Roiter, Fulvio
*1926, Italien

Lungomare Marconi 28
Venezia-Lido
Italy

Nachdem er Chemie studiert hatte, wurde Fulvio Roiter 1949 Mitglied der venezianischen Fotografenvereinigung *La Gondola*. 1953 begann er als Berufsfotograf zu arbeiten, seine Aufnahmen erschienen in Magazinen wie *DU, Réalités, Schöner Wohnen*, aber schon 1954 konzentrierte er sich dann auf die Illustration von Bildbänden. Ständig in verschiedenen Ländern unterwegs, beschäftigte er sich z.B. 1964 mit den Riten der afrikanischen Volksstämme und 1966 erschien sein Buch *Naguane*, das den Versuch darstellt, ein Kapitel der Prähistorie in Bilder zu übersetzen. Fulvio Roiter wurde insbesondere für seine ausdrucksstarken Fabrfotografien bekannt.

After finishing his studies in chemistry in 1949, Fulvio Roiter became a member of the Venetian photographers *La Gondola*. He started his career as a freelance photographer in 1953, and his photographs were published in magazines such as *DU, Réalités, Schöner Wohnen*. However from 1954 on his main activity became the illustration of books. Travelling widely, in 1964 he studied the rites of the African people and in 1966 he published the book *Naguane*: his attempt to translate a chapter of prehistory into imagery. Fulvio Roiter especially became known for his color photography of great evocative power.

Rössle, Marcus
*1957, Deutschland

Frankfurter Landstr. 116
6100 Darmstadt
West-Germany

Rössle studierte Fotodesign an der Fachhochschule in Darmstadt und seit er 1984 seinen Abschluß machte, arbeitet er als freier Werbefotograf, spezialisiert auf "People" und Porträts, in Darmstadt und Düsseldorf. Seit vier Jahren fotografiert er in Farbe, es entstand u.a. eine Serie über Blumen und Vasen auf Polaroid-Material. Auf mehreren Ausstellungen wurden bereits seine frei inszenierten, 1x2 m großen Farbfotografien gezeigt.

Rössle studied photo design in Darmstadt. Since his graduation in 1984 he has been working as a freelance advertising photographer in Darmstadt and Düsseldorf, specialized in people and portraits. Four years ago Rössle began to work in color. On Polaroid material he did a still life series on flowers and vases. His staged, large-size color photographs have already been shown in a number of exhibitions.

Ruetz, Michael
*1940, Deutschland

HBK
Broitzewerstr. 230
3300 Braunschweig
West-Germany

Ruetz studierte bis 1965 Sinologie und Publizistik in Freiburg, München und Berlin. Als Gasthörer bei Heinz Hajek-Halke gewann er zunehmendes Interesse an der Fotografie. 1969–74 war er dann Redaktionsfotograf des *Stern* und gab diese Anstellung auf, um ungebundener arbeiten zu können. 1978 publizierte er die Bildbände *Auf Goethes Spuren* und *Nekropolis*, 1979 *Im anderen Deutschland, Mit Goethe in der Schweiz*, etc. 1984 erschien in die USA *Eye on America*. Seit 1982 ist Ruetz Professor an der Hochschule für Bildende Künste in Braunschweig.

Unitl 1965 Michael Ruetz studied sinology and journalism in Freiburg, Munich and Berlin. During the next four years he attended the lectures of Heinz Hajek-Halke and took a growing interest in photography. In 1969 Ruetz joined the staff of the magazine *Stern* in Hamburg, but decided to leave in 1974 in order to produce work of a more personal nature. In 1978 he published the picture books *Auf Goethes Spuren* and *Nekropolis*; in 1979, *Im anderen Deutschland, Mit Goethe in der Schweiz* etc. In 1984 *Eye on America* came out as well as other books on Goethe. Ruetz has been a professor at the Academy of Fine Arts in Braunschweig since 1982.

Ruting, Peter
*1938, Niederlande

Linneausstraat 25
1093 EE Amsterdam
The Netherlands

Studierte an der Kunstgewerbeschule in Amsterdam und begann 1960 seine Karriere als Fotograf. Zunächst war Peter Ruting hauptsächlich mit Architektur- und Industriefotografie beschäftigt, dann fotografierte er zahlreiche Werbekampagnen. Seit einiger Zeit macht er nur noch so viel kommerzielle Arbeiten, wie er für den Lebensunterhalt braucht und widmet sich hauptsächlich dem freien Stilleben. Seine aus wenigen Elementen arrangierten Farbstilleben entstehen oft in wochenlanger Arbeit, wobei er die einzelnen Etappen des Gestaltungsprozesses in Polaroidfotos festhält, bevor er den Film für das Original schließlich belichtet.

Peter Ruting studied at the Institute of Arts and Crafts in Amsterdam and started his career as a photographer in 1960. Initially he mainly did architectural and industrial work but later undertook several advertising campaigns. Nowadays he earns his keep with commercial projects but dedicates himself to still life photography, composed from a minimum of objects. These images often take him weeks to complete and he captures the individual stages in Polaroid images, before actually taking the final photograph.

Rutledge, Richard
*c.1920, USA

Im zweiten Weltkrieg arbeitete Richard Rutledge in einer Firma, die Kriegsmaterial herstellte. Er wählte die Nachtschicht, um tagsüber Fotografie an der *Art Center School* in Los Angeles studieren zu können. Bei Kriegsende zog Rutledge nach New York, wo er von Condé·Nast als Fotograf engagiert wurde. Ende der 40er Jahre schickte ihn der Verlag von *Vogue* und anderen Magazinen für zwei Jahre nach Paris, wo er für die französische *Vogue* fotografierte und fotografische Experimennte betrieb.

When WW II began, Richard Rutledge took a job in a war plant, choosing the night shift in order to be free during the daytime to study photography at the *Art Center School* in Los Angeles. At the end of the war Rutledge moved to New York, where the Condé Nast Publications hired him as a photographer. Four years later the company sent him to Paris, where he worked for French *Vogue* and carried out photographic experiments.

Růžička, Drahomir Josef
1870,(CSSR), † 1960, USA

Růžička hatte in Wien Medizin studiert und emigrierte um 1900 in die USA, wo er als Arzt arbeitete. 1904 machte er seine ersten, unter dem Einfluß der Kunstfotografie stehenden fotografischen Versuche. 1911 lernte er Clarence H. White kennen, der ihn fotografisch ausbildete. Růžička fotografierte Stilleben und Aktstudien, wandte sich dann von den Edeldruckverfahren der Kunstfotografie ab und der Neuen Sachlichkeit zu. 1921 wurden seine Fotografien erstmals in einer größeren Ausstellung in der CSSR gezeigt. In den 20er Jahren ging von Růžička Arbeiten ein wichtiger Einfluß auf die tchechische Fotografie aus.

Růžička studied medicine in Vienna and around 1900 emigrated to the States where he served as a doctor. In 1904 he had his first experiences with photography, being heavily influenced by Pictorial Photography. He met Clarence H. White in 1911 and underwent a training with him. Růžička took photographs of still lifes and nudes, then abandoned Pictorial in favor of Straight Photography. In 1921 the first large exhibition of his photographic work took place in the CSSR and during the 1920's his work was of major influence on Czech photography.

Sachs, Gunter
*1932, Deutschland

Wehrlestr. 13
8000 München 80
West-Germany

Sachs beschäftigte sich während seiner Studienzeit in Lausanne (1952-1955) mit experimenteller Schwarzweißfotografie. 1963-70 produzierte und drehte er sieben Dokumentarfilme. 1972 wandte er sich wieder der Fotografie zu. Für die *photokina* '74 fotografierte er das offizielle Plakat und er stellte dort auch seine farbigen Mädchenfotos aus. Gleichzeitig erschien der Bildband *Mädchen in meinen Augen*, 1981 kam *Licht Bilder* heraus. Seit 1975 fotografiert Sachs Mode, hauptsächlich für die französische und deutsche *Vogue*, und realisiert Kalender und Werbeaufnahmen.

While a student in Lausanne (1952-55) Sachs practised black-and-white experimental photography. Between 1963-70 he produced and directed seven documentaries. In 1972 he again turned to photography, now working in color. He photographed the official poster for *photokina* '74 where he exhibited his color photographs of girls. The same year his photo book *Mädchen in meinen Augen* appeared, and in 1981 *Licht Bilder* was published. Since 1975 he photographs fashion mainly on commission for the French and German editions of *Vogue*. He also does calendar and advertising pictures.

Ságl, Jan
*1942, CSSR

Chodská 31
12000 Praha 2
CSSR

1961 zog Jan Ságl nach Prag und seit 1964 ist er dort als Berufsfotograf tätig. Er fotografiert für Kunstmagazine, und von 1967-76 auch für Musikgruppen. 1969 reiste er durch die USSR, die Fotos von dieser Reise erschienen in Katalogen und Kunstmagazinen. 1974-1977 fotografierte er in der Slowakei die Reste des traditionellen Landlebens und Milieus. 1979 begann Ságl in Farbe zu arbeiten, es entstehen seitdem drei Zyklen: Landschaften in extremer Beleuchtung, über Licht und Reflexionen, über die Beziehungen von Fotografie und bildender Kunst.

Jan Ságl moved to Prague in 1961, working there as a professional photographer since 1964. He photographed on commission for art magazines and during 1967-76 for music groups. In 1969 he travelled in the USSR; the results of this journey appeared in catalogues and magazines. During 1974-77 he recorded the traditional environment and village life of Slovakia. Ságl started to work in color in 1979 with three series: landscapes in extreme lighting; light and reflections; and the relationships between photography and the fine arts.

Samaras, Lucas
*1936, Griechenland

57 West 71st Street
New York, N.Y. 10023
USA

1939 wanderte sein Vater in die USA aus, Samaras folgte 1948 mit seiner Mutter. Er besuchte dann in West New York die Schule. 1955 wurde er amerikanischer Staatsbürger und begann Kunst zu studieren, 1959 besuchte er die Vorlesungen über Kunstgeschichte von Meyer Schapiro. Seit 1964 lebt Samaras als Künstler und Fotograf in New York. Seine ersten *Autopolaroid* Fotografien entstanden 1970, die ersten *Photo-Transformations* 1973. Fünf Jahre später realisierte er die 8 x 10″ Polaroidaufnahmen zu *Sittings* und 1983 produzierte er die Serie *Panoramas*. Samaras stellt sich meist auf seinen Fotos selbst dar.

In 1939 Lucas Samaras' father emigrated to the States; his wife and son followed in 1948. Samaras was educated in West New York and he was naturalized in 1955. He studied art and attended Meyer Schapiro's lectures in art history. Since 1964 Samaras has been an artist and photographer, living in New York City. His first *Autopolaroid* photographs were taken in 1970, and he started to work on the *Photo-Transformations* in 1973. Five years later he realized *Sittings*, a series of 8 x 10″ Polaroid photos and the *Panoramas* series in 1983. Lucas Samaras portrays himself in most of his photographic work.

Saroldi, Marco
*1957, Italien

Lungopo Antonelli 143
10153 Torino
Italy

Seit 1982 ist die Fotografie sein Beruf; er arbeitet als Reportage- und Industriefotograf, außerdem ist er Spezialist für die Ausarbeitung von Cibachromeabzügen. Das Interesse an der Farbfotografie begann schon 1979 und bis heute hat Saroldi eine Vorliebe für die theatralischen Aspekte des täglichen Lebens, die er in seinen Fotografien herausarbeitet durch die Schwärze des Hintergrundes, die Leuchtkraft der Farben und die starken Kontraste.

Since 1982 Saroldi has been a professional photographer, specialized in reportage and industrial work, as well as in Ciba printing. His interest in color dates back to 1979 and he has a tendency towards the theatrical aspects of everyday life. He expresses this with black backgrounds, brilliant colors and sharp contrasts.

Sato, Akira
*1930, Japan

1-5-17 Aobadai, Meguro-ku
Tokyo 153
Japan

1953 schloß Akira Sato sein Ökonomiestudium an der Universität von Yokohama ab und begann im folgenden Jahr als Modefotograf zu arbeiten. 1959 begründete er zusammen mit →Hosoe, →Kawada, →Narahara und anderen die Gruppe VIVO. 1961 hatte er mit einer Serie über Frauen seine erste Einzelausstellung und 1966 wurde Sato mit dem Preis der japanischen Fotokritik ausgezeichnet. Er fotografierte u.a. die Mitternachtssonne, Mailand und das Ägäische Meer. Sato arbeitet auch mit Videofilm.

In 1953 Akira Sato graduated in economics from Yokohama University and he started his work as a fashion photographer the following year. In 1959 he was the co-founder of the VIVO group, together with →Hosoe, →Kawada, →Narahara and others. Sato held his first solo exhibition in 1961 with a series on women and he won the Japanese Photo Critic Prize in 1966. His photographic work includes a series on the midnight sun; Milan and the Aegean Sea. Sato also works with video film.

Saudek, Jan
*1935, Tschechoslowakei

Vlnita 16, Praha 4
CSSR

Anfang der 50er Jahre machte Jan Saudek mit einer einfachen Box-Kamera seine ersten Aufnahmen. Tief beeindruckt von dem Katalog der *Family of Man* Ausstellung entstand etwa zehn Jahre später Saudeks erste ernsthafte fotografische Arbeit. Seit dem Ende der 60er Jahre benutzt er einen Keller als Studio, dessen Wand den ständig wiederkehrenden Hintergrund zu Ver- und Entkleidungsszenen bildet. Saudeks meist handkolorierte Fotografien handeln von der verinnenden Zeit: Von der Zeit zwischen den Aufnahmen einer Sequenz oder den Jahren zwischen zwei Porträts von ein und derselben Frau. Die Spuren, die das Leben auf den Körpern und Gesichtern hinterläßt sind Saudeks Hauptthema. Erst kürzlich fing Saudek, der bekannteste tschechische Fotograf, an, unmittelbar in Farbe zu fotografieren.

Jan Saudek took his first photographs in the early 1950's with a cheap box camera. Deeply impressed by the catalogue of the *Family of Man* exhibition, a decade later he produced his first serious photographs. Since the end of the Sixties he has used a cellar as his studio, the wall which reappears as the background for his dressing and undressing scenes. Saudek's handcolored photographs are about the passing of time: about the time between the exposures during a sequence, or the years between two portraits of the same woman. The traces of life on bodies and faces are Saudek's main interest. Only recently Saudek, the most famous Czech photographer, started to work directly in color.

Schnakenwinkel, Gerd
*1941, Deutschland

Neptunstr. 24
2720 Rotenburg/Wümme
West-Germany

Studierte Pädagogik und Naturwissenschaften in Bielefeld, Tübingen und Münster. Er arbeitete als Ornithologe und ist seit 1972 im Schuldienst tätig. 1963 begann er intensiver zu fotografieren, bevorzugt Naturaufnahmen, 1977 spezialisierte er sich auf die Landschaftsfotografie in Farbe. Seit 1981 werden seine Fotografien auf Ausstellungen gezeigt.

Schnakenwinkel studied Pedagogics and Natural Science in Bielefeld, Tübingen and Münster. He worked as an ornithologist and since 1972 has been a school teacher. Way back in 1962 he started to photograph seriously, mostly pictures of nature and in 1977 he specialized in color landscapes. His work has been exhibited regularly since 1981.

Schrager, Victor
*1950, USA

73 Warren Street
New York, N.Y. 10007
USA

Schrager studierte in Harvard und an der Florida State University, wo er 1975 seinen Magister in Kunsterziehung erhielt. Seit 1978 fotografiert er in Farbe und hatte viele Ausstellungen als künstlerischer Fotograf. Er spezialisierte sich auf Stilleben, wobei er meist verschiedene bedruckte Papiere kombiniert und dann fotografiert, so das eine Art plastische Collage entsteht.

Victor Schrager graduated from Harvard University and received his Master of Fine Arts degree from Florida State University in 1975. Since 1978 he has been working in color and his artistic works have been exhibited widely. Schrager specialized in photographing still lifes, mainly combinations of various printed papers, resembling three dimensional collages.

Schulthess, Emil
*1913, Zürich

Langacker 5
8127 Forch/Zürich
Switzerland

Als ausgebildeter Grafikdesigner nahm Schulthess 1932 Fotounterricht bei Hans Finsler an der Kunstgewerbeschule in Zürich. Er arbeitete dann als Grafiker, zunächst frei, ab 1937 als Angestellter bei Conzet & Huber, dem Verlag, der ab 1941 das kulturelle Monatsmagazin *DU* herausbrachte. Schulthess machte das Layout von *DU*, dann arbeitete er als Bildredakteur und Fotograf, bis er 1957 *DU* verließ. Seitdem widmet er sich der Veröffentlichung eigener Bildbände. Schon seine Landschafts- und Naturaufnahmen hatten weite Beachtung gefunden, doch bekannt wurde Schulthess insbesondere durch seine Panoramafotografien. Schon 1949 hatte er Panoramen der Sonne vom Auf-zum Untergang fotografiert, ab 1970 entstanden dann Panoramen von Städten und von den Alpen.

Trained as a graphic designer, Emil Schulthess took photographic lessons under Hans Finsler at the school of Arts and Crafts in Zurich. He worked as a graphic designer, freelance at first, but in 1937 he joined Conzett & Huber. In 1941 their monthly magazine *DU* was born and Schulthess was responsible for the layout. Later on he served as editor and photographer until he left the magazine 1957. Since that time he has devoted himself entirely to the publication of his books. A skilled landscape and nature photographer, Schulthess especially became known for his panoramic images. As early as 1949 he photographed the sun from sunrise to sunset. Then from 1970 he did panoramic views of cities and of the Alps.

Schumacher, Jacques
*1933, Niederlande

Nach einer Fotografenlehre studierte Schumacher Grafikdesign. Dann unterrichtete er von 1955 bis 1957 an der Werkkunstschule in Bielefeld, bevor er nach Paris übersiedelte, wo er als Grafikdesigner arbeitete. 1963 eröffnete er in Hamburg ein eigenes Studio, und seitdem fotografiert er erfolgreich im Auftrag von Werbeagenturen und Zeitschriften. Sein Spezialgebiet: "Mädchenfotografie".

Following an apprenticeship as a photographer, Jacques Schumacher studied graphic design. After his graduation he lectured at the *Werkkunstschule* Bielefeld during 1955-57. He then moved to Paris, France, where he worked as a graphic designer. He opened a photographic studio in Hamburg in 1963 and since then has successfully been working for advertising agencies and magazines. He specializes in photographing girls.

Schürmann, Wilhelm
*1946, Deutschland

Hans Heyden-Str. 195
Dortmund
West-Germany

Schürmann studierte von 1966 bis 1971 Chemie an der TH in Aachen. Während des Studiums begann er als Autodidakt zu fotografieren und er arbeitete bis 1973 für die *Neue Rheinische Zeitung* als Lokalreporter. 1973 gründete er zusammen mit Rudolf Kicken die Galerie Lichttropfen, die dann 1976 in Galerie Schürmann und Kicken umbenannt wurde. Die Tätigkeit als Fotogalerist gab Schürmann zwei Jahre später auf und begann Fotografie an der Fachhochschule Aachen zu lehren. Als Fotograf wurde er in den 70er Jahren bekannt durch seine Schwarzweißfotografien von Häusern in Belgien und Aachen. Seit einigen Jahren Fotografiert er auch in Farbe.

Wilhelm Schürmann studied chemistry at the Technical College in Aachen 1966-71. As a student he taught himself photography and until 1973 did news shots for the *Neue Rheinische Zeitung*. In collaboration with Rudolf Kicken in 1973 he founded the photo-gallery Lichttropfen in Aachen, the name of which was changed to Galerie Schürmann und Kicken in 1976. Schürmann left the gallery in 1978 and started to lecture at the Technical College in Aachen the following year. In the 1970's he became known for his black & white photographs of houses, taken in Belgium and Aachen. In recent years he also photographs in color.

Sentís, Marta
*1949, Spanien

Via Layetana 6
08003 Barcelona
Spain

Sentís studierte Französisch an der Sorbonne, Englisch in Cambridge und Italienisch an der Universität von Florenz. 1976 begann sie mit einer Dokumentation über die Malediven ihre Arbeit als freiberufliche Reisefotojournalistin. Ihre Intention ist es, Gefühle und Stimmungen von Menschen unterschiedlicher Kulturkreise einzufangen. Deshalb fotografiert sie auch in Farbe, weil diese mehr Informationen über die jeweilige Kultur vermittelt und weniger Raum läßt für eine beliebige Interpretation der Aufnahmen. Zur Zeit arbeitet Marta Sentís an einer Dokumentation über die *Afrikanische Diaspora*.

Marta Sentís studied French at the Sorbonne, English in Cambridge and Italian at Florence University. She started her career as a freelance travel photo-reporter in 1976 with a documentary on the Maldives Islands. She is interested in capturing the moods and feelings of people of different cultures. She uses color, because this "gives more cultural information and leaves less room for dreamy interpretations." Her work in progress is a documentary on the *African Diaspora*.

Sherman, Cindy
*1954, USA

59 Walker Street
New York, N.Y. 10004
USA

Sherman studierte am *State University College* in Buffalo und schon mit 22 Jahren hatte sie ihre erste Einzelausstellung. In den letzten Jahren wurde sie dann international bekannt. Sie ist Fotografin und Performance-Künstlerin, wobei sie beides vereint: Ihre Aufnahmen sind stets Selbstinszenierungen, das Besondere daran aber ist, daß sie weniger sich selbst, als vielmehr Rollenklischees und Alltagsmythen in ihren Arbeiten reflektiert. 1983 erschien in München ein Buch mit ihren Fotoarbeiten.

Cindy Sherman graduated from State University College in Buffalo. Already at the age of 22 she had her first exhibition and she has gained international recognition during recent years. She is both a photographer and a performence artist and she combines the two in her work. Her photographs are always self-productions, only she does not primarily portray her true self but everyday myths and clichés. Her book of photographs appeared in 1983.

Shinoyama, Kishin
*1940, Japan

9-6-17 Akasaka
Minatu-ku, Tokyo 107
Japan

Shinoyma studierte Fotografie an der Nihon Universität in Tokio und fing schon als Student an, für eine Werbeagentur zu arbeiten. 1968 machte er sich als Fotograf selbständig und arbeitet seitdem für Magazine, fotografiert Mode und Werbeanzeigen. 1970 wurde er mit einer Aktserie bekannt und vier Jahre später arbeitete er an einer Serie über traditionelle japanische Tätowierungen. 1976 wurden seine Farbaufnahmen der japanische Wohnformen erstmals ausgestellt, die Serie heißt *The Meaning of the House* (Die Bedeutung des Hauses). Seitdem hat Shinoyama etliche Bücher mit Farbfotgrafien publiziert.

Kishin Shinoyama studied photography at Nihon University, Tokyo. Already as a student he started to work for Light Publicity Company in Tokyo and since 1968 he has been a freelance photographer, working for magazines in the field of advertising and fashion. In 1970 he became known for a series of nude studies and four years later he worked on a series of traditional tattoos. In 1976 his color photographs of Japanese home interiors were shown for the first time; the series is entitled *Meaning of the House*. Since then Shinoyama has published several books of color photographs.

Shore, Stephen
*1947, USA

Shore fotografiert seit 1953, seit 1956 in Farbe. 1970 begann Shore mit der Großformatkamera in Farbe zu arbeiten und gut zehn Jahre später erschien das Buch *Common Places* mit seinen dokumentarisch schlichten Farbfotos von Straßenkreuzungen, Tankstellen, usw. 1977 bis 1982 fotografierte er im Auftrag des Metropolitan Museum in New York den Garten des impressionistischen Malers Claude Monet in Giverny. Diese Aufnahmen kamen 1983 in den USA als Buch heraus.

Stephen Shore took his first photographs in 1953; the first ones in color in 1956. In 1970 he started to load a view camera with color plates and a decade later his book *Common Places* was published, including his documentary color photographs of street crossings, gas stations, etc. From 1977-1982 Shore was commissioned to photograph the gardens of the impressionist painter, Claude Monet in Giverny, France – by the Metropolitan Museum, New York.

Sieff, Jeanloup
*1933, Frankreich

87, rue Ampère
75017 Paris
France

Sieff begann 1954 als Fotojournalist zu arbeiten, er fotografierte für *Elle* und trat für ein Jahr *Magnum Photos* bei. 1959-61 hielt er sich in New York auf, wo er für amerikanische und europäische Modejournale arbeitete. 1966 ließ er sich wieder in Paris nieder, wo er seitdem ein Studio für Mode sowie Werbefotografie und –Film unterhält. Seine freien Akte, Landschafts- und Porträtaufnahmen entstanden häufig unter Verwendung eines Weitwinkelobjektivs. 1983 erschien in München eine Monografie über sein fotografisches Werk.

Jeanloup Sieff started to work as a photo-journalist in 1954, joining *Magnum* agency for one year and collaborating with the magazine *Elle*. During 1959-61 he stayed in New York, working for U.S. and European fashion journals. He returned to Paris, where he has had a studio since 1966 and specializes in fashion and commercial photography and film. His personal nude studies, landscapes and portraits in black & white were mainly done with a wide-angle lens. His photographic work has been featured widely, including in a monograph, published 1983.

Siegel, Arthur
*1913, USA, † 1978, USA

Siegel begann sich 1927 für die Fotografie zu interessieren und 1935 fing er an, als Industrie- und Zeitschriftenfotograf zu arbeiten. 1937/38 besuchte er den Fotounterricht von Laszlo Moholy-Nagy am New Bauhaus und dort entstanden seine ersten abstrakt-experimentellen Fotografien. Nach dem Krieg arbeitete Siegel als freier Fotograf für *Time, Life, Fortune* und andere Illustrierte. Er gehörte damals zu den Pionieren der Kleinbildfarbfotografie. 1946-78 lehrte er am Institute of Design in Chicago (dem ehemaligen New Bauhaus) und ab 1968 gab er die aktive Fotografie zugunsten der Lehre langsam auf. 1981 veranstaltete die Chicago Historical Society eine große Retrospektive auf Siegels fotografisches Lebenswerk.

Arthur Siegel's interest in photography began in 1927 and he started to work as a magazine and industrial photographer in 1935. During 1937/38 he attended the lessons of Laszlo Moholy-Nagy at the New Bauhaus, where he took his first abstract experimental photographs. Following the war, Siegel worked as a freelance photographer for such magazines as *Time, Life, Fortune*. At that time he was one of the pioneers of 35mm color photography. Siegel taught at the Institute of Design in Chicago (the former New Bauhaus) during 1946 to 1978 and in fact abandoned active photography after 1968 in favor of teaching. In 1981 the Chicago Historical Society organized a large retrospective on Siegel's lifetime of photographic work.

Šimánek, Dušan
*1948, Tschechoslowakei

Kubelikova 24
13000 Prague 3
Czechoslovakia

Nach einer Ausbildung als Bühnenbildner studierte Šimánek bis 1978 Fotografie an der Filmhochschule in Prag. Seitdem arbeitet er als Werbe- und Modefotograf. Seit 1979 fotografiert er verlassene Häuser, die vor dem Abriß stehen. Die Farben seiner fast abstrakt wirkenden Fotografien sind sehr fein und nuanciert, fast undefinierbar.

Following a training as a stage designer, Dušan Šimánek enrolled at the College of Cinema in Prague, where he studied photography until 1978. Since that period he has been working professionally as a fashion and advertising photographer. Since 1979 he has been photographing abandoned houses, before they were pulled down. The colors of his nearly abstract photos are very delicate and sometimes rather undefinable.

Simpfendoerfer, Thomas
*1959, Deutschland

Waldschmidtstr. 17
6000 Frankfurt
West-Germany

Simpfendoerfer begann 1979 in Darmstadt Kommunikationsdesign mit dem Schwerpunkt Fotografie zu studieren, ab 1981 hauptsächlich bei Hans Georg Puttnies. 1983 arbeitete er als Layout Assistent bei einer Werbeagentur in Frankfurt und im Jahr darauf schloß er das Studium als Diplom-Designer ab. Seine großformatigen Farbaufnahmen, auf denen er meist selbst mit abgebildet ist, wurden bereits auf verschiedenen Ausstellungen vorgestellt.

Simpfendoerfer started to study communication design in Darmstadt in 1979, working mainly under Hans Georg Puttnies since 1981. In 1983 he worked in an advertising agency as a layout assistant and received his diploma as a designer the following year. His large format color prints, which often portray himself, have been shown in various exhibitions.

Singh, Raghubir
*1942, Indien

11, rue de Siam
75016 Paris, France

1957 schenkte ihm ein Onkel seine erste Kamera. An der Universittät von Delhi immatrikuliert, arbeitete er, statt zu studieren, für *Life* und die *New York Times.* Singh studierte dann Kunst am *Hindu College* in Neu Delhi. 1965-69 fotografierte er den Ganges, 1972-73 Calcutta, dann die Provinz Rajasthan bis 1975. Seitdem lebt Singh in Paris, kehrt aber häufig nach Indien zurück, um dort Aufnahmen zu machen. Nur in Indien und Südasien fotografiert er in Farbe. Er hat mehrere Bildbände veröffentlicht.

Raghubir Singh's uncle gave him a camera in 1957. He later enrolled at Delhi University, but instead of attending lectures he took on photographic assignments for Life and the New York Times. Singh also studied art at the Hindu College in New Delhi. During 1965-69 he photographed the Ganges river, 1972-73 Calcutta and then the region of Rajasthan until 1975. Since that year he has been living in Paris, but he often returns to India in order to photograph in his native country. Only in India and South Asia does he work in color. Singh has published a number of picture books.

Sinsabaugh, Art
*1924, USA, † 1983, USA

Sinsabaugh studierte von 1945 bis 1949 Fotografie bei Moholy-Nagy und → Harry Callahan am *Institute of Design* in Chicago. Von 1951-59 war er selbst Lehrer an diesem Institut und ab 1959 Professor an der Universität von Illinois. In den 60er Jahren fotografierte Sinsabaugh Panoramen der Präric und Plateaus im Mittleren Westen. Ab 1980 arbeitete er an einer Landschaftsserie in Farbe mit einer 12x20″ Kamera. 1978 wurde am Indiana University Art Museum das Art Sinsabaugh Archiv gegründet, in dem sich alle seine Arbeiten seit 1937 befinden.

Art Sinsabaugh studied photography under Moholy-Nagy and → Harry Callahan at the Institute of Design in Chicago, from 1945-49. Later he became a teacher of photography there (1951-59). From 1959 on he was a professor at the University of Illinois. In the Sixties Sinsabaugh did panoramic views of the prairies and plateaus of the Midwest. In 1980 he started a series of landscapes in color, using a 12x20″ camera. In 1978 the Art Sinsabaugh Archive was established at Indiana University Art Museum in Bloomington, where all his photographic works since 1937, are to be found.

Siwik, Hans
*1933, Deutschland

Grenzstr. 9
6370 Oberursel 4
West-Germany

Nach dem Volontariat bei einem Zeitungsverlag in Frankfurt begann Hans Siwik als freier Journalist zu arbeiten. Unter anderem war er drei Jahre lang in Bonn für verschiedene Zeitungen des In- und Auslandes tätig. Seit Anfang der 70er Jahre arbeitet Siwik als freier Fotodesigner; neben Kalendern und Anzeigenaufnahmen realisiert er vor allem freie Projekte. *Venedig - Menschen hinter Masken* wurde als Buch verlegt, in Japan fotografierte er eine Serie über "Kyudo" und ein Porträt der Menschen und Landschaften Islands befindet sich 1986 in Arbeit.

After a two year apprecticeship with a newspaper publisher in Frankfurt, Hans Siwik started to work as a freelance photo journalist. For three years he stayed in Bonn, photographing for various German and foreign newspapers. Since the early Seventies he has been active as a freelance photo designer; he carries out calendar and advertising projects but is mainly involved in personal projects such as *Venedig - Menschen hinter Masken*, a book on the carnival in Venice, Italy. In Japan he photographed a series on 'Kyudo' and his work in progress in 1986 is a portrait of the people and landscapes of Iceland.

Skoglund, Sandy
*1946, USA

Während ihres Studiums begann Skoglund als Konzeptkünstlerin zu arbeiten. Bis 1976 war sie dann mit der Minimal Art beschäftigt, wandte sich schließlich von diesen gedanklichen Kunstprozessen ab und drehte einen Dokumentarfilm. Die Kamera benutzte sie zuerst, um ihre Konzept-Kunst zu dokumentieren, dann brachte sie Kontaktpapier in den Ecken von Räumen an, auf denen dann Muster und Farben die Positionen der Objekte im Raum angaben. Schließlich stellte sie in jüngerer Zeit Objekte wie Fische aus Ton und Katzen aus Pappmaché selbst her, um sie dann in arrangierten Interieurs zu fotografieren.

During her studies, Sandy Skoglund started to work as a concept artist. Until 1976 she was involved in Minimal Art, but she then turned away from such artistic processes and made a documentary film. She initially made use of a still camera to document her conceptual artworks, but then she started to stick contact sheets in the corners of rooms, so that the patterns and colors on them would define their actual spatial positions. More recently she modelled objects like ceramic fish or paper maché cats and photographed them in staged interiors.

Slavin, Neal
*1941, USA

62 Green Street
New York, N.Y. 10012
USA

1955-59 besuchte er die Hochschule für Musik und bildenden Kunst in New York, bis 1963 studierte er anschließend Malerei, Grafikdesign und Fotografie an der Cooper Union in New York. Seit 1963 arbeitet er als freier Fotograf für Magazine und Werbung. Neben seiner kommerziellen Arbeit realisiert er freie Projekte, seit 1972 fotografiert er sie in Farbe. Ab 1973 entstand als freies Projekt eine Serie von formellen Farbporträts amerikanischer Gruppen und Vereine; *When Two or More are Gathered Together* erschien 1976 als Buch. Zehn Jahre später beendete Slavin ein vergleichbares Projekt über *die Britten*, das ebenfalls in Buchform veröffentlicht wurde.

Educated at the Music and Art High School, New York (1955-59), Neal Slavin studied painting, graphic design and photography at Cooper Union, New York until 1963. Since 1963 he has worked as a freelance photographer for magazines and advertising. Besides his commercial work, he undertakes a lot of personal projects and since 1970 also lectures. Slavin started working in color in 1972 and a year later began his series of posed formal color portraits of American social and professional groups, published in book form as *When Two or More are Gathered Together* in 1976. In 1985 he photographed English groups and associations and his book, *The Britons* was published in 1986.

Smith, Clinton
*1944, USA

Diente 1963-71 in der US Air Force und begann sich zunehmend für die Fotografie zu interessieren. Ab 1971 widmete er sich ganz der Fotografie und im Jahr darauf gründete er die "Light Impressions Gallery", die erste reine Fotogalerie in Süd-Kalifornien. 1975 zog er nach Monterey Peninsula und arbeitete als Dunkelkammerassistent von →Wynn Bullock bis zu dessen Tod Ende 1975. 1978 begann er in Farbe zu fotografieren und 1981 damit Workshops abzuhalten. 1983 fing er an, selbst Cibachrome und Dye Transfer Abzüge herzustellen, seit 1984 experimentiert er mit dem Carbon Pigment Prozeß. Seine in der Tradition der "Straight Photography" stehenden Landschaftsaufnahmen wurden in zahlreichen Ausstellungen gezeigt.

Clinton Smith served in the US Air Force and became increasingly interested in photography. In 1971 he turned to photography full-time and a year later founded 'Light Impressions Gallery', the first purely photographic gallery in Southern California. He moved to Monterey Peninsula and worked as a darkroom assistant to →Wynn Bullock until Bullock's death in late 1975. In 1978 he began working with color and since 1981 teaches at photographic workshops. In 1983 he began making his own Cibachrome and Dye Transfer prints and in 1984 his experiments with the Carbon Pigment Process, began. His traditional Straight Photography landscapes have been extensively exhibited.

Snowdon (Anthony Armstrong-Jones)
*1930, Großbritannien

22 Lanceston Place
London W8 5 RL
Great Britain

Armstrong-Jones ging in Eton zur Schule und studierte dort bis 1950 Architektur. Seit 1951 arbeitet er als Fotograf für *Harper's Bazaar, Sunday Times, Picture Post, Queen.* 1953-61 hatte er ein Fotostudio in der Pimlico Road in London. 1960-78 war er mit Prinzessin Margaret verheiratet und erhielt 1961 den Titel Viscount Linley, 1st Earl of Snowdon. Seit 1962 ist Snowdon Fotograf und künstlerischer Berater der *Sunday Times.* Neben seinen Fotoreportagen entstanden seit 1968 mehrere preisgekrönte Dokumentarfilme für das Fernsehen. Snowdon engagiert sich besonders für geistig und körperlich Behinderte.

Anthony Armstrong-Jones attended Eton School and studied architecture until 1950. Since 1951 he has been a freelance photographer, working for *Harper's Bazaar, Sunday Times, Picture Post, Queen.* He maintained a studio in Pimlico Road, London, during 1953-61. From 1960 to 1978 he was married to Princess Margaret and received the title Viscount Linley, 1st Earl of Snowdon in 1961. Since 1962 Snowdon has been the photographer and artistic advisor of the Sunday Times. Besides his reportages, he also produced several award-winning TV-documentaries. Snowdon is particularly involved in aiding mentally and physically handicapped people.

Somoroff, Michael
*1957, USA

Dorotheenstr. 176
2000 Hamburg 60
West-Germany

Michael Somoroff studierte an der *New School for Social Research* und an der *Parsons School for Design,* beide in New York. Er leitete dann u.a. das Studio seines Vaters, des Fotografen Ben Somoroff, und arbeitete als Kameramann und Regisseur von Werbespots. Seit 1980 hat Somoroff ein Studio in Hamburg und erledigt Werbeaufträge in ganz Europa.

Michael Somoroff studied at the New School for Social Research and at Parsons School of Design, both in New York. He then worked as a studio manager, e.g. for his father, the photographer Ben Somoroff. He also worked as a director and cameraman for TV commercials. Since 1980 Somoroff runs a photographic studio in Hamburg, West-Germany, working on commercial assignments throughout Europe.

Souza, Al
*1944, USA

415 Meadow Street
Amherst, MA
USA

Souza studierte Ingenieurwesen und arbeitete als Luftfahrtingenieur in Connecticut. Gleichzeitig besuchte er drei Jahre lang die *Art Students League* in New York und machte 1972 seinen Magister in Kunsterziehung an der *School of Visual Arts* in New York. Seine Arbeiten sind im Bereich der konzeptuellen Fotografie anzusiedeln; Souza benutzt vorzugsweise Sequenzen, ein Mittelding zwischen Einzelfoto und Film. Zu den die Wahrnehmung thematisierenden Fotosequenzen fügt er teilweise gemalte Elemente hinzu.

Al Souza studied engineering and then worked as an aviation engineer in Connecticut. At the same time he attended the Art Students League for three years and in 1972 he received his Master of Fine Arts degree from the School of Visual Arts in New York. His photographic work more or less belongs to the field of Concept Art. Souza mainly uses sequences, a medium between single images and film. He often adds painted elements to his sequences, which are about perception.

Spring, Anselm
*1943, Deutschland

Museumsstr. 5
8910 Landsberg
West-Germany

Eigentlich wollte er Maler oder Musiker werden, doch nachdem er als Tourist in den USA fotografiert hatte, arbeitete er bald als Mode- und Werbefotograf. Da er seinen eigentlichen Berufswunsch nicht ganz aus den Augen verlor, produzierte er zwischendurch drei Langspielplatten. Bekannt wurde er vor allem durch seine sehr ästhetisierten, farbigen Landschaftsaufnahmen. 1980 publizierte er *Babylon*, einen Bildband mit Farbfotos, die er in den USA gemacht hatte. Seitdem arbeitet er u.a. für *Geo, Stern, Merian,* das *Frankfurter Allgemeine Magazin*, fotografierte für Kalender, Tonbildschauen und will sich in Zukunft wieder mehr der Malerei und der Musik widmen.

Anselm Spring originally intended to become a painter or musician; instead he established himself as a fashion and commercial photographer, after having taken pictures as a tourist in the USA. He however did not forget his initial ambitions and recorded three LP's while working as a landscape photographer. In 1980 he published *Babylon*, a book of photographs he had taken in the States. Nowadays he regularly contributes to *GEO, Stern,* the *Frankfurter Allgemeine Magazin* and also takes pictures for calendars and audiovisual shows. In future he intends to spend more time on his music and painting.

Steenwijk, Jan van
*1938, Niederlande

11 Warwick Road
Belmont, MA 02178
USA

Aufgewachsen in Holland und Indonesien ging Jan van Steenwijk 1960 nach Dänemark, um dort als Fotograf zu arbeiten. 1968 eröffnete er in Kopenhagen ein eigenes Studio und zählt heute zu den führenden Fotografen in Dänemark. 1970 gründete er "Multi Vision, Inc.", ein Studio, in dem hauptsächlich Diaschaun und Videofilme produziert werden. Steenwijk ist außerdem Redakteur der *Dansk Fotografisk Tidsskrift* und von *RF-Avisen*, einem Magazin für Werbefotografen. Er schrieb zwei Bücher über die USA: *USAROUND - A Personal Meeting* und das selbstverlegte *Always on the Road*. Er lebt in Dänemark und den USA.

Raised in Holland and Indonesia, Jan van Steenwijk went to Denmark in 1960, where he began working as a photographer. In 1968 he opened his own studio in Copenhagen and he is now one of the leading photographers in Denmark. In 1970 he established 'Multi Vision, Inc.', primarily to produce slide programs and video productions. Steenwijk additionally serves as editor to *Dansk Fotografisk Tidsskrift* and *RF-Avisen*, a Danish magazine for commercial photographers. He wrote two books about the United States: *USAROUND - A Personal Meeting* and the self published book *Always on the Road.* He lives in Denmark and the States.

Steichen, Edward
*1879, Luxemburg
† 1973, USA

Im Alter von 16 Jahren begann Steichen zu fotografieren, während er gleichzeitig in einer Lithografieanstalt arbeitete und Kunstunterricht nahm. Zwischen 1900 und 1922 lebte er abwechselnd in Frankreich und den USA; malte und gehörte zu den bekanntesten Vertretern der Kunstfotografie. Ca. 1922 gab er die Malerie auf und arbeitete als Cheffotograf für *Vogue* und *Vanity Fair* bis 1937. Zehn Jahre später wurde er Leiter der Fotografieabteilung am Museum of Modern Art in New York. Dort startete er 1955 die von ihm organisierte Wanderausstellung *The Family of Man*; 1962, im Alter von 83 Jahren zog er sich aus dem Berufsleben zurück.

Edward Steichen's interest in photography began when he was 16 years old, then worked in a lithography company and attended art classes in the evenings. Between 1900 and 1922 he mainly resided in France, where he became known as a painter and pictorial photographer. Around 1922 Steichen abandoned painting in favor of photography and served as chief photographer for *Vogue* and *Vanity Fair* until 1937. In 1947 he became director of the department of photography at the Museum of Modern Art, New York. It was there that he curated the famous traveling exhibition *The Family of Man*, which opened in January 1955. Steichen retired in 1962, at the age of 83.

Stepan, Peter
*1955, Deutschland

Durch seine Eltern, die beide Fotografen sind, ist er von Kindheit an mit der Fotografie vertraut. Er begann 1976 in Tübingen und München Kunstgeschichte, Archäologie und Germanistik zu studieren. 1982 wurde er zum Dr. phil. promoviert. Er ist tätig als Fotograf, aber auch als freier Lektor, Feuilleton-Korrespondent sowie als Lehrbeauftragter für Kunstgeschichte an der Universität München.

Both parents being photographers, Peter Stepan got acquainted with this medium early in life. In 1976 he began to study art history, archeology and German literature at Tübingen and Munich universities. He received his Ph.D. in 1982. Stepan works as a photographer, as well as a freelance publisher's reader and newspaper correspondent and has been lecturer in the Faculty of Art History at the University of Munich.

Sternfeld, Joel
*1944, USA

Sternfeld erhielt 1965 den Abschluß in Kunsterziehung am Dartmounth College in New Hampshire; er fotografiert seit 1970 in Farbe. 1976-78 entstanden Schnappschüsse in Farbe von Straßenpassanten, die 1977 in der Zeitschrift *Camera* veröffentlicht wurden. 1978 erhielt er ein Guggenheim Stipendium, um die Jahreszeiten in der amerikanischen Landschaft zu fotografieren. Sternfeld kaufte eine Großbildkamera und reiste alleine mit einem VW-Campingbus durch die USA. Er erhielt weitere Stipendien und fotografiert das Leben in Amerika, Landschaften und Porträts.

Joel Sternfeld received his Bachelor of Fine Arts degree from Dartmounth College, New Hampshire in 1965. He has been working in color since 1970. During 1976-78 he did a series of candid street photographs in color, of which a portfolio was published by the magazine *Camera* in 1977. Sternfeld received a Guggenheim Fellowship in order to photograph the American landscape in all seasons, in 1978. He bought a 8x10" view camera and in a VW camping bus, he travelled throughout the United States. He received several more grants and has been portraying the American life style, people and landscapes.

Strand, Paul
*1890, USA
† 1976, Frankreich

Paul Strand besuchte von 1904 bis 1909 den Fotounterricht von Lewis Hine an der *Ethical Culture School* in New York. Berühmt wurde Strand als Vorreiter und Vertreter der "Straight Photography": 1916 stellte Alfred Stieglitz in seiner Galerie *291* Paul Strands "direkte", nicht malerisch verfremdete Fotografien aus. Nach seinen Aufnahmen aus Mexiko waren vor allem das 1980 wiederaufgelegte *Time in New England* von 1950 oder *Tir a'Mhurain – Outer Hebrides* von 1962 wichtige Bücher in der Geschichte der schwarzweißen Landschaftsfotografie. Von 1951 bis zu seinem Tode lebte Strand in Frankreich – er war nicht nur ein außergewöhnlicher Fotograf, er hat sich parallel immer auch mit Film befaßt.

Paul Strand attended the photo courses of Lewis Hine at the Ethical Culture School in New York during 1904 to 1909. He became famous as a pioneer and promoter of straight photography: In 1916 Stieglitz exhibited Strand's photographs of New York in his legendary Gallery *291.* Following his pictures taken in Mexico, Paul Strand's books *Time in New England* (1950, 1980) or *Tir a'Mhurain – Outer Hebrides* (1962) have been milestones in the history of black & white landscape photography. Strand moved to France in 1951, where he resided until his death. He was not only an outstanding photographer, but a fine film-maker as well.

Streetman, Evon
*1932, USA

1010 S.W. 21st Avenue
Gainesville, Florida 32601
USA

Erhält 1954 den Bachelor of Arts von der Florida State University, wo sie Malerei studierte. Nach einem zweijährigen Aufbaustudium in Malerei und Werbegrafik wurde sie Assistentin von Eugene Cook. 1960 machte sie sich dann als Werbefotografin mit einem eigenen Studio selbständig. Seit 1977 ist sie Associate Professor of Art an der Universität von Florida. Ihre freien Fotoarbeiten entstehen häufig aus einer Kombination verschiedener Techniken, so malt sie z.B. über Aufnahmen oder fotografiert Materialcollagen.

Evon Streetman studied at Florida State University and took her B.A. degree in 1954. A two-year graduate study in painting and advertising followed and subsequently she was appointed as assistant to Eugene Cook. In 1960 she established herself as a commercial photographer with her own studio in Tallahassee. Since 1977 she has been Associate Professor of Art at the University of Florida. Her private work often involves a combination of techniques, e.g. she paints over her prints or photographs collages.

Suister, Ed
*1934, Niederlande

Goudsbloemstraat 108
1015 JS Amsterdam
The Netherlands

Suister wollte erst Lehrer werden, besuchte dann aber von 1952 bis 1956 das Institut für Kunsthandwerk, die heutige Rietveld Akademie. Ab 1956 arbeitet er sechzehn Jahre lang als Werbefotograf, wobei er wirklich alles fotografierte: vom Waschmittel bis zur Haute Couture. Seitdem fotografiert er für Verlage und Firmen, insbesondere hat er zahlreiche Kochbücher illustriert. 1975 stellte er Fotos von Häusern an der Algarve aus, von denen das Stedelijk Museum einige ankaufte, er fotografierte die Kunst in die U-Bahn Stationen von Amsterdam, sowie das Projekt *Beautiful Garbageplan*.

Ed Suister first attempted to become a teacher, but soon decided to continue his studies at what is known today as the Rietveld Academy. For 16 years, from 1956 he worked as an advertising photographer, doing anything from washing-powder to haute couture. Since then he has worked for publishers and corporations, especially illustrating a number of cookbooks. His photos of houses at the Algarve, Portugal, exhibited in 1975 are now part of the collection of the Stedelijk Museum, Amsterdam. He also documented the art presented in the subway stations of Amsterdam, and his last personal project is entitled *Beautiful Garbageplan*.

Székessy, Karin
*1939, Deutschland

Haynstr. 2
2000 Hamburg 20
West-Germany

Sie studierte von 1958 bis 1960 am Institut für Fotojournalismus in München und lebt seit 1960 in Hamburg. Dort fotografierte Karin Székessy zunächst Prominentenporträts: Von 1962 bis 1967 entstand die Serie *Zeitgenossen*. Gleichzeitig arbeitete sie als Fotojournalistin für *Kristall*. 1971 heiratete sie den Künstler Paul Wunderlich, mit dem sie schon vorher zusammengearbeit hatte, und 1977 erschien ihr gemeinsames Buch *Korrespondenzen*. Karin Székessy wurde bekannt für ihre Aktaufnahmen, aber sie fotografierte auch weiterhin Porträts und für die Werbung.

Karin Székessy studied at the Institute of Photo Journalism in Munich 1958-60 and has been living in Hamburg since 1960. There she initially portrayed prominent persons: during 1962-67 she did her series *Contemporaries*. At the same time she worked as a photo journalist for *Kristall*. In 1971 she married the artist Paul Wunderlich, with whom she had collaborated in previous years, and in 1977 their book *Correspondences* was published. Karin Székessy became known for her nude studies, but she also continued to do portraits and advertising work. In 1983 she started the preparation of a book on her husband's sculptures.

Taconis, Kryn
*1918, Niederlande
† 1977, Kanada

Taconis lernte das Fotografieren bei Paul Germoen und war von 1942-45 Assistent von → Carel Blazer. 1948-50 war er Korrespondent von *Time-Life* für die Benelux Länder, von 1950 bis 1960 und wiederum ab 1973 arbeitete er als Fotojournalist mit der Agentur *Magnum* zusammen. Ab 1959 lebte er in Kanada.

Kryn Taconis studied photography with Paul Germoen and was the assistant of → Carel Blazer during 1942-45. He served as a correspondent for Benelux countries for *Time-Life* from 1948 to 1950 and as a photo-journalist he cooperated with *Magnum* agency from 1950 to 1960 and again from 1973 on. Since 1959 he lived in Canada.

Talbot, Henri
*1920, Deutschland

23 Bay St.
Mosman, 2088
Australia

Studierte in Berlin, England und ab 1940 in Melbourne. 1956 gründete er zusammen mit →Helmut Newton ein Fotostudio, in dem er nach wie vor arbeitet. 1962-63 war Talbot Präsident des *Institute of Victorian Photographers*. Er lehrte am *Preston Institute of Technology* und ab 1977 am *Phillip Institute of Technology*. Seine Arbeiten befinden sich in zahlreichen bedeutenden Sammlungen.

Henri Talbot studied in Berlin, in England and from 1940 in Melbourne. In 1956 he formed a partnership with →Helmut Newton and commenced working in their own photographic studio. During 1962-63 he was president of the *Institute of Victorian Photographers*. He lectured at Preston Institute of Technology and from 1977 was senior lecturer at the Phillip Institute of Technology. His work is part of several noted collections.

Tenneson, Joyce
*1945, USA

114 West 24th Street
New York, N.Y. 10001
USA

Joyce Tenneson, Doktor der Philosophie, hat ein besonderes Interesse daran, wie Kunst von Künstlern verstanden wurde. Sie ist aktiv als Fotografin, Autorin und unterrichtet auch. 1978 gab sie das Buch *In / Sights* mit Selbstporträts von Fotografinnen heraus und 1983 erschien in Frankreich ein Buch mit ihren eigenen fotografischen Arbeiten, das waren in den letzten Jahren vor allem sehr helle, zarte Porträts und Aktstudien.

Joyce Tenneson holds a Ph. D. degree and has a special interest in the way art is conceived by artists. Active as a photographer, writer, editor and teacher, she in 1978 edited *In / Sights – Self-Portraits by Women*. In 1983 her monographic book *Joyce Tenneson Photographs* came out in France. During the past years she became known for her very bright and tender toned portraits and nude studies.

Thompson, Bill
*1947, USA

300 Mercer Street
New York, N.Y. 10003
USA

Thompson schloß 1969 sein Studium am *Rochester Institute of Technology* ab und erhielt den ersten Preis im Fach Fotografie. Anschließend lebte er bis 1977 in Paris, seitdem in New York. Thompson macht Panoramaaufnahmen, die er auf Cibachrome Material vergrößert, fotografiert aber auch in Schwarzweiß. Seine erste Ausstellung hatte er 1975 im American Cultural Center in Paris und 1982 stellte ihn das französische Fernsehen in der Sendung über neue Richtungen in der Fotografie vor.

In 1969 Bill Thompson graduated from Rochester Institute of Technology, winning a first prize in photography. Following his studies he lived in Paris from 1977 and later in New York. He has produced panoramic images, which he enlarges on Cibachrome material, but he also works in black & white. His first exhibition took place in the American Cultural Center in Paris in 1975 and in 1982 the French television presented his work in a feature film on new trends in photography.

Thornton, John
*1946, Australien

The Turret, 3 Fulham Park
Road, London SW 6
Great Britain

Thornton arbeitete in diversen Jobs bevor er Assistent in einem Fotostudio wurde. Nach der Ausbildung beschäftigte er sich mit Sportfotografie. Er zog 1969 nach London und ist dort seitdem ein erfolgreicher Werbefotograf. Durch die Veröffentlichung seiner surrealistisch-phantastischen Mädchenfotos in allen führenden Fotozeitschriften und Magazinen, sowie in Buchform (*Pipe Dreams*, 1979), wurde er auch außerhalb der Werbeszene bekannt.

John Thornton worked in different jobs before he became an assistant in a photo studio. Following his photographic training, he worked as a sports photographer. In 1969 he moved to London and has been a successful commercial photographer since that time. He became popular outside the advertising field because of his surrealistic-phantastic photographs of girls, published in all major photographic magazines and other journals. He published his monographic book *Pipe Dreams* in 1979.

Toscani, Oliviero
*1942, Italien

Toscani stammt aus einer illustren Fotografenfamilie und fotografierte erstmals im Alter von sechs Jahren. Später erhielt er dann eine Ausbildung an der Kunstgewerbeschule in Zürich. Toscani ist ein sehr erfolgreicher kommerzieller Fotograf, dessen Arbeiten in allen wichtigen Magazinen erschienen. Er lancierte sogar einmal Arbeitskleidung als Modetrend. Er wurde als Fotograf "mit dem Geist eines Revolutionärs" bezeichnet, "der an permanente Umwälzungen und Veränderungen glaubt."

Oliviero Toscani was born into an illustrious family of photographers, and has been taking photos since he was six years old. He later graduated from the Academy of Arts and Crafts in Zurich, Switzerland. Toscani is a very sucessful commercial photographer, whose work has been published by all the major magazines. He was also influential in promoting working clothes as fashion. He was referred to as a photographer 'with a revolutionay spirit who believes in continuous upheaval and change'.

Tourdjman, Georges
*1935, Marokko

60, rue Pauline Borghèse
92200 Neuilly
France

Nach der Schulzeit in Casablanca arbeitete Tourdjman von 1956 bis 1962 als Regieassistent beim Film. 1963 ging er nach New York, um das Fotografieren zu erlernen und wurde dort Schüler von Alexey Brodovitch. 1964 zog er nach Paris – er ist französischer Staatsbürger – und etablierte sich dort als Fotograf. Er fotografiert im Auftrag von französischen und ausländischen Magazinen, aber hauptsächlich arbeitet er für die Werbung. 1976 hielt er auf den R.I.P. in Arles seinen ersten Workshop über Porträtfotografie ab und seitdem hat er sich außer mit dem Porträt auch intensiv mit der Aktfotografie befaßt.

Georges Tourdjman attended school in Casablanca and during 1956 to 1962 worked as assistant director of films. He left for New York in 1963 in order to learn photography and studied with Alexey Brodovitch. As a French citizen, Tourdjman moved to Paris in 1964 and established himself as a freelance photographer with assignments from French and foreign magazines, but mainly working for advertising agencies. In 1976 he conducted his first workshop on portraiture at the R.I.P. in Arles. More recently besides portraits, Tourdjman also concentrated on nude studies.

Tress, Arthur
*1940, USA

2 Riverside Drive
New York, N.Y. 10023
USA

Tress studierte Kunstgeschichte und unternahm dann als ethnologischer Fotograf Studienreisen nach Japan, Indien, Mexiko, Alaska und Afrika, um die Bräuche anderer Völker zu dokumentieren. 1971 wurde seine Fotofolge *Theater of the Mind* ausgezeichnet und 1972 *The Dream Collector.* Tress Fotos aus den 70er Jahren sind tendenziell der surrealistischen Fotografie zuzurechnen. In den 80er Jahren entstanden dann großformatige abstrakte und experimentelle Farbarbeiten. 1986 erscheint eine Monografie über Tress unter dem Titel *Talisman*.

Arthur Tress graduated in art history and travelled as an ethnographic photographer in Japan, India, Mexico, Alasca and Africa, in order to document the habits of other races. In 1971 Tress received a grant for his *Theater of the Mind* series, and another one for *The Dream Collector.* His photographs, done in the 70's are mainly of a surrealistic nature. In the 80's he produced large size abstract and experimental color works. In 1986 a monograph on Tress, entitled *Talisman* will be published.

Tritschler, Alfred
*1905, Deutschland
† 1970, Deutschland

Presse-Bildarchiv
Dr. Paul Wolff & Tritschler
Blöchlestr. 24
7600 Offenburg

Nach dem Ersten Weltkrieg absolvierte er in seiner Heimatstadt eine Fotografenlehre. Er besuchte dann die Münchner Fotografische Lehranstalt, aus deren kinematografischer Abteilung er in das Versuchslabor der Ufa nach Babelsberg geholt wurde. Hier lernte er auch die Leica kenne, die dann zu seinem Berufsgerät wurde, nachdem er Kompagnon von →Paul Wolff in Frankfurt geworden war. Neben den Fotos, die er zu Wolffs Büchern beisteuerte, veröffentlichte Tritschler auch eigene Publikationen, so 1949 das damals populäre Buch *Kleiner Wagen auf großer Fahrt* über den Volkswagen oder auch *Unser Schicksal, die deutsche Industrie* von 1952. 1963 zog sich Tritschler aus dem von ihm nach Wolffs Tod weitergeführten Geschäft zurück.

After World War II, Tritschler became a photographer's apprentice. Following this period he enrolled at the Photographic Academy in Munich, where he studied cinematography and was hired by the UFA to work in their experimental laboratories in Babelsberg. There Tritschler first saw the Leica camera, which later became his tool as a professional photographer. Tritschler became →Paul Wolff's associate and maintained the studio and photo agency after Wolff's death until he retired in 1963. Besides contributing to books published by Wolff, Tritschler published several of his own including the popular *Kleiner Wagen auf großer Fahrt*, a book on the Volkswagen, published in 1949 and *Unser Schicksal, die deutsche Industrie* in 1952.

Trültzsch, Holger & Vera Lehndorff
*1939, Deutschland

74, rue Marcadet
75018 Paris
France

Trültzsch studierte erst Malerei, dan Soziologie. 1969 war er Mitbegründer der Musikgruppe Popul Vuh und traf mit Vera Lehndorff zusammen, die unter dem Namen Veruschka als Fotomodell sehr populär war. 1970 begann Trültzsch zu fotografieren und gleichzeitig die künstlerische Zusammenarbeit mit Vera Lehndorff: der Film und die Fotoserie *Body Paintings* entstanden. 1977 wurde die Teamarbeit fortgesetzt; Trültzsch experimentierte mit Emulsionen und entwickelte die *Oxydographie*-Technik. 1982 fotografierte er Baumstrukturen und seit 1984 ist er als Dokumentarfotograf in der Mission DATAR in Frankreich tätig.

Trültzsch studied painting and sociology. In 1969 he became co-founder of the electronic music group, Popul Vuh and met Vera Lehndorff, a popular model working under the name of Veruschka. Trültzsch started to photograph and collaborate with Vera Lehndorff in 1970 and this resulted in a film and a photographic series entitled *Body Painting*. This cooperation was started up again in 1977. Trültzsch experimented with emulsions and developed his *Oxydography* technique. He worked on *Tree Structures* in 1982 and since 1984 has been employed as a documentary photographer for the DATAR Mission in France.

Tu, Alan David
*1949, Großbritannien

Willemstraat 32A
1015 JD Amsterdam
The Netherlands

Ausgebildet am *St. Martins College of Art* in London, begann er 1976 als Fotograf zu arbeiten. Seine ersten Aufträge erhielt er von der englischen *Vogue*. 1977 fing Alan David Tu an zu reisen, wobei er als Fotograf und Designer arbeitete, aber den Stil seiner Arbeiten dem Diktat des Zufalls überließ. Er machte "Glamour-Fotografie" genauso wie Architekturaufnahmen, arbeitete im Bereich Public Relations und für das Musikgeschäft. 1986 fotografierte er im Auftrag von Magazinen und Londoner Werbeagenturen.

Educated at St. Martins School of Art and at the Royal College of Art in London, Alan David Tu has worked as a photographer since 1976. His first professional assignments were for the English *Vogue*. He started travelling in 1977 – working as a photographer and designer – letting circumstances dictate the style of work. These assignments included glamour, photography, architecture, public relations, the music business. In 1986 he undertook assignments for magazines and advertising agencies in London.

Turner, Pete
*1934, USA

154 West 57th Street
New York, N.Y. 10019
USA

Nachdem Pete Turner seine Ausbildung am *Rochester Institute of Technology* abgeschlossen hatte, begann er seine steile Karriere als kommerzieller Fotograf, wobei er sich auf die Kleinbildfotografie in Farbe spezialisierte. Turner fotografierte für alle möglichen Zwecke, das reicht von der Werbeanzeige zum redaktionelle Beitrag in Illustrierten und da wiederum von der Illustration zum Foto-Essay. Mittlerweile haben wirklich alle führenden Magazine in der Welt Fotos von ihm publiziert. Turner hat ein Studio im Gebäude der Carnegie Hall und will sich in Zukunft mehr seinen freien Arbeiten widmen zu können.

After graduating from Rochester Institute of Technology in 1956, Pete Turner began his freelance career. Within a few years he became one of America's prominent commercial photographers, specialized in 35 mm, color imagery. Turner has produced photographs for a considerable variety of purposes, ranging from advertising to editorial assignments for magazines, and he has done many photo essays. By now his work has been published in virtually all the major magazines around the world. Having opened a studio in the Carnegie Hall Building, Turner nowadays tries to concentrate more and more on his personal work.

Ueda, Shoji
*1913, Japan

82 Suehirocho
Sakaiminato-shi
Tottori 684
Japan

1933 eröffnete Ueda ein Studio in seiner Heimatstadt. Bei seinen freien Arbeiten prägte er einen persönlichen, eben den Ueda-Stil, der sich durch strenge Komposition und Raumaufteilung auszeichnet. Ueda gilt als der Poet unter den japanischen Fotografen. Seine Motive sind die Menschen und die Landschaft seiner Region. 1967-78 entstanden die eher dokumentarischen Reisejournale, 1971 publizierte er ein Buch über Kinder und 1978 *Sand Dunes*, seine wohl bekanntesten Fotos. In jüngerer Zeit ist er, seit 1975 Professor an der Kynsha Sangy Universität, fasziniert von der Verwendung weichzeichnender Linsen für Farbfotos.

Shoji Ueda established his own studio in 1933 in his home town. Besides his commercial work he carried out personal projects in his special Ueda style, which is characterized by strong compositions and spatial relationships. Ueda is called the poet among Japanese photographers; his subjects are the people and landscapes of his native region. During 1967-78 he photographed his more documentary *Travel Journals*. In 1971 he published a book on children and *Sand Dunes* – probably his best known work – in 1978. More recently Ueda, a professor at Kynsha Sangy University since 1975, has been fascinated by the use of soft focus lenses for his color photographs.

Uelsman, Jerry
*1934, USA

5701 S.W. 17th Drive
Gainesville, Florida 32608
USA

Uelsman studierte Fotografie am Rochester Institute of Technology, u.a. bei Minor White und dann bis 1960 an der Indiana University. Seitdem lehrt er, seit 1969 als Professor in Gainesville. 1962 gründete er, zusammen mit → Ansel Adams u.a., die *Friends of Photography* in Carmel. Uelsman wurde bekannt für seine schwarzweißen Landschaftsfotografien, die er meist aus mehreren Negativen kombiniert, und die in ihrer Bildwirkung der surrealistischen Malerei verwandt sind. 1982 erschien ein Bildband über seine 25jährige fotografische Karriere.

Jerry Uelsman studied photography at Rochester Institute of Technology, under Minor White amongst others, and until 1960 at Indiana University. Uelsman has been lecturing since 1960 and has been a professor in Gainesville since 1969. Back in 1962 he was the co-founder, together with → Ansel Adams and others, of the *Friends of Photography* in Carmel. Uelsman gained recognition for his black & white landscape work, which consists mainly of a combination of several negatives, resembling surrealistic painting. In 1982 a retrospective monograph on his 25 year career as a photographer, was published.

350

Ulay/Abramović
*1943, Deutschland
*1946, Jugoslawien

Zoutkeetsgracht 116
1013 II Amsterdam
The Netherlands

Ulay studierte zunächst Ingenieurwesen und dann von 1962 bis 1968 Fotografie. Marina Abramović erhielt ihre Ausbildung an der Kunstakademien in Belgrad und Zagreb. Ab 1972 realisierte sie Sound-Environments, seit 1975 beschäftigt sie sich mit Performance, Video und Film. In Amsterdam lernte sie 1975 den deutschen Künstler Ulay kennen, mit dem sie seither zusammenarbeit und mit dem sie inzwischen verheiratet ist. Ursprünglich wurden ihrer beider Performances auf Video augezeichnet, doch seit 1980 dokumentieren sie ihre "Body Language" auf großformatigem Polacolorfilm.

Ulay studied engineering and later photography from 1962-68. Marina Abramović attended art academies in Belgrad and Zagreb. From 1972 on she produced sound environments and in 1975 her involvement with performance, video and filming began. That same year in Amsterdam she met the German artist Ulay – now her husband – and they started their collaboration. Originally their performances were recorded on video, but since 1980 they have documented their 'body language' work on large format Polacolor film.

Vachon, John
*1941, USA, † 1975, USA

John Vachon gehörte zur "zweiten Generation" der für die Historical Section der Farm Security Administration tätigen Fotografen und Bemerkenswerterweise war dies seine erste fotografische Erfahrung. 1936 war er von der FSA als Bote eingestellt worden und später drückte ihm Roy Stryker eine Kamera in die Hand, weil er sich einen Fotografen nach seinen Vorstellungen heranbilden wollte. Vachon entwickelte dann seinen eigenen Stil als er im Westen der USA die Prärie fotografierte, wobei nahezu abstrakte Aufnahmen entstanden. Wie einige andere, so fotografierte auch Vachon gegen Ende des FSA-Projektes kurze Zeit in Farbe. Jahre später wurde Vachon Fotograf bei *Look* (1948-71), aber seine besten Arbeiten bleiben die aus der FSA-Zeit.

John Vachon was among the 'second generation' of photographers working for the Farm Security Administration's Historical Section and, quite remarkably, it was his first experience with a camera. He had been hired by the FSA as a messenger in 1936, and later Roy Stryker, who had decided to mold a photographer in his own image, put a camera in Vachon's hand. Vachon then developed is own style while photographing the plains, producing abstract photographs.Like some other FSA-colleagues, Vachon did a little color work towards the end of the project. In later years he was on the staff of *Look* magazine for quite a period (1948-71), but his best achievements were done in his FSA period.

Veen, David van 't
*1941, Niederlande

Knalhutteweg 13
7541 PA Enschede
The Netherlands

An der Kunstakademie in Enschede absolvierte er eine Ausbildung zum Grafikdesigner. Ursprünglich Aquarellmaler, spezialisierte er sich 1976 auf die Sofortbildfotografie. Am liebsten arbeitet er für Zeitschriften und sein bevorzugtes Tätigkeitsfeld ist die anspruchsvolle erotische Fotografie. Er ist Dozent für Polaroid Fotografie an der Kunstakademie in Enschede.

Trained as a graphic designer at the art academy in Enschede, David van't Veen initially did aquarell painting. Since 1976 he has specialized in instant photography, and presently teaches Polaroid photography at the Art Academy in Enschede. He prefers working for magazines and his favorite subject is sophisticated erotic photography.

Velde, Peter van der
*1936 Amsterdam

Oranje Nassaulaan 27
1075 AS Amsterdam
The Netherlands

Seit seinem zwölften Lebensjahr war er ein engagierter Amateurfotograf, wurde aber zunächst Steward bei der KLM. Zu Beginn der 60er Jahre lernte er den holländischen Fotografen Kees Scherer kennen, dessen Arbeiten er sehr bewunderte, und 1969 wurde er dann Scherers Assistent. Seit 1973 arbeitet Peter van der Velde nun als selbständiger Fotograf; Aufträge erhält er vor allem von den Zeitschriften *Avenue, Margriet* und *Nieuwe Revu*. Neben Reisereportagen fotografiert er seit kurzem auch für die Werbung und er illustrierte mehrere Bücher über Wein.

Peter van der Velde became an enthusiastic amateur photographer at the age of twelve years. Initially he worked for KLM as a flight steward and this gave him ample opportunity to develop his interest in photography. Then at the beginning of the Sixties, he was introduced to the Dutch photographer, Kees Scherer, whose work he fervently admired and in 1969 he finally started to work as Scherer's assistant. Since 1973 Peter van der Velde has been a freelance photographer, mainly contributing to the magazines, *Avenue, Margriet* and *Nieuwe Revu*. In addition to his travel reportages, he has recently begun to do advertising work and also illustrates a number of books on wine.

Vincenzo, Roberto di
*1954, Italien

Via Tiburtina 80
65100 Pescara
Italy

Von 1972 bis 1978 studierte Vincenzo Philosophie, Literatur und Anthropologie an der Universität von Florenz. Seit 1978 arbeitet er als Anthropologe. Ein Jahr zuvor hatte er angefangen in Schwarzweiß zu fotografieren und 1980 hatte er mit seiner Serie *Tracce* (Spuren) seine erste Einzelausstellung. Dann arbeitete er auch in Farbe und 1983 fand die erste Ausstellung mit den von ihm selbst gefertigten Cibachrome Abzügen statt.

Roberto di Vincenzo studied philosophy, literature and anthropology at Florence University 1972-78. Since then he works as an anthropologist in Pescara. He had started to photograph in 1977 and in 1980 held his first solo exhibition with his black-and-white series *Tracce* (traces). Vincenzo has also been working in color and in 1983 he held his first exhibition of color work. His prints are Cibachromes, which he himself produces.

Vink, John
*1948, Belgien

Von 1968 bis 1971 studierte John Vink Fotografie am La Cambre in Brüssel. Seine erste Einzelausstellung hatte er 1973 in der Galerie Wilde in Köln, die auch ein Portfolio seiner Schwarzweißarbeiten vertrieb. Ab 1977 konzentrierte sich Vink dann auf die Reportagefotografie und begann an einem Buch über Belgien zu arbeiten. Seit Anfang der 80er Jahre arbeitet er für *Time, Fortune* und verschiedene Theaterzeitschriften.

John Vink studied photography at La Cambre in Brussels during 1968-1971. His first exhibition took place in 1973 at the Gallery Wilde in Cologne, which also distributed a portfolio of Vink's work in black & white. Since 1977 he concentrates on reportage and started to work on a book about Belgium. From the beginning of the Eighties Vink has been collaborating with *Time, Fortune*, and several theater magazines.

Vogler, Hans
*1921, Österreich

Ruemann Platz 17/2/4
1100 Vienna
Austria

Vogler war von Jugend an beruflich und freischaffend eng mit der Fotografie verbunden. "Nicht das Experiment ist ihm das Wesentliche; er will gezielt einen bestimmten Ausdruck finden bezeichnet seine Arbeit als abstrakte Wiedergabe von Gefühlen und Sehnsüchten." Vogler nennt seine Fotografie selbst "abstrakt-meditativ".

From his early youth, Hans Vogler was involved with photography, both as a hobby and professionally. 'Experimenting is of no essence to him. He aims to determine a specific expression and describes his work as an abstract reproduction of feeling and longing.' Vogler has also referred to his work as being 'abstract-meditative'.

Vogt, Christian
*1946, Schweiz

Augustinergasse 3
4051 Basel
Switzerland

Vogt studierte Fotografie an der Kunstgewerbeschule in Basel und eröffnete 1970 in Basel ein Studio. 1976 begann er an seiner roten Serie zu arbeiten, bei der er Personen zusammen mit einem roten Tuch im Studio fotografierte. 1980 erschien bei RotaVision in Genf die erste Monografie über ihn. Es entstand die Farbserie *Onlookers*, bei der eine bekannte Landschaft den Hintergrund abgibt und der Vordergrund jeweils die Rückenansicht einer Person zeigt.

Christian Vogt studied photography at the School of Decorative Arts in Basle, where he opened his own studio in 1970. In 1976 he started his red series, in which he photographed people with a piece of red fabric. In 1980 the first monograph on his work was published by RotaVision, Geneva. Vogt then worked on *Onlookers*, a series of color images with familiar landscapes in the background and a person photographed from behind in the foreground.

Volz, Wolfgang
*1948, Deutschland

Birkenstr. 118-120
4000 Düsseldorf 1
West-Germany

Volz beendete 1974 sein Architektur- und Fotografiestudium an der Folkwangschule in Essen. Seitdem arbeitet er als Fotojournalist. Er hält sich häuftig in New York auf und entsprechend fotografierte er für deutsche und amerikanische Zeitschriften. Seit 1971 kooperiert er mit dem Verpackungskünstler Christo, indem er für die fotografische Aufzeichnung der vergänglichen Projekte verantwortlich ist. In Buchform erschienen seine Dokumentationen über den *Running Fence* und die *Wrapped Walkways*, sowie *Christo – Surrounded Islands*.

In 1974 Wolfgang Volz finished his studies in architecture and photography at the Folkwangschule in Essen. Since that time he has been working as a photo journalist. He often stays in New York und therefore photographs for both German and U.S. magazines. In 1971 his cooperation with the wrap-up artist Christo initially began. Volz has been responsible for the photographic documentation of Christo's perishable projects. His photographs of the *Running Fence*, the *Wrapped Walkways* and the *Surrounded Islands* have been published in books.

Vormwald, Gerhard
*1948, Deutschland

52, rue Penuely
75014 Paris
France

Nach einer Lehre als Offsetdrucker begann Vormwald 1966 an der Werkkunstschule in Mannheim Gebrauchsgrafik, Malerei und plastisches Gestalten zu studieren. Als Fotograf Autodidakt, arbeitete er gleichzeitig am Nationaltheater in Mannheim. In seinem 1971 eröffneten Studio fotografierte er u.a. Titel für *Pardon, Stern, Zeitmagazin*. 1982 verlegte er sein Studio nach Paris. Neben seinen Aufträgen realisiert Vormwald auch freie Arbeiten, die dann wiederum häuftiger von Magazinen wie dem *Stern* und dem *Playboy* publiziert werden.

Following his apprenticeship as an offset printer Gerhard Vormwald enrolled at the art school in Mannheim in 1966, studying graphic design, painting and sculpturing. Self taught in photography he simultaneously worked at the National Theater in Mannheim. In his own studio, which he set up in 1971, he produced cover photographs for the magazines *Pardon, Stern, Zeitmagazin*. Since 1982 he maintains a studio in Paris and besides his commercial work he realizes personal projets, which often are published by magazines such as *Stern* and *Playboy*.

Wackerbarth, Horst
*1950, Deutschland

Rheinalle 168
4000 Düsseldorf 11
West-Germany

Wackerbarth besuchte die Akademie für Bildende Kunst in Kassel und war Herausgeber der Materialien zur Documenta 6 *Kunst und Medien*. 1979-84 fotografierte er *Das rote Sofa*, ein Projekt, das er zusammen mit →Kevin Clarke konzipiert hatte und das 1984 als Buch erschien. Wackerbarth reiste mit den Sofa durch die USA und porträtierte darauf prominente und unbekannte Menschen. Er arbeitet als Werbefotograf in Düsseldorf und Los Angeles.

Horst Wackerbarth attended the fine arts academy in Kassel, Germany, and edited *Kunst und Medien*, materials for Documenta 6. During 1979 to 1984 he worked on *The Red Couch* project, which he developed together with →Kevin Clarke and which resulted in a book in 1984. For this Wackerbarth travelled throughout the States, portraying prominent and other persons on this couch. Horst Wackerbarth has been working as a commercial photographer in Düsseldorf and Los Angeles.

Walther, Pan
*1921, Deutschland

Billerbecker Straße
4425 Billerbeck-Bombeck 23
West-Germany

Lernte die Fotografie durch seinen Vater kennen, besuchte die Waldorfschule und erlernte dann das Fotografenhandwerk in Den Haag und Dresden, wo er 1945 ein Atelier gründete. Nach der Meisterprüfung 1946 und der Berufung in die GDL 1949, zog er 1950 nach Westfalen. Neben seinen Aktivitäten als freier Fotograf lehrte er in Münster, Köln, seit 1963 an der Fachhochschule Dortmund, wo er die Fachgruppe Foto-Film-Design gründete. Pan Walthers eigenwillige Persönlichkeit zeigt sich in seinen Aufnahmen ebenso, wie sie ihn als Lehrer auszeichnet.

Pan Walther was introduced to photography by his father, attended the Waldorf School and learnt the craft in The Hague and later Dresden, where he established a studio in 1945. He got his Master degree in 1946, was appointed member to the GDL in 1949 and moved to Westphalia in 1950. Besides his activities as a freelance photographer he taught in Münster, Cologne and since 1963 at the *Fachhochschule Dortmund*, where he established the Foto-Film-Design Department. Pan Walther's slightly eccentric personality shows up in his photographs and makes him an outstanding teacher.

Walther, Thomas
*1949, Deutschland

451 Broome Street
New York, N.Y. 10013, USA

Walther besuchte die Waldorfschule und studierte von 1970 bis 1975 Architektur in Berlin. 1976-77 hielt er sich in London auf, wo er den Fotografenberuf erlernte, anschließend unternahm er ausgedehnte Reisen. 1980 zog er nach New York, wo er heute lebt und arbeitet.

Thomas Walther attended the Waldorf school and during 1970 to 1975 studied architecture in Berlin. He then went to London for one year, where he underwent a training as a photographer. He traveled widely and in 1980 moved to New York, where he now mainly lives and works.

Wangenheim, Chris von
*1942, Deutschland
† 1981, USA

Mit 12 Jahren fing Chris von Wangenheim an, zu fotografieren und im Alter von Zwanzig beschloß er, Fotograf zu werden. 1965 ging er nach New York und arbeitete dort bis 1967 als Assistent. 1968 erhielt er die ersten Aufträge von *Harper's Bazaar* und zwei Jahre später auch von *Italien Bazaar*. Ab 1972 arbeitete er hauptsächlich für *Vogue*, neben er amerikanischen auch für die frazösischen, deutschen und italienischen Ausgaben. Er publizierte außerdem im *Interview Magazine, Playboy, Esquire* und *Viva*. Neben Mode fotografierte er auch für Werbezwecke.

At the age of twelve, Chris von Wangenheim took his first photographs and when he was twenty years old, he decided to become a photographer. He went to New York in 1965 and worked as a photographer's assistant for two years. In 1968 he got his first assignment from *Harper's Bazaar* and two years later also from the *Italian Bazaar* magazine. Since 1972 he mainly does work for American *Vogue*, but he also had publications in *Vogue's* French, German and Italian editions, as well as in such magazines as *Interview, Playboy, Esquire* and *Viva*. Besides fashion photography, Chris von Wangenheim also worked in the field of advertising.

Warhol, Andy
*1928, USA

860 Broadway
New York, N.Y. 10003, USA

Warhol ist tschechischer Abstammung und studierte 1945-49 am *Carnegie Institute of Technology*. 1952 ging er nach New York und arbeitete dort als Werbegrafiker. Er wandte sich 1959 der Kunstproduktion zu und wurde in den 60er Jahren zur einflußreichsten Gestalt der Pop Art. Bekannt wurden vor allem seine seriellen Vervielfältigungen von Konsumgegenständen (Suppendosen) und die *Images* von Elvis Presley, Marilyn Monroe und anderen Kultfiguren. Seit Mitte der 70er Jahre entstehen Porträts berühmter Leute, von denen Warhol Sofortbilder macht, die er dann überarbeitet und in Siebdrucke umsetzt. 1979 erschien *Andy Warhol Exposures,* das Schwarzweiß Schnappschüsse von Prominenten enthält.

Andy Warhol, who orgined from Czechoslovakia, studied at Carnegie Institute of Technology during 1945-49. He went to New York City in 1952 and worked as a commercial artist. He turned to art multiples in 1959 and was the most influential figure of Pop Art in the 1960's. Particularly popular became his serialized reproductions of consumer goods such as soup tins, and his *Images* of Elvis Presley, Marilyn Monroe and other idols. In the mid-Seventies Warhol started his series of portraits of prominent persons, based on altered and manipulated instant pictures. In 1979 his photo book *Andy Warhol Exposures* containing black & white snapshots of prominent persons, was published.

Webb, Alex
*1952, USA

Während er an der Harvard Universität Literatur studierte, nahm Alex Webb gleichzeitig Fotounterricht. 1974 begann er dann als Fotojournalist zu arbeiten, seit 1976 in Kooperation mit der Fotoagentur *Magnum*, deren Mitglied er 1979 wurde. Im Jahr zuvor hatte Webb erstmals in der Karibik und in Mexiko in Farbe fotografiert. Diese "subjektive Reportagefotografie" setzte Webb bis heute in der Karibik und in den Ländern der Dritten Welt fort. Webb arbeitet vorzugsweise für *GEO* und das *New York Times Magazine*.

While majoring in literature at Harvard University, Alex Webb attended courses in photography. He began working professionally as a photojournalist in 1974, cooperating with *Magnum* agency since 1976 to become a full member in 1979. The year before, Webb started his 'subjective reportage' work in color in the Carribean and Mexico, which he continues to pursue today, travelling to many Third World nations as well as to the places mentioned above. Webb mainly collaborates with the magazine *GEO* and the *New York Times Magazine*.

Webb, Boyd
*1947, Neuseeland

Red Door 2b Heneage Street
London E1
Great Britain

Webb studierte Bildhauerei an der Canterbury Universität in Neuseeland, ging 1972 nach London und besuchte dort das *Royal College of Art*. Zuerst fotografierte Webb seine Skulpturen, dann wurde das Fotografieren langsam wichtiger als die Bildhauerei und nun kam auch die Farbe ins Spiel. Er benutzt, wie er sagt, "die Techniken eines Versandhauskatalogfotografen". Dabei entstehen im Bereich der Konzeptkunst angesiedelte Tableaus, die vom Betrachter eine Entzifferung verlangen.

Boyd Webb studied sculpture at Canterbury University, New Zealand and in 1972 went to London, where he attended the Royal College of Art until 1975. Webb first used photography to record his sculptures, but 'gradually the photographs became more important than the sculpture' and color became inevitable. He uses, what he calls 'the techniques of the mail-order catalogue photographer'. Boyd Webb creates Concept Art tableaus which demand interpretation by the observer.

Wegman, William
*1942, USA

Erhielt seine Ausbildung am Massachusetts College of Art, Boston, B.F.A. 1965, und 1965-67 an der University of Illinois, Urbana, M.F.A. 1967. Bis 1972 lehrte er an verschiedenen Universitäten, und ließ sich dann als freischaffender Künstler in New York nieder. Er zeichnet, dreht Videofilme und fotografiert, von 1969-78 fast nur in Schwarzweiß, ab 1978 benutzte er zusätzlich Polaroid Farbmaterial für Großbildkameras. 1970-82 entstanden die witzigen, oft absurden Fotos mit seinem Hund *Man Ray*, benannt nach dem Künstler und Fotografen. Die gute und produktive Zusammenarbeit mit *Man Ray* endete mit dem Tod des Hundes 1982. Im selben Jahr erschien *Man's Best Friend* in New York, ein Buch mit Zeichnungen und Fotografien.

William Wegman was educated at the Massachusetts College of Art, Boston, B.F.A., 1965 and at the University of Illinois, Urbana, M.F.A. in 1967. Until 1972 he taught at various universities, then settled as a freelance artist in New York. He paints, draws, produces video films and photographs – from 1969-78 mainly in black & white. Since 1978 he has also been working with color Polaroid material. Between 1970-82 he created the amusing, often absurd color photographs, featuring his dog, *Man Ray*, named after the artist and photographer. The excellent and productive collaboration with *Man Ray* ended in 1982 when the dog died. That same year the book, *Man's Best Friend* with drawings and color photographs of *Man Ray*, appeared.

Weston, Cole
*1919, USA

P.O. Box 22155
Carmel, CA 93922
USA

Cole Weston ist der jüngste Sohn des Fotografen →Edward Weston und er erhielt 1935 von seinem Bruder →Brett die erste Kamera. Er studierte Theaterwissenschaften und arbeitete dann für eine Flugzeugfirma. 1946-58 wohnte er in Carmel und assistierte seinem Vater. Angeregt durch dessen Experimente mit Farbfilm, begann er selbst in Farbe zu fotografieren: 1957 machte er die ersten Farbfotos von der Küste von Monterey. 1958 wurde er der Verwalter des väterlichen Nachlasses und in den 60er jahren leitete er ein Kulturzentrum in Carmel, dann begann er, weite Schiffs- und Segeltouren zu unternehmen, auf denen Naturfotos und Filme entstehen.

Cole Weston ist the youngest son of the photographer →Edward Weston and he received his first camera from his brother →Brett in 1935. In 1940 he graduated in theater arts, worked with an aircraft corporation and joined the Navy. During 1946 to 1958 he resided in Carmel and assisted his father. Animated by his father's color experiments, he himself started to use color material. In 1957 Cole Weston began to photograph views of the Monterey coastline in color and the following year he took over as executor of the Edward Weston Estate. In the Sixties Cole Weston was the director of a cultural center in Carmel, before undertaking long sailing expeditions, photographing and filming nature along the way.

Weston, Edward
*1886, USA, † 1958, USA

1920 machte er seine ersten Fotos und 1906 beschloß er, als Fotograf zu arbeiten. 1909 heiratete er Flora May Chandler, sie bekamen vier Söhne: Chandler, Brett, Neil und →Cole. 1911 eröffnete er ein Studio in Topico, doch die freie künstlerische Arbeit gewann für ihn zunehmend an Bedeutung. 1919-21 experimentierte er mit Abstraktionen und Aktedetails. 1922 ging er nach Mexiko, wo er bis 1928 mit Unterbrechungen lebte und fotografierte. Ende der 20er Jahre enstanden dann die berühmten Nahaufnahmen von Muscheln und Paprika. 1928 begann er in der Mojave Wüste zu fotografieren, 1929 am Point Lobos. 1932 wurde die Gruppe f/64 gegründet. Die größmögliche Schärfentiefe und die präzise Abbildung von Details wurde zum Programm der "Straight Photography", zu deren Meistern neben Weston auch →Ansel Adams und →Paul Strand zählen. 1947 machte Weston Experimente mit Farbfilm.

Weston took his first photographs in 1902 and by 1906 had decided to become a photographer. In 1909 he married Flora May Chandler and they had four sons: Chandler, Brett, Neil and →Cole. Weston opened a studio in Topico in 1911 but free, creative photography became of growing importance to him. During 1922-28 he lived and worked mainly in Mexico. At the end of the 1920's he started close-up photography, and his famous shots of shells and peppers date back to that period. Around that time he also did his series on the Mojave Desert and on Point Lobos. In 1932 the Group f.64 was established. Great depth of field and precision of detail became the photographic program of Straight Photography, with Weston, →Adams and →Strand as its masters. By 1947 Weston was experimenting with color film.

Wiesenhofer, Hans
*1954, Österreich

Karolinengasse 6-34
1040 Wien
Austria

Bekannt wurde Hans Wiesenhofer durch seine Arbeit für Time-Life; für die Fotobuch-Länderserie fotografierte er in Australien, Deutschland, Frankreich, Italien, Kanada, Osteuropa, Spanien and exklusiv den Bildband über Israel. 1983 erschien in Wien sein Buch *Durch Deutschland*, für das er die Motive nach Farbstimmung und Gestaltungskriterien auswählte. Neben den Buchprojekten widmet sich Wiesenhofer der Erstellung von Fotokunst-Kalendern sowie der Arbeit für Magazine und Agenturen.

Hans Wiesenhofer became known for his collaboration with Time-Life. For the illustration of the Time-Life book series on countries, he photographed in Australia, Germany, France, Italy, Canada, East Europe, Spain and he did all the shots for the picture book on Israel. In 1983 his book, entitled *Durch Deutschland* (Through Germany) was published in Vienna. For this book he selected photographs with special color atmosphere and formal composition. Besides his book projects, Hans Wiesenhofer dedicates himself to the production of photo art calendars; he also works for magazines and photo agencies.

Williams, Daniel
*1942, USA

1975 machte Williams seinen abschluß am Brooklyn College, 1965 hatte er seinen M.F.A. von der Universität in Oregon erhalten. Während der letzten Jahre reiste Williams durch die USA und fotografierte die Emancipation Day Feierlichkeiten. Seine Früheren Arbeiten waren u.a. Stilleben aus symbolischen, in Beziehung zu seiner Erfahrung als Schwarzer stehenden Objekten und Texten.

Daniel Williams received his B.A. from Brooklyn College in 1975, his M.F.A. from the University of Oregon in 1965. Since 1968 Williams has taught at Ohio University, Athens, Ohio. For the past several years, Williams has traveled across America to attend and photograph Emancipation Day celebrations. Earlier photographic work includes still-life collages composed of symbolic objects and printed matter pertinent to the black experience.

Willmann, Manfred
*1952, Österreich

Fotogalerie
im Forum Stadtpark
Stadtpark 1
8810 Graz
Austria

Willman studierte an der Kunstgewerbeschule in Graz und seit 1975 leitet er die Fotogalerie im Forum Stadtpark in Graz und veranstaltet seit 1979 jährlich ein Symposium über Fotografie. Seit 1980 gibt er die Fotozeitschrift *Camera Austria* heraus und seit 1977 ist er auch als freischaffender Fotograf tätig. Seine Aufnahmen wurden u.a. in den monografischen Bildbänden *Schwarz und Gold* (1981), *Die Welt ist schön* (1983) und *Ich über mich* (1983) veröffentlicht.

Manfred Willman studied at the Graz school of Arts and Crafts and since 1975 has been director of the *Fotogalerie im Forum Stadtpark*, where since 1979 he organizes the yearly Symposium on Photography. Since 1980 he is the editor of the magazine, *Camera Austria*. Back in 1977 he started to work as a freelance photographer. He published his monographs *Schwarz und Gold*, *Die Welt ist schön* and *Ich über mich*.

Wolf, Reinhardt
*1930, Deutschland

Kleiner Kielort 4
2000 Hamburg 13
West-Germany

Der für seine "Still-life", "Food" und Architekturaufnahmen bekannte Fotograf Reinhardt Wolf studierte bis 1954 Psychologie, Literatur und Kunstgeschichte in New York, Paris und Hamburg und legte zwei Jahre später seine Meisterprüfung als Fotograf ab. Seit 1969 arbeitet er in Hamburg in einem von ihm erbauten Studio-Haus, in dem sich auch eine Werbefilm-Produktion befindet. Ende der 70er Jahre fotografierte Wolf mit einer Großformatkamera die *Gesichter von Gebäuden* und die Türme der Wolkenkratzer in New York. Seine Serie *Castillos. Burgen in Spanien* erschien ebenfalls als Buch. Wolf hat neben diesen Bildbänden auch einige Kochbücher illustriert, außerdem arbeitet er viel für *GEO* und den *Stern*.

Well-known for his still life, food and architectural photographs, Reinhardt Wolf studied psychology, literature and art history in New York, Paris and Hamburg until 1954. Two years later he received his 'Meister' degree as a photographer. In 1969 he established his studio in Hamburg in a building constructed by himself, where he also runs a production firm for TV-commercials. At the end of the 1970's Wolf photographed the *Faces of Buildings* as well as the towers of the New York City skyscrapers. His series on castillos in Spain was published in 1983. Besides his own picture books, Wolf has illustrated a number of cookery books, and he also does a good deal of editorial work for *GEO* and *Stern*.

Wolf, Silvio
*1952, Italien

Via Compagnoni 3/a
20129 Milano
Italy

Nach einem Jahr Psychologiestudium ging Wolf 1972 an das London College of Printing, wo er bis 1974 Fotografie studierte. 1976 eröffnete er in Mailand ein Studio und begann für Presse und Werbung zu arbeiten. Seine freien Arbeiten, die dem Bereich der Concept Art zuzurechnen sind, stellte er 1979 in Ferrara erstmals aus. Er beschäftigt sich vorzugsweise mit visuellen und räumlichen Phänomenen, so in der Arbeit *Interieur, Exterieur.* Seit 1980 unternahm er zahlreiche Reisen und 1985 kaufte das Museum für moderne Kunst in Mailand eine seiner Arbeiten an.

Silvio Wolf studied psychology for a year and in 1972 subsequently enrolled at the London College of Printing in London, where he took his diploma in advanced photography in 1974. Two years later he opened a studio in Milan and started to work as a freelance photographer in the field of press and publicity. He exhibited his private work, which belongs to the Concept Art trend, in Ferrara in 1979 for the first time. Wolf is concerned with visual and spatial phenomena, as seen in his work, *Inside, Outside*. Since 1980 he has been traveling a lot and in 1985 the Museum of Contemporary Art in Milan bought one of his works for its permanent collection.

Wolff, Paul
*1887, Deutschland
† 1951, Deutschland

Presse-Bildarchiv
Dr. Paul Wolff & Tritschler
Blöchlestr. 24
7600 Offenburg
West-Germany

Wolff studierte Zahnmedizin in Straßburg und promovierte kurz vor dem Ersten Weltkrieg. Nach dem Krieg wurde ihm die Niederlassung als Arzt im Elsaß verweigert und er zog nach Frankfurt. Dort etablierte sich bald als gefragter Fotograf. Bei der Gründung des Studios und der Bildagentur wurde →Alfred Tritschler sein Kompagnon. Anfang der 30er Jahre beschäftigten Wolff & Tritschler bereits 18-20 Mitarbeiter; die Firma lieferte Fotos für alle Bereiche. Wolff selbst wurde vor allem als Propagator der Kleinbildfotografie mit der Leica bekannt. 1934 erschien *Meine Erfahrungen mit der Leica*, 1942 *Meine Erfahrungen ... farbig*. 1944 wurde Wolffs Haus und fast sein gesamtes Archiv durch die Bomben zerstört.

Wolff studied dentistry in Strasbourg and received his M.D. degree shortly before World War I. After the war, when Alsace was French territory, he was not allowed to practise medicine, so he moved to Frankfurt, where he established himself as a photographer. He set up a studio and a photo agency and made his former assistant, →Alfred Tritschler, his partner. In the early 1930's, Wolff & Tritschler already employed 18-20 people, working in various fields of photography and illustration. Paul Wolff himself especially gained recognition as a promoter of 35 mm photography with the Leica. In 1934 a book on his experiences with this technique appeared, which was followed by a photo book with Leica images in color, in 1942. In 1944 his archives were almost totally destroyed by bombs.

Wolff-Purcell, Rosamond
*1942, USA

121 Allston Street
Medford, Mass. 02155
USA

Wolff studierte Französisch an der Universität in Boston und von 1965 bis 1969 unterrichtete sie Geschichte in Cambridge. 1969 heirate sie Dennis W. Purcell, der ihr eine Polaroid Kamera schenkte und sie so zum Fotografieren animierte. Wolff-Purcell illustriert seitdem Bücher des Verlages Houghton Mifflin und fotografierte Kinderszenen für Polaroid. Seit 1976 hat sie zahlreiche Workshops und Vorlesungen gehalten. 1981 war sie Fotografin in den Universal Studios in Hollywood bei dem Film *Ghost Story.* In letzter Zeit arbeitet sie mit der Polaroid 50x60 Kamera.

Rosamond Wolff studied French literature at Boston University and she taught history in Cambridge during 1965-69. In 1969 she married Dennis W. Purcell, who gave her a Polaroid camera und thus her involvement with photography began. She started a collaboration with the publisher Houghton Mifflin, illustrating books, and she also did photographs of children for Polaroid Corporation. She has lectured extensively since 1976 and in 1981 she was photographer in the Universal Studios for the film *Ghost Story.* More recently she has worked with the Polaroid 20x24″ camera.

Worth, Don
*1924, USA

38 Morning Sun Ave.
Mill Valley, CA 94941
USA

Studierte Musik und gab die Musik als Beruf erst 1958, nach 17 Jahren als Pianist, Lehrer und Komponist, zugunsten der Fotogafie auf. 1953 hatte er begonnen, sich ernsthaft mit der Fotografie auseinanderzusetzen und seit 1955 stellt er seine Aufnahmen aus. Seit 1962 lehrt er Fotografie an der San Francisco State University. 1973 fand im San Francisco Museum of Art eine Retrospektive mit 150 seiner Arbeiten statt. 1974-75 erhielt er ein Guggenheim Stipendium, um die amerikanische Landschaft zu fotografieren. Dabei legte er 28.000 Meilen zurück und fotografierte im Westen von Kanada und die USA, in Mexiko und in Zentral-Amerika. 1985 stellte er Stilleben in Farbe vor, die ihn als Meister des "trompe l'oeil" und der Farbfotografie ausweisen.

Don Worth studied music but terminated his musical career as a pianist, composer and teacher after 17 years and in 1958 turned his full attention to photography. Some years before he had become seriously involved with photography and regularly exhibited his work. Since 1962 he has been teaching photography at San Francisco State University. In 1973 a retrospective exhibition of 150 photographs took place at San Francisco Museum of Art. Don Worth was awarded a Guggenheim Fellowship to photograph American landscapes in 1974-75. He travelled over 28,000 miles through western Canada, western USA, Mexico and Central America. In 1985 he produced a series of still life pictures which distinguished him as a master of 'trompe l'oeil' and of color photography.

Würfel, Joachim
*1952, Deutschland

Schwabstr. 2
7000 Stuttgart
West-Germany

Nach seiner Ausbildung zum Mode- und Werbefotografen, u.a. als Assistent bei →Franz Lazi, begann Würfel seine Praktikantenzeit in den USA. Bei seinen Aufenthalten an beiden Küsten des Kontinents entstanden Farbaufaufnahmen von einer gewissen formalen Strenge, bei denen Würfel einige Partien von einem Retuscheur herausarbeiten ließ. In den USA fotografierte er auch die ersten seiner skurrilen, inszenierten Bilder mit ausgestopften Tieren; die Serie setzte er dann in Stuttgart fort. Würfel arbeitet als selbständiger Fotograf vor allem im Modebereich, macht aber auch Werbeaufnahmen.

After his training as a fashion and advertising photographer with →Franz Lazi in Stuttgart, Würfel worked as a photographer's assistant in the USA. During this stay on both of the American coasts, he took photographs which were rather formal and precise and which he had retouched. In the USA he also photographed the first of his farcical, staged works with stuffed animals; a series he continued back in Stuttgart. Würfel works as an independent photographer, predominantly in the fashion world, but he also does advertising assignments.

Yavno, Max
*1911, USA, † 1985, USA

Yavno studierte am City College of New York wo er 1932 B.S. erhielt, und an der Columbia Universität. Als Mitglied der Photo League in New York begann er sich der sozialdokumentarischen Fotografie zuzuwenden. Nach dem Zweiten Weltkrieg ließ er sich in Kalifornien nieder und machte als kommerzieller Fotograf Karriere. Er stellte nicht mehr aus, bis er sich 1975 entschloß, sich nur noch der künstlerischen Arbeit zu widmen. Seine Fotografen sind klare, detailreiche und vorurteilslose Darstellungen des Alltags in den USA.

Max Yavno studied at City College in New York (where he received his B.S. in 1932) and briefly at Columbia University. As a member of the Photo League in New York, he started his social documentary photographic work. Following WW II, he settled in California, developing his career as a commercial photographer. After the Forties, Yavno did not exhibit again, until 1975 when he decided to devote himself full-time to creative work. His photographs are clear and detailed documents, revealing aspects of the daily urban life in America, without criticism.

Yoshida, Ruiko
*1938, Japan

2-4-5 Gotokuji
Setagaya-ku
Tokyo, Japan

Arbeitete nach dem Studium in Japan als Ansagerin bei Funk und Fernsehen. Als Fulbright-Stipendiatin studierte sie dann Publizistik an amerikanischen Universitäten. Das Fotografieren erlernte sie bei Lisette Model, und sie arbeitete für Eugene Smith. Nach vier Jahren in einer New Yorker Werbeagentur kehrte sie 1971 nach Japan zurück und ist seitdem als Fotoreporterin in aller Welt unterwegs. Ihr Interesse gilt den Minderheiten, die sie vor allem in den USA fotografierte, und der Politik: sie fotografierte und interviewte u.a. Fidel Castro, Sadat, Kim Dae Jung und zuletzt Oberst Gaddafi zur Zeit des amerikanischen Bombenangriffs auf Tripolis im April 1986.

Ruiko Yoshida graduated from Keio University and then worked as a radio and TV announcer. As a Fulbright Exchange Student she studied journalism at U.S. universities. She underwent a photographic training with Lisette Model and has worked for Eugene Smith. For four years she was employed by an advertising agency in New York and following that period, in 1971, she returned to Japan where she has worked and travelled as a photo-journalist ever since. Her main interests were the minority groups she saw and photographed in the USA, and politics: she interviewed and photographed Fidel Castro, Sadat, Kim Dae Jung and lately Colonel Gaddhafi during the U.S. bombing incident of Tripoli in April 1986.

Yuste, Juan Ramón
*1952, Spanien

Bola 8
Madrid 28013
Spain

Yuste begann 1972 als Autodidakt zu fotografieren und arbeitete gleichzeitig bis 1974 als Korrespondent der Fotozeitschrift *Nueva Lente*. 1981 war er Bildredakteur des Magins *Dezine*. Er leitete verschiedene Fotokurse und Projekte. 1986 gab er die Publikation *La Fotografia Existe* der Zeitschrift *La Luna* heraus.

Juan Ramón Yuste taught himself photography in 1972 and he also worked as a correspondent to the photo magazine, *Nueva Lente* until 1974. By 1981 he served as a picture editor to the magazine *Dezine*. He conducted numerous workshops photographic projects. In 1986 he edited the publication *La Fotografia Existe* of the magazine *La Luna*.

Zurborn, Wolfgang
*1956, Deutschland

Lange Fuhr 47
4600 Dortmund 1
West-Germany

Machte 1975 das Abitur in Ludwigshafen und studierte 1977-79 an der Bayrischen Staatslehranstalt für Fotografie in München, dann bis 1984 an der Fachhochschule in Dortmund Fotografie-/Filmdesign bei Hans Meyer-Veden. Seinen Abschluß machte er mit einer Arbeit über Freizeitparks in Deutschland. 1985 erhielt er das Otto Steinert Stipendium der DGPh für das Projekt *Menschenbilder-Bildermenschen*.

Wolfgang Zurborn finished college in 1975. From 1977-79 he studied at the Bavarian State School for Photography in Munich to then continue his studies in Dortmund at the Technical High School, where he took film design and photographic lessons from Hans Meyer-Veden. In 1984 he graduated with a series on leisure grounds in Germany. In 1985 he received the Otto Steinert Fellowship in order to photograph the project entitled *Menschenbilder-Bildermenschen* (People Pictures - Picture People).

Die biografischen Angaben, soweit sie nicht von den Fotografen und Galeristen kamen, oder aus Monografien über die Fotografen entnommen wurden, stammen hauptsächlich aus folgenden Büchern:

The biographical data, unless submitted by the photographers themselves or by galleries, stems primarily from the following publications:

Auer, Michèle and Michel (ed.):
Photographers Encyclopaedia International, 1938 to the present,
Hermance, Switzerland 1985.

Das Aktfoto. Ästhetik, Geschichte, Ideologie,
hrsg. von Michael Köhler und Giesela Barche,
Katalog, München 1985.

Contemporary Photographers.
Walsh, Naylor, Held (ed.),
Encyclopaedia, New York 1982.

Eauclaire, Sally:
The New Color Photography,
New York 1981.

Krichbaum, Jörg (Hrsg.):
Lexikon der Fotografen,
Frankfurt 1981.

Liberman, Alexander (ed.):
The Art and Technique of Color Photography.
A Treasure of Color Photographs by the Staff Photographers of Vogue, House & Garden and Glamour,
New York 1951.

Lichtbildnisse. Das Porträt in der Fotografie,
Klaus Honnef (Hrsg.),
Katalog, Köln 1982.

Chronik 1936-1986

Chronology 1936-1986

1936	Im August kommen in den USA die Kodachrome Kleinbild- und "Bantam"-Filme heraus, im November erscheint der Agfacolor-Neu Kleinbildfilm auf dem deutschen Markt. Zur Sommerolympiade in Berlin brachte Agfa noch eine hochempfindliche Agfacolor-Ultra Kornrasterplatte heraus. In Dresden wird die Mikut Farbkamera gebaut, in den USA als eine der ersten dortigen Dreifarbenkameras (Strahlenteiler-Prinzip) die Royal One-Shot. Das deutsche Duxochrom-Verfahren für Papierbilder wird in den USA als "Colorstil" eingeführt.	The Kodachrome 35 mm and 'Bantam' films appear in the USA in August; Agfacolor-Neu 35 mm Film is launched on the German market in November. Agfa brings out another high-sensitivity Agfacolor-Ultra grain screen plate for the summer Olympics in Berlin. The Mikut color camera is produced in Dresden, and the Royal One-Shot in the USA, one of the first three-color cameras (beamsplitter principle) to appear there. The German Duxochrom process for color prints is introduced in the USA as 'Colorstil'.
1937	Optikotechna, Prerov, CSR, stellt die Coloretta Strahlenteilerkamera für Kleinbildfilm her. Die Ives Color Processes Inc., Philadelphia, USA, beginnt mit der Produktion von Farbvergrößerungen nach eigenem Verfahren.	Optikotechna of Prerov, Czechoslovakia, produces the Coloretta one-shot camera for 35 mm film. Ives Color Processes Inc., Philadelphia, USA starts production of color enlargement, using a process of its own.
1938	Die Empfindlichkeit bei Agfacolor wird von 7/10 °DIN auf 15/10 °DIN erhöht, und es kommt auch ein Agfacolor Kunstlichtfilm heraus. Der Entwicklungsprozeß für Kodachrome wird auf die "farbige Nachbelichtung" umgestellt und dadurch vereinfacht. Kodachrome Professional Planfilme für Berufsfotografen kommen auf den US-Markt. In den USA bringen die Devin Colorgraph Company, New York, die International Research Labs. (Adrian Le Roy), New York, die Thomas S. Curtis Labs., Huntington Park, Ca., und die National Photocolor Corp., New York, eine Reihe verschiedener Strahlenteilerkameras heraus und richten zum Teil auch eigene Farbbild-Kopierdienste ein. Die Curtis Color-Scout und die Devin Tricolor Camera (Aufnahmeformat: 6,5 x 9 cm) sind handliche Apparate auch für den Amateurgebrach.	The sensitivity of Agfacolor is increased from 7/10° DIN to 15/10°DIN, and an Agfacolor film for artificial light is also produced. The Kodachrome development process is simplified by a changeover to 'color postexposure'. Kodachrome Professional sheet films for professional photographers appear on the US market. In the USA, the Devin Colorgraph Company and International Research Labs. (Adrian Le Roy) of New York, the Thomas S. Curtis Labs. of Huntington Park, California, and the National Photocolor Corp. of New York produce a number of different one-shot cameras, and in some cases also set up their own color printing services. The Curtis Color Scout and the Devin Tricolor Camera (exposure size: 6.5 x 9 cm) are convenient cameras intended for amateur use as well.
1939	Das Agfacolor Negativ/Positiv-Verfahren wird als erstes seiner Art zunächst für Kinofilme eingeführt. In der Tschechoslowakei kommt die Spektaretta Farbkamera als Nachfolgerin der Coloretta in den Handel. Curtis in den USA bietet sein Orthotone-Verfahren für Farbbilder an.	The Agfacolor negative/positive process, the first of its kind, is introduced initially for cinefilms. In Czechoslovakia, the Spectaretta color camera, a successor to the Coloretta, appears on the market. Curtis in the USA offers its Orthotone process for color pictures.
1940	Der Sakura Natural Color Diafilm (nach dem Kodachrome-Verfahren) von Konishiroku ist der erste japanische Farbfilm. Die deutsche Tricroma Farbkamera von Walch ist die letzte mit schnellem Plattenwechsel für die Aufnahme von drei Farbauszugen. In den USA werden die Verfahren Curtis Neotone und Chromax-Dyeset von Tricol Color Products, New York, für farbige Papierbilder eingeführt.	Konishiroku's Sakura Natural Color transparency film (using the Kodachrome process) is the first Japanese color film. The German Tricroma Color Camera from Walch is the last to use quick-change plates for shooting three color separations. The Curtis Neotone and Chromax-Dyeset color print processes are introduced in the USA by Tricol Color Products of New York.
1941	Kodak ermöglicht die Anfertigung von Aufsichtsbildern nach Kodachrome-Dias für Amateure (Minicolor Print) und für Berufsfotografen (Kotavachrome Print). Kodachrome Filme werden im beschränktem Umfang auch von der Kodak Limited in Harrow, England, produziert. Der für die militärische Luftbildfotografie hergestellte Kodacolor Aero Reversal Diafilm ist das erste Material nach dem von Kodak seit 1937 ausgearbeiteten zweiten modernen Farbverfahren (mit ölgeschützten, wasserunlöslichen Farbkupplern). Das Condax-Dyetrol System of Imbibition Color Printing der Condax-Speck Inc., New York, ist eine Verbesserung des 1935 von Kodak herausgebrachten Eastman Wash-Off Relief Process für Farbbilder und damit Vorläufer des späteren Dye Transfer Prozesses. In Japan stellt Fuji die Color Bi-Pack Dry Platte für zweifarbige Aufnahmen als ihr erstes Farbfotomaterial vor.	Kodak introduces process for the preparation of color prints from Kodachrome slides for amateurs (Minicolor Print) and professional photographers (Kotavachrome Print). Kodachrome films are also produced on a limited scale by Kodak Limited in Harrow, England. Kodacolor Aero Reversal slide film, produced for aerial photography for military purposes, is the first film to use the second modern color process devised by Kodak since 1937 (using oil-protected, water-insoluble color couplers.) Condax-Speck Inc. of New York introduces the Condax-Dyetrol System of Imbibition Color Printing, an improved version of the Eastman Wash-Off Relief Process for color photographs brought out by Kodak in 1935, and thus a precursor of the later dye transfer Process. In Japan, Fuji launches its first material for color photography – the Color Bi-Pack Dry plate.
1942	Als erster Farbnegativfilm für Amateurfotos kommen im Januar in den USA Kodacolor Rollfilme mit zugehörigem Colorpapier auf den Markt. Im Oktober stellt die Agfa das Agfacolor Negativ/Positiv-Verfahren für Papierbilder in Dresden offiziell vor.	In January, the first color negative film for amateur photographs appears on the USA market – Kodacolor Roll films supplied with color paper. In October, Agfa officially launches the Agfacolor negative/positive Process for color prints in Dresden.

1942	Ferrania (heute 3M) bringt in Italien den ersten Ferraniacolor Diafilm (nach dem Agfacolor-Verfahren) heraus. Agfa Ansco Inc., Binghamton, N.Y., USA beginnt mit der Produktion eines eigenen Ansco Color Diafilms in Planfilmformaten für die Selbstverarbeitung (zunächst nur für die US Army). Ebenfalls für militärische Zwecke stellt sie das Gasparcolor Opaque Printing Material für farbige Aufsichtsbilder nach dem Silberfarbstoff-Bleichverfahren her. Die Firma Farbenphoto Coloprint, Wien, gibt ihr Coloprint Farbbild-Verfahren für Amateure frei; damit können Aufsichtsbilder von Agfacolor-Dias angefertigt werden.	In Italy, Ferrania (now 3M) brings out the first Ferraniacolor Slide Film (using the Agfacolor process). Agfa Ansco Inc., of Binghamton, N.Y., USA begins producing its own Ansco Color Film in sheet film sizes for self-processing (initially restricted to the US Army). It also produces the Gasparcolor opaque printing material for color prints, using the silver dye bleaching process, again for military purposes. Farbenphoto Coloprint of Vienna discloses its Coloprint color slide process for amateurs, enabling prints to be made from Agfacolor slides.
1943	Der Kodacolor Negativfilm erhält eine die Farbsättigung in den Kopien erhöhende Silbermaske (in einer besonderen Zwischenschicht). In den USA wird Ansco Printon für Farbbilder nach Ansco Color und Kodachrome Dias vorgestellt.	A special undercoat containing a silver mask which increases the color saturation in prints is added to Kodacolor negative film. Ansco Printon for color prints from Ansco Color and Kodachrome slides is introduced in the USA.
1944	Das Großlabor der Pavelle Color Inc., New York, ist der erste moderne Fotofinishing-Betrieb im heutigen Sinne (er verarbeitet Ansco Printon). Ansco Color Planfilme sind frei erhältlich.	Pavelle Color Inc.'s industrial-scale laboratory in New York is the first modern photo-finishing plant in the present-day sense (processing Ansco Printon). Ansco Color sheet films are readily obtainable.
1945	Das Agfacolor-Verfahren wird durch die Siegermächte über Deutschland allgemein zugänglich gemacht.	The Agfacolor process is made generally accessible throughout Germany by the victorious powers.
1946	Kodak startet das Ektachrome Diafilm-Sortiment mit Planfilmen (Process E-1). In den USA erscheinen auch Ansco Color Roll- und Kleinbildfilme. Die Minicolor Bilder von Kodak werden in "Kodachrome Print", die Kotavachrome-Vergrößerungen in "Kodachrome Professional Print" umbenannt.	Kodak inaugurates the Ektachrome range of slide films with sheet films (process E-1). Ansco Color Roll and 35 mm films also appear in the USA. Kodak's Minicolor prints are renamed 'Kodachrome Print' and the Kotavachrome enlargements become 'Kodachrome Professional Print'.
1947	Kodak bringt auch Ektachrome Rollfilme heraus. Gevaert Photoproducten N.V. Mortsel, Belgien, stellt ihren ersten Gevacolor Diafilm (Agfacolor-Verfahren) her. Auch in der Sowjetunion wird mit der Produktion von Farbfilmen nach dem Agfacolor-Verfahren begonnen. In Japan werden Sakura Color Umkehrfilme regulär hergestellt. Kodak führt den Dye Transfer Process für Farbvergrößerungen ein.	Kodak adds roll films to the Ektachrome range. Gevaert Photoproducten N.V. of Mortsel, Belgium, produces its first Gevacolor slide film (Agfacolor process). In the Soviet Union, too, production of color films using the Agfacolor process begins. Sakura Color reversal films are produced on a regular basis in Japan. Kodak introduces the dye transfer process for color enlargements.
1948	Der Kodak Ektacolor Planfilm für Kunstlichtaufnahmen ist der erste Negativfilm mit Farbmasken (Azo-Maskenkuppler nach Dr. Wesley T. Hanson, Kodak – heute allgemein verwendet). Es erscheinen weitere Diafilme nach dem Kodachrome-Verfahren: in England Ilford Colour, in Japan Fujicolor. Die französische Kodak-Pathé S.A. nimmt ebenfalls die Produktion von Kodachrome Filmen auf. Die Ansco Corp. bringt in den USA ihre Plenacolor Negativ/Positiv-Materialien für Amateure heraus und experimentiert dabei auch mit Silber- und Farbmasken.	The Kodak Ektacolor sheet film for artificial-light photography is the first negative film with color masks (azo mask couplers as developed by Dr. Wesley T. Hanson of Kodak – now in general use). More color films are produced using the Kodachrome process: Ilford Colour in England, Fujicolor in Japan. The French Kodak-Pathe S.A. also begins production of Kodachrome films. In the USA the Ansco Corp. brings out its Plenacolor negative/positive films for amateurs, and also experiments with silver and color masks.
1949	Nach der Produktionsaufnahme von Agfacolor Negativfilm und Papier im Bayerwerk Leverkusen wird das Negativ/Positiv-Verfahren in der Bundesrepublik Deutschland und bald auch in Europa eingeführt. Die Materialien werden ebenfalls von der Filmfabrik Agfa Wolfen in der DDR hergestellt. Die Azo-Farbmasken werden ebenfalls für den Kodacolor Film übernommen. Es erscheint auch ein Kodacolor Type A Kunstlichtfilm und sind nun auch Kodacolor Vergrößerungen erhältlich. Ferrania, Italien, beginnt, nach dem Agfacolor-Verfahren auch Ferraniacolor Negativfilme und Papier herzustellen. In New York und Hollywood werden Labors für Gasparcolor Bilder nach Amateurdias eingerichtet (Materialhersteller: Du Pont de Nemours, USA). In der Sowjetunion wird der erste Farbdiafilm aus eigenener Produktion "CO-1" herausgebracht.	Following the start-up of production of Agfacolor negative film and paper at Bayerwerk, Leverkusen, the negative/positive process is introduced in the Federal Republic of Germany, and in the rest of Europe shortly afterwards. The materials are also produced by the Agfa film factory at Wolfen in the German Democratic Republic. The azo color masks are also adopted for Kodacolor film. A Kodacolor Type A artificial-light film appears, and Kodacolor enlargements, too, are obtainable. In Italy, Ferrania begins producing Ferraniacolor negative films and paper by the Agfacolor process. Laboratories are set up in New York and Hollywood for the production of Gasparcolor print from amateur slides (materials produced by Du Pont de Nemours, USA). The first Russian-made color transparency film – "CO-1" – is produced in the Soviet Union.
1950	Weitere Negativfilme und Colorpapiere nach dem Agfacolor-Verfahren erscheinen: in England durch den deutschen Emigranten Dr. Kurt I. Jacobson (Marken: Alfacolor, Fotocolor, später vor allem Pakolor) und in der Schweiz von der Tellko AG, Fribourg (Telcolor ist der erste Universalfilm für Tages- oder Kunstlicht). Im Grand Central Terminal, dem größten Bahnhof in New York City, wird das 18 x 60′ große Kodak "Colorama" als größtes Farbfoto-Transparentbild der Welt, fotografiert auf Ektacolor Planfilm und kopiert auf Ektacolor Print Film, ausgestellt.	More negative film and color papers using the Agfacolor process appear: In England, from the German immigrant Dr. Kurt I. Jacobson (brands: Alfacolor, Fotocolor, and especially – later – Pakolor) and in Switzerland from Tellko AG in Fribourg (Telcolor is the first universal film for daylight or artificial light). In New York City's biggest station, Grand Central Terminal, the world's biggest color transparency is put on display: the giant Kodak 'Colorama' measuring 18 feet x 60 feet, photographed on Ektacolor sheet film and printed on Ektacolor print film.
1951	Gevaert, Belgien, liefert auch Gevacolor Negativfilme und Papier. Ferrania bringt wieder einen (verbesserten) Ferraniacolor Diafilm heraus. Dr. Ralph M. Evans, Kodak, entwickelt den ersten Datenspeicher für Printer-Kopiermaschinen. Der Linienraster der seit 1935 erhältlichen englischen Dufaycolor Diafilme wird erheblich verbessert. In England werden die Eves Strahlenteiler-Farbkameras gebaut.	Gevaert of Belgium begins supplying Gevacolor negative films and paper. Ferrania again launches an (improved) Ferrania color slide film. Dr. Ralph M. Evans of Kodak develops the first data store for printer copying machines. The line screen of the English Dufay color slide films available since 1935 is substantially improved. The Eves one-shot color cameras are constructed in England.

1952

Agfa, Leverkusen, ergänzt ihr Agfacolor-Sortiment wieder um einen Diafilm. Der Agfa Labomat ermöglicht die maschinelle Verarbeitung von Colorpapier in Blattware.
Der verbesserte Alticolor Kornraster-Rollfilm von Lumière, Frankreich, löst den Lumicolor Film – Nachfolger der früheren Autochrome Platte- ab.
Der französische Fresson Prozeß wird zum Mehrfarbenverfahren ("Quadrichromie"-Aufsichtsbilder) weiterentwickelt.

Agfa of Leverkusen again extends as its Agfacolor range, to include a slide film. The Agfa Labomat makes it possible to process color paper by machine in cut-film form. The improved Alticolor grain screen roll film from Lumière of France replaces the Lumicolor Film – successor to the previous Autochrome Plate.
The French Fresson process is further developed to give a multi-color process ('Quadrichromie' prints).

1953

Oriental Color sind die ersten japanischen Negativ/Positiv-Materialien überhaupt und ein Diafilm (nach dem Agfacolor-Verfahren).
Tellko, Schweiz, bringt auch einen Telcolor Diafilm heraus.
Mit dem Johnsons Colour Screen Process wird in England wieder ein Kornrastermaterial für Dias nach dem Vorbild des in den dreissiger Jahren bekannten Finlay-Colour vorübergehend eingeführt.
Mc. Gregor Products Co., Rochester, N.Y., bringen erstmals einen weiteren nach dem Kodachrome-Verfahren hergestellten Diafilm (Mc. Gregor Color) in den USA auf den Markt; er ist der Vorläufer der späteren Dynachrome Filme.
In England nimmt der Ilford Colour Print Service die Herstellung von Amateurbildern nach dem Silberfarbstoff-Bleichverfahren auf (Vorgänger von Cibachrome).

Oriental Color are the first Japanese negative/positivie materials of any kind, a slide film (using the Agfacolor process).
Tellko of Switzerland also brings out a Telcolor slide film.
Johnson's color screen process, a grain screen material for slides based on the Finlay-Colour, familiar in the 1930's, is temporarily reintroduced in England.
Mc.Gregor Products Co. of Rochester, N.Y., first introduces another slide film produced by the Kodachrome process (Mc.Gregor Color) in the USA; this is the precursor of the later Dynachrome films.
In England, the Ilford Colour Print Service begins using the silver dye bleach process for producing amateur photographs (a predecessor of Cibachrome).

1954

Mit seinen damals höchstempfindlichen Agfacolor-Ultra Filmen (16/10 °DIN beim Dia- und 17/10 °DIN beim Negativfilm) erreicht der VEB Filmfabrik Agfa Wolfen, DDR, erstmals die Standardempfindlichkeit von Schwarzweißfilmen.
Lumière, Paris, bringt noch die höher empfindlichen Filmcolor Ultra Rapide Type A Kornraster-Planfilme auf den Markt.

Agfa's VEB Film Works at Wolfen in the German Democratic Republic matches the standard sensitivity of black and-white films for the first time, with its Agfacolor-Ultra Films 16/10°DIN in slide form and 7/10°DIN in the negative film), the most sensitive films of the day.
Lumière of Paris follows by marketing the even more sensitive Filmcolor Ultra Rapide type A grain screen sheet films.

1955

Höher empfindliche Diafilme (ASA 32) werden auch von Kodak (Ektachrome, Process E-2) und Ansco (Anscochrome) in den USA produziert; die Anscochrome Filme können als erste "gepusht", das heißt empfindlichkeitssteigernd entwickelt werden.
Kodak führt den später weitverbreiteten Enwicklungsprozeß C-22 für Farbnegativfilme ein, womit auch für Kodacolor Filme die Selbstverarbeitung möglich wird, und bringt die neuen Papiere Kodak Color Print Type C (für Bilder von Negativen) und Type R (für Bilder von Dias) heraus.
Als zweites deutsches Farbfilmfabrikat erscheint der Adox Color CNT Negativfilm der Dr. C. Schleussner GmbH, Frankfurt (Main).
PAKO, USA, bietet den ersten frei käuflichen Printer (Kopiermaschine für Color-Rollenpapier) an.

More sensitive slide films (SA 32) are also produced by Kodak (Ektachrome, Process E-2) and Ansco (Anscochrome) in the USA; the Anscochrome films are the first which can be "pushed", in other words have their sensitivity increased during development.
Kodak introduces the C-22 developing process for color negative films, later to become widespread, which makes self-processing possible even for Kodacolor films, and also produces the new Kodak Color Print Type C papers (for pictures from negatives) and Type R (for pictures from slides).
Germany's second color film product appears – the Adox Color CNT Negative film from Dr. C. Schleussner GmbH of Frankfurt/M.
PAKO in the USA markets the first commercially available printer (printing machines for color roll).

1956

Agfa, Leverkusen, führt den hochempfindlichen Agfacolor CN 17 Negativfilm als "Universalfilm" für Tages- oder Kunstlicht sowie für Farb- oder Schwarzweißbilder ein. Ektacolor erscheint auch als Planfilm für Tageslichtaufnahmen (Type S, ASA 32).
Auch in Spanien werden Farbfotomaterialien hergestellt: Valcolor Negativfilm und Papier (Agfacolor-Verfahren) der Sociedad Española de Productos Fotograficos Valca S.A., Bilbao.

Agfa of Leverkusen produces the high-sensitivity Agfacolor CN 17 Negative Film as a 'universal film' for daylight or artificial light and for color or black-and-white pictures. Ektacolor also appears in the form of a flat film for daylight photography (Type S. ASA 32).
Materials for color photography are produced in Spain, too: Valcolor Negative Film and Paper (Agfacolor process) from the Sociedad Española de Productos Fotograficos Valca S.A., Bilbao.

1957

Die ersten Diafilme mit 18 DIN (Agfacolor CUT 18, später "CT 18") und 21 DIN Empfindlichkeit (Super Anscochrome von Ansco, USA) kommen auf den Markt.
Icicolor von Imperial Chemical Industries (ICI), England, ist der erste in Europa hergestellte Negativfilm mit Farbmasken (unabhängig von Kodak-Patenten).
Konishiroku in Japan bringt Konicolor Negativfilm und Papier in den Handel; in der CSSR beginnt Fotochema in Hradec Králové mit der Produktion von Fomacolor Papier (alle nach dem Agfacolor-Verfahren).

The first slide films with 18 DIN (Agfacolor CUT 18, later 'CT 18') and 21 DIN sensitivity (Super Anscochrome from Ansco, USA) appear on the market.
Icicolor from Imperial Chemical Industries (ICI), Britain, is the first negative film with color masks produced in Europe (independently of Kodak patents).
Konishiroku in Japan begins to market Konicolor negative film and papers; in Czechoslovakia, Fotochema of Hradec Králové starts production of Fomacolor Paper (all using the Agfacolor process).

1958

Auch Fuji folgt in Japan mit einem Farbnegativfilm (Fujicolor N 32) und Colorpapier (Agfacolor-Verfahren). Als weiterer westdeutscher Hersteller führt Perutz, München, den Perutz Color C 18 Diafilm ein. Kodacolor wird auch als Kleinbildfilm erhältlich. Die Produktion des vorläufig letzten Farbrasterfilms des Weltmarkts, Dufaycolor, wird eingestellt.
Kodak stellt zum erstenmal ein Farbpapier unter dem Namen Ektacolor vor, daß dem Kodak Color Print Type C gleich kommt.

Fuji follows suit in Japan with a color negative film (Fujicolor N 32) and color paper (Agfacolor process). Another West German manufacturer, Perutz of Munich, introduces the Perutz Color C 18 slide film.
Kodacolor becomes available in 35 mm form. Production of Dufaycolor, at this state the last lenticulated film on the world market, is discontinued.
Kodak markets color paper under the 'Ektacolor' brandname for the first time, as a supplement to Kodak Color Print Type C in the photofinisher sector.

1959

Weitere Empfindlichkeitssteigerungen: bei den Diafilmen mit Kodak High Speed Ektachrome (Tageslichttyp ASA 160/23 DIN; Kunstlichttyp ASA 125/22 DIN) und bei den Negativfilmen mit Ori-Color (ASA 50/18 DIN) von Oriental Photo Industry Co. Ltd., Tokyo, Japan und Konicolor Universal von Konishiroku, Japan, auf ASA 50/18 DIN.
Kodak bringt verbesserte Ektachrome Planfilme und neue Ektachrome Professional Rollfilme (neuer Verarbeitungsprozeß E-3) auf den Markt.
Schleussner ergänzt sein Sortiment um den Diafilm Adox Color C 15.

Further increases in sensitivity: among slide film, Kodak High Speed Ektachrome (Daylight) type ASA 160/23 DIN; Artificial-Light Type ASA 125/22 DIN), and among the negative films Ori-Color from Oriental Photo Industry Co. Ltd. of Tokyo, Japan.
Kodak markets improved Ektachrome sheet films and new Ektachrome Professional roll films (new E-3 processing method).
Schleussner extends its range to include the slide film Adox Color C 15.

1960

Ilford führt in England auch Negativ/Positiv-Materialien (Ilfacolour) ein.

Ilford also introduces negative/positive materials (Ilfacolour) in England.

1961

Die neuen Kodachrome II Filme besitzen eine höhere Empfindlichkeit (ASA 25/15 DIN beim Tageslicht- und ASA 40/17 DIN beim Kunstlichtfilm) und eine verbesserte Bildqualität (klarere Farbtrennung, noch höhere Schärfe). GAF (früher Ansco) entwickelt für Farbaufnahmen im Weltraum den höchstempfindlichen Ultra Speed Anscochrome Film (ASA 200/24 DIN).
Fujicolor R 100 ist (noch nach dem Agfacolor-Verfahren arbeitend) der erste mit ASA 100/21 DIN hochempfindliche Diafilm in Japan.
Der reguläre Verkauf der Dynachrome Filme (Kodachrome-Verfahren) von Dynacolor Corp., Rochester, N.Y., USA, beginnt in Canada; dieses Filmmaterial verbreitet sich dann vor allem unter verschiedenen Handelsmarken.

The new Kodachrome II films have higher sensitivity (ASA 25/15 DIN for daylight and ASA 40/17 DIN for artificial-light film) and improved image quality (clearer color separation, even better sharpness). GAF (formerly Ansco) develops the high-sensitivity Ultra Speed Anscochrome Film (ASA 200/24 DIN) for color photography in space. Fujicolor R 100 (still using the Agfacolor process) is the first high-speed slide film in Japan, with ASA 100/21 DIN. Dynacolor Corp. of Rochester, N.Y., USA begins regular marketing of Dynachrome Films (Kodachrome process) in Canada; this film material then becomes particularly widespread under various commercial brandnames.

1962

Das Kodak Ektachrome Umkehrpapier (Process Ektaprint-R) löst das Kodak Color Print Type R Material ab. Der höher empfindliche Ektacolor Film Type L (ASA 50/18 DIN) erscheint.
Agfacolor CT 18 wird wesentlich verbessert.
Als erstes "fremdes" Material für den Entwicklungsprozeß C-22 kommt in den USA der Anscocolor Rollfilm (mit nur 1 Farbmaske) in den regionalen Verkauf.
In der CSSR wird der Fomacolor Negativfilm herausgebracht.

Kodak Ektachrome reversal paper (Ektaprint-R process) replaces the Kodak Color Print Type R material. The faster Ektacolor Film Type L (ASA 50/18 DIN) appears.
Agfacolor CT 18 is greatly improved.
Anscocolor Roll Film (with only 1 color mask) is put on sale regionally in the USA as the first 'foreign' material for the C-22 developing process.
Fomacolor Negative Film is produced in Czechoslovakia.

1963

Die farbige Sofortbildfotografie beginnt mit den Polacolor Rollfilmen Type 38 und 48 sowie Packfilm Type 108 von Polaroid.
Zwei Kassettensysteme erleichtern das Filmeinlegen: "Instamatic" oder "Pak" (Konfektionierungssorte 126; Aufnahmeformat: 28 x 28 mm) von Kodak und "Rapid" von Agfa. Kodak führt auch dazu eine vollständige neue Filmgeneration mit auf ASA 64/19 DIN gesteigerter Empfindlichkeit ein (Ektachrome-X, Kodachrome-X und Kodacolor-X). Der Kodak Ektacolor Professional Film Type S (Tageslicht, ASA 80/20 DIN) kommt heraus.
Fujicolor N 64 ist der erste japanische Negativfilm mit Farbmasken (nach dem Kodak-Prinzip).
Auch Agfa (Agfacolor CN 17 M) und Gevaert (Gevacolor-Mask) beginnen mit der Produktion maskierter Negativfilme.
Das Cibachrome-Print System (Aufsichtsbilder nach dem Silberfarbstoff-Bleichverfahren) wird vorgestellt.

Instant color photography begins with the Polacolor Type 38 and 48 roll films and Type 108 film pack from Polaroid.
Two cassette systems make it easier to insert films: Kodak's 'Instamatic' or 'Pak' (packaging grade 126; picture size: 28 x 28 mm) and Agfa's 'Rapid'. Kodak also brings out a completely new generation of films, with the speed boosted to ASA 64/19 DIN (Ektachrome-X, Kodachrome-X and Kodacolor-X). The Kodak Ektacolor Professional Film Type S (daylight, ASA 80/20 DIN) comes out.
Fujicolor N 64 is the first Japanese negative film with color masks (on the Kodak principle).
Agfa (Agfacolor CN 17 M) and Gevaert (Gevacolor-Mask) also start production of masked negative films.
The Cibachrome-Print system (color prints using the silver dye bleach process) is launched.

1964

Als ersten Farbnegativfilm mit der heutigen Standardempfindlichkeit ASA 100/21 DIN bringt Konishiroku, Japan, den damals doch unmaskierten Sakuracolor N 100 heraus. Anscochrome 200 ist mit ASA 200/24 DIN der zur Zeit höchstempfindliche Farbfilm.
Die Agfacolor Materialien aus Wolfen werden in "Orwocolor" umbenannt; zugleich erscheinen neue Negativfilme Orwocolor NC 16 (Universaltyp) und NK 16 (erster deutscher Film mit Farbmasken).
Polaroid bringt den Polacolor Planfilm Type 58 auf den Markt.
Ciba richtet als Praxistest in der Schweiz einen Cibachrome-Service für Amateurbilder ein.

Konishiroku in Japan brings out Sakuracolor N 100, the first color negative film with today's standard speed of ASA 100/21 DIN, though at this stage the film is unmasked. Anscochrome 200 is the fastest color film of its day at ASA 200/24 DIN.
Agfacolor materials from Wolfen are named 'Orwocolor'; new negative films appear at the same time – Orwocolor NC 16 (universal type) and NK 16 (first German film with color masks).
Polaroid markets the Polacolor Type 58 flat film.
Ciba sets up a Cibachrome service for amateur photographs in Switzerland as a practical test.

1965

Ilford führt eine neue Farbfilmgeneration ein: Diafilme Colourslide und Super Colourslide sowie Negativfilm Colourprint.
Der VEB Filmfabrik Wolfen, DDR, stellt erstmals seinen hochempfindlichen Diafilm Orwochrom UT 21 her und beginnt damit die Umstellung seiner Umkehrfilme auf eine andere Filmemulsion und eine andere Verarbeitung.
3M führt das elektrofotografische Kopierverfahren Electrocolor ein.
Die Arbeiten an der Dreifarben-Holographie werden begonnen.

Ilford launches a new generation of color films: Colourslide and Super Colourslide slide films and Colourprint negative film.
The VEB film factory at Wolfen in the German Democratic Republic produces its high-speed Orwochrom UT 21 slide film for the first time, marking the start of the changeover of its reversal films to a different film emulsion and a different processing method.
3M introduces the Electrocolor electro-photographic printing process.
Work begins on three-colour holography.

1966

Hochleistungsprinter von Agfa-Gevaert und von Kodak können rund 2.000 Farbbilder/Stunde anfertigen.
Neue Verarbeitungsprozesse vereinfachen und verkürzen die Entwicklung: E-4 von Kodak löst E-2 ab und verringert bei nunmehr 29,5 °C Bädertemperatur die Gesamtzeit von 71 auf 47 Minuten, der Papierprozeß Ektaprint-C ersetzt P-122; der Agfacolor Papierprozeß "Pa" ist mit nur 17 Minuten "Naßzeit" bei 25 °C der schnellste seiner Art.
Das neue Kodak Ektacolor Papier Type 1878 bringt eine wesentlich erhöhte Farbstabilität.
In der Fotochrome Color Camera (USA) kann direkt auf Anscochrome Printon (für Ausichtsbilder) fotografiert werden.

High-speed printers from Agfa-Gevaert and Kodak are capable of processing about 2000 color pictures/hour.
New processing methods make developing simpler and shorter: Kodak's E-4 replaces E-2 and, with a bath temperature of 29.5°C, reduces the total time from 71 to 47 minutes; the Ektaprint-C paper process replaces P-122; the Agfacolor 'Pa' paper process is the fastest of its type, taking only 17 minutes 'wet time' at 25°C.
The new Kodak Ektacolor type 1878 paper brings greatly increased color stability.
The Fotochrome Color camera (USA) can be used for photographing direct only Anscochrome Printon (For color prints).

1967

Anscochrome 500 (ASA 500/28 DIN) (später "GAF 500 Color Slide") ist der höchstempfindliche Farbfilm des Weltmarkts.
In der Volksrepublik China beginnt die Produktion eigener farbfotografischer Materialien.
Cibachrome-Print wird als Fachmaterial international eingeführt.

Anscochrome 500 (ASA 500/28 DIN) (Later 'GAF 500 Color Slide') is the fastest color film on the world market.
The People's Republic of China begins producing its own materials for color photography.
Cibachrome-Print materials for professionals are launched internationally.

1968	Agfacolor CNS Negativfilm (mit Farbmasken nach Agfa- und Gevaert-Patenten) wird eingeführt. Kodak Ektacolor 20 RC ist das erste Colorpapier mit kunststoffbeschichteter Unterlage (RS = resin coated). Es folgen die entsprechenden neuen Ektachrome RC Umkehrpapiere. Durch diese in den nächsten Jahren auch von weiteren Herstellern übernommene Papiersorte verringern sich die Wässerungs- und Trocknungszeiten; die Hochglanzoberfläche ist fabrikationsseitig gleich vorhanden, aus Wettbewerbsgründen werden diese Papiere in mehreren verschiedenen Oberflächen angeboten.	Agfacolor CNS negative film (with color masks based on Agfa and Gevaert patents) introduced. Kodak Ektacolor 20 RC is the first color paper with a plastic-coated base (RC – resin coated). It is followed by the equivalent new Ektachrome RC reversal papers. These paper grades are also adopted by other manufacturers during the next few years, reducing washing and drying time; the high-gloss surface is produced initially in the factory, but for competitive reasons these papers are offered with various different surfaces.
1969	Weitere Hersteller übernehmen das zweite Kodak-Farbverfahren (Kodacolor/Ektachrome) zu Gunsten einer weltweit einheitlichen Entwicklung: Fujicolor N 100 (Exporttyp) und 3M Color Print Negativfilme für Process C-22; Fujicolor Papiere Type 8904 für Ektaprint-C und Fujichrome R 100 Diafilm für E-4. Die Ansco Farbmaterialien werden in "GAF Color", die Ferraniacolor Materialien in "3M" umbenannt. In der CSSR wird nun auch ein Diafilm produziert (Fomachrom). In den USA werden die Schnellverarbeitungsprozesse Rapid Access Color und Unicolor für Farbpapierbilder eingeführt. Cibachrome-Transparent für lichtstabile Großdias kommt heraus, und Cibachrome-Print wird verbessert.	Other manufacturers adopt the second Kodak color process (Kodacolor/Ektachrome) in the interests of standardizing developing methods worldwide: Fujicolor N 100 (export type) an 3M Color Print negative films for the C-22 process; Fujicolor Type 8904 papers for Ektaprint-C and Fujichrome R 100 slide film for E-4. The Ansco color materials are renamed 'GAF Color' and the Ferraniacolor materials become '3M'. A slide film is now produced in Czechoslovakia also (Fomachrom). In the USA; the high-speed Rapid Access Color and Unicolor processing methods are introduced for color prints. Cibachrome-Transparent is brought out for light-stable large-scale slides, and Cibachrome-Print is improved.
1970	Mit dem Ektaprint-3 Prozeß von Kodak (für das neue Ektacolor Papier 30 RC) verringern sich die Anzahl der chemischen Bäder auf drei und die Dauer auf rund 8 Minuten. Agfa-Gevaert führt die neuen Diafilme Agfachrome Professional 50 S und 50 L ein und stellt sein Agfachrome CU 410 Material für das Silberfarbstoff-Bleichverfahren vor. Mit der Produktionsaufgabe für Dynachrome verschwinden die letzten "fremden" Farbfilme nach dem Kodachrome-Verfahren vom Markt. Es erscheinen weitere elektrofarbfotografische Systeme zur Herstellung von Aufsichtsbildern, z.B. O/G Chroma Color, können sich aber nicht allgemein durchsetzen.	Kodak's Ektaprint-3 process (for the new Ektacolor 30 RC paper) reduces the number of chemical baths to three and the duration to about 8 minutes. Agfa-Gevaert introduces the new Agfachrome Professional 50 S and 50 L slide films, and launches its Agfachrome CU 410 materials for the silver dye bleach process. Production of Dynachrome ceases, thus removing from the market the last 'foreign' color films produced by the Kodachrome process. More electro-photographic systems for producing color prints appear, such as O/G Chroma Color, but fail to become generally established.
1971	Auch Agfa-Gevaert führt einen 3-Bad-Prozeß (85) für Colorpapier ein. Kodak bringt das hochempfindliche Ektachrome 14 RC Papier aus französischer Produktion und die ersten Vericolor Professional Negativfilme (für die Versamat-Maschinenentwicklung) auf den Markt.	Agfa-Gevaert also brings out a 3-bath process (85) for color paper. Kodak markets the high-speed Ektachrome 14 RC paper, made in France, and the first Vericolor Professional negative films (for the Versamat development machine).
1972	Kodak führt die Pocket-Kassette (110) und mit ihr den verbesserten Kodacolor II Film für den neuen Process C-41 ("Flexicolor") ein; letzterer verringert die Gesamtverarbeitungszeit von 51 Min. (C-22) auf 30 Min. Kodacolor II enthält erstmals DIR-Kuppler zur Verbesserung der Bildqualität (Schärfe, Körnigkeit, Farbreinheit), was dem kleinen Aufnahmeformat der "Pocket" (13 x 17 mm) zugutekommt. Der Weltverbrauch an Colorpapier holt den von Schwarzweiß-Fotopapier ein. Polaroid stellt sein SX-70 Sofortbild-System vor; es arbeitet mit nur einem Blatt und somit abfallfrei sowie mit metallisierten Farbstoffen zu Gunsten der Farbenhaltbarkeit. Die zusammenklappbare Polaroid SX-70 Land Kamera ist eine neuartige Konstruktion mit einem Spiegelreflexsystem. Mit dem neuen herkömmlichen Polacolor Film Type 88 (für Polaroid Colorpack Kameras) entfällt das Aufziehen der Bilder auf Kartonunterlage).	Kodak introduces the pocket cassette (110), and with it the improved Kodacolor II film for the new C-41 ('Flexicolor') process; this reduces the total processing time from 54 minutes (C-22) to 30 minutes. Kodacolor II is the first to contain DIR couplers to improve the image quality (sharpness, grain, purity of color), which benefits the small 'pocket' picture size (13 x 17 mm). World consumption of color paper overtakes that of black-and-white photographic paper. Polaroid launches its SX-70 Instant Picture System; it uses only single sheets, making it waste-free, and also uses metalized dyes to promote color stability. The collapsible Polaroid SX-70 Land camera is a novel design using a mirror-reflex system. The new standard Polacolor Type 88 (for Polaroid Colorpack cameras) makes it unnecessary to mount the pictures on a cardboard base.
1974	Die neuen Kodachrome Filme 25 und 64 mit erhöhter Farbreinheit lösen Kodachrome II und -X ab. Kodacolor II kommt auch in weiteren Filmkonfektionierungen auf den Markt und weitere Farbnegativfilme für den Prozeß C-41 folgen (Kodak Vericolor II Professional, Fujicolor F-II). Polaroid SX-70 wird weltweit eingeführt.	The new Kodachrome 25 and 64 films, with increased color purity, replace Kodachrome II and Kodachrome-S. Kodacolor II is also marketed in other film packages, and more color negative films follow for Process C-41 (Kodak Vericolor II Professional, Fujicolor F-II). Polaroid SX-70 is launched worldwide.
1975	Weitere C-41 Negativfilme erscheinen (3M Color Print und Sakuracolor II). Ilford beginnt mit der Einführung von Cibachrome-A für Amateure und Cibachrome-Print 2 zuerst in den USA. Polaroid führt als erstes völlig selbst hergestelltes Polacolor-Sofortbildmaterial den Typ 2 mit ebenfalls metallisierten Farbstoffen zuerst in den USA und England ein.	More C-41 negative films appear (3M Color Print and Sakuracolor II). Ilford begins introducing Cibachrome-A for amateurs and Cibachrome-Print 2 initially in the USA. Polaroid introduces its Type 2, the first Polacolor instant photographic material produced entirely by Polaroid, again using metalized dyes; initially, type 2 is launched in the USA and Britain.
1976	Kodak beginnt – zuerst im Professional-Sortiment – mit der Einführung der völlig neuen Ektachrome Filmgeneration für den neuen Verarbeitungsprozeß E-6 (33 Min. bei 38 °C): Typen 64 und 200 für Tageslicht-, 50 und 160 für Kunstlichtaufnahmen. Fujicolor F-II 400 ist der erste höchstempfindliche Farbnegativfilm mit ASA 400/27 DIN. Die 2-Bad-Verarbeitung Ektaprint-2 von Kodak für Colorpapiere ergänzt Ektaprint-3. Kodak führt sein Sofortbildverfahren Instant Color Picture Process zuerst in Nordamerika ein. Der New XS-70 Land Film von Polaroid besitzt eine bessere Farbwiedergabe. Das Polaroid 8 x 10-System erleichtert die Arbeit im Fotostudio.	Kodak begins to introduce – initially in the professional range – the completely new generation of Ektachrome films for the new E-6 processing method (33 minutes at 38°C): Types 64 and 200 for daylight, 50 and 160 for artificial light. Fujicolor F-II 400 is the first high-speed color negative film of ASA 400/27 DIN. Kodak's Ektaprint-2 two-bath processing for color papers supplements Ektaprint-3. Kodak introduces its Instant Color Picture Process for instant pictures, initially in North America. Polaroid's New SX-70 Land film gives better color reproduction. The Polaroid 8 x 10-System makes studio work easier.

1977	Weitere ASA-400-Farbnegativfilme folgen: Kodacolor 400, 3M High Speed Color Print, Sakuracolor 400. Kodak Ektacolor 74 RC ist das erste hochempfindliche Colorpapier. Der Weltverbrauch an Colorpapier ist nun dreimal so hoch wie der von Schwarzweißpapier.	More ASA-400 color negative films follow: Kodacolor 400, 3M High Speed Color Print, Sakuracolor 400. Kodak Ektacolor 74 RC is the first high-speed color paper. World consumption of color paper is now three times as high as that of black-and-white paper.
1978	Agfacolor CNS 400 ist der erste Film von Agfa-Gevaert für eine sog. kompatible, d.h. vereinheitlichte Verarbeitung (Prozeß C-41). Mit Kodak Ektachrome 400 erscheint der erste Diafilm der Empfindlichkeitsklasse ASA 400/27 DIN. Fuji und Konishiroku bringen auch Diafilme für den Prozeß E-6 heraus. Das Cibachrome-Copy System und das Cibachrome RC Papier werden eingeführt. Polaroid bringt den verbesserten SX-70 Land Film mit schnellerer Entwicklung heraus. Das Nimslo-System mit plastisch wirkenden Farbbildern (3D-Linsenrasterverfahren, ohne Betrachtungsbrille) wird vorgestellt. Die LaserColor Laboratories, West Palm Beach, Florida, USA, setzen einen Printer mit Laserstrahlen als Kopierlicht ein ("LaserColor Art Print").	Agfacolor CNS 400 is Agfa-Gevaert's first film for 'compatible' i.e. standardized processing (C-41 process). Kodak's Ektachrome 400 is the first slide film in the ASA 400/27 DIN speed range. Fuji and Konishiroku also bring out slide films for the E-6 process. The Cibachrome-Copy System and Cibachrome RC paper are introduced. Polaroid brings out the improved SX-70 Land Film with quicker development. The Nimslo-System of 3D-effect color photographs (3D Lenticular screen process, no goggles needed) is introduced. LaserColor laboratories, West Palm Beach, Florida USA, introduce a printer which uses laser beams as printing light ('LaserColor Art Print').
1979	Der Colormator-Printer 7565 von Agfa-Gevaert ist mit stündlich 14.000 Farbbildern der zur Zeit schnellste der Welt. Verbesserungen beim Sofortbild: Mit dem zuerst in Florida eingeführten Polaroid Time-Zero Supercolor film verkürzt sich die Bildentstehung bei SX-70-System auf 1 Minute; Kodak bringt den Instant Color Film PR 10-2 mit besserer Bildqualität und kürzerer Entwicklungszeit. Ilford führt die Cibachrome Materialien PS-Brilliant und RC-Pearl sowie das Type A RC Papier (für Amateure) ein.	Agfa-Gevaert's Colormator-Print 7565 is the world's fastest, handling 14,000 color pictures per hour. Improvements in instant photography: the Polaroid Time-Zero Supercolor film, initially introduced in Florida, cuts down the time taken to produce a picture under the SX-70 System to 1 minute; Kodak brings out the PR 10-2 Instant Color Film with improved picture quality and reduced processing time. Ilford introduces the Cibachrome PS-Brilliant and RC-Pearl materials and the Type A RC paper (for amateurs).
1980	Kodak bringt den lichtstabilen Duratrans Display Farbpositivfilm auf den Markt. Der Cibachrome Prozeß P-3 mit "Selbstmaskierung" wird eingeführt; dafür wird auch das neue Cibachrome-Transparent Material TD Type II hergestellt. Polacolor ER mit erweitertem Belichtungsspielraum ergänzt das Polacolor 2 Sortiment.	Kodak markets the light-stable Duratrans display color-positive film. The Cibachrome P-3 process 'with self-masking' is introduced; the new Cibachrome-Transparent TD Type II material is also produced for it. Polacolor ER with increased exposure range is added to the Polacolor 2 range.
1981	Sony stellt auf der Berliner Funkausstellung den Prototyp einer Fotokamera mit Bildaufzeichnung auf einem Magnetspreicher vor (Mavica). Mit 3M Color Slide 640T (ASA 640/29 DIN) erscheint ein höchstempfindlicher Kunstlicht-Diafilm. Das Kodak Ektaflex PCT System bringt die Farbbildverarbeitung (vom Negativ oder Dia) mit nur einem Bad auf der Grundlage der Sofortbild-Technologie. Fuji führt in Japan sein Sofortbildsystem Fotorama mit Fuji Instant Color Film FI-10 (entsprechend dem Kodak Instant Color Picture Process) ein. Polaroid führt zuerst in den USA sein neues 600 Sofortbildsystem mit dem höchstempfindlichen 600 High Speed Color Land Film (ASA 600/29 DIN) ein. Die neuen Kameras regulieren automatisch das auch das Tageslicht bei jeder Aufnahme ergänzende Blitzlicht.	At the Berlin Radio Exhibition, Sony launches the prototype of a photographic camera which records images on a magnetic storage medium (Mavica). An ultra-high-speed slide film for artificial light appears – 3M Color Slide 640T (ASA 640/29 DIN). The Kodak Ektaflex PCT System offers color processing (from negative or slide) with a single bath, using the instant picture technology. In Japan, Fuji introduces its Fotorama Instant Picture System using Fuji Instant Color Film FI-10 (equivalent to the Kodak Instant Color Picture Process). Polaroid introduces – initially in the USA – its new 600 Instant Picture System using the ultra-high-speed 600 High Speed Color Land Film (ASA 600/29). The new cameras automatically regulate the flash which supplements daylight for every exposure.
1982	Kodak bringt die Disc-Bildscheibe heraus und verkleinert damit das Aufnahmeformat für Negative auf 8 x 10,5 mm; der dafür geschaffene Kodacolor HR Disc Film ist das erste Material mit hochauflösender "high resolution"-Emulsion und ISO 200/24° Empfindlichkeit. Das Disc-System wird noch im selben Jahr auch von Fuji übernommen. Kodacolor VR 1000 ist der erste Negativfilm des Weltmarkts mit ISO 1000/31° Empfindlichkeit; er verwendet tafelförmige Silberhalogenide ("T Grains") als lichtempfindliche Filmbausteine. Mit der Einführung von Agfachrome 200 (für Prozeß E-6) beginnt Agfa-Gevaert auch bei Diafilmen mit der Aufgabe des alten Agfacolor-Verfahrens. Agfa-Gevaert präsentiert sein Agfachrome Speed 1-Bad-Verfahren für Aufsichtsbilder von Dias in Sofortbild-Technologie. Kodak Vericolor III Professional Film Typ S mit höherer Empfindlichkeit (ASA) 160/23°), besserer Bildqualität und längerer Lagerstabilität der Negative wird vorgestellt. Kodak führt das neue Kodamatic Instant System mit hoher empfindlichen Sofortbildfilm (ISO 320/26°) und Kameras mit automatischer Blitzlichtdosierung ein. Sony stellt den Mavigraph Printer vor, mit dem Mavica-Fotos Thermographisch (Farbstoff-Übertragung unter Wärmeeinwirkung) als Papierbild ("Mavigram") gedruckt werden.	Kodak brings out the disc camera, thus reducing the picture size of negatives to 8 x 10.5 mm; the Kodacolor HR Disc Film made for this is the first material to have high-resolution emulsion and ISO 200/24°C speed. The disc system is also adopted by Fuji in the same year. Kodacolor VR 1000 is the first negative film on the world market with a speed of ISO 1000/31°; it uses T-shaped silver halides ('T Grains') as photo-sensitive film components. The introduction of Agfachrome 200 (for the E-Process) marks the start of Agfa-Gevaert's abandonment of the old Agfacolor process even for slide films. Agfa-Gevaert introduces its Agfachrome Speed 1-bath process for color prints from slides by the instant-print technology. Kodak Vericolor III Professional Type S film is introduced, with greater speed (ISO 160/23°), improved picture quality and longer storage life for the negative. Kodak introduces the new Kodamatic Instant System with high-speed instant print film (ISO 320/26°) and cameras with automatically metered flash. Sony introduces the Mavigraph Printer, with which Mavica photographs are printed thermographically (by color transfer under the action of heat) as prints ('Mavigram').
1983	Fuji und kurz darauf auch Kodak führen als erste Herstelle Farbnegativfilme der aus den Disc-Filmen abgeleiteten neuen Generation mit neuen Silberhalogenid-Kristallen und anderen weiterentwickelten Filbausteinen (u.a. neue DIR-Kuppler) ein: Fujicolor HR 100 und HR 400; Kodacolor VR 100, VR 200 und VR 400. Agfa-Gevaert folgt mit den Agfacolor XR Filmen und löst Agfachrome CT 18 durch den CT 64 ab. Fuji beginnt als erste Filmherstellerin mit der Einführung einer neuen Emulsionsgeneration für Diafilme (Fujichrome 50 D, 100 D und 64 T). 3M Color Slide 1000 ist der erste Diafilm mit ISO 1000/31° Empfindlichkeit.	Fuji, soon followed by Kodak, are the first manufacturers to introduce color negative films of the new generation derived from the disc films, with new silver halide crystals and other sophisticated film components (including new DIR couplers): Fujicolor HR 100 and HR 400; Kodacolor VR 100, VR 200 and VR 400. Agfa-Gevaert follows suit with Agfacolor XR films and replaces Agfachrome CT 18 with CT 64. Fuji is the first film manufacturer to start introducing a new generation of emulsions for slide films (Fujichrome 50 DT, 100 D and 64 T). 3M Color Slide 1000 is the first slide film with a speed of ISO 1000/31°.

1983

Polaroid führt sein Autoprocess System für schnell entwickelnde Diapositive ein und greift dabei für den Polachrome CS Film auf das alte, schon für den Polavision-Schmalfilm (1977) wesentlich verfeinerte Linienraster-Verfahren zurück, kombiniert mit der Sofortbildchemie (Silbersalzdiffusions-Verfahren).
Konishiroku Photo Industry Co. Ltd., Tokyo, geht – zunächst für den nordamerikanischen Markt – auf die neue Marke "Konica" (statt "Sakura") über und beginnt mit der Einführung der neuen Konica Color SR Filme.
Die von Kodak geschaffene DX-Filmcodierung zur Erkennung des Filmtyps bei Belichtung und Verarbeitung der Filme wird vorgestellt und allen Filmherstellern lizenzfrei angeboten. Kodak führt den Kodamatic Trimprint Film mit ablösbarem und somit dünnerem Sofortbild ein.

Polaroid introduces its Autoprocess system for fast-developing slides, resorting, for the Polachrome CS film, to the old line screen process which had already been greatly upgraded for the Polavision narrow-gauge film (1977), combined with instant-print chemistry (silver salt diffusion process).
Konishiroku Photo Industry Co. Ltd. Tokyo switches to the new 'Konica' brand (instead of 'Sakura') – initially the North American market – and begins launching the new Konica Color SR films.
The DX film coding for recognizing the film type during exposure and processing, developed by Kodak, is introduced and offered to all film manufacturers free of licensing fees. Kodak introduces the Kodamatic Trimprint Film with a detachable and hence thinner instant print.

1984

Neue Colorpapiere mit ("jahrhundert-") langer Farbstabilität (Agfacolor Type 8, Kodak Ektacolor Plus und Konica Color PC Type SR "Century Print") werden herausgebracht.
Agfa-Gevaert führt sein neues Professional Filmsortiment (mit Agfachrome Filmen Type RS und Agfacolor Filmen Type XRS, einschließlich Filmen mit ISO 1000/31° Empfindlichkeit) zuerst in den USA ein.
Die ausnutzbare Filmempfindlichkeit steigt weiter: Kodak führt den Ektachrome P 800/1600 Professional Film (Prozeß E-6P mit "gepushter" Entwicklung) ein; Fuji stellt für die Sommerolympiade in Los Angeles und für Japan Fujichrome 1600 Professional (Spezialprozeß) "PZ") her und bringt den Fujicolor HR 1600 Negativfilm (Empfindlichkeit: ISO 1600/33°) heraus.
Kodak bereichert das Kodachrome Sortiment um Professional Kleinbildfilme mit ausgewählter Qualität und kurzfristiger Entwicklung.
Polaroid führt den inzwischen verbesserten Polachrome Diafilm international ein und bringt einen neuen 600 Supercolor Film mit verbesserter Farbwiedergabe heraus.
Kodak ersetzt den Ektachrome 64 Amateurfilm durch den neuen Ektachrome 100.
Fuji ergänzt sein Sofortbildsortiment in Japan um das Fotorama 800 System mit höchster Filmempfindlichkeit (ISO 800/30°) und Kameras mit automatischer Blitzlichtdosierung.
Kodak stellt den Instagraphic-Sofortdiafilm vor.
Das Sakura Nice Print System von Konishiroku ist das erste wasserfrei arbeitende Minilab.

New color papers with ('centuries') long color stability (Agfacolor Type 8, Kodak Ektacolor Plus and Konica Color PC Type SR 'Century Print') are brought out. Agfa-Gevaert produces its new Professional film range (using Agfachrome Type RS films and Agfacolor Type XRS films, including films of ISO 1000/31°), initially in the USA.
The usable film speed continues to increase: Kodak launches the Ektachrome P 800/1600 Professional film (Process E-6P with 'pushed' development); produces Fujichrome 1600 Professional (special process) 'PZ' for the Los Angeles Summer Olympics and for Japan, and brings out the Fujicolor HR 1600 negative film (speed: ISO 1600/33°).
Kodak extends the Kodachrome range to include professional 35 mm films of select quality and short development time.
Polaroid launches its (now improved) Polachrome slide film internationally, and brings out a new 600 Supercolor film with improved color reproduction.
Kodak replaces the Ektachrome 64 Amateur film with the new Ektachrome 100.
Fuji extends its instant picture range in Japan to include the Fotorama 800 System with ultra-high film speed (ISO 800/30°) and cameras with automatically metered flash.
Kodak introduces the Instagraphic-Instant Slide film.
Konishiroku's Sakura Nice Print System is the first Minilab to work without using water.

1985

Agfacolor XRS 1000 und Agfachrome 1000 RS Professional sind als erste Filme dieser Empfindlichkeitsklasse auch in Rollfilm-Konfektionerung erhältlich.
Ein neuer Fujichrome P 1600 Professional Film kan nun auch nach dem Prozeß E-6P verarbeitet werden.

Agfacolor XRS 1000 and Agfachrome 1000 RS Professional are the first films with this speed rating which are also obtainable in roll-film make-up.
A new Fujichrome P 1600 Professional film can now also be processed by the E-6P process.

1986
Stand Juli/*as of July*

3M Color Print HR II Rollfilm, die Kodacolor Gold Filme (in den USA "VR-G") und die Fujicolor Super HR Filme läuten die zweite Generation der Negativfilme mit "HR"-Technologie ein und bringen vor allem sattere Farben. Konishiroku folgt mit dem neuen Konica Color SR-V-100 Film.
Agfa-Gevaert vergrößert bei dem verbesserten Agfacolor Maxi XR 100i Kleinbildfilm und bei Agfachrome CT 100 die Aufnahmeanzahl von 24 auf zusätzliche drei Bilder und erste Muster eines Kodachrome Rollfilms 120 (64 Professional) werden verteilt.
Kodak führt die neuen Ektacolor Papiere 2000 (für den Prozeß EC-1) und 2001 (zunächst für die neuen Kodak Minilab Systeme mit "RA"-Chemikalien ein; Gesamtverarbeitungszeit hierbei unter 4 Min.); ein hochempfindlicher Kodachrome 200 Film wird angekündigt.
3M geht – zunächst in Nordamerika – mit verbesserten Filmen zur neuen Marke "Scotch" über.
Kodak unterliegt Polaroid im Patentrechtstreit um sein Sofortbildverfahren und gibt es auf.
Polaroid führt in de USA sein neues, ursprünglich unter der Typenbezeichnung 7000 angekündigtes neues Sofortbildsystem "Spectra" (in Europa "Image") mit kompakter, hochelektronisierter Kamera und einem verbesserten film mit nunmehr rechteckigen Bildern (7,3 x 9,1 cm) ein.
Canon führt in den USA sein "SVS" Still Video System für "filmlose" farbige Stehbilder, aufgenommen auf floppy disc Speicher, ein. Der Canon RP-601 Printer stellt farbige Aufsichtsbilder nach dem Ink-Jet-Druckverfahren von den Aufnahmen mit der Canon RC-701 Kamera und anderen Video-Bildquellen her.

3M Color Print HR II roll film, Kodacolor Gold films ('VR-G' in the USA) and Fujicolor Super HR films announce the second generation of negative films with 'HR' technology, and – in particular – offer richer colors. Konishiroku follows suit with the new Konica Color SR-V-100 film.
Agfa-Gevaert increases the number of exposures from 24 to 27 for its improved Agfacolor Maxi XR 100i 35 mm film and Agfachrome CT 100.
Kodak introduces new Ektacolor papers – 2000 (for the EC-1 process) and 2001 (initially for the new Kodak Minilab Systems with 'RA' chemicals; total processing time less than 4 minutes); a high-speed Kodachrome 200 film is announced, and the first samples of a Kodachrome 120 roll film (64 Professional) are distributed.
3M adopts the new brandname 'Scotch' for its improved films, initially in North America.
Kodak is defeated by Polaroid in a patent case relating to its new instant-print process, and abandons it.
Polaroid introduces its new 'Spectra' ('Image' in Europe) instant-print system, originally announced under the type designation 7000, with a compact, highly electronicized camera and an improved film which now gives rectangular pictures (7.3 x 9.1 cm).
In the USA Canon introduces its 'SVS' Still Video System for 'filmless' color stills, taken on floppy-disc storage media. The Canon RP-601 printer produces color prints by the ink jet printing process from pictures taken by the Canon RC-701 camera and other sources of video pictures.